In No Strange Land
The Embodied Mysticism of Saint Philip Neri

Jonathan Robinson of the Oratory

In No Strange Land

*The Embodied Mysticism of
Saint Philip Neri*

First published
by Angelico Press, 2015

© Jonathan Robinson, 2015

All rights reserved

No part of this book may be reproduced or transmitted,
in any form or by any means, without permission.

For information, address:
Angelico Press
4709 Briar Knoll Dr.
Kettering, OH 45429
angelicopress.com

978-1-62138-134-1

Cover image: Johann Friedrich Overbeck (1789–1869)
Saint Philip Neri (1826)
Cover design: Michael Schrauzer

"*In No Strange Land*"

O world invisible, we view thee:
O world intangible, we touch thee:
O world unknowable, we know thee:
Inapprehensible, we clutch thee.

Not where the wheeling systems darken,
And our benumbed conceiving soars:
The drift of pinions, would we harken,
Beats at our own clay-shuttered doors.

The angels keep their ancient places—
Turn but a stone, and start a wing!
'Tis ye, 'tis your estranged faces
That miss the many-splendoured thing.
                    FRANCIS THOMPSON

et ei amor ipse est intellectus
(*and love itself is understanding for him*)
                    WILLIAM OF THIERRY[1]

---

1. William of St. Thierry, *The Golden Epistle, A Letter to the Brethren at Mont Dieu.*

To Abbot Eugene Hayes, O. Praem.
and the Norbertine Community of
St. Michael's Abbey, California

. . . there are varieties of service, but the same Lord.

1 Corinthians 12:5

CONTENTS

Acknowledgments ii
Preface: People Not Arguments 1
Introduction: An Embodied Mysticism 15

PART I *Light in Florence*
 1 Using This World Well 49
 2 Chastity and Charity 71
 3 Reform in Florence: St. Catherine and Savonarola 87
 4 Art, Irony, and Eros 109
 5 The Philip Who Left Florence 127

PART II *The Mystical Assault: Clouds and Light in San Germano and Rome*
 6 San Germano 139
 7 Studies and Books 157
 8 The Catacombs and the Apostolate 175

PART III *Light from the Darkness*
 9 The Darkness of God 195
 10 Towards an Account of St. Philip's Embodied Mysticism 217
 11 The Apostle of Rome 241

Appendix I: Julian of Norwich on Laughter 273
Appendix II: The Net of Love 274
Bibliography 275
Index 289

ACKNOWLEDGMENTS

My first debt is to the members of the Toronto Oratory for their patience and support and for all they have taught me about St. Philip.

I have to thank in a special way Fr. Philip Cleevely, Fr. Derek Cross, Fr. Daniel Utrecht, and David Warren, all of whom read the entire manuscript of this book while it was being written. With great kindness, not unmixed with a quiet irony, they have been the cause of a good deal of tightening up of both argument and style. I must add that, in spite of all this help, the flaws that remain are all my own doing.

My friend Dennis Crowley, who in spite of bad health has been unfailing in his encouragement, and who has placed his first-hand knowledge of Renaissance music and art at my disposal: I am very grateful for this. My thanks also go to Professor Bruce Redford, who also helped me on many aspects of the history of art. Dr. Edward Goldberg, the Founder of the Medici Archives Project, and his successor, Dr. Alessio Assonites, were always there to answer questions about why and where in sixteenth-century Florence, and I do thank them for their kindness.

I am also very much in the debt of Professor Lorenzo Polizzotto of the University of Western Australia, who has very generously drawn on his vast learning of Renaissance Florence to help and encourage a complete stranger.

Dr. Stephanie Treloar and the staff of the library at the Centre for Reformation and Renaissance Studies at the University of Toronto have been unfailing in courtesy and helpfulness.

The Reverend Brother Domenic Viggiani, F.S.C., and Robert Pontisso, have both been generous in helping with the translation of some of the Italian texts.

Preface
People Not Arguments

Perhaps, then, the memory of anyone distinguished in life would be enough to fill our need for a beacon light and to show us how we can bring our soul to the sheltered harbor of virtue where it no longer has to pass the winter amid the storms of life or be shipwrecked in the deep water of evil by the successive billows of passion. It may be for this reason that the daily life of those sublime individuals is recorded in detail, that by imitating those earlier examples of right action those who follow them may conduct their lives to the good.

St. Gregory of Nyssa[1]

The heart is commonly reached, not through the reason, but through the imagination, by means of direct impressions, by the testimony of facts and events, by history, by description. Persons influence us, voices melt us, looks subdue us, deeds inflame us.

J. H. Newman[2]

THIS BOOK is an essay on the life of St. Philip Neri, written from the viewpoint of the development of his mystical life. This account has, therefore, both a biographical aspect and an element of what has come to be known as "historical theology." Christians believe that their faith is based on the truth of God's revelation in Jesus Christ, but the reception of this revelation has an essentially historical character. The divine truth is believed, heard, and developed by real men and women living in the everyday world of time and space.[3] This believing is through God's gift

---

1. St. Gregory of Nyssa, *Life of Moses*, 13.
2. J. H. Newman, *An Essay in Aid of a Grammar of Assent*, Chapter 4, section 3.
3. Karl Rahner writes of "the essentially historical character of dogma as divine truth heard, believed and formulated by man in this world and as a living function of the Church, which must receive, explicate and proclaim the truth that is given to her—guaranteed by God himself—according to the ever varying understanding (ability to hear) of the world around her, a process essentially historical and socially structured." Rahner, "History of Dogma," in *Theological Dictionary*.

of grace; what is believed comes from what has been heard from the Church. *Fides ex auditu* is what St. Paul teaches,[4] but the development of the life of prayer, under grace, is inescapably personal and historical.

It follows from this principle—that is, the principle that development in the life of prayer is inescapably personal and historical—that the only way we will see how this development really takes place is by examining individual lives. There may, of course, be general aspects to be discovered as a result of such an inquiry, but if we leave out the examination of the time-bound experience of those who have actually prayed, then we will end up by prescribing, in terms of theory, how prayer should develop, rather than describing how it does in fact begin, and how it sometimes flowers into the experience of the mystics.

In this book I attempt to show how the mysticism of St. Philip Neri developed during his lifetime and was the source of his influence. I have chosen to use this particular life not to illustrate a concept of mysticism that has already been established, but to probe the question of how prayer sometimes develops into what I have termed "embodied mysticism."

In North America, St. Philip's life and significance hardly register in the awareness of contemporary Catholics. Even those who have heard about the Saint take him for a practical joker who was suspicious of book learning and had a flair for dealing with young men and aristocratic ladies. Some know that he was reported to have been something of a mystic and took a long time saying Mass. This all adds up to something slightly more than nothing. Rather than being brought face-to-face with Philip—the friend of God and living witness to the unseen—we glimpse an eccentric priest who for largely unexplained reasons was an important figure in sixteenth-century Rome. First, then, it is necessary to amplify this inadequate impression with a biographical delineation.

St. Philip was born in Florence in 1515. He lived through most of the sixteenth century and died in 1595. He left his native city and came to Rome in 1533 or 1534 (when he was eighteen or nineteen) and spent the rest of his life there. He began as a kind of hermit, living in the city, earning a little money by tutoring, studying at two of the Roman universities, and praying by night in the catacombs. Gradually he began to preach and teach, and he gathered a little group around him to pray and converse about spiritual things. There was also a practical side to these meetings. Philip organized visits to the hospitals and laid foundations for a large-scale charity to care for pilgrims to Rome.

Philip was ordained, at his confessor's insistence, in 1551, when he was

---

4. Romans 10:17.

thirty-five years old. He went to live at the Church of San Girolamo della Carità, where his little group, attracted by his personal influence, began to grow. They came regularly to pray with him, to go to confession to him, and to listen to talks on the lives of the saints and the development of the Christian virtues. Later, he had some of his followers ordained to help in this work of praying, confessing, and instructing.[5] But it was the larger, secular group of laymen who constituted the first Oratory.

From these modest and unpremeditated beginnings, Philip's influence grew until he was the confessor of popes and cardinals, of dukes, bankers, and princesses—but also, and still, of the artisans and washerwomen who had been with him in the beginning. Now what, today, are we to make of such a life? We can see that St. Philip's life and work is of great historical interest; it remains important today as an example of ecclesial reform that works within the established hierarchical and juridical structures of the Church. For just as Ignatius won back large parts of Europe for the Church, so Philip, in the same generation, instituted a deep spiritual reform in Rome itself. Beginning very simply, and with no fixed scheme, he ended by becoming, as he came to be called, the Second Apostle of Rome. And then, quite unexpectedly and almost of itself, the sphere of Philip's activities and his influence continued to grow until, in the words of Ludwig Pastor:

> ... in the time of Gregory XIII it included the whole of Rome, and at last the whole Church; until cardinals and popes, science and art paid him homage, and what is more, thousands venerated him as the author of their happiness in time and in eternity.[6]

In *The Idea of a University*, Cardinal Newman, who spent half of his long life as a member of the Oratory that Philip had founded, wrote some dazzling pages on the Saint. After an extended and moving account of Philip's influence, he ends with a question:

> And who was he, I say, all the while, but an humble priest, a stranger in Rome, with no distinction of family or letters, no claim to station or to office, great simply in the attraction with which a Divine Power had

---

5. These ordained followers developed into an organized body officially recognized by the Church. In 1575 Gregory XIII erected the group into a *Congregation of Secular Priests*. "Its members actually lived together, they were priests, or those who were training for the priesthood, and they served the Church. [That is, the particular Church to which they were attached.] It was this Community which was erected into a Congregation, under the title of the Congregation of the Oratory." Murray, "Newman's Oratory Papers," in *Newman the Oratorian*, 164.

6. Pastor, *The History of the Popes*, Volume 19, 195–196.

gifted him? And yet thus humble, thus unennobled, thus empty handed, he has achieved the title of Apostle of Rome.[7]

These are words of high praise, but they also provide a sober, truthful recounting of an extraordinary, personal, unstructured, non-institutionalized influence that is almost unique in the history of the Church. And Newman is asking a real question. It is difficult to bridge the gap between these accounts of Philip's influence and much that has been written about him. Most biographies leave us puzzling over why he became the Apostle of Rome and the counselor of popes; nor is it made clear how he is supposed to have reformed the Curia. Newman has given us at least the form of the answer: Philip was "great simply in the attraction with which a Divine Power had gifted him." I think this is right, and Newman had the right focus. It was the grace of God operating through the sacramental and liturgical life of the Church that formed Philip into one of the great mystics of the Catholic Church. The "Divine Power," though, was given to Philip not merely for his own edification, but so that through sharing in that power he helped to bind up the wounds of Christ's body, which is the Church. It is in this mysticism that we find the explanation of St. Philip's power both in his own time, and, perhaps more secretly, in ours as well.[8]

Philip's life and influence are a lesson in the importance of personal influence in spreading the truth. The need for this personal influence is vital today if the Christian revelation is to catch even the attention, much less the assent, of our contemporaries. It is a commonplace to say that we live in a world in which the language of traditional Christianity is a dead letter. The intellectual framework, the images, and the moral teaching of the faith no longer color the ordinary consciousness. We inhabit, as a modern English philosopher puts it, "a scientific and anti-metaphysical age in which the dogmas, images, and precepts of religion have lost much of their power."[9] It is this weakening of the religious mind that is intended when the word *secularization* is used; modern society has been secularized and so has the consciousness of those whose lives it shapes.

It is to this secularized world that Christianity is expected to speak. In one of her short stories, Edith Wharton describes, in a few words, this bleak sense of the unreality of the values that many once treasured:

---

7. See above, Preface, 3 (Newman, *The Idea of a University*, 241).
8. See below, 6–7.
9. Murdoch, "Against Dryness," *Existentialism and Mystics*, 287.

Outside, the immense black prospect of New York, strung with its myriad lines of light, stretched away into the smoky edges of the night. He showed it to her with a gesture.

"What do you suppose such words as you've been using—'society,' 'tradition,' and the rest—mean to all that life out there?"[10]

If the man had been a Christian, he might have said: "What do you suppose such words as you've been using—'Faith,' 'Jesus Christ,' the 'Sacraments,' and the rest—mean to all that life out there?" In our darker moods we are tempted to say, "Not very much."

Charles Taylor has written that our modern secular age "is one in which faith, even for the staunchest believer, is one human possibility among others."

> I may find it inconceivable that I would abandon my faith, but there are others, possibly some very close to me, whose way of living I cannot in all honesty just dismiss as depraved, or blind, or unworthy, who have no faith (at least not in God or the transcendent). Belief in God is no longer axiomatic. There are alternatives. And this will also likely mean that at least in certain milieux, it may be hard to sustain one's faith. There will be people who feel bound to give it up, even though they mourn its loss.[11]

That seems an accurate description of our world in the West; faith has become an option.[12]

Sometimes, though, the word secularization is used to describe the cause of this condition. People seem to be convinced that secularization is a kind of force, an irresistible current sweeping away faith, but that is a completely different claim. We must be careful to distinguish between the *fact* of secularization and the *process* of secularization. I hold that, however it may be that we have become secularized, it was not an inexorable development from primitive societies, which are believing and unsecularized, to our own, which is unbelieving and secularized. The evidence does not support this sweeping conclusion, and there are serious anthropologists who maintain that it is totally false to say that primitive man is by nature religious, or that unbelief is to be found only in modern society. Consider, for example, this robust statement from the distinguished English anthropologist Mary Douglas:

---

10. Wharton, "Autre Temps," 145.
11. Taylor, *A Secular Age*, 3.
12. But while agreeing with Taylor's description, we needn't accept everything he says about what it was like to believe in officially believing societies, or his understanding of Catholicism.

> Secularization is... an age-old cosmological type, a product of a definable social experience, which need have nothing to do with urban life or modern science.... The contrast of secular with religious has nothing whatever to do with the contrast with traditional or primitive. The idea that primitive man is by nature deeply religious is nonsense.[13]

Yet even if there have always been unbelieving societies, we must ask how the Faith of the Church is to be presented to this modern, unbelieving, secularized world. Part of the answer is that the glory of God breaks through the carapace of unbelief and indifference by means of the holiness of the saints. One of the reasons we are given the Saints is so that each of them, in his own way, may strike us, through the force of his own personality, with the reality and truth of Christ. Sanctity is something lived, and the lives of the saints are important because in the end, as Newman said, it is people we trust and not arguments.[14] In this he was echoing Aristotle, who maintained that:

> We believe good men more fully and more readily than others; this is true generally whatever the question is, and absolutely true where exact certainty is impossible... his character may almost be called the most effective means of persuasion he possesses.[15]

In the fifth of his *University Sermons*, "Personal Influence, the Means of Propagating the Truth," Newman argued that the "inspired word being but a dead letter (ordinarily considered) needs to be transmitted from one mind to another, and this is done only through committed individuals who live what they preach."

> ... it [is] difficult to estimate the moral power which a single individual, trained to practice what he teaches, may acquire in his own circle, in the course of years. While the Scriptures are thrown upon the world, as if the common property of any who choose to appropriate them, he is, in fact, the legitimate interpreter of them, and none other.... While he is unknown to the world, yet, within the range of those who see him, he will become the object of feelings different in kind from those which mere intellectual excellence excites.[16]

The lives and personalities of the saints exhibit Newman's point. The saints are men and women who have "become the object of feelings different in kind from those which mere intellectual excellence excites." This personal influence of the saints has different notes, which domi-

---

13. Douglas, *Natural Symbols*, 18.
14. Newman, *An Essay in Aid of a Grammar of Assent*, 89.
15. Aristotle, *Rhetoric*, 1356 a 6.
16. Newman, *Sermons Preached Before the University of Oxford*, 74.

nate, in different ways, the mystery of personal influence. In some cases, it is a heroic charity for the poor and the outcast; in others, it may be selfless sacrifice, through administration, for the good of the Church. Again, there is the witness of the blood of the martyrs. There is, also, the personal influence, based on a mystical awareness of the presence of God. This is the case of St. Philip.

The contention that Philip's mysticism was the source of his influence will be an empty formula until some notion is provided as to how the term "mystical" is being used. Yet, to provide even a working definition of mysticism is not so easy as might first appear. In talking about mysticism, or the mystical, we are not dealing with a series of experiences, or possibly a practice, that everyone agrees constitutes the subject and now requires only a tighter definition. On the contrary, there is the widest possible disagreement about what it is that we should try to investigate and define.[17]

The natural tendency is to look for a meaning, or perhaps essence of the word, and then to see how it works out in different cultures and people. This is the wrong way to go about it. The notion that there is a common meaning to mysticism, which can be examined in isolation from a particular religious tradition, is, I think, false. Mysticism, that is, ought to be looked on as an element or aspect of the practice of a particular religion. The mystic is first of all a Jew, or a Muslim, or a Christian, and it is out of the ordinary practice of a religion that mystical experience sometimes grows.[18] I will return to the question of how we are to understand these experiences, or even if "experience" is the best word. Here, I want only to oppose the *a priori* assumption that mysticism has

---

17. "What is 'mysticism'? What is 'experience'? The latter question seemed to me to be too difficult; the former to be a blind alley, for I do not know of any discussions which shed less light on the subject of 'mysticism' than those many which attempt *definitional* answers to the question 'what is mysticism?' For it seems that answers generally fall into two categories: those which are *stipulative* and whose relation with actual mysticism is at best contingent; and those which are merely *descriptive* of the various actual mysticisms, the question of which varieties are included in the canon being left to convention or intuition. Neither way of answering the question seems very satisfactory in principle, nor do they shed much light on the subject in practice." Turner, *The Darkness of God*, 2.

18. "It was perhaps the greatest insight of Friedrich Baron von Hügel's great book, *The Mystical Element in Religion*, to emphasize that mysticism is only one part or element of a concrete religion and any particular religious personality. *No mystic before the present century (i.e., the twentieth century) believed in or practised 'mysticism.' They believed in and practised Christianity (or Judaism, or Islam, or Hinduism) that is, religions that contained mystical elements as parts of a wider historical whole.* These elements, which involve both belief and practices, can be more or less important to the wider body of believers." McGinn, *The Foundations of Mysticism*, vol. I, xvi (emphasis added).

one meaning, exemplified in the same way every time the word is used. This may seem counterintuitive today—to say that the practice of an actually existing religion must be examined if we are going to track a viable sense of mysticism—but that is hardly an objection. St. Philip's mysticism grew out of, and was nourished by, the ordinary practice of his Catholicism. It is unintelligible without this reference. Let us call this rootedness, in the liturgical and sacramental life of his Faith, an "embodied mysticism."

Further still, this ordinary practice of Catholicism is itself profoundly influenced and molded by the social and cultural environment in which it finds itself at any particular time and place. The practice of Catholicism in the Renaissance Florence of Philip's boyhood and youth combined, in an uneasy conjunction, a range of attitudes and convictions stretching from those based on the memories of Savonarola's apocalyptic preaching to those that are to be found, for example, in Francesco Guicciardini, and that saw Catholicism as little more than a necessary qualification for service to the Florentine state.[19] This principle, that the Catholicism that nourished Philip in Florence united within itself a complex of often competing influences, extends to the Church during his life in Rome. The mix was on a larger scale, and included many different elements from those that affected the Church in Florence; but, once again, there is no understanding of Philip's mysticism without an awareness of this historical background. It follows from this that we will have to know something about the social and cultural environment of the Catholicism within which Philip's embodied mysticism took root and began to grow; that must be followed by a discussion of the Catholicism of sixteenth-century Rome, which continued the shaping, begun in Florence, of Philip's spiritual life. It follows, then, that while Philip's development can only be understood within the context of the ordinary practices of Catholicism, it also has to be understood that this Catholicism itself was fraught with tensions, conflicting ideals, and a troubled political and social situation.

If we are going to understand the embodied mysticism of St. Philip, we have, first of all, to see it as growing out of the ordinary practices of his Catholicism, but that will not tell us much until we grasp that these

---

19. "I know no man who dislikes more than I do the ambition, the avarice, and the lasciviousness of the priesthood: not only because each of these vices is odious in itself, but also because each of them separately and all of them together, are quite unsuitable in men who make profession of a life dedicated to God.... And yet the position I have served under several popes has obliged me to desire their greatness for my own self-interest and were it not for this, I would have loved Martin Luther as myself...." Guicciardini, *The History of Italy*, Editor's Introduction, xvi.

ordinary practices were profoundly influenced by their development within the historical, social, and, more narrowly, religious environment of late fifteenth- and early sixteenth-century Florence and Rome. So instead of trying to provide a definition of mysticism, I have set down some of the aspects of the word and its cognates with reference specifically to St. Philip.

First, I will emphasize that mystical experience is an experience of the activity of God. The writer of the *Cloud of Unknowing* wrote of the "drawing of this love and the voice of this calling."[20] St. John of the Cross teaches the same doctrine and says, "First it must be known that, if a soul is seeking God, its beloved is seeking it much more."[21] He goes on to say:

> When, therefore, the soul reflects that God is the principal agent in this matter, and the guide of the blind self Who will take it by the hand and lead it where it could not of itself go (namely, to the supernatural things which neither its understanding nor its will nor its memory could know as they are), then its chief care will be to see that it sets no obstacle in the way of the guide, who is the Holy Spirit, upon the road by which God is leading it.[22]

Newman's phrase "the attraction with which a Divine Power had gifted him" draws our attention to this divine initiative. Moreover, his words anticipate a contemporary concern. They look ahead to a very fruitful discussion of revelation, and of mystical experience, as a gift of God.[23] A gift is not something created by the recipient's expectations, but is dependent on the will of the donor. The recipient may refuse to accept it, but he neither creates the gift, nor is able to control whether or when it is offered. This perspective of the divine initiative in the mystical is one very important aspect of my use of the word "mystical" in connection with St. Philip.

Secondly, mysticism is used in connection with an experience or a practice of human beings. While mysticism is associated with and grows out of a particular religion, it is, nonetheless, something that individual men and women do practice, or better, something that happens to

---

20. Anonymous, *The Cloud of Unknowing and Other Treatises* (1952), chapter 2: "What weary wretched heart and sleeping in sloth is that, the which is not wakened with the drawing of this love and the voice of this calling?" The writer is here insisting that the *drawing* and the *calling* are the work of God on the individual.
21. St. John of the Cross, "Living Flame of Love," *Complete Works*, vol. III, 66.
22. Ibid.
23. The work of Jean-Luc Marion is of great importance in this regard. See Marion, *Étant donné*.

them. If we are going to understand what they practiced, or what happened to them, then we will have to know something about the individuals themselves. That is to say, if we want to understand mysticism, then we will have to become involved in biography and history. In saying this, I am not denying that it is possible to distil common elements in the experience of Catholics who have been mystics. Indeed, some such effort should always be made. Anyone writing a book that deals with mystical experience has to use universal terms that apply beyond the experience of a particular individual. The universal aspects of the experience are provided by a particular religious tradition, and we must trace what these might be. But if we don't consider the particular histories, the narratives of individuals, then our search for an understanding of an embodied mysticism, like St. Philip's, will be a lost cause. We will lack the primary data to grasp how the liturgical and sacramental aspects of Catholicism worked in the embodiment of Philip's mysticism. The life and times of St. Philip Neri are not a series of convenient coat hooks upon which to hang generic truths about mysticism. On the contrary, unless we stay close to his life and times, we will never get it. We will never understand how the initiative of God was encountered by Philip, in the accessible reality of the sacramental and liturgical life of the Church.

Thirdly, the Christian mystic is driven by his contact with the hidden God to share with others what he has learned in the darkness. The summit of Christian mysticism is not an experience of the self but a participation in the love of God that led to the redemption of the world through the life and death of Christ.[24] This participation, being a sharing in the love of God for this world, is an activity in self-giving. The mystic has learned nothing new at the verbal level, and so he has nothing specific to communicate. "I no longer know what to do or say, if Thou help me not, my Jesus"[25] is St. Philip's way of making this point. The Christian mystic has nothing of his own to communicate. Why? Because to some degree he has become the icon, or monstrance, of the presence of the invisible God. I don't mean by this to imply that mystics cannot write in an authoritative way about mysticism; after all, St. Gregory, St. John of the Cross, and St. Teresa of Avila wrote extensively on the sub-

---

24. See, for example, Daniélou, *Platonisme & Théologie Mystique*, 327.

25. Neri, prayer #52. "Prayers which the Blessed Philip Neri, my spiritual father, taught me, although I have always been an unworthy, intractable and proud son. He many times recommended me to say, in the form of a chaplet, that is instead of the Pater and Ave, one or other of these ejaculatory prayers, which the said Father valued exceedingly." Francesco Zazzara quoted in Ponnelle and Bordet, *St. Philip Neri*, 596.

ject. But people took what these mystics wrote seriously because it was clear from the sort of people they were that they knew what they were talking about, and in the end it is people, not arguments, we trust. The experience in an overpowering way of the love of God in the darkness beyond concepts and words was what they communicated, and what authenticated what they wrote about. These considerations have much to do with explaining the influence of the Second Apostle of Rome.

God took possession of Philip's soul, and the presence and the action of God in Philip's soul was recognized by his contemporaries. But this whisper of the eternal—just because it was of the eternal—can still be heard by us. Philip's life was "hid with Christ in God,"[26] and so he could say "it is no longer I who live, but Christ who lives in me."[27] Philip lived in an embattled Church, at war all too often with herself as with the world. We, too, live in such a Church, divided and faced with a hostile and unbelieving world. Philip had no formulas for saving either the Church or the world. His sanctity is a reflection of the sanctity of Christ; a sanctity that belongs no more exclusively to the sixteenth century than to the twenty-first.

After centuries of research, the historical background of Philip's life is now firmly established.[28] I intend to use the basic outlines of this story, although I do have serious difficulties with some of the ways these outlines have been interpreted.[29] I will use the received account of the life and times of Philip Neri with a view to deepening our understanding of his embodied mysticism. I will look for this understanding by considering some of the influences we know were brought to bear on him, and how he dealt with them. I am convinced that his mysticism is the source of his perennial fascination and enduring influence. This fascination and influence reminds us that the ordinary sacramental and liturgical life of the Church, open to all Catholics, continues to present "the riches of his glory, for the vessels of his mercy, which he has prepared beforehand for his glory."[30]

In brief, my book is historical because it considers influences on St. Philip that we do know, or conjecture about with reasonable certainty. Yet, it is also a series of meditations on Philip's assimilation and reaction to those influences, done within the framework of the development of

---

26. Colossians 3:3.
27. Galatians 2:20.
28. See next page, "A Note on the Sources of Philip's Life."
29. For example, I think the anti-intellectualist Philip, with whom we are often presented, is a false one. See chapter seven, "Studies and Books."
30. Romans 9:23.

his embodied mysticism. It is best understood, therefore, as an essay in historical theology.

A Note on the Sources of Philip's Life

Over the centuries, the foundations of an inquiry into Philip's embodied mysticism have been laid in sound and scholarly biographies, and I have used these biographies to explore the inner dynamics and abiding influence of Philip's life and deeds. Our knowledge of the historical circumstances of St. Philip's life is based on two sources. First, there are the early seventeenth-century lives by the Oratorians Antonio Gallonio[31] and Pietro Giacomo Bacci.[32] For the next two centuries, these two biographies provided the basic material for many books on St. Philip. The second source for first-hand historical information is in the testimonies of the hundreds of witnesses recorded in *The First Process for Philip's Beatification*.[33] Gallonio and Bacci were familiar with this material and used it extensively in their work.

Newman's all-too-brief writings on St. Philip, in the middle of the nineteenth century, are a brilliant effort to recast the seventeenth-century hagiographies into a compelling account of Philip's life and influence. Under Newman's guidance, Philip appears as a recognizable human being. On the other hand, Newman's sources are the conventional ones, and he never realized his hope of writing a full-length life of the Saint.[34] Cardinal Capecelatro,[35] who had been Superior of the Oratory in Naples, produced at the end of the nineteenth century a life of the saint which has been called "a labor of love." It is easy to underestimate the value of this book, written by a distinguished Oratorian, as it is often hagiographical in just the sort of way Newman objected to and so successfully avoided in his own remarks. Nonetheless, Capecelatro not only understood from the inside, as it were, the Italian setting of Philip's

---

31. Antonio Gallonio, *The Life of Saint Philip Neri*, trans. Jerome Bertram (Oxford: Family Publications, 2005). This was first published in 1600.

32. Pietro Giacomo Bacci, *The Life of Saint Philip Neri*, new and revised edition, ed. and trans. by Frederick Ignatius Antrobus (London: Kegan Paul, Trench, 1902).This was first published in 1622.

33. Giovanni Incisa Della Rocchetta and Nello Vian, *Il Primo Processo per San Filippo Neri*, Four Vols. (Città del Vaticano: Biblioteca Apostolica Vaticana, 1957–1963).

34. There exists material for such a biography: in Newman's "The Mission of St. Philip Neri," which is Sermon XII of *Sermons Preached on Various Occasions*, and in a sketch of Philip's early life in "Newman's Oratory Papers," published in *Newman the Oratorian*, 156–171. There is also Newman's lovely testimony to Philip the Saint in *The Idea of a University*, 239–241.

35. Alfonso Cardinal Capecelatro, *The Life of Saint Philip Neri*, trans. T.A. Pope (London: Burns, Oates & Washbourne Ltd., 1926).

work, but he also had insights into the importance of the intellectual life in the early Oratory. This is a precious gift, as all too often Philip is presented as someone who at best tolerated studies and the pursuit of learning.

It was not until the early twentieth century that two French priests, Louis Ponnelle and Louis Bordet, the former of whom was killed in the First World War, produced a new book by direct investigation of archival material.[36] Their book, *St. Philip Neri and the Roman Society of his Times*, brought a breath of fresh air to the study of St. Philip. It rescued him from the straitjacket of the seventeenth-century lives, and it remains the standard authoritative work on Philip's life. Father Ralph Kerr of the London Oratory translated the book into English and added a series of learned and incisive footnotes, designed to correct a strain of unnecessary skepticism about the supernatural elements in Philip's life.

Since the work of Ponnelle and Bordet, several excellent shorter lives of Philip have been published, but they all depend on the tradition of the seventeenth century as mediated and developed by the work of the two Frenchmen, with an occasional glance at Newman. A notable exception is *San Filippo Neri*[37] by Nello Vian, one of the editors of the four volumes for the first process of St. Philip's canonization. In this series of essays, Vian, who wears his learning very lightly, sheds valuable new light on many aspects of the Saint's life and times. In particular, several of his essays correct the view that Philip sailed through life in a happy-go-lucky way:

> Vian mette in guardia dal rischio di rappresentare la spiriualità di Filippo solo come Christiana letizia, dimenticadone il carattere spesso irrequieto, talvolta drammatico. (Vian warns us of the risk of looking on the spirituality of Philip as only one of Christian joy, forgetting its restless and sometimes dramatic character.) [38]

Philip's experience of God was given to him for the sake of others. In his lifetime Philip became a light shining in the darkness of unbelief and a living icon of the reality and importance of the unseen. Furthermore, just as Philip's experience of God was for the benefit of others, so that experience itself was awakened, nourished, and brought to fruition within the religious tradition into which he was born and from which he lived.

---

36. Louis Ponnelle and Louis Bordet, *St. Philip Neri and the Roman Society of His Times*, trans. Ralph Francis Kerr of the London Oratory (London: Sheed & Ward, 1922).

37. Nello Vian, *San Filippo Neri, Pellegrino Sopra La Terra* (Brescia: Morcelliana, 2004).

38. Ibid., Introduction by Massimo Marocchi, 9 (author's translation).

Introduction
An Embodied Mysticism

The Bride speaks: "Upon my bed by night I sought him whom my soul loves ... but found him not. I called him, but he gave no answer." How indeed could she reach with a name the one who is above every name?
St. Gregory of Nyssa[1]

PHILIP was one of the great mystics of the Church, and his embodied mysticism was the source of his influence. This gives us a problem from the start, for the word "mysticism" is widely viewed with suspicion and has been anathematized as "hateful, modern and ambiguous."[2] Cardinal Newman shared this suspicion, and he is often identified as the author of the *bon mot* that mysticism begins with mist and ends in schism.[3] I cannot find the phrase in Newman, and think it is much more likely to derive from G.K. Chesterton or Monsignor Ronald Knox, who have also been credited with the aphorism. But the message is in line with Newman's attitude, even if it is much too "clever" (in the bad sense) to have originated with him.

Used with care, however, the term is a necessary tool for understanding St. Philip's life and influence. There is a vast literature on mysticism that compels our acknowledgment. I am not trying to produce any sort of summary of what the tradition of Catholic mystical theology has to say,[4] or is supposed to have said, nor am I trying to review all past and current discussions.[5] For the moment, it is less important to prove the correctness of what I say than to show how I am using the term. There is not

---

1. St. Gregory of Nyssa, *Commentary on the Song of Songs*, 6
2. Chapman, "What *Is* Mysticism," *Spiritual Letters*, 297.
3. E.g., Louth, *The Origins of the Christian Mystical Tradition*, 201.
4. As for example in Garrigou-Lagrange, *The Three Ages of the Interior Life*, vol. I, 225.
5. Bernard McGinn's as yet incomplete five-volume work, *The Foundations of Mysticism*, is an example of this approach.

much point in discussing any sort of mysticism without stipulating the role to be played by the word itself, and the adjectives used to qualify it.

Those who write on mysticism tend to take it as an experience that happens *to* people, or as an activity done *by* people: as either experience or act. William James is the best-known exponent of the experiential view,[6] while St. Thomas Aquinas may be taken as teaching that mysticism follows from an intellectual sort of activity. In fact, mysticism in Thomas's view is a special sort of theology.[7] Neither view on its own, as usually presented, can provide an adequate basis for an understanding of St. Philip's embodied mysticism.

Thomas teaches that mystical experience arises out of a consideration or contemplation of the truths of Catholicism. This teaching will have to be a foundational element in any theory of Christian mysticism. On the other hand, mysticism is not only an activity in which the mystic's contribution to the experience is the focus of attention. The experience, or mystical activity, begins with human acts but moves into a condition where the awareness of God, and of his activity, begins to be the dominant element.[8] This awareness introduces an aspect of passivity, or of experience in a broad sense, into any consideration of mysticism that will be anything more than a paper theory.

There is a clear description of this development—from a concentration on human acts to an awareness of God's activity—in *The Cloud of Unknowing*.[9] In his discussion of the virtue of meekness, the author says that we must "swinke & swete"[10] to get a true knowledge and sense of ourselves. But this activity on our part is sometimes met in "the overabundant love and the worthiness of God in himself,"[11] which so dominates the experience that all sense of the self is lost, and only an awareness of the activity of God remains:

> ...full oft it may befall that a soul in this deadly body—for the abundance of grace in multiplying of his desire, as oft and as long as God vouchsafeth to work it—shall have suddenly and perfectly lost and for-

---

6. James, *The Varieties of Religious Experience*.
7. This change from a theological to an experiential interpretation is one of the major themes of Denys Turner's *The Darkness of God*. The last chapter, "From Mystical Theology to Mysticism" (252–273), summarizes the main themes of his book and traces the development from a mysticism centered on the quest for the hidden God to a mysticism based on the experiences of the mystic.
8. See Preface, 9.
9. Anonymous, *The Cloud of Unknowing* (1982), chapters 13–16.
10. "Toil and sweat" (author's translation).
11. Anonymous, *The Cloud of Unknowing* (1982), chapter 13.

gotten all knowing and feeling of his being, not considering whether he have been holy or wretched.[12]

Mystical activity moves from ordinary, readily accessible activities within a religious tradition to an overwhelming sense of the presence of God. Yet awareness is always a particular person's, and therefore some consideration of individual experience must be given. The element of passivity is most apparent in the physical phenomena of mysticism, such as ecstasies, levitations, and the like. Such things do not define the nature of mystical experience, but they are so intimately connected with it that they cannot be ignored. Furthermore, they serve as a constant reminder that mysticism is a facet of the experience of determinate individuals living within a particular religious tradition.

Von Balthasar criticized Garrigou-Lagrange for his failure to deal with these physical phenomena.[13] But the eminent Dominican is hardly in a class of one. The subject is generally found to be distasteful and out of harmony with the clean lines of a properly theological inquiry. And yet, these purportedly distasteful things happen. Furthermore, they happened to men and women who are saints of the Church and were living exponents of the most sublime sanctity. It is not enough merely to ignore these physical phenomena or to say they are irrelevant or even hostile to real sanctity. Over and over again, we see them as elements in the embodied mysticism of Catholicism.

Unless we provide some account of how mysticism works out in actual, individual cases, it becomes difficult to see how the mystical life of an individual, such as St. Philip, could be of use in convincing an unbelieving world of the reality of God, the Redemption of the world by his Son, and the continuing presence of the Holy Spirit at work in our lives. The emphasis of William James on experience has, at the very least, to be taken into account.

The best way of uniting these different facets of mysticism dealt with by William James and St. Thomas—of experience and of human act—is to say that mysticism is embodied: embodied in a particular person, a particular subject. But the particular subject is himself ensconced, involved in, a complex communal, linguistic, and symbolic order of beliefs and practices. Furthermore, this order of beliefs and practices is always an aspect of a wider societal context. For St. Philip Neri, these

---

12. Ibid., chapter 13.
13. Balthasar praises Garrigou-Lagrange "for linking the missions of prophets far more securely to the order of charity (and criticizes for withdrawing the extraordinary charismata from consideration in his greatly influential work, *Perfection chrétienne et contemplation*)." Nichols, *Divine Fruitfulness*, 283.

beliefs and practices were situated in the mystical body of Jesus Christ, which is the Church. Yet the Catholic Church as he experienced it was, first, that of Renaissance Florence, and then of Papal Rome, with their own particular appropriation of Christianity. It was a Church with its own glories, but haunted by its own violent history.

This preliminary discussion of some of the requirements for an adequate use of the word mysticism, and a method of discussing them, must now be fleshed out. We must deal with the view that mysticism is a sort of experience that can be found in all religions, and even sometimes in those with no religion. William James takes that approach. Then we have to look at St. Thomas's view of mysticism, which lays no emphasis whatsoever on experience. Then we must seek to reconcile and balance these opposing insights. Finally, we must turn to the tradition of the three ways of the mystical life, for this provides the best framework for a discussion of the embodied mysticism of St. Philip.

William James and Mystical States of Consciousness

Today most people understand mysticism as the experience of individuals, forms of experience which have no intrinsic connection with the particular religious tradition to which the mystic belongs. In its most common form, this view goes back to William James's *The Varieties of Religious Experience*.[14] In his Gifford lectures, he adopted the following description of religion:

> Religion ... as I shall ask you arbitrarily to take it, shall mean for us *the feelings, acts, and experiences of individual men in their solitude, so far as they apprehend themselves to stand in relation to whatever they may consider the divine.*[15]

At the heart of this personal religion are what James calls "mystical states":

> One may say truly, I think, that personal religious experience has its root and center in mystical states of consciousness.[16]

So religion is taken to be a personal relation with whatever a man thinks of as God, and at the center of this experience are "mystical states of consciousness." James enumerates "four marks which if an experience has them, may justify us in calling it mystical for the purpose of the present lectures."[17] These are: ineffability, noetic quality, transiency, and

---

14. James, *The Varieties of Religious Experience*.
15. James, ibid., 32 (emphasis added).
16. Ibid., 370.
17. Ibid., 371. The following quotes about the four marks all come from the same source, 371–372.

passivity. It is worth seeing what James intends by these terms as, partly no doubt through his influence, they summarize relatively well our contemporary view of religion and mysticism.

"Ineffability," he says, is the "handiest of the marks" by which a state of mind can be classified as mystical; this mark is a negative one:

> The subject of it immediately says that it defies expression, that no adequate account of it can be given in words. It follows from this that its quality must be directly experienced; it cannot be imparted or transferred to others. In this peculiarity mystical states are more like states of feeling than like states of intellect.

The "noetic quality" means that those who experience mystical states, in spite of the fact that they are like states of feeling, also take them for states of knowledge:

> They are states of insight into depths of truth unplumbed by the discursive intellect. They are illuminations, revelations, full of significance and importance, all inarticulate though they remain; and as a rule they carry with them a curious sense of authority for after-time.

By "transiency," James means that mystical states cannot be sustained for long; "except in rare instances," for half an hour, and then they fade into the light of common day:

> Often, when faded, their quality can but imperfectly be reproduced in memory; but when they recur it is recognized; and from one recurrence to another it is susceptible of continuous development in what is felt as inner richness and importance.

Finally, there is "passivity"; this means the mystic is not in total control of the experience:

> Although the oncoming of mystical states may be facilitated by preliminary voluntary operations, as by fixing the attention, or going through certain bodily performances, or in other ways which manuals of mysticism prescribe; yet when the characteristic sort of consciousness once has set in, the mystic feels as if his own will were in abeyance, and indeed sometimes as if he were grasped and held by a superior power.

If we accept James's starting point, that mysticism is essentially about "states of consciousness," then he has given a fair description. Each of James's four criteria for recognizing mystical states could be illustrated from the life of St. Teresa. I do not mean that St. Teresa can be used to support James's view, although it has often been pointed out that she leaves herself open to the charge of an overly experiential view of mysticism.[18] Nonetheless, she describes such states in ways that bear out James's description, even if his use of her writings betrays a radical distaste for institutional religion, and Catholicism in particular.[19]

Religion is essentially personal for James, and it follows that churches, creeds, and even other people are, at best, of secondary importance.[20] It is worth spelling out that if mysticism is recognized by the possession of James's four characteristics, then the notion of any objective referent by which the experience could be authenticated or evaluated becomes irrelevant, if not meaningless. The experience is self-authenticating: it either has the four marks or it doesn't. On James's definition of mysticism, we can't ask if the experience conforms or relates to something outside itself. It is itself, and not another thing.

There are many today who, like James, think mysticism is at the heart of all the varieties of religious experience, and that this central core is worth investigating for any number of reasons. For those interested in an academic point of view, there is a vast amount of material to be studied from epistemological and metaphysical angles.[21] Then again, mystical experience has provided an endless series of case studies for the psychologist.[22] For those who do not care for religion, the thought that some

---

18. "... though Teresa certainly denied that such 'experiences' are constitutive of true contemplation, she was rather more inclined than John liked to distinguish the different stages of spiritual development (the 'Mansions' of her *Interior Castle*) in terms of the 'experiences' typically associated with them...." Turner, *The Darkness of God*, 251.

19. "... one thing he [James] has trouble getting his mind around is Catholicism. His wide sympathies fail him, for instance, when it comes to St. Teresa of Avila. She is one of his sources, and he quotes her at length (408–410), but at another point he says in some exasperation that 'in the main her idea of religion seems to have been that of an endless amatory flirtation—if one may say so without irreverence—between the devotee and the deity' (347–348)." Taylor, *Varieties of Religion Today*, 23.

20. "... it is evident that out of religion in the sense in which we take it, theologies, philosophies, and ecclesiastical organizations may secondarily grow ... we shall hardly consider theology or ecclesiasticism at all." Ibid., 32.

21. For example the work of Steven T. Katz: *Mysticism and Language* and *Mysticism and Sacred Scripture* (see bibliography). See also Forman (Ed.), *The Problem of Pure Consciousness, Mysticism and Philosophy*; Sells, *Mystical Languages of Unsaying*; and Nelstrop, Magill, and Onisha, *Christian Mysticism: An Introduction to Contemporary Theoretical Approaches*.

22. The work of Jean-Martin Charcot (1825–1893) on hysteria and mysticism is famous. There is an interesting historical account in Talar (Ed.), *Modernists and Mystics*, 10–13, of this interaction between psychiatry, and especially of the treatment of hysteria, with mystical experience. It seems unfortunate that the diagnosis of hysteria has been formally eliminated "from the plethora of psychiatric syndromes and diseases that make up the increasingly elephantine *Diagnostic and Statistical Manual* published by the American Psychiatric Association ... after more than two millennia on the medical scene, hysteria was officially euthanized in 1980." Scull, Review of *Modernists and Mystics*, 30.

psychotic experience is at its heart is too attractive to resist. And mysticism is viewed by some as a useful spiritual exercise which, if properly handled, will be of great benefit in recovering a sense that life is worth living. This contention often goes with talk about the wisdom of the East.

Thus, in addition to appearing intuitively right, James's view of mysticism has both popular and academic weight behind it. But it is not the only view. For this experiential approach runs counter to the much older way of understanding mysticism as an action taking place within a well-defined context of belief and practice—what I have called an embodied mysticism.

Aquinas and a Word Bursting Forth in Love

So if mysticism does not reduce to exceptional experiences, as James teaches, what is its subject matter? For a better description, and a better method of investigation, one might turn to mystical theology.[23] St. Thomas is often taken as the outstanding exponent of this approach. In what follows, I am not trying to give a short lesson in Thomas's theology. Rather, I am concerned with illustrating an older and largely unfamiliar approach to mysticism.

It is hard to know how to write about St. Thomas today, because even the most basic concepts he uses are foreign to most readers. We must think slowly through ideas that once seemed almost self-evident, especially to a Thomist. And we must get into sympathy with these ideas in order to comprehend them. This is because any discussion of Thomas's writings that assumes knowledge of his terminology will not only lose people, but it will also destroy any attraction the Angelic Doctor's work might have had for them. Very few, anyway, are very interested in the secret garden of rarefied scholastic discourse. Therefore, let us begin with a sketch of the way he uses words.

Thomas's View of Mystical Theology

Thomas does not explicitly discuss mystical theology, but there is enough in his work to point us in the right direction.[24] In the *Prima Pars*, Question 43 (that is, on the Missions), he asks how we are to

---

23. This is one of the major themes of Turner's *The Darkness of God*; the last chapter, "From Mystical Theology to Mysticism," 252–273, summarizes the main themes of his book and traces the development from a mysticism centered on the quest for the hidden God to a mysticism based on the experiences of the mystic.

24. Cardinal Journet asks "Whether St. Thomas Aquinas took Mystical Theology into Account," and, while he concludes that he did, he makes it clear that the question is not clearly answered where we might expect it to be. Journet, *The Dark Knowledge of God*, 89.

understand *The sending of the persons of God*.²⁵ In article 5, which deals with "whether it belongs to the Son to be sent invisibly," St. Thomas says that the Son is the Word: "not, however, just any word, but the Word breathing love; *The Word as I want its meaning to be understood is a knowledge accompanied by love*. Consequently, not just any enhancing of the mind indicates the Son's being sent, but only that sort of enlightening that bursts forth into love."²⁶

The Latin word translated as "bursting forth" is *prorumpat*. An enlightening that bursts forth into love is a striking expression.²⁷ More: it goes some way to capturing an awareness that is not only intellectual but also suffused with a desire to become one with what is being thought about. The knowledge that bursts forth into love is said to be a sort of experiential awareness, and this precisely is what wisdom is, a knowledge that, as it were, is tasted.²⁸ Mystical theology is this sort of knowledge; it is experienced and bursts forth into love.

Mystical theology, for St. Thomas, is thus an intensified knowledge that breaks out into love for what the intellect is considering. We can see from the phrase "mystical theology" itself that mysticism is looked on as a kind of theology; a way of doing theology or carrying out theological investigations. The point is that mysticism is no longer a noun or a substantive. The word is being used to qualify what is a noun or a substantive, that is, theology. Theology, no matter how the word is used, requires at least a view or theory about God. It is a view that must be articulated in language if it is to be shared, discussed, and developed. St. Thomas sometimes refers to theology as *quasi sermo de Deo*, "something like talk about God."²⁹ Talking about God is an intellectual activity, and it follows that we are going to begin our analysis by considering the mind's involvement with what it believes to be true and not with ineffable experiences.

---

25. This is McDermott's translation of *de missione divinarum personarum*.

26. Aquinas, *Summa Theologiae* Ia, 43, 5, ad 2.

27. "The phrase *prorumpere in amorem* is a curious expression that captures Thomas's notion of love as a vital motion that impels the one who loves out of himself towards the object of his love." Merriell, *To the Image of the Trinity*, 231. The author continues: "It does not appear to come from Augustine's *De Trinitate*, for Augustine usually speaks of love as the force that connects and yokes together, and he does not draw attention to the explosive quality of love. I do not know where Thomas got this expression."

28. "... perceptio autem experimentalem quandam notitiam significat et haec proprie dicitur sapientiae, quasi sapida scientia. ..." *Summa Theologiae* I a, 43, 5, ad 2.

29. "... what a science discusses is its subject. In this case the discussion is about God; for it is called theology, as it were, talk about God—quasi sermo de Deo." Aquinas, *Summa Theologiae, Prima Pars* I, 7. Thomas has a more general term, *sacra doctrina*

Some may object that the discussion of mysticism has just been sidetracked by an inquiry into an intellectual discipline called theology. Theology is presumed to be an intellectual discipline, and we did not set out to fit mysticism into it. Instead, we wanted to know what distinguishes mysticism from other activities. To say that it is a sort of thinking is to give the wrong sort of answer. Perhaps we liked James's fundamental assumption that there is a phenomenon called mysticism that is essentially the same in all religions. It is, anyway, not immediately clear how mysticism should be regarded as theology. If mystical theology only meant that there ought to be a study of the sort of thing James talks about within a theological framework, then maybe we could accept this. But it is important to see that the claim is much stronger than that. The claim is that mysticism requires theology for its existence.[30] It is theological reflection that triggers an experience that is something more than merely meditating on, or contemplating, the truths of faith.

A passage from St. Bonaventure will help us to grasp this. At the end of his *Itinerarium Mentis in Deum*, or *The Soul's Journey into God*, there is a description of an intensified knowledge breaking forth into love.[31] The first six chapters of the *Itinerarium* contain a detailed and rigorous intellectual analysis of the soul's ascent to God through what Bonaventure calls contemplation. This contemplating is clearly the practice of *sermo de Deo* in a prayerful way on the part of the believer.[32] We begin by contemplating God through his vestiges in the universe, then through his image stamped on our natural powers, until we reach, in the sixth chapter, a very difficult contemplation on "the Most Blessed Trinity in His Name which is Good." In the seventh chapter, though, contemplation is replaced by "spiritual and mystical ecstasy," and rest is given to our intellect when:

"holy teaching,"' which is sometimes translated as Christian Theology. It has been suggested that he chose this less definite word because *theologia* is said by Aristotle to be the highest part of metaphysics. "[Metaphysics] does not reach to truths in the light of divine revelation, and there the theology he [Thomas] is going to investigate differs in kind from the theology which is the culmination of philosophy." Thomas Gilby in vol. 1, appendix 5, section 9 of the Blackfriars *Summa Theologiae*, 63.

30. The reverse is also true; that is, that theology requires mysticism for its creativity and depth. I take it that this is at least part of the message of Von Balthasar.

31. Bonaventure, *The Soul's Journey into God*, 110.

32. This preliminary effort to describe contemplation relies heavily on St. Thomas's discussion in 2a, 2ae q. 182 on the active and contemplative life. That discussion, in its turn, is based on Aristotle's view of contemplation being essentially intellectual. This view of contemplation leads Aquinas to argue that "... the contemplative life becomes man in according to that which is best in him, namely the intellect, and according to its proper objects, namely things intelligible." 182, art 1.

> In this passing over,
> if it is to be perfect
> all intellectual activities must be left behind
> > and the height of our affection
> must be totally transferred and transformed
> > into God.
> This, however, is mystic and most secret,
> > which *no one knows*
> > except him who receives it,
> > no one receives
> > except him who desires it,
> > and no one desires except him
> who is inflamed in his very marrow by the fire of the Holy Spirit
> > whom Christ sent into the world.
> > And therefore the Apostle says that
> This mystical wisdom is revealed
> By the Holy Spirit.[33]

This passage illuminates in a telling way Thomas's view that mystical theology begins with thinking in a prayerful way (that is, contemplating) and that the experience of "spiritual and mystical ecstasy" follows upon it. Still, while Thomas points us in the right direction, it is not very clear to what we are being pointed. Does Thomas mean that mystical theology, the *quasi-cognitio experimentalis*, is merely a kind of heightened or intensified knowing in which the affective aspect is dominant? Or does he mean that the "sort of enlightening that bursts forth into love" puts us into contact with God in a way that is inaccessible to theology as such?

On the face of it, given Thomas's view that we can only love what we know, it would seem that mystical theology can only be a particularly intensified form of an intellectual activity, a heightened sort of *sermo de Deo*. But if so, then mystical theology does not really open any new avenue to God, or leave room for what we might call an affective cognition. By affective cognition I mean a sort of knowing, or awareness, which is not an awareness of the otherness of objects. This is sometimes described as an awareness disclosed to the will alone. It is not, however, a rejection of the presence of reason in experience. Affective cognition instead goes beyond analytical reasoning to direct apprehension. This notion of an awareness that is more than intellectual, what F. H. Bradley called immediate experience, provides at least a helpful

---

33. Bonaventure, *The Soul's Journey into God*, 113.

analogy in thinking about the sort of embodied mysticism that I have attributed to St. Philip.

Immediate Experience and the Gift of Wisdom

When we first think about experience we tend to imagine a subject who sees, or hears, or feels, or even remembers or thinks about a something: a something that is set apart, an other, or more simply, an object. If we try to understand the knowing that bursts forth into love on this model, we will be frustrated. This is so because, whatever else mystical theology might be, it involves love, and love involves some sort of union between the lover and what is loved.

We are wrong to assume that all experience has to be understood in terms of subject and object. We need only think of the experience of a man with a bad toothache, or overwhelmed by an aesthetic or emotional experience of great depth, to know that it cannot be described as the subject's awareness ("here") of an object ("over there"). There is nothing particularly religious in this assertion, and the point is clearly put by F.H. Bradley as a philosophical principle:

> We have ... experiences in which there is no distinction between my awareness and that of which it is aware. There is an immediate feeling, a knowing and being in one, with which knowledge begins; and, though this in a manner is transcended, it nevertheless remains throughout as the present foundation of my known world.[34]

Bradley called experiences like this immediate, and it would be foolish to deny their existence. Immediate experience is an awareness either so intense, or so dream-like, that the *I* in the experience falls away. T.S. Eliot wrote:

> For most of us, there is only the unattended
> Moment, the moment in and out of time,
> The distraction fit, lost in a shaft of sunlight,
> The wild thyme unseen, or the winter lightning
> Or the waterfall, or music heard so deeply
> That it is not heard at all, but you are the music
>   While the music lasts.[35]

The experience of someone half asleep in a deck chair on a summer day hardly aware of himself, and who is conscious in a dreamy way of

---

34. Bradley, "On our Knowledge of Immediate Experience," *Essays on Truth and Reality*, 159–160.
35. Eliot, "The Dry Salvages," *Four Quartets*, 30. Eliot wrote his dissertation for Harvard on Bradley.

the humming of the bees and the smell of newly cut grass, would be another example. Again, to assert the existence of immediate experience is not to argue for irrationalism. In each of these cases, there still has to be a center of consciousness for the experience even to be possible. Nonetheless, at the time of the experience there is no explicit awareness of either the object or the subject. Once the subject begins to think about the experience, or remembers it later on, or compares it with similar experiences, he becomes aware of himself as a subject, set over and against the experience itself. But note that it is wrong to describe the experience, as it was given, in terms of subject and object.

The *quasi-cognitio experimentalis* of Thomas's mystical theology can be understood on the model of immediate experience. This is borne out by his discussion of the gift of wisdom. In the book of Isaiah there is a passage predicting the coming Messiah:

> And the Spirit of the Lord shall rest upon him.
> the spirit of wisdom and of understanding,
> the spirit of counsel and might,
> the spirit of knowledge and the fear of the Lord.[36]

In the Septuagint version that St. Thomas used, there was found a seventh gift, that of piety: εὐσέβεια. These gifts are given so that we can be moved by the Holy Spirit in a way that will help us to obtain the beatific vision.[37] We possess the gift as a quality of the soul, a quality that endows us with a new dimension. But it is a dimension only God can put into action.

The gift that most concerns us is that of wisdom. St. Thomas associates it with the virtue of charity.[38] What characterizes a wise man? The

---

36. Isaiah 11:2.

37. The gifts are given to us by God at baptism and they really do become an aspect of, or qualify, the human soul. Part at least of their function is to supplement both the acquired and the infused virtues in such a way that they will be able to conform to standards of operation that they could not hope to attain without this added help. The gifts provide the spiritual organism with the means to act in a God-like way. The gifts are put into operation by what St. Thomas usually calls an *instinctus* of the Holy Spirit. This *instinctus* is sometimes translated as a *prompting* (of the Holy Spirit); prompting not in the sense of an actor's being reminded of lines he has forgotten, but prompting in the sense we say he was prompted by a generous impulse to give money to a poor man. "... reason by itself is not sufficient to direct man to his ultimate and supernatural end without the prompting of the Holy Spirit from above. Thus it is written, *They that are led by the Spirit of God are sons of God and heirs*; and, *Your good Spirit will lead me into a right land*." Aquinas, *Summa Theologiae*, 1a, 2ae, 68, 2.

38. "All through the *Summa* he has noted the structural difference between knowing and willing, seeing and loving. His effort here is to bind them together. His basic insight

wise man knows what makes things work; he knows what is behind things. In the final analysis, what lies behind everything is God, and so the wise man in an unqualified sense is "he who knows the cause that is simply the highest without qualification, namely God, (and such a man) is called wise without restriction."[39] There is more to it than this, however. The wise man not only knows the highest cause, God, but he also "judges and puts in order all things according to God's rules."[40]

> He comes to such judgment through the Holy Spirit: *A spiritual man is able to judge the value of everything,* says St. Paul, because (as he notes in the same chapter) *the Spirit reaches the depths of everything, even the depths of God.*[41]

To talk about judging seems almost over-intellectual. It fails to capture the mystery and obscurity conveyed by the word mysticism. If we are disappointed to see Thomas maintaining his fundamental conviction that human experience is essentially rational, then we will just have to be disappointed. To put his position in a different way: I do not see how any experience can be called human that does not involve language. This does not mean we have always to be talking, either to ourselves or to others. It does mean that without the possibility of recognition, identification, and discrimination, the experience is less than human. Recognition, identification, and discrimination require language.

The mind did not suddenly put in an appearance when we began to reflect on the immediate experience; it must have been in some way operative in the awareness itself. But while human experience requires reason in order to be human, that does not mean that the reason involved is always like the subject-object awareness of ordinary consciousness. Some judging has about it the aspect of affinity, or of being immediate. Wisdom, Thomas says, "implies a certain rightness in judging according to divine norms."[42] This, he continues, can come about

---

is this: knowledge of the goodness of an object causes us to love it; love then brings about a different and a better kind of knowledge; this new appreciation deepens the love which, in turn, intensifies the appreciation, and so on." Thomas R. Heath O.P. in vol. 35, appendix 4 of the Blackfriars *Summa Theologiae,* 200.

39. Aquinas, *Summa Theologiae,* 2a, 2ae, 45, 1.
40. Ibid., 2a, 2ae, 45, 1. "... dicitur sapiens simpliciter: inquantum per regulas divinas omnia potest judicare et ordinare."
41. Ibid., 2a, 2ae, 45, 1.
42. Ibid., 2a, 2ae, 45, 2.

through a perfect use of reason.[43] It can also come about through "a certain natural kinship with the things one is judging about."[44]

> Thus in matters of chastity, one who is versed in moral science will come to a right judgment through rational investigation, another who possesses the virtue of chastity will be right through a kind of instinctive affinity. So it is with divine things. A correct judgment made through rational investigation belongs to the wisdom which is an intellectual virtue. But to judge aright through a certain fellowship with them belongs to that wisdom which is the gift of the Holy Spirit. Dionysius says that Hierotheus is perfected in divine things for *he not only learns about them but suffers them as well*. Now this sympathy or connaturality with divine things, results from charity which unites us to God; *he who is joined to the Lord is one spirit with him*.[45]

We now have all the elements we need to begin understanding St. Thomas's doctrine of mystical theology. It is a quasi-experiential knowledge of a Divine Person in the soul, a knowledge that is tied to the Divine Missions. This awareness of the Persons is itself made possible by the presence in the soul of *gratia gratum faciens*: grace that makes us pleasing (to God). Further, along with sanctifying grace come the gifts of the Holy Spirit, which make it possible for us to receive the divine prompting, that is the *instinctus*, of the Holy Spirit. When God prompts the gift of wisdom into operation, the soul has a quasi-experiential knowledge of a Divine Person. This quasi-experiential knowledge is mystical theology.

Theology itself is a *quasi-sermo*, a kind of talking. And mystical theology, no matter how deeply the one doing theology is identified through love with the divine presence, will always have an aspect of this *quasi-sermo*. What then of the many descriptions by mystics that suggest their experiences are so overpowering and immediate, so sudden and unrelated to anything that ever happened to them before? Does that make the whole idea that somehow they are dependent on, or closely related to any sort of talking, or *sermo de Deo*, seem absurd?

---

43. Wittgenstein rephrases Aristotle's doctrine of practical reason in the following way: "What one acquires here is not a technique; one learns correct judgments. They are also rules but they do not form a system, and only experienced persons can apply them right. Unlike calculating rules, what is most difficult here is to put this indefiniteness, correctly and unfalsified, into words." Cited in Nussbaum, "An Aristotelian Concept of Rationality," *Love's Knowledge*, 54.
44. "... propter connaturalitatem quamdam ad ea de quibus iam est judicandum." Aquinas, *Summa Theologiae*, 2a, 2ae, 45, 2.
45. Ibid.

The Weight of God[46]

In St. Thomas's understanding of mystical theology, there is no space given to the experiential aspect of mystical theology.[47] The root of the intensified and loving knowledge that characterizes mystical theology lies beyond the psychological sphere. An authoritative author on mysticism has written:

> Hence the essence of supernatural faith, the deification of our spiritual existence, and the vision of the divine in revealed truths which it effects, is not bound up with a special psychological happening.[48]

If the heart of mystical theology lies beyond the reach of psychological categories, and so it seems to be for St. Thomas, then what are we to make of the sort of experiences that James writes about? Or the astonishing but well-documented events connected with the lives of many of the saints, including St. Philip? The question has not disappeared with modern times, as if our more rigorous standards of proof have shown that the accounts of paranormal phenomena need not be taken seriously. In our own times there is the case of Padre Pio.[49] The authorities of the Church were extremely suspicious and even unfair in their dealing with him, and they did their best to prove he was either deluded or a fraud. Yet the reality of the whole range of the physical phenomena of mysticism finally had to be acknowledged as genuine. What we are to make of these experiences is another question. But there is enough hard evidence to suggest we should not be satisfied with any explanation that says they are based only on the credulity of the half-educated or a lack of respect for ordinary standards of proof. We should try to make the attitude of Fr. Herbert Thurston, S.J., our own. He disliked and distrusted

---

46. The expression is Cardinal Daniélou's. Daniélou, *God and the Ways of Knowing*, 126–127.

47. This sort of observation extends beyond his treatment of mystical theology. Cornelius Ernst, O.P., for example, writes: "If a theology of grace may be said to fulfill three functions, moral, existential and metaphysical, it is clear that while St. Thomas is strong on metaphysics and is in fact strong on morals too, he is not very satisfying existentially, in the sense of offering a personal reading of the human condition." Cornelius Ernst, O.P., Introduction to "The Gospel of Grace," Blackfriars *Summa Theologiae*, vol. 30, xxv.

48. Stolz, *The Doctrine of Spiritual Perfection*, 176. Similarly: "There is no hint in St. Thomas to the effect that he associates the connatural tasting and experiences of divine truths by means of the Gifts of the Holy Ghost with a special psychological happening." Ibid., 190.

49. There is a clear and authoritative biographical account of Padre Pio's life, which includes an account of the physical phenomena that accompanied his mystical life, in the biographical essay of Padre Pio's *Letters* (English version, Father Gerardo di Flumeri, Ed.), 14–65. See also Cirri and Malatesta, *Nel Nome del Padre*.

mysticism, but he was prepared to investigate and weigh up these experiences in a sober and careful way.[50]

James is wrong in taking these physical phenomena to define what he calls mysticism, but it does not follow from his error that extraordinary occurrences such as levitation, bilocation, and visions have no connection with the intensified and loving knowledge of mystical theology. Has St. Thomas so purified the nature of mystical experience that the baby has been thrown away with the bathwater? Has he left us with more than an "unearthly ballet of bloodless categories"?[51] One does not have to be William James to ask such questions.[52]

It is impossible to consider the life of Philip without taking account of what has been called "the physical phenomena of mysticism"[53] in the life of the saints. Bacci has an entire section (Book III) on "The Gifts which God Vouchsafed to him."[54] These six chapters survey Philip's raptures and ecstasies, Philip's visions, and Philip's gift of prophecy—he predicts the death of many persons and the recovery of many more. He prophesies to several that they will be Cardinals or Popes. Philip is also said to have had the gift of healing others of both physical disease and mental infirmities.

These phenomena centered around, or found their source in, an experience in the Catacombs on Pentecost 1544, when he saw the Holy Spirit as a ball of fire entering his mouth and which he then felt expand-

---

50. "Il se méfiait du mysticisme sous quelque forme que soit, le considérant comme la porte ouverte aux déceptions; il est impossible de tirer de ses écrits quelques enseignements qui approche le spirituel autrement que par le bon sens." *Dictionnaire de Spiritualité*, vol. 15, column 912.

51. The expression is taken from F.H. Bradley, *The Principles of Logic*, vol. II, 591. Bradley is arguing against the view he attributed to Hegel that "existence should be the same as understanding strikes us as cold and ghost-like as the dreariest materialism ... if the glory of this world ... hides some colorless movement of atoms, some spectral woof of impalpable abstractions, or unearthly ballet of bloodless categories.... They can no longer *make* the whole which commands our devotion, than some shredded dissection of human tatters *is* the warm and breathing beauty of flesh which our hearts found delightful."

52. St. Thomas does discuss rapture or ecstasy (*raptus*) in his discussions of prophecy. The experiences of *raptus* are unexpected and bear a witness to the truth of the prophet's sayings. On the other hand, they have no connection with the holiness or otherwise of the prophet, and so Thomas's discussion needs development if it to be used as a basis for an understanding of St. Philip's embodied mysticism.

53. This is the title of a collection of a series of studies on the physical phenomena of mysticism written by Fr. Herbert Thurston between 1919 and 1938 (see Thurston, *The Physical Phenomena of Mysticism*). The expression itself seems to be that of the editor, Fr. J.H. Creehan, S.J. See also Thurston, *Surprising Mystics*.

54. Bacci, *The Life of Saint Philip Neri*, vol. 1, 337–392.

ing in his breast. The experience had physiological consequences which were observable during the rest of his life. "In moments of excitement there appeared externally on his breast a swelling to leave room for the extraordinary beating of the heart."[55] This event at Pentecost has been compared to the stigmata of St. Francis; and at the autopsy after Philip's death, "they discovered an organic lesion corresponding to this swelling."[56]

We cannot, therefore, disregard either the reality or the strangeness of what was at very least the paranormal, in our saint's experience. This is so, even if it is also true that we must not try to understand his mysticism solely in terms of the paranormal. There does, then, seem to be something missing in St. Thomas's analysis of mysticism. This contention is widely shared, if by no means universally accepted.

> The precepts of Aquinas were not sufficient to determine in any satisfactory scientific way the specific nature of the mystical state. On the contrary it can be shown that the saint either failed altogether to recognize the mystical state as something distinctive in the soul or, at any rate, deemed it unworthy of scientific investigation.[57]

My analysis is based on St. Thomas's teaching on mystical theology. But I think this teaching must be broadened to understand contemplation in a more extended sense than the prayerful reception of the truth.[58] Without altering or attenuating the aspect of *sermo de Deo*, I want it to be understood to include the reception of God's revelation in Christ by not only the intellect but also the whole person. Von Balthasar's definition of contemplation is helpful:

> Contemplative prayer is the reception of revealed truth by one who believes and loves and therefore desires to apply to it all his powers of reason, will and sense. Consequently, the form of the truth itself must always determine and prescribe the mode of reception. Knowledge of the basic truths of theology helps contemplation, for theology, by formulating precisely what the contemplative experiences personally, enables him to avoid being led into false or devious paths. Conversely, anyone practiced in prayer will welcome all the central insights he gains from theology as a means of enriching his own prayer.[59]

---

55. Ponnelle and Bordet, *St. Philip Neri*, 127.
56. "The two first 'false' ribs had become detached from the cartilages which normally unite them to the breastbone; at the point of fraction, the free ends, both ribs and cartilages, projected outwards towards the skin." Ibid.
57. Stolz, *The Doctrine of Spiritual Perfection*, 164.
58. See above, this chapter, pages 23 and 28.
59. Von Balthasar, *Prayer*, 242.

Balthasar asserts that contemplative prayer is a kind of knowledge. What kind? Surely it is a knowledge based on what used to be called divine and Catholic faith. This dependence on theological truth is one aspect of an embodied mysticism. But it is a human being who believes, and the structure of his faith is not distinct from the natural act of what the scholastics call *fides scientifica,* which "rests on a natural perception of credibility."[60] So the *quasi-experimentalis cognitio,* the knowledge that bursts forth into love,[61] has the same psychological structure as other non-supernatural experiences of connaturality, of the kind I outlined in connection with the gift of wisdom.[62] Stolz then lays down a principle of great importance:

> In this sense mystical experience can be described by a rather paradoxical expression as "transpsychological" experience.[63]

Mystical experience is held to be something that goes along with, or is found within, psychological experience. We might now want to ask, what sort of psychological experience? Stolz means, in part, that mystical experience happens to real human beings whose faculties do not need to be distorted or damaged before they are capable of a loving and direct awareness of the divine indwelling and the truths of faith. We are not dealing with "abnormal psychology."

These experiences occur, as Denys Turner puts it, "within the ordinariness of the individual Christian life, whether in liturgy, private prayer, ascetical practice, Christian learning and theology, the reading of Scripture or the duties of religious observance."[64] Mysticism is not a practice by itself, with its own particular set of objects. It happens alongside, or in conjunction with, specifically Christian practices.

The effort to define mysticism, and then see how this definition works out in the experience of the particular mystic, is thus fundamentally wrong-headed. The mystic has "experiences," but these are the result of his encounter with God; they are not the means by which he comes into contact with God. The contemporary emphasis on experi-

---

60. Stolz, *The Doctrine of Spiritual Perfection,* 177. Stolz continues by emphasizing that this *fides scientifica* is "infinitely distinct from a supernatural vision springing from the deified being of the knowing faculty."

61. See above, this chapter, 22.

62. ". . . the new vision and tasting of the truth which deepens the insight common to all believers is not structurally different from similar activities, and in essence is not outside the boundaries of what can be established in a purely psychological manner." Stolz, *The Doctrine of Spiritual Perfection,* 177.

63. Ibid.

64. Turner, *The Darkness of God,* 269.

ence misplaces the focus away from God to what seems to be of interest in what Turner calls "the rather closed, anti-intellectual world of Christian 'spiritualities.'"[65]

The danger with the approach of Stolz or Turner—or of St. Thomas, for that matter—is that they could be taken as leaving nothing of the "quasi-experience" of the divine indwelling except the intellectual aspect. Von Balthasar put the perspective right when he wrote about St. John of the Cross that the mystic is one who, with God's grace, comes to participate in the life of God himself,[66] and if the mystic participates in the life of God himself, that must surely be the key to understanding mysticism. It is not a question of various techniques to obtain more or less satisfying experiences. It is God himself who desires the creature to share in the life of the creator. God, to use Von Balthasar's words, is "pure, radiant love,"[67] and actively desires mankind's participation in the same love. But this sharing only becomes possible when the mystic gives himself up to God totally, and so "divine love becomes the loving action of the creature itself."[68] This process, by which the mystic hands himself over, is only possible because God has already made his presence known to the soul. This principle is taught in the Book of Revelation:

> Behold, I stand at the door and knock; if any one hears my voice and opens the door, I will come to him and eat with him, and he with me.[69]

For the mystic, this knocking at the door becomes more and more insistent. The voice most of us hardly ever hear becomes what, for the mystic, is impossible to ignore. Past a certain point, he has no choice in the matter: in the dialectic of knowledge and love, it is love that takes over. Both the knocking and the voice remove any awareness in the soul of anything but the dark presence of God. This insistent and finally overwhelming character of the experience of God's power upon the soul is what Cardinal Daniélou calls the *weight of God*:

---

65. Ibid., 8.
66. "God alone suffices. Man is created, called, endowed with grace, for the sake of the vision of God, for participation in the inner, triune life of eternal love. Man, who is relative, is what he is for the sake of the Absolute, and inasmuch as the Absolute outweighs the relative, so in human desire God must outweigh all created things." Von Balthasar, *The Glory of the Lord*, vol. III, 108.
67. God's love, Balthasar goes on to say, is "a love that is open to the creature and desires its participation in the absolute and ontological unity of the Godhead." Ibid.
68. Ibid.
69. Revelation 3:20. See above, *Preface*, 9.

This weight of God upon the heart has a name; it is mystical experience. The mystic is one who experiences the reality of the living God. But he cannot bear it—and that is exactly what he feels. The brightness of the divine light is too intense for sight to endure without perishing. This is why St. John of the Cross says that it is darkness. The abyss of God is too dazzling for sight to fathom, and this is why St. Gregory of Nyssa speaks of being dazzled by the divine essence.[70]

It is often said that before the sixteenth century and the writings of the two Carmelites St. Teresa of Avila and St. John of the Cross, little attention was paid to the question of experience. On the face of it, this is untrue. Even an elementary knowledge of the early Cistercians makes nonsense of such a claim.[71] The real issue is the significance or value to be set on this personal experience. Hegel maintained, for example, that what he called subjectivity in religion entered into the modern consciousness through the German Reformation. The result of this reformation, properly understood, Hegel taught, was that "Reason and the Divine commands are now synonymous." Through the "time honored and cherished sincerity of the German people" what Hegel called externality in religion was abolished. By externality he meant "that the specific embodiment of Deity ... is in no way present and actual in an outward form, but as essentially spiritual is obtained only by being reconciled to God—in faith and spiritual enjoyment." Faith becomes "the subjective assurance of the Eternal, of Absolute Truth, of the Truth of God."[72] The step from this contention to the all too familiar view that real religion is only about authenticity, sincerity, and inwardness is both short and almost irresistible. The personal and the subjective [in Hegel's sense], are not words that point in the same direction. Embodied mysticism has an ineluctably personal aspect, but, in St. Paul's words, "we have his treasure in earthen vessels, to show that the transcendent power belongs to God and not to us."[73] It is the weight of God on the individual that is at the heart of the matter. The individual and his experiences only have significance within this framework of God's activity.

It is evident from St. Thomas's analysis that some of the highest mystical experiences, using the word to mean a direct experience of God, of

---

70. Daniélou, *God and the Ways of Knowing*, 126–127.

71. Consider, for example, this (typical) passage from William of St. Thierry: "Yearnings, strivings, longings, thoughts and affections, and all that is within me, come and let us go up to the mountain or place where the Lord sees and is seen." William of St. Thierry, *On Contemplating God, Prayer Meditations*, 1:36.

72. Hegel, *The Philosophy of History*, 414–423.

73. 2 Corinthians 4:7.

which God is the source, fall under the category of *raptus*.[74] They are the result of a sudden incursion of a power which brooks no opposition. The experiences of *raptus* are unexpected. They are not the result of any sort of ascetical or intellectual preparation.

This analysis of *raptus* will be useful in understanding other sorts of mysticism, and I want now to lay the groundwork for this understanding. First of all, I want to suggest that while the category of *raptus* covers a well-defined area of mystical experience, it doesn't cover other experiences of the highest forms of mysticism. The culmination of mystical development as traced out, for example, by St. Teresa and St. John of the Cross differs in significant ways from that of *raptus*. For the Carmelites, this culmination is not characterized by a violent and unexpected incursion of an exterior force, even though the mystic is passive in the hands of God. Moreover, the experiences St. John of the Cross writes about are consequent on a long ascetical and intellectual preparation.[75] This preparation, although it does not cause or bring about the experiences,[76] is essential for a Catholic mystical life. So, unlike the experience of *raptus*, the good, even saintly moral character of the mystic is a vital aspect of the mystical journey. Genuine mystical experience finds its ultimate sense in God's use of the mystic as an instrument for the good of a wounded and suffering humanity.[77] Embodied mysticism falls into the category of what Cardinal Journet calls "charismatic graces." They do not directly sanctify the person receiving them but instead are given so that the recipient can help others.[78] Still, it must be emphasized that, unlike the charismatic graces given to the prophets, the lives of the great mystics are the lives of saints.

Although the mystic is passive in the hands of God, the final outcome is not characterized by a violent and unexpected incursion of an exterior force. St. Teresa says that in the final stage, or mansion, of the mystical journey, there "are hardly any of the periods of aridity or interior disturbance in it which at one time or another have occurred in all the rest, but the soul is almost always in tranquility."[79]

---

74. Aquinas, *Summa Theologiae*, 2a, 2ae, q. 175, articles 3–6, inclusive.
75. See below, this chapter, 36–37, and Part I, "Light in Florence."
76. See Part Two, "Clouds and Light in San Germano and Rome."
77. See Part Three, "Light From the Darkness."
78. "We shall end with a word on what are called 'charismatic graces.' . . . [These are] graces *not directly sanctifying* the person receiving them, graces that simply enable him to perform acts which assist others along the road to sanctifying grace. They are useful socially." Journet, *The Meaning of Grace*, 31.
79. St. Teresa of Jesus, "Interior Castle," *Complete Works*, vol. II, 342.

So tranquilly and noiselessly does the Lord teach the soul in this state and do it good that I am reminded of the building of Solomon's temple, during which no noise could be heard; just so, in this temple of God, in this Mansion of His, He and the soul alone have fruition of each other in the deepest silence. There is now no need for the understanding to stir, or to seek out anything, for the Lord Who created the soul is now pleased to calm it....[80]

In the *Living Flame of Love*, St. John of the Cross describes the culmination of the mystical ascent in a similar way. He also says that the condition for this final stage of the mystical life is a willingness to submit to what he calls the dark night of the spirit, through a readiness to suffer in the darkness the apparent absence and even rejection by God. The obstacles to a whole-hearted and total obedience to the demands of the Gospel are so deeply ingrained in human nature that they cannot be remedied even with good will and divine grace. They can only be destroyed by the direct action of God on the soul, and progress in the love of God can only be obtained by a willing payment of a high price. That price is a loving acceptance of a suffering that reflects the agony in the garden and the desolation of the Cross. So few reach the summit of the mystical life because so very few will accept these trials:

> And here it behooves us to note why it is that there are so few that attain to this lofty state. It must be known that this is not because God is pleased that there should be few raised to this high spiritual state—on the contrary, it would please Him if all were so raised—but because he finds few vessels in whom He can perform so high and lofty a work. For, when He proves them in small things and finds them weak and sees that they at once flee from labor, and desire not to submit to the least discomfort or mortification, or to work with solid patience, He finds that they are not strong enough to bear the favor which He was granting them when He began to purify them, and goes not farther with their purification, neither does He lift them up from the dust of the earth, since for this they would need greater fortitude and constancy.[81]

The flame of God's love assaults and wounds the soul, and if the recipient of these graces does not run away from these dark and bitter experiences, then God will heal it and bring it into his presence.

> For Thou slayest and Thou giveth life and there is none that can flee from Thy hand. But Thou, oh, Life Divine, never slayest save to give

---

80. Ibid.
81. St. John of the Cross, "Living Flame of Love," *Complete Works,* vol. III, 46.

life, even as Thou never woundest save to heal. Thou hast wounded me, oh, hand Divine, in order to heal me, and thou hast slain in me that which would have slain me, but for the life of God wherein now I see that I live.[82]

The purpose of trials in the mystical life is to do away with everything in the soul that is at enmity with God and stands in the way of union of the soul with its creator. In the end, after the storms and near shipwreck, these divine assaults, or touches, bring peace and tranquility:

Oh, delicate touch of the Word, delicate, yea, wondrously delicate, to me, which, having overthrown the mountains and broken the stones of Mount Horeb with the shadow of Thy power and strength that went before Thee, didst reveal Thyself to the Prophet with the whisper of gentle air. Oh, gentle air, thou art so delicate and gentle! Say how Thou doest touch the soul so gently and so delicately when Thou art so terrible and powerful? Oh, blessed, twice blessed, the soul whom Thou dost touch so gently though Thou art so terrible and powerful![83]

The concept of rapture or ecstasy understood as a violent incursion of the supernatural will not explain every instance of mystical experience. It will certainly prove inadequate for an understanding of Philip's embodied mysticism.

The Three Ways

This discussion of an embodied mysticism should maintain a theological outlook while, at the same time, avoiding any *a priori* theory of how the theological principles work out in practice. We still need, though, a framework to organize the discussion of the many and varied topics to which I have alluded. Such a framework must be theological in nature but also leave room for a discussion of the actual experiences of the mystics. The tradition of the three ways is such a framework: it is theological in nature, and it throws light on the development of the experience of the individual as it is lived out in the Church. Yet it is not arbitrary or narrow.

The tradition maintains that there are characteristic ways which the soul has of acting, and re-acting, to the presence of God in its moral life, in its effort to understand the truths that are the foundation of its life, and in the development of its sacramental and liturgical life. It teaches that these ways can be understood as stages, or focuses of attention, in the progress of the individual Christian's relationship to God. In *Denys*

---

82. Ibid., 42.
83. Ibid., 43.

the Areopagite there is a triad of purification, illumination, and union; this classification "was destined to have great impact on subsequent Christian tradition."[84] St. Thomas has another three-fold classification and talks about the way of beginners, the way of those making progress, and the way of the perfect.[85]

There are other ways of talking about growth in the knowledge and love of God. A seventeenth-century French Dominican, Louis Chardon, wrote a book called *The Cross of Jesus*, which is faithful to the teaching of St. Thomas but speaks about the spiritual life "in terms of the negative aspect of suffering and purgation and the positive aspect of growth in grace and the invisible missions."[86] It is important to notice the possibility of other classifications, such as Chardon's, as it may help to counter the temptation to think that God always acts in the same way on individuals, or worse, that if there is no evidence of the triple scheme in a particular case, the writer may be dismissed as not up to scratch.

It should be said that the doctrine of the three ways has been seriously criticized in more modern times, and both Von Balthasar and Rahner were reluctant to accept it. Von Balthasar had the commendable conviction that God deals with each soul in a unique and irreplaceable way. The Holy Spirit is to be allowed to work in souls as he freely wills. "That he chooses conditions and missions according to the uniqueness of each person is why Balthasar to a degree mistrusts the *developmental* accounts of mystical prayer offered by the doctors of sixteenth-century Carmel (and their modern disciples like Garrigou-Lagrange)."[87] Balthasar also had reservations about what he regarded as the Neo-Platonic origins of the divisions.[88]

---

84. See Louth, *Denys The Areopagite*, 40–42. Louth points out that the origin of the threefold division is to be found partly in the pagan mystery religions, and that Plato "picked up" such language in discussing the development of opinion to true knowledge.

85. The Latin word translated here as way is *studium*. A *studium* can also be translated as something like "focus of attention" or "main concern." I do not think anything rigid or fixed is indicated by Thomas's use of *studium* or in his discussion of our growth in charity. A focus of attention does not eliminate everything else. For example, concentrating on trigonometry does not eliminate our knowledge or need for arithmetic, nor does it mean that the time and energy spent in early life on learning to add and subtract was a waste of time. See Robinson, *On the Lord's Appearing*, 78–84.

86. Aumann, "Introduction," Chardon, *The Cross of Jesus*, xx.

87. Nichols, *Divine Fruitfulness*, 284.

88. "The identification of this forty days of contemplation [that is, of many of the prophets and of Christ himself] with the Greek idea of the contemplative ascent to God was first made by Origen and his followers ... but it is not an altogether happy one." Von Balthasar, *Prayer*, 192.

Karl Rahner, in his "Gradual Ascent to Christian Perfection," is even harder on the very possibility of such a classification:[89]

> ... the usual conception of the step-by-step development of the spiritual life presupposes that there is a kind of growth and enrichment in the realm of the *empirical* ego and its experiences. This is, however, rather obviously dependent on the indicated non-moral causes and circumstances (to which of course belong also heredity, the basic vital and psychical constitution, the "*complexio*" of old people, and everything which influences these things in the course of one's life).[90]

Simon Tugwell, O.P., finds another aspect of these difficulties. He argues that the earliest monastic tradition knew nothing of the threefold developmental view, and in this it was much closer to reality:

> The monastic tradition ... more or less took it for granted that it is only gradually that we make progress in our Christian lives, and that we may never get any further than oscillating between falling and getting up again. As likely as not, our whole life will be one long battle and, when all else fails, we may end up simply saying to God, "Lord save me, whether I like it or not; dust and ashes that I am, I love sin."[91]

This passage will strike a chord in many reader's hearts today. It should be handled with care. Of course, progress is gradual. But if we think "oscillating between falling and getting up again" means that it is pointless even to think about moral and spiritual progress, then we are very close to the way some people understand Luther. That is to say, we are teaching the fruitlessness of moral effort in the life of faith. Attractive as this turn in the road may be, it usually ends in not even trying and talking about "the filthy rags of righteousness." Nonetheless, this note of unease about the tradition of the three ways should not be ignored, even when we have greater reservations about its critics. Their hesitations introduce a welcome note of reality and common sense into what sometimes seem to be abstract and *a priori* discussions of Christian perfection.[92]

The disagreement between those who adopt the traditional view of development and those who reject it can blind us to the crucial truth:

---

89. Karl Rahner, *Theological Investigations*, 3.
90. Ibid., 19.
91. Tugwell, *Ways of Imperfection*, 37.
92. My procedure is not open to the sort of strictures urged by Rahner against the twofold classification of the three ways—that is whether they are really talking about the same thing—nor the difficulties with both approaches in themselves. I am writing about the experiences of one saint, and trying to understand these experiences within a well-defined sacramental and liturgical life.

the presence of God's action both in initiating and maintaining genuine mystical experience.[93] Whether we think that the Christian's relationship with God is best described by a version of the three ways or think it is a humdrum matter of working the same set of factors over and over, we must keep alive the truth that God is active. If God is active, then it is also true that we are not in complete charge of our dealing with him. We should allow an element of passivity on our part towards this action of God's:

> ... purification, illumination and union are operations that happen to us: we *are* purified, we *are* illuminated, we *are* perfected. We do not achieve this movement towards God ourselves, by our own efforts: we depend on God's gracious movement towards us.[94]

It is a good question to what extent this action of God in our lives can be perceived. Some of the hesitations expressed about the three ways show a tendency to resist proponents of the doctrine who equate, in a direct way, "experiences" with the action of God. Nonetheless, it does not follow from this misreading that the doctrine itself is useless, nor that we can dismiss such experiences as being always irrelevant and misleading.

With these cautions in mind, let us proceed with the doctrine of the three ways, both as a framework for the historical aspects of St. Philip's life and for the development of his relationship with God. I have taken much of what I say on the three ways from one of the Greek Fathers. Newman, in a litany to St. Philip, called him "Man of primitive times." The early Fathers of the Church fascinated Philip and, although he knew his St. Thomas well, there is often a freshness and immediacy about the Greek Fathers that we find again in St. Philip. This is particularly true of Gregory of Nyssa, whose doctrine of perpetual progress catches something of Philip's own free and attractive communion with the unseen God.[95]

In chapter three of his Letter to the Philippians, St. Paul asks for the righteousness of God that depends on faith, so that he may know Christ Jesus and the power of his resurrection. He asks that he may share Christ's sufferings, becoming like him in his death, so that if possible he may attain the resurrection from the dead. He then says:

---

93. See above, Preface, 9
94. Louth, *Denys the Areopagite*, 41.
95. I should make I make it clear that I am not buying into St. Gregory's extraordinary views about human nature. Even after Daniélou's sympathetic and careful handling, they do seem to have a bizarre aspect to them.

> Not that I have already obtained this or am already perfect; but I press on to make it my own, because Christ Jesus has made me his own. Brethren, I do not consider that I have made it my own; but one thing I do, forgetting what lies behind and straining forward to what lies ahead, I press on toward the goal for the prize of the upward call of God in Christ Jesus.[96]

This continual striving after transformation into the likeness of God in Christ is central to Gregory's thinking. For most of Greek philosophy, becoming was an imperfection, and this was true of Origen. Yet for Gregory it was no imperfection, because becoming itself was the only way spiritual progress was made. This stretching towards what is ahead, in zest and excitement, fits Philip's own journey into God. The words of a contemporary Orthodox scholar about St. Gregory give what I believe to be the right perspective on Gregory's relation to Origen, and to Greek philosophy, on the question of change and becoming:

> In the history of human thought Gregory appears as the one who broke the cycles of ancient thought (still traceable in Origenism), who rehabilitated becoming, who gave time a positive value as the apprenticeship of love, and supremely the one who showed that human beings have no other definition than to be indefinable, because they are made by God's infinitude and created for it.[97]

Gregory's "rehabilitation" of becoming does away with the temptation to look on the three ways as a succession of fixed steps with no room for the ups and downs of individual lives, nor for the heights and depths of the soul's response to the approach of the God who makes all things new.[98]

Gregory uses the life of Moses as an example of how an individual man was led from the darkness of false and deceptive ideas about God into a loving awareness of the divine presence.[99] God's manifestation to Moses began with light:

> And the angel of the Lord appeared to him in a flame of fire out of the midst of a bush; and he looked and lo, the bush was burning, yet it was not consumed.[100]

This shows us, explains Gregory, that the spiritual life begins with a

---

96. Philippians 3:11–14.
97. Clement, *The Roots of Christian Mysticism*, 339.
98. "And he who sat on the throne said, 'Behold I make all things new,'" Revelation 21:5.
99. See Gregory of Nyssa, *The Life of Moses* and *Commentary on the Song of Songs*.
100. Exodus 3:2

withdrawal from false, deceptive ideas about God and is thus a turning from darkness towards light. Our baptism brings us from the darkness of sin and error into the life of light and grace. The first stage of the spiritual life, the purgative way, is learning to live in this light and grace. The sacrament of Penance is the way that those who sin after baptism return to the condition of baptismal innocence. St. Paul says that "once you were darkness, but now you are light in the Lord; walk as children of light (for the fruit of light is found in all that is good and right and true)."[101] This is the task of the first way: to learn to walk as children of light. We enter into the way of light through our baptism. Following Origen, Gregory associates the first way with the Book of Proverbs, in which the soul is like a pupil who is being taught.

> The instruction in Proverbs provides words fit for the person who is still young, adapting its words of admonition to that period of life. "Hear my son, your father's instructions and reject not your mother's teaching." You see here the soul is at a stage of life where it is tender and easily formed. Moreover, it still needs maternal instruction and paternal admonition.[102]

But after the light, there comes obscurity and darkness, and God spoke to Moses through a cloud:

> And the people stood afar off, while Moses drew near to the thick cloud where God was.[103]

Gregory understood this to mean that after living a moral and free life in the grace of God, we begin to discern previously hidden depths of our faith. We begin to seek this reality we sense, beyond the appearances of everyday life and, he continues, this "more careful understanding of hidden things leads the soul through appearances to God's hidden nature which is symbolized by a cloud overshadowing all appearances and which little by little accustoms the soul to behold what is hidden."[104] This stage of illumination about hidden truth is associated with the sacrament of confirmation. By this sacrament the baptized:

> are more perfectly bound to the Church and are enriched with a special strength of the Holy Spirit. Hence they are, as true witnesses of Christ, more strictly obliged to spread and defend the faith by word and deed.[105]

---

101. Ephesians 5:8.
102. Gregory of Nyssa, *Commentary on the Song of Songs*, the first homily, 45.
103. Exodus 20:21
104. Gregory of Nyssa, *Commentary on the Song of Songs*, the eleventh homily, 202.
105. *Catechism of the Catholic Church*, 1285.

We have need of being more perfectly bound to the Church, and of a special strength to persevere in our efforts to contemplate "the secret and hidden wisdom of God," which "no eye has seen, nor ear heard, nor the heart of man conceived."[106] If we are to witness to the truth of Christ, we must, according to our capacities and the grace given to us, persevere in the often lonely search for the light shining in the darkness. Gregory associates this search for hidden truth with the Book of Ecclesiastes:

> ... Solomon adds the philosophy contained in Ecclesiastes for the person who has been sufficiently introduced by proverbial training to desire virtues. After having reproached in that book men's attitude towards external appearances, and after having said that everything is vain and passing ... Solomon elevates above everything grasped by sense the loving movement of our soul towards invisible beauty.[107]

Finally, "having risen higher and having become more perfect, Moses saw God in darkness":[108]

> Then Moses went up on the mountain, and the cloud covered the mountain ... and Moses entered the cloud, and went up on the mountain.[109]

This shows us, says Gregory, that finally the soul is led on high. "Forsaking what human nature can attain, the soul enters within the sanctuary of divine knowledge where she is hemmed in on all sides by the divine darkness."[110] Gregory presents the dominant theme of this third, unitive way not as knowledge but as love. For this reason, he associates the way of union with the Eucharist, the sacrament of our Lord's love through which we are united in a real way with the God we have been seeking from the beginning.

We have, then, three different sets of interrelated concepts for interpreting development in the mystical life. First, there is one modeled on the sacraments: Baptism and Penance, Confirmation, and the Eucharist.[111] Secondly, there is an account based on the experience of the individual: the purgative way, the illuminative way, and the unitive way. And third, there is an approach that unites both the ecclesial dimension

---

106. 1 Corinthians 2:6 and 2:9
107. Gregory of Nyssa, *Commentary on the Song of Songs*, 47.
108. Gregory of Nyssa, *Commentary on the Song of Songs*, 202
109. Exodus 24:15 and 24:18
110. Gregory of Nyssa, *Commentary on the Song of Songs*, 202.
111. In this manner the three ways are firmly attached to what the Church calls *The Sacraments of Christian Initiation*. "The sacraments of Christian initiation—Baptism,

and the experience of the individual: Proverbs, Ecclesiastes, and the Song of Songs.

To obtain a balanced view of the mystical life, we should keep all three of these sets of concepts for describing it in play. To discuss the purgative, illuminative, and unitive ways in isolation from the sacramental life of the Church, and in abstraction from any biblical foundation, is to invite the sort of criticisms levelled by Karl Rahner and Simon Tugwell. On the other hand, the different classifications do highlight different aspects of spiritual theology, and one of these aspects is often better adapted to grasping a particular mystic's life and teaching than another. In this book, we are trying here to understand the development of one particular mystic, St. Philip Neri, and not mysticism in general. Therefore, I have used the account of the three ways that highlight the development of the individual's experience as the best way of describing Philip's own journey.

Confirmation and the Eucharist—lay the *foundations* of every Christian life. 'The sharing in the divine nature given to men through the grace of Christ bears a certain likeness to the origin, developing and nourishing of natural life. The faithful are born anew by Baptism, strengthened by the sacrament of Confirmation, and receive in the Eucharist the food of eternal life. By means of these sacraments of Christian initiation, they thus receive in increasing measure the treasures of the divine life and advance towards the perfection of charity.'" *Catechism of the Catholic Church*, 1212.

PART ONE
Light in Florence

And if the flame by which the soul of the prophet was illuminated was kindled by a thorny bush, even this fact will not be useless in our inquiry. For if truth is God and truth is light—the Gospel testifies by these sublime and divine names to the God who made himself visible to us in the flesh—such guidance of virtue leads us to know that light which has reached down even to human nature. Lest one think that the radiance did not come from a material substance, this light did not shine from some luminary among the stars but came from an earthly bush and surpassed the heavenly luminaries in brilliance.

St. Gregory of Nyssa[1]

IN the *Introduction* to this book, I outlined how the discussion of St. Philip's embodied mysticism would be structured on the tradition of the three ways.[2] This tradition holds that the roots of the mystical life are the same as the foundations of Christian living, and St. Philip's mysticism began in learning virtue and fighting vice. This struggle to dominate pride, anger, lust, and the other passions, as well as to build up patterns of Christian behavior, was called by Origen the purgative way, by St. Thomas the way of beginners, and by Gregory of Nyssa the way of light. In calling it the way of light, Gregory meant that while the struggle against the passions, and to build good habits, is long and difficult, nonetheless, it is a transition out of the darkness of sins and error into God's own marvelous light.[3]

It is God's truth as light, a light shining in the darkness of confusion,

---

1. St. Gregory of Nyssa, *Life of Moses* II, 19, 59.
2. See Introduction, "An Embodied Mysticism," 37–44. A balanced view of this tradition, I pointed out, has to keep in mind three different sets of interrelated concepts. These are one modeled on the sacraments, the next on the experience of the individual, and the third, which unites both the ecclesial dimension and the experience of the individual.
3. Cf. 1 Peter 2:9.

sin, and error, that dominates Gregory's understanding of the way of beginners and the spiritual combat that is its defining characteristic. This "virtue ethics," as it is called nowadays, is sometimes criticized as formalistic and impersonal, and no doubt it can degenerate into rote responses and insensitivity to the contingencies of life. But the spiritual combat is the foundation of all Christian living. It is also the foundation, and remains an essential element, of the mystical life. It is a touchstone of the reality of one's commitment to the fundamental obligations of a life in Christ.

This focus on day-to-day living of Christianity is found all through St. Paul, and St. Peter has the same focus:

> Finally, all of you, have unity of spirit, sympathy, love of the brethren, a tender heart and a humble mind. Do not return evil for evil or reviling for reviling; but on the contrary bless, for to this you have been called, that you may obtain a blessing. For
> "He that would love life and see good days...
> Let him turn away from evil and do right;
> Let him seek peace and pursue it."[4]

These foundations of mysticism have nothing to do with a superior attitude towards "unenlightened and ordinary" morality. This all-too-common attitude ruins our understanding of the mystical life because, to put it bluntly, without a serious effort to live ordinary Christianity there is no possibility of extraordinary Christianity. This view of the foundations of Christian living is in sharp contrast to a good deal of writing about the saints. Instant perfection, or spectacular conversions, still seem, all too often, to be taken as the norm. It has been said that Catholic hagiography deals either with the lives of reformed rakes or people out of stained glass windows. St. Augustine, St. John of God, St. Camillus of Lellis, and even St. Ignatius of Loyola are taken as belonging to the first class, while the great majority seem to have stepped out of a stained-glass window. There is, for example, the account of the birth of St. Nicholas, of whom it is reported: "and leaping from his mother's womb he cried: God be glorified."[5]

St. Philip was not a reformed rake, but neither was he a figure out of the world of stained glass; he was a man of flesh and blood whose early life exemplified a particularly successful training of his nature. This resulted in defeating the domination of the passions as well as establish-

---

4. 1 Peter 3:8–11.
5. This is from Eric Crozier's libretto for Benjamin Britten's cantata *Saint Nicolas* (1948).

ing a loving freedom with God. The spiritual combat, and a sense of familiarity with God, are the foundations of all Christian living. They also remain as an essential aspect of the mystical life. Fighting sin does not come naturally; it has to be taught; it requires an education in Christian truth. St. Paul said squarely: "What have you that you did not receive? If then you received it, why do you boast as if it were not a gift?"[6] To receive something requires a giver, to learn something requires a teacher, and St. Gregory of Nyssa, as we have seen, links the beginning of a life deeply committed to Christ with receiving and being taught.

This stage of life begins with Baptism, and it should be understood as a working out of the consequences of this sacrament of initiation. These consequences involve not only the spiritual combat against sin and error, but also the "putting on of the new man, created after the likeness of God in true righteousness and holiness."[7] For Gregory, the successful outcome of the spiritual combat is *apatheia* and *parrhesia*.[8] The first of these is the capacity to live in a state of grace and in detachment from worldly distractions, while the second is the possession of a loving familiarity with and childlike confidence in God.[9] These endowments are prerequisites of a mystical life that is genuinely Christian.

The training Philip received in fighting the vices and developing the virtues was one aspect of what I have described as an embodied mysticism. This mysticism does not exist save as an aspect of a complex of communal, linguistic, and symbolic order of beliefs and practices.[10] The ascetical dimension itself, the element of being trained, and training oneself, in Christian living, is embedded in this order. The other two strands of this embodied mysticism are the theological and the sacramental, or liturgical. The seeds of the mystical life are sown, take root, and begin to flower in the ascetical aspect of Christianity. It is also, though, the case that this ascetical dimension is itself an aspect of theological truth and Catholic liturgical practice.[11] Mysticism is not a prize for a successful moral life—whatever that might mean exactly. On the other hand, the ascetical life is required to make Christian mysticism possible.

6. 1 Corinthians 4:7.
7. Ephesians 4:24.
8. Ἀπαθεία and παρρησία.
9. See chapter five, "The Philip who Left Florence," 129.
10. See Introduction, "An Embodied Mysticism," 23.
11. Without this theological and liturgical setting, the ascetical life is all too liable to fall into self-deception and hypocrisy. Francois Mauriac's *A Woman of the Pharisees* is only one example in a long line of tales of Christian morality gone wrong. See Robinson, *Duty and Hypocrisy in Hegel's Phenomenology of Mind*.

The *First Way* of the mystical life, Origen's *Purgative Way*, or Gregory's *Way of Light*, or St. Thomas's *Way of Beginners*, was the foundation of Philip's holiness, and this foundation was laid during his life in Florence. Philip did not begin as a saint, and if we are to catch even a glimpse of how the boy born in Florence, in difficult times, and of a not particularly happy family, developed into Saint Philip Neri, then we have to understand some of the influences that went to shape him and his reaction to them. He became a great mystic who moved from the shadows of an ordinary background into the center of the Catholic world. But that was not how it was in the beginning. In the five chapters of part one, I show how the foundation of Philip's mysticism was laid during his early life.

First, there is a chapter on Philip's growing up in Florence and the attitude he began to develop, to borrow an expression of Newman's, of *using this world well*. This is followed by a discussion on the development of the Christian virtues, especially that of chastity. I go on to apply the results of this discussion to Philip. Then I outline some of the teachings of St. Catherine of Siena and Savonarola on the soul's relationship to God and on the nature of reform in the Church. Both of these Dominican saints had a profound and lasting influence on Philip. Next there is a chapter that deals with art, irony, and eros as aspects of what I have called Philip's worldliness. Once again, it was his Florentine background that provided the raw material for his own inimitable fusion of what he learned from, and how he reacted to, his early environment. Finally, there is a discussion of Philip's character as it was by the time he left Florence, when he was seventeen or eighteen.

It was in St. Philip's devotion to, and absorption in, the ordinary life of the Church—a Church which has to be understood as having a historical dimension—that we find his mystical practice and the key to his influence. In Turner's happy phrasing, it was in "the 'hiddenness' of the divine transcendent within the public, accessible, common cult,"[12] that Philip grew from an unknown boy into a great saint. Yet the great saint was always Philip Neri; the Philip Neri who was born and educated in Florence. His participation in God's own love for his creation was always mediated, or filtered, through Philip's own human, and therefore limited and particular, nature. To understand Philip's embodied mysticism requires not only knowledge of the religious and social environment that formed him but also the recognition that Philip's mysticism, being embodied in a particular individual, had its own unique character.

---

12. Turner, *The Darkness of God*, 258.

1

Using This World Well

> We attain to heaven by using this world well, though it is to pass away; we perfect our nature, not by undoing it, but by adding to it what is more than nature, and directing it towards aims higher than its own.
>
> J. H. Newman[1]

THE WORLD that Philip learned to use well was no abstraction or general idea. It was the world of Florence. Philip grew up in a city proud, some would say inordinately so, of its history and of its citizens. By the time of Philip's birth, the external political power of fifteenth-century Florence was on the wane, and its internal stability had all but disappeared. Yet he was born into a society that had no small estimate of its own merits.

The history of Florence and the intellectual and cultural development of Renaissance Italy have been carefully studied over the centuries, and even today the discipline is still something of a growth industry.[2] The focus of this research has changed through the years, and the relative weight given to artistic and philosophical aspects, or to economic and political factors, has been and remains fluid. Yet regardless of differing approaches, this continuing research is evidence enough that Renaissance Florence was a very special place and that its citizens were marked by what they had created. Philip was no exception, and the Roman saint bore the impress of his Florentine boyhood to the end. He never rejected this upbringing, and, as Newman put it, the path to his sanctity

---

1. J.H. Newman, *The Idea of a University*, 147.
2. "Mountains of new scholarship have appeared in the last two generations.... All this scholarship, which has grown beyond the realistic possibility of both mastering the work of the past and keeping up with what emerges every month, sometimes feels like an avalanche in which one can easily be buried." Najemy, *A History of Florence*, 4.

lay through using this world well; and this world, to emphasize the point, was the city of Florence.

The following excerpts, from a panegyric of the city and of its citizens[3] by Leonardi Bruni, were written a century before Philip's birth. Yet the attitudes the passage conveys—despite the dramatic changes in the power and prestige of Florence externally and the internecine strife which all but ruined it internally—still characterized its citizens. First Bruni points out the difficulty of describing his city:

> Nothing more beautiful or more splendid than Florence can be found anywhere in the world.... The splendor of the city is so remarkable that no eloquence could begin to describe it.... If you consider the beauty and the magnificence of the city, you would think that there is nothing more deserving with which to begin a speech. If, on the other hand, you take into account its power and wealth, you would think it right to start an oration with these topics. Furthermore if you look at its deeds both in the present and in the past, nothing could appear more important than to begin here. But if you focus on its customs and institutions, nothing could seem more worthy of distinction.[4]

Bruni then tells us about the inhabitants of Florence:

> As it sometimes happens that a son's resemblance to his parents is immediately noticeable, so the Florentines resemble their most noble and illustrious city to such a degree that one is led to believe that they could never have lived anywhere else, nor could Florence ever have had any other kind of inhabitants. Just as these citizens far excel all other people by virtue of their natural genius, prudence, wealth, and magnificence, so Florence, whose site was most carefully chosen, is superior to all others in splendor, beauty and cleanliness.[5]

The writing of panegyrics was a recognized literary form, and it would be difficult to say how far the writer or his readers accepted everything said. But Bruni believed there was enough truth in what he said to save him from looking ridiculous, and he thought that what he said would resonate with what his hearers thought about themselves. Behind Bruni's words there lay what has been called *The Myth of Florence*.[6]

This myth was expressed by Girolamo Benivieni, one of Lorenzo de'

---

3. *Laudatio florentinae urbis* cited in Baldassari and Sauber, *Images of Quattrocento Florence*, 39.
4. Ibid., 40–41.
5. Ibid., 41.
6. See chapter one, "The Myth of Florence," in Weinstein, *Savonarola and Florence*, 27.

Medici's friends, who assured Florence that she had a universal mission to play and that all the world would come to the city:

> All peoples and all nations, wrote Benivieni, would conform to the one true religion of Florence, and the world would be united in one sheepfold under a single shepherd. In the new age Florence would extend her hegemony in a benevolent *imperio* because she was the city of the elect and of the true religion. All those who returned voluntarily to rest between the paws of the lion would be blessed with temporal and spiritual rewards, while any who disdained her future glory would be accursed.[7]

This myth of Florence had important repercussions for the Catholicism of the city. Whatever Benevieni may have meant by "the one true religion of Florence," the belief that Florence was predestined to play a central role in history was taken up and used by the Dominican reformer Girolamo Savonarola in his attempt to establish a Christian Commonwealth in which Jesus Christ was to be the sovereign and the Gospel the law.[8] Savonarola had no doubt about the nature of "the true religion of Florence." It was Catholicism as understood by the strictest of the Reforming party in the Church. Savonarola's few years of power in Florence altered not only the political complexion of the state but also introduced a strong and often strident reforming current into its Church, a current that continued after his death. Philip's family had been taken up by this reforming current, and Philip himself always held the memory of Savonarola in veneration.[9]

Philip was born on July 22, 1515, at two o'clock in the morning, and the same day he was taken to the baptistery of San Giovanni in Florence to receive the sacrament of Baptism. Through his baptism, he also became a member of his native city, and it was this city that nurtured and formed him in many different ways. Before the Council of Trent, at least in Italy, only the cathedral of a diocese, or a special building associated with it (as in Florence), had a baptismal font. When a twelfth-century canon:

---

7. Ibid., 31.
8. See chapter three, "Reform in Florence: St. Catherine and Savonarola," 95–97, on how Savonarola used the myth.
9. "...we may conjecture that in the great religious conflict which had so recently agitated Florence, the Neri had taken the part with Savonarola; and this conjecture is strengthened by the fact that our saint showed great affection to the friars of S. Mark, and held in much honour the memory of the austere and impetuous reformer." Capecelatro, *The Life of Saint Philip Neri*, 6.

...of the Cathedral of Bergamo was asked about the relation of the Cathedral to its baptistery, he explained that the two were a single entity, and since the baptism for the city were performed in one, both together formed the Ecclesia Matrix, the Mother Church. Baptism, above all else, identified the first church of the city.[10]

This arrangement made clear the communal aspect of the sacrament; the child was incorporated into a local church, and the situation had not changed at the time Philip was baptized. In *The Divine Comedy*, when Dante encounters his ancestor Cacciaguida in heaven, "he speaks to him of their native city, [and] refers to his fellow Florentines as the 'flock of San Giovanni,' the offspring of the city baptistery."[11] It was this same baptistery in which Philip was baptized and that still stands today, with its great bronze doors as an abiding example of the marvels of Florentine art.

Baptism is a great deal more than the adoption of the child into a local community; it is also his incorporation into the life-giving death of Christ, the beginning of the Christian life, and the foundation of all the other sacraments. But for now, let us consider only its societal aspects in Florence. It was Florence that formed Philip, and in spite of having spent most of his life in Rome, he always considered Florence his native land.[12]

Philip's Boyhood

On the twelfth of July, 1596, Elisabetta Cioni appeared before the vicar of the Cardinal Archbishop of Florence, Alessandro de' Medici,[13] as a witness in the canonical process inquiring into the sanctity of Philip Neri, who had died the year before in Rome. Elisabetta had already testified on May eleventh of the same year before a Diocesan Tribunal, and her testimony in July was virtually identical[14] to her earlier deposition. No doubt, though, she must have been listened to with more than ordinary attention. She was Philip Neri's sister.

Elisabetta was born on the seventh of February, 1519, four years after

---

10. See Thompson, *Cities of God*, 26.
11. Ibid., 27.
12. "... in the last letter but one of his which we possess, he speaks of her [Florence] as his native land." Ponnelle and Bordet, 67, n. 4. Ponnelle and Bordet say, "He was never to see Florence again [after his departure at age eighteen], and he soon forgot it...." No evidence is given for this statement, and I do not see how it can have been true. See also the chapter entitled "Fiorentinità de San Filippo" in Vian, *San Filippo Neri*, 111.
13. Della Rocchetta and Vian, *Il Primo Processo per San Filippo Neri*, vol. 3, 399.
14. "... identiche nella sostenza e nella forma, meno in qualche espressione e nell'ordine di alcune parte." Ibid., n. 2416.

Philip's birth, and had married Antonio Cioni, a widower, who had died in 1558, leaving her childless but in comfortable circumstances. Tullia Animuccia, a niece of the great musician Giovanni Animuccia, had lived in Florence for a year and a half as a teenager, had known Elisabetta, and said she was "a much honored lady of leisure who lived in a lovely apartment."[15] Not a great lady, certainly, but respected within Florentine society, especially among those who revered the memory of Savonarola.[16]

Elisabetta Neri had re-established herself by marriage into the social background from which she and Philip had come. Meriol Trevor, in her biography of Philip, assures us that Philip's background "was definitely middle class,"[17] and if she means in saying this that it was not working class, this is certainly true. But it is also true, as Ponnelle and Bordet maintain, that the family was broke, and that Philip "grew up among very unimportant people." His mother, Lucrezia da Mosciano, was the daughter of a carpenter. He hardly knew her, for she died shortly after the birth of her fourth child, Antonio, who was born in September, 1520, and who does not seem to have survived himself. Of her two daughters, Caterina was older and Elisabetta younger than Philip.

Lucrezia had brought some modest measure of affluence to the family. Besides a property at Monteperstoli, her own mother, Lena, had given her a dowry of fifty gold florins. To his own property at Castelfranco, Francesco Neri thus added that of his wife, and he and his family would have been in easy circumstances if Francesco had not been a seeker after the philosopher's stone; he was an alchemist. For the sake of the "grand art," he neglected his fortune and his children.[18]

Whatever the attention paid by the tribunals who heard Elisabetta in 1596 may have been, her testimony fixed the understanding of Philip's early life in Florence from that time until the present. From Antonio Gallonio's first biography, which was finished in time to be printed for the Holy Year of 1600, through Bacci (1622) and the modern works of Ponnelle and Bordet, of Father Cistellini, and of everyone else, the words of Elisabetta speak to us.

---

15. This is my somewhat free translation of: "... era donna molto honarata et comodissima e stava in un bel casamento...." Della Rocchetta and Vian, *Il Primo Processo per San Filippo Neri*, vol. 3, 114.

16. Her father was said to have been a good man who had venerated Fr. Girolamo. P.C. III, 399, n. 2416.

17. Trevor, *Apostle of Rome*, 10; she continues: "The family had a burial vault at San Michele, a genealogical table of their descent and a coat of arms—Philip, who was to give up all worldly connections, nevertheless had a seal with his three stars on it, which after his death was kept by Antonio Gallonio."

18. Ponnelle and Bordet, 50.

Elisabetta was seventy-seven or seventy-eight when she testified, and her eyesight was so bad she could no longer read. She had her wits about her, but she had not seen Philip for nearly sixty-five years, and she would have been fifteen at the most—but perhaps only thirteen—when he left Florence. Her memory may have been accurate enough, but what did she know about her brother's life in Florence outside of their home? More importantly, what did she understand about what she did know? Gallonio takes several points from her deposition, and these have been repeated over and over with varying degrees of enthusiasm.

The first of these is the story of Philip and the donkey. It is the first thing after the account of Philip's baptism that Gallonio relates; its prominence serves to emphasize Philip's predestination to sanctity:

> In about the twenty-second year of this century, or the following year, when Hadrian VI was Pope, it happened that a countryman was leading a donkey laden with apples to Philip's house from a farm belonging to his father Francesco Neri. Philip, who was then eight or nine years old, climbed on its back, whereupon both he and the donkey promptly fell down from a high place straight into a wine cellar. His parents were horrified, and ran to him, imagining that they would recover a lifeless body, but found him alive and unharmed, with no injuries anywhere, which was a remarkable grace of God, who had destined him from birth to bring many to salvation.[19]

Next there is the account of his saying the psalms with Elisabetta when their sister Catherine...

> ...bounded up to them to annoy them. Our boy wanted to be rid of this nuisance to both himself and Elizabeth and so pushed Catherine away gently, but their father was very cross when he heard about it. The holy child was so upset by this that he washed away his fault (if you could really call it that in one so young) with floods of tears.[20]

These incidents gave Elisabetta the opportunity to remark on Philip's gentleness, his contrition over even a minor fault, and his desire to please his father. It also allowed her to add that although he was pious he did not overdo it, as he didn't go in for the construction of toy altars or speak about becoming a monk or a priest.

> He was called Philip "the good" by his companions. Unlike many pious boys, he had no taste for dressing up as a priest or making little altars

---

19. Gallonio, *The Life of Saint Philip Neri*, 1.
20. Ibid. Gallonio says that Catherine was "their younger sister"; she was in fact the oldest of the three children, born on January 25, 1513.

where he could pretend to offer Mass, nor is he known ever to have expressed any desire to be a priest or religious.[21]

Ponnelle and Bordet dismiss Elisabetta's account of Philip's religious tendencies as so much gossip; and it is hard to be impressed with what she actually did remember and easy to be disappointed about what she did not. There is also something about the voice that comes through that is not altogether attractive to at least one modern reader of her deposition.

Elisabetta had been brought up by an improvident father who had completed the ruin of the family fortunes that Philip's grandfather and great-grandfather (who had been in the debtors' prison) had begun.[22] When her father died, she had taken the precaution of accepting her inheritance only on the condition that the debts did not exceed the assets. She had married herself back into a secure place in society, and in spite of the family coat of arms, about which a great deal of heart-searching seems to have gone on, she was, if one dares to say it, a petit-bourgeois whose horizons were limited by her respectability.

There is, too, a second reason for finding the voice less than compelling. She had no conception of whom she was talking about. She knew, or thought she knew, that her brother had been a good boy in Florence; she had heard over the years that he had developed into a good man during his life in Rome; she probably understood that he had become very important; and she now knew that many thought him a saint. Yet, somehow, she missed the point. That is not to blame her; those closest to Christ seem also to have been constantly missing the point. But unlike the disciples, she was not close to Philip. Nonetheless, she first laid down the hallowed tropes, the almost ritual incantations, about Philip's years in Florence, and these tropes leave much unsaid. How were the foundations of a great sanctity laid in this good-looking young Florentine? How did Philip Neri, born of a family fallen on hard times, raised by a morose father who was an unsuccessful notary and a ruined fortune-seeker, become a figure whose life touched the whole Catholic world of his time, and continues to do so? How are we to understand a youth spent in a brilliant but in many ways dissolute Florence, a Florence torn with civil and religious strife? How did such a background contribute to the creation of a saint?

---

21. "Era chiamato da compagni Filippo buono, e, se bene era devoto, non mostrava singolarità di devotione, con altarini o simil cose, come sogliono fare i fanciulli, e non ragionava mai d'esser prete o religioso." Della Rocchetta and Vian, *Il Primo Processo per San Filippo Neri*, vol. 3, 403.

22. See Ponnelle and Bordet, 49.

Elisabetta's testimony in 1596 gives us a tiny window onto Philip's early life, but the passage of sixty years had blotted out a good deal of what might once have been seen. Older people often vividly remember vignettes from their early life at the cost of context and chronology. Perhaps this was the case with Elisabetta, or perhaps, as I have suggested, she never saw very much.

She spoke about her brother as she remembered him, but she was speaking to people who had known him in his maturity and old age as a great saint. Her recollections are presented to us, and what she said was understood, as though Philip's fully developed virtues and holiness must have already been present in the boyhood and adolescence of the young Florentine. Right from the beginning, we are given to understand that the "finished product," was already present. So Gallonio writes:

> You could not find anyone more decent, affectionate and good looking than Philip. He behaved respectfully to grown-ups, got on easily with contemporaries, and was kind to the little ones, apparently incapable of anger. The result of all this was that he was universally popular, and was commonly called "Pippo bono," "Good Pippin," a nickname which simply meant that Philip was a good-living boy.[23]

Can it really have been like that? I think not. In saying this I am not doubting the sincerity of those who built up this picture, nor am I denying that Philip's sanctity developed out of his early life in Florence. I do want to insist that development in the moral life involves progressive growth; it is not there "ready made" from the beginning. The raw material of sanctity is not the finished product. I am in no way trying to denigrate Philip's sanctity or deny even his special place among the saints. Philip's sanctity was not there from the beginning, and it had to be worked for by struggling against the vices and developing the virtues. Philip was not, to put it in another way, exempt from the spiritual combat that every serious Christian has to face. Yet to say that Philip was not perfect from the beginning may appear offensive to pious ears. It is not meant to be, but we will never find a real man beneath the pretty pictures unless we try to see a life development and struggle.

Philip's Secularity

We have seen that Philip as a child had no interest in becoming a

---

23. Gallonio, *The Life of Saint Philip Neri*, 2. This is Father Bertram's translation: The Italian for "good living boy" reads, "Non fa udito dir mai male d'altrui, nè meno veduto far cosa, che no fusse da farsi, o non buona" (8). "It was never known that others spoke badly of him, nor was he ever seen to do anything that would draw attention to himself or anything bad."

cleric.²⁴ It was not until he was thirty-six that he yielded to his confessor's insistence that he should be ordained.

> The Almighty ... put it into the heart of F. Persiano Rosa, Philip's confessor, to persuade him to be ordained priest, and to undertake the charge of hearing confessions, that he might be the better able to win souls. When Philip first heard the proposal, he brought forward all manner of reasons to excuse himself from it, trying his best to prove to his confessor his inability and unfitness *and especially urging the strong desire he had to serve God as a layman.*²⁵

There was a question of principle behind this "strong desire." Philip came to believe explicitly, however clear he may have been about it while still in Florence, that while sanctity or Christian perfection is all-important, it is not necessarily bound up with any particular way of life. "The great thing," as he used to say later in life, "is to become saints,"²⁶ but becoming a saint did not entail living in the religious state. His mysticism had nothing essentially to do with being a cleric, and even after he was ordained, he considered himself to be a secular priest whose vocation was to live in the world:

> He was once at the house of the Marchesa Rangona, when the Countess d'Olivarez, the wife of the Spanish ambassador, was there. After some conversation, the Countess asked him how long it was since he had left the world. Philip answered, "I do not know that I have ever left the world...."²⁷

Philip did not stay in the world because he lacked the zeal or ability to become a monk or a friar. He stayed because he had no inner conviction that doing the will of God required him to live as a cleric; instead he believed that God wanted him to become a saint as a layman. Later in life, he made this point explicitly and taught it to his disciples:

> Let persons in the world sanctify themselves in their own houses, for neither the court, professions, nor labor, are any hindrance to the service of God.²⁸

Philip's contention is an important one: he is convinced that there is a universal call to holiness. The Second Vatican Council would affirm this strongly:

---

24. See above, 54–55.
25. Bacci, *The Life of Saint Philip Neri*, vol. 1, 39 (emphasis added).
26. Neri, Maxim for November First in *The Maxims and Counsels of St. Philip Neri*, 95.
27. Bacci, *The Life of Saint Philip Neri*, vol. 1, 296.
28. Neri, Maxim for January 24 in *The Maxims and Counsels of St. Philip Neri*, 7.

> It is ... quite clear that all Christians in any state or walk of life are called to the fullness of Christian life and to the perfection of love, and by this holiness a more human manner of life is fostered also in earthly society. In order to reach this perfection the faithful should use the perfection dealt out to them by Christ's gift, so that, following in his footsteps and conformed to his image, doing the will of God in everything, they may wholeheartedly devote themselves to the glory of God and to the service of their neighbor.[29]

Philip's attitude toward the world was more complex than his conviction that it was not necessarily a hindrance to sanctity; he was more positive. He stayed in the world because there were things in the world he thought valuable, not only in themselves but also in his own search for God. Cardinal Capecelatro brings this out in his discussion of the Saint's relations with an illiterate Capuchin lay brother, Saint Felice of Cantalice. Capecelatro points to the large overlap in the ascetical and mystical lives of the two saints. He shows Philip's esteem and love for the humble lay brother but then adds, almost in passing, the following significant passage:

> With the aid of divine grace [Fra Felice] knew how to love God and his neighbor better than many who are learned in many sciences; and in that science of good and evil which regards the spiritual life, his mind was an inexhaustible treasure of wealth. Hence Philip loved him so tenderly. *If to this supernatural wealth there had been added the gifts of lofty genius and wide culture, Philip might perhaps have loved him yet more....*[30]

Capecelatro means that in spite of Fra Felice's great holiness, there was, for Philip, something lacking. Lady Amabel Kerr, in her life of St. Felice,[31] misses the Cardinal's point completely; after quoting the Cardinal, she writes:

> But we venture to think that it was because Felix was precisely what he was that St. Philip held him in such affection; for nowhere else could he have found one who, to such a preeminent degree, owed everything to God and nothing at all to nature. Rough, uncouth, unlettered, and uncultured, it required a St. Philip to gauge the heavenly wisdom possessed by the holy lay-brother.[32]

I am sure Capecelatro would have had no trouble in agreeing that it

---

29. *The Dogmatic Constitution of the Church*, chapter 5, no. 40.
30. Capecelatro, *The Life of St. Philip Neri*, 402–403 (emphasis added).
31. Kerr, *A Son of St. Francis*, 126.
32. Ibid.

required a St. Philip to recognize these depths. But the Cardinal was making an altogether different and more interesting point: he was maintaining that if Felice had not been "rough, uncouth, unlettered and uncultured," Philip would have loved him more. Why? Because Philip thought "lofty genius and wide culture" were important in themselves, and that for some people, himself included, they added to sanctity, as well as being a help towards its attainment.

There is a tendency in those who take faith seriously to restrict what is valuable in human experience to what is unambiguously religious. Such people may recognize that some place must be given to other aspects of life. They do not deny that people have to earn a living, or that they need to be governed; they do not want to deny the whole network of social and political relationships that have to, as it were, be staffed by human beings; and most would admit that some sort of education, and even cultural activities such as music and art, might serve a purpose. Nonetheless, society, the state, education, and the arts—all of them are, when properly viewed, according to these ultra-supernaturalists, of little importance. Activities that do not immediately serve the ends of religion are judged to be irrelevant distractions that deflect our attention from what really matters; or worse, they are obstacles to keeping God and his laws from the first place in our minds. Compared with the demands of the Gospel, as the single-minded perfectionists understand them, everything else should fade into insignificance. It is clear that such an understanding of Christian perfection never attracted Philip, and he believed that one could find, and joyfully do, the will of God in the lay state.

This exclusive concentration on God and his law in a way that depreciates the value of God's creation and of human endeavor will not do as a general prescription for Christian holiness. At its best, when actually put into practice by some of the saints, and along with heroic efforts to carry out the second great commandment of loving our neighbor, it has an austere grandeur; a grandeur that sharply reminds the sinful and the sloppy of the reality of the law of God. Nonetheless, something is radically wrong with this approach to Christian living; if, that is, we understand it as a prescription or ideal that is supposed to apply to everyone.

What has gone awry is not the true premise that, in Newman's words, the Cross of Christ is "the measure of the world," but the conclusion drawn from this premise that nothing else "really matters" for the Christian. We can agree with Newman that the Cross is a standard of value by which we are to evaluate what counts in the long run, but it in no way follows that this standard automatically shows which human activities are important. Newman himself never drew such a conclusion.

In one of Newman's Anglican sermons, he makes the striking statement that "it is the death of the Eternal Word of God made flesh, which is our great lesson how to think and how to speak of this world."

> His Cross has put its due value upon every thing which we see, upon all fortunes, all advantages, all ranks, all dignities, all pleasures; upon the lust of the flesh, and the lust of the eyes, and the pride of life.... It has taught us how to live, how to use this world, what to expect, what to desire, what to hope. It is the tone into which all the strains of this world's music are ultimately to be resolved.[33]

This is the principle shared by both St. Philip and St. Felice. What St. Philip shared, and St. Felice did not, was Newman's lifelong conviction that human activity not obviously connected with God mattered, and that God's gifts must be cultivated in the here and now. This belief in no way contradicts his principle that the Cross is the standard by which life is to be judged. Newman, for instance, argues that a university exists to cultivate the intellect; a university is not a seminary, nor is it a school for training in the professions:

> ... it contemplates neither moral impression nor mechanical production; it professes to exercise the mind neither in art nor in duty; its function is intellectual culture; here it may leave its scholars, and it has done its work when it has done as much as this. It educates the intellect to reason well in all matters, to reach out towards truth, and to grasp it.[34]

It is not necessary to accept Newman's theory of university education to grasp his broader point: that we achieve our final destiny through the cultivation of the gifts given us by God.

> We attain to heaven by using this world well, though it is to pass away; we perfect our nature, not by undoing it, but by adding to it what is more than nature, and directing it towards aims higher than its own.[35]

Newman's teaching that "we attain to heaven by using this world well" and that "we perfect our nature, not by undoing it, but by adding to it" is one of the central themes of Christian humanism. When Cardinal Capecelatro wrote that St. Philip would have loved St. Felice more if Felice had possessed "gifts of lofty genius and wide culture," he was at the same time reminding us that total self-abnegation is not the only

---

33. Newman, "The Cross of Christ the Measure of the World," *Parochial and Plain Sermons*, 1240.
34. Newman, "Knowledge Viewed in Relation to Learning," *The Idea of a University*, 149.
35. Ibid., "Knowledge Its Own End," 147.

road to sanctity, and that there have been saints, St. Philip among them, who thought that a love of God's creation and the works of man had a role to play in a life that was both fully human and fully Christian. The following lines, written probably in the ninth century, are a moving expression of this perennial theme:

> Live, and be famed and happy; all the praise
> Of honored life to thee.
> Yea, all this world can give thee of delight,
> And then eternity.[36]

Philip's Schooling and Renaissance Humanism

This quiet, untroubled sense of a harmony between "all this world can give thee of delight, and then eternity" was something Philip's Florence conspicuously lacked. Florence was the pre-eminent city of Renaissance Humanism, and Renaissance Humanism was a spirit with a divided soul. It was a spirit that was profoundly Catholic but had not succeeded in integrating that Catholicism with the new intellectual and cultural movement that developed in Italy from the middle of the fourteenth century to the end of the fifteenth. Humanism was initiated and carried on by men of letters, historians, moralists, and statesmen in opposition to the philosophy of their time. Modern philosophy, they thought, was overly concerned with logic and argument; they were in fact reacting against the nominalistic logic of the fourteenth century.[37] The humanists insisted that man's education must be based on the disciplines that are closely connected with the nature and conduct of man, such as poetry, history, ethics and politics, rhetoric.[38] None of this is in itself un-Catholic, much less anti-Catholic. But divergent interests and tendencies must be held together in a practical or existential way, even when there is no serviceable theoretical synthesis ready to hand. We must accept the unwelcome truth that sometimes, perhaps often, there is no apparent reconciliation available to us, and we must try to hold on to all the elements of a given situation if we are even to begin to deal with or understand it. Petrarch, the key figure of Renaissance Humanism, illustrates this.

---

36. "Written by Colman the Irishman to Colman returning to his own land," *Mediaeval Latin Lyrics*, 85.
37. See Abbagnano, "Renaissance Humanism," *Dictionary of the History of Ideas*.
38. "... humanism may be regarded: as a body of knowledge; a care for the beauty of words and verbal structures; as a source and measure of moral values; and, in close connection with the last, as a complex of human achievement standing in ambivalent relation to the Christian message." Foster, *Petrarch, Poet and Humanist*, 157.

The tensions that result in a man's intellectual life may be destructive. They may lead to fence-sitting and indecision—a sort of intellectual dithering. On the other hand, the effort to hold on to unreconciled and apparently disparate elements may be the source of a deeper and more complex grasp of reality. I think it was like that with Petrarch, because he was true to all the elements of reality of which he was aware, and so he avoided any facile and shallow systematization of reality. It is easy, if we come up against apparently contradictory features in our understanding of reality, to force a false coherence on our view by ignoring those elements which do not fit into our own particular take on the way things are. Rather than accepting the often messy, apparently contradictory nature of things, we give up trying to see things steadily and to see them whole, and we subtract from the picture. The only alternative is to accept the unpleasant fact that there is no apparent reconciliation, without letting go of any particular truth. Foster has this right when he says:

> Petrarch's Latin writings are still of great interest in a number of ways, but in none more conspicuously than in the marvelous witness they severally bear to the tensions set up in the mind of the greatest scholar of the late middle ages between a passionate attachment to classical antiquity and a sincere Christian faith. To speak of Petrarch's "humanism" is, for me, to speak of that tension and vice-versa....[39]

Our interest here is in the influence Petrarch and his humanist followers had on the education Philip received in Florence. It is not too difficult to trace this influence in outline and to indicate something about the curriculum that resulted from the work of the humanists. Note that the fundamental attitude, or spirit, of trying to see things steadily and to see them whole, and the reluctance to arrive at reality by subtraction, provides an important insight into Philip's own character.

> The humanists of the fifteenth century created a seismic shift in education: They discarded the late Medieval Latin curriculum of verse grammars and glossaries, morality poems, a handful of ancient poetical texts, and *ars dictaminis*. In its place they substituted grammar, rhetoric, poetry, and history based on Latin classical authors and texts just discovered or newly appreciated. Above all they inserted the letters of Cicero as the Latin prose model.[40]

The revolution was achieved by educating the sons of the powerful and the rich in Northern Italy. Then, with this example before them, parents of less exalted social and financial strata, as well as the communal coun-

---

39. Foster, *Petrarch, Poet and Humanist*, x.
40. Grendler, *Schooling in Renaissance Italy*, 404.

cils, adopted the new Latin humanistic curriculum. The humanists' revolution was so successful that by "about 1450 schools in a majority of northern and north-central Italian towns taught and studied the *studia humanitatis*."[41] The Latin schools thus became humanistic and were commonly called "schools of oratory, poetry, and grammar":

> Italian pedagogues had effected a curriculum revolution, one of the few in the history of Western education, in the relatively short time of about fifty years—1400–1450. They solidified their triumph by 1500. Boethius, *Graecismus, Facetus, Theodulus,* and the rest of the curriculum authors gave way to Cicero, Terence, and Caesar. The *studia humanitatis* replaced *ars dictaminis*. The *auctorista* disappeared; the humanist took his place.[42]

By the time Philip was born, the Florentine schools were humanistic in this sense. Ponnelle and Bordet say that Philip grew up like any other young Florentine, and that "he attended the ordinary schools."[43] There are several things we should notice about this assertion. First, it must be understood that Philip grew up like any other young Florentine of the professional classes, or those destined for managerial roles in trade and commerce. Early Renaissance Florence had an extraordinarily high rate of vernacular literacy "not seen again in Europe for another three or four centuries,"[44] but even so, it has been estimated that in 1480 only about a third of the adult male population could read and write.[45] So while Philip's family may have belonged to the genteel poor, Philip was provided with an education that was as good as could be obtained anywhere at the time.

Again, we must not imagine that Philip went to anything like the parochial or private Catholic school of later times. The organization of primary and secondary education was a secular enterprise. Although little is known about the early Middle Ages, it is clear that the church had relinquished most of its educational role by 1300.

> After 1300 the church educated only the limited number of youths destined for the religious life—and far from all of these—plus a small number of girls in convents. The close association between church and

---

41. Ibid., 404.
42. Ibid., 141.
43. Ponnelle and Bordet, 50.
44. Witt, "What did Giovanni Read and Write," 83–114.
45. "A somewhat conservative overall literacy (reading and writing) estimate of thirty percent to thirty-three percent seems reasonable for the Florentine male population in 1480." Grendler, *Schooling in Renaissance Italy*, 76.

school typical of fourteenth- and fifteenth-century England, and possibly elsewhere, did not prevail in the Italian peninsula.[46]

Communal councils and parents stepped in to found the schools of Renaissance Italy. After the collapse of church schools, parents in the fourteenth century provided for society's needs by paying numerous laymen and clerics to teach their sons as independent masters, either in small neighborhood schools of ten to thirty pupils or as household tutors. Communal councils, especially in smaller urban centers, also contracted with a master to teach a limited number of boys. This structure of Italian schooling was set in the fourteenth century. It did not change for three centuries.[47]

Two different sorts of schools were organized based on what was taught: either a curriculum based on Latin or one devoted to the skills needed for commerce, which were called *abbaco*; either a humanist sort of education, or what we would call today a "vocational" one. The Latin schools trained the future leaders of society and the professionals, chiefly lawyers and secretaries, who would assist them. The communes strongly supported the abbaco schools as they trained boys in the skills needed for commerce. The Latin schools, with few exceptions, did not teach mathematics and ignored abbaco completely because "it added nothing to the social status and career goals of their students."[48] Philip went to a Latin school and would have acquired the same skills as those who would assist the leaders of society in the future; indeed, the same as those leaders themselves.

The teacher in the Latin school Philip went to was called Clemente.[49] He was said to have been a celebrated professor of Greek.[50] If the school followed the norm, it would have had between ten and thirty pupils. The academic year traditionally began in the fall but remained in ses-

---

46. Ibid., 11.
47. Ibid., 404.
48. Ibid., 311.
49. "Non so da dove Gallonio abbia tratto questo notizia, registrata anche nella *Vita lat*, p. 3, ma tralasciata nella sua deposizione cit., e non segnalata de alcun altro testimone. Sempre de Gallonio la trasse D. Manni *Ragionamenti* . . . , che indentificò il personaggio nel maestri Chimenti, lettore di Greco alla Badia fiorentina negli anni 1535–1556, ricordato de V, Borghin, *Ricordi intorno alla sua vita*, in: *Opuscoli inediti o rari di classici a approvati scrittori* . . . , Firenze, 1844, p. 5." Gallonio, *La Vita di San Filippo Neri, Edizione critica, con introduzione e note di Maria Teresa Bonadonna Russo* (Roma: Presidenza Del Consiglio Dei Ministri, 1995), 9, n. 7.
50. Why Gallonio bothered to include the mention of Clemente's mastery of Greek is not clear; certainly he did not pass his knowledge on to his pupil, as it seems clear that Philip knew no Greek.

sion all year long, Monday through Friday or Saturday. There were numerous holidays, of which *Carnevale*, the days before Lent began, was the longest. It has been estimated that the academic year had about 190 days if the school did not meet on Saturday, and 240 if it did.

The school day was long but flexible. The commune organized the school day "around universal reference points that fluctuated according to the seasons,"[51] and the schools organized by parents did the same:

> For example, Pistoia in 1511 ordered its communal teachers to present themselves at their schools at sunrise and to teach until the hour of the midday meal. After a lunch break of an unspecified length, school resumed until an hour before sunset in the winter and until two hours before sunset in summer. However, between 1 March and 1 September the teacher should allow students to stop for the afternoon snack (*merenda*) "as is the custom" at the ringing of the vespers bell sometime in mid-afternoon. After the *merenda* break (probably short) students returned for the rest of the day. Other towns followed this pattern with minor variations.[52]

At this school, Philip learned Latin, and he knew it fairly well.[53] But this brings us to what else he learned. It is impossible to say anything very meaningful about the content of Philip's education, either in Florence or, later, in Rome, without returning to the question of the tension between the appeal of antiquity and the Christian faith. The curriculum used in Philip's education had been determined by the humanists. Many writers use the phrase Christian humanism, or simply Humanism, in their discussions of Philip's attitude towards learning and culture without telling us very much about what they understand by the term. Often enough, *humanism* is used in an approving way to indicate a variety of attitudes of which the writer approves and in which Philip is thought to have shared. Meriol Trevor gives us an example of this:

> Philip, if he was anything, was certainly of the humanist school; Scripture was first and last his interest. Indeed, though, although he never despised any sort of learning, and insisted on young men studying as

---

51. Grendler, *Schooling in Renaissance Italy*, 34.
52. Ibid., 34. It was the Jesuits in the sixteenth century who, after some experimentation, introduced a five- or six-hour school day divided between mornings and afternoons.
53. Ponnelle and Bordet say: "Enough to read easily the Fathers and Scholastics, but certainly not as a humanist. In 1574 though at a sermon in the Oratory, he cites Ovid." *St. Philip Neri*, 56. It is not clear why they say his Latin was not up to humanist standards, or even what they mean by it.

66   IN NO STRANGE LAND

thoroughly as possible, Philip himself was too intent on the love of God to throw himself completely into a scholarly career.[54]

Sometimes this remark, that Philip was "of the humanist school," is coupled with the assertion, which is thought to follow from it, that Philip found Plato more congenial than he did Aristotle. This baseless assertion seems to find its source in Capecelatro and is repeated by Ponnelle and Bordet.[55] These larger questions will be dealt with later, but here we must consider how humanism had a bearing on what Philip was taught in school. What was taught in a school of sixteenth-century Florence was the consequence of the success of the humanist movement. Paul F. Grendler remarks that education always reflects the society it serves, and that Italian Renaissance schooling suggests several characteristics of its age.[56] He explains that both the Latin and vernacular schools attempted to instill personal and social values based on classical and Christian sources. But the education itself was secular. It inculcated civic morality for the ruling class and the professionals who served them. This should not be understood to mean that education was anti-Christian, or even that the schools were "neutral" in regard to Catholicism. The point is that they were controlled by laymen and that laymen did the teaching. Their Catholicism was that of the humanists who had succeeded in reforming the curriculum of secondary education, and not the well-defined Counter-Reformation sort. Schools did not stress Christian religious doctrine and practices until the advent of the Catholic Reformation.

> The Church played no institutional role in Renaissance education until the late Renaissance. Indeed, most clergymen seem to have received the same education as laymen. This may help explain the nature of ecclesiastical life in the renaissance, and why churchmen often behaved like laymen.[57]

The Catholicism of the humanists is, as we have seen, a large, much worked over, and disputed subject. But it is a mistake to think of the stance of the humanists as overtly or consciously anti-Christian. The sort of school Philip went to would have taught morality through classical and Christian examples, ignoring what now seem to us the contradictions between these two approaches to life. Schooling:

---

54. Trevor, *Apostle of Rome*, 23.
55. See chapter four, "Art, Irony, and Eros," 122, and chapter seven, "Studies and Books," 168.
56. Grendler, *Schooling in Renaissance Italy*, 409.
57. Ibid., 409–410.

... united Italians and played a major role in creating the Renaissance. Humanistic pedagogues developed a new educational path very different from education in the rest of Europe in the early fifteenth century. Thereafter, Italy's élite of rulers, professionals, and humanists shared the language of classical Latin. They shared a common rhetoric, and they drew from the same storehouse of moral attitudes and life examples learned in school.[58]

Grendler maintains that this schooling provides us with the key concept for understanding renaissance humanism: it was not individualism, as Burkhardt argued—"He would have been better advised to look into the schoolroom for the spirit of the age."[59]

Grendler's remark is important for understanding Philip's own attitude to learning and culture. Philip was a humanist not because he hated Aristotle and loved Plato, but because, like Petrarch, he shared the spirit of the age, an age that lived the tension between a heightened sense of the past and of individuality, and a deeply reflexive Catholicism. Philip later on in his life said that he had never left the world, and the world he first knew and in which he learned to live his faith was Florence—a Florence that might not have been quite up to Bruni's description, but which was and remained for Philip a very special place. It was the place where he had been schooled, but in a more fundamental way, it had endowed him with a sense that this world mattered. The complex cultural and political reality that was his Florentine inheritance taught him the truth of Terence's words: "I am a man, I count nothing human foreign to me";[60] words he may actually have heard in school, as Terence was a favorite of the Humanists.[61] But whether or not he knew them, they characterized his approach to life. For, as Newman said, "we attain to heaven by using this world well, though it is to pass away."

The rich unity of Philip's character, like Petrarch's, came from holding together different certainties about how life was to be lived and how the world was viewed. Petrarch held together his genuine Christian faith with his passion for the classical past. Philip's humanism was also the product of such a tension between different poles, although they were

58. Ibid., 410.
59. Ibid.
60. Publius Terentius Afer, c. 190–159 BC: "Homo sum, humani nil a me alienum puto."
61. "Medieval scholars and teachers did not know Terence nearly as well as they did Vergil [sic]. In contrast, Renaissance teachers from the beginning gave Terence a prominent pedagogical role.... Sixteenth-century editors, commentators, and even translators praised Terence as a teacher of good style and good morals." Grendler, *Schooling in Renaissance Italy*, 250–251.

not the same as Petrarch's. For Philip, the task was holding together a lived Christianity with the life and culture of the Florence of his own time. While the elements were less complex, their synthesis was no easier. Petrarch's antiquity was not a present reality. To experience it required an imaginative effort, which Petrarch and his followers were free not to make. Philip's Florence was in the here and now, and it forced itself onto Philip's consciousness as a given; it required no imagination to be felt. Philip's achievement was to maintain and practice a deeply traditional and orthodox Catholicism together with a vivid sense of the human condition in the here and now, a present which could not be left aside or transcended in a search for some hidden absolute.

The Facezie of Arlotto

One window onto the world Philip grew up in is the work of an unknown writer who collected the jokes and sayings of Arlotto Mainardi, better known as Piovano Arlotto.[62] Nello Vian says the book was Philip's favorite,[63] and Ponnelle and Bordet add, although it is not clear on what evidence, that he first read the *Facezie*[64] during his school days:

> It was from this Florentine of the fifteenth century that Philip drew his peculiar humor. In him we find a manner of dealing with things and persons that is brusque, easy, and slightly facetious, which is yet compatible with perfect goodness of heart.[65]

This is a much more extensive claim than the assertion that Philip was fond of Arlotto. Ponnelle and Bordet maintain that it had a deep influence on his character. Both of these assertions are important, but they must be handled with care. We do not really know when Phillip first read Arlotto, and it is a large claim to say it was formative. Unless the claim is seriously qualified, it is false.

Ponnelle and Bordet present us with a curiously anodyne picture of Arlotto's behavior and character. The Arlotto of the *Facezie* is much rougher, and his behavior and interests more explicitly sexual, than they suggest. The grosser elements were recognized later in the sixteenth century, and the edition in Philip's possession when he died was one that had

---

62. See Arlotto, *Facezie*. Piovano was a parish priest whose church, exceptionally, had a baptismal font. See above, 51.
63. "... il prediletto Piovano Arlotto." Vian, *San Filippo Neri*, 73. The index to the book spells out that Arlotto was Philip's favorite reading: "lettura preferita di F."
64. "... and no doubt then [i.e., during his school days in Florence] he read ... the Facezie del Piovano Arlotto." Ponnelle and Bordet, *St. Philip Neri*, 56.
65. Ibid., 61–62.

been expurgated by the Inquisition.[66] That does not, of course, prove that Philip did not read an earlier, unexpurgated edition in his youth, but without other evidence, this is a large assumption. The point of introducing the *Facezie* here is to portray something about the Florence in which Philip grew up and developed the virtues. The *Facezie* tell us a good deal about Florence, but they certainly do not show us that Philip was a clone of Arlotto's. The two men may have shared certain characteristics, but to larger questions of Philip's character and humor we will return. The two men may have shared certain characteristics; this was more likely due to their both having been Florentines than to conscious imitation on Philip's part. To maintain that Arlotto's character provided a model for a future saint seems to me to be without foundation.

Arlotto was, like Philip, the son of a notary and became a parish priest in the Diocese of Fiesole.[67] His collection is only one example, though one of the best, of a genre of collections of *facezie* (jokes or pleasantries) written in fifteenth-century Italy.[68] The book may not seem particularly funny to modern English-speakers. Some of the stories are surprisingly earthy, and not all of them are kind. Here is a short excerpt that gives the flavor:

> In the time of Pope Callistus, who was a Catalan, Piovano Arlotto was in Rome to expedite certain matters and needs at the Papal Court. A galley slave came up to him and said: Give me alms for the love of God and the Blessed Virgin, because I have escaped from the hands of the Catalans. Piovano replied: I think it is you who should give me the alms because it is I who have now fallen into their hands.[69]

Not all the stories are as bland. A large number involve sex. One such account relates how Arlotto, when young and vigorous (*giovane* and *gagliardo*), went to a brothel and was so put off by the wares on display that after various offers on the woman's part, he paid her for her time

---

66. "L'edizione, che compregende le facezie di Arlotto ... è purgata, essendone state levate 'quelle che allo Inquisitore sono parse troppo libere.'" Vian, *San Filippo Neri*, 73.

67. "An anonymous biography preceding the early editions of the collection identifies Arlotto as a 'plebano della plebe,' the son of a Florentine notary who abandoned his career in the wool industry to be a priest in a poor church in the contado (Santo Cresci a Maciuoli)." McClure, *The Culture of Profession in Late Renaissance Italy*, 31.

68. "Boccaccio had ... given over all of Day VI to verbal wit, *motti e facezie*, in which the Florentines ... excelled. Little wonder, then, that one finds collections of jokes and humorous anecdotes ... the masterpiece is *Motti e facezie del Piovano Arlotto*, by an anonymous admirer of Arlotto Mainardi (1396–1484) who never wrote anything down except himself except for his own epitaph...." Brand and Pertile, Eds., *The Cambridge History of Italian Literature*, 157.

69. Arlotto, *Facezie*, 184.

and left, so the writer assures us, without having sinned.[70] Then there is the tale, which leaves very little to the imagination, of Arlotto's encounter, when he was young and good-looking and not yet a priest, with a nun who was enamored with him.[71] Or the account of how Arlotto, by accusing the Ambassador of the Duke of Ferrara of leaving a good-looking and well-born boy to sleep in the stables, traps him into admitting the boy is sleeping every night with the ambassador in his own bed.[72]

Other stories convey a different aspect of Arlotto's character; he is presented as a folk hero who rights wrongs and defends the innocent.[73] He was clearly curious about how people earned their livings and about the ethical implications of their work. But this curiosity is a commonplace of *facezie*. Another popular contemporary work, that of Ludovico Domenici, deals with the trades and the professions. The two books even share some jokes, although they focus on different professions: Domenici's is the elite world of lawyers and doctors, while Arlotto's is lower- and middle-class.

> Arlotto's anthology contains several jokes that deal with tangible issues of professional practice, working conditions, and malpractice—particularly in the realm of the artisan and merchant classes. His identification with the lower classes is apparent throughout his collection.[74]

The stories manifest an unabashed interest in the everyday life of fifteenth-century Florence and an intense enjoyment of what Italians still call *La Vita*. Philip's enjoyment of them, in whatever version he may have read, would indicate a fairly robust appreciation of the absurdities, injustices, and amusements of everyday Florentine life. They describe the world in which Philip grew up and that he learned to use well. Yet alongside this worldliness of St. Philip was also the reality of God and the presence of Christ's Church; as yet I have hardly touched on the specifically Catholic elements in the complex pattern of Philip's sanctity.

---

70. "Dopo averla salutata, se ne andò senza aver commesso peccato." Ibid., 42. The comment of the writer shows the more relaxed attitude towards sexual morality that seems to have been common before the Council of Trent.

71. Ibid., 139. It is difficult to know quite what Ponnelle and Bordet mean when they assert that Arlotto was chaste (Ponnelle and Bordet, *St. Philip Neri*, 61).

72. "... egli sta in camera nel mio letto, e ogni notte lo tengo a dormire con me in queste mie braccia." Ibid., 132.

73. "Piovano Arlotto is presented as a Florentine folk hero, beloved by men and women of all social classes for his shrewd quick-wittedness. Through him, the author presents the old republican values that Dante praises—sobriety, hard work, and fraternity—and have all but disappeared in a grasping, competitive society in which money measures worth. For the Piovano, religion and virtue mean practical works of mercy for the desperately poor people of Florence, and first of all his own parishioners." Brand and Pertile, Eds., *The Cambridge History of Italian Literature*, 157.

74. McClure, *The Culture of Profession in Late Renaissance Italy*, 31.

2

Chastity and Charity

> Thy decrees are very sure;
> Holiness befits thy house,
> O Lord, for evermore.
> Psalm 93

THE SPECIFICALLY Catholic elements in Philip's sanctity come almost entirely from his relationship with the Dominicans. I say "almost" entirely, as there would also have been elements in his formation as a Catholic that he acquired at home and from his local parish church. This early training would have served as a foundation to what he learned later from the Friars. Ponnelle and Bordet paint a somber picture of Philip's life at home;[1] while Capecelatro, in his zeal to see Philip's sanctity present from the beginning, paints a very different view. In Capecelatro's view Philip's sanctity overflowed, submerging the other members of his family:

> ... there was a great peace in that home, a pure and serene air cheered and gladdened that Christian household; and hence that self-restraint and composed gentleness of words and ways which rendered it so dear to all its members.[2]

It could have been like this, but with the father, Francesco Neri, trying to turn lead into gold and ruining the family finances and imperiling its social status, I can't think it was. Yet whichever picture we take of Philip's home life, it was there that he learned the rudiments of his Christianity, and these would have been reinforced by the liturgical and sacramental life of his local parish, S. Pier Gattolino.

It was to the Dominicans, however, that Philip owed both his education in the spiritual combat and his reflective knowledge of Catholicism. St. Philip's Catholicism is entirely Dominican in its ascetical and doctri-

---

1. See chapter one, "Using this World Well."
2. Capecelatro, *The Life of Saint Philip Neri*, 10.

nal dimensions, and he saw these aspects of his Catholicism incarnated in someone who had died twenty years before he was born, Girolamo Savonarola. That does not mean he adopted the political aspects of the great Friar's Catholicism, nor, as we have seen, did he think the religious life was the only way to sanctity. On the other hand, he knew Savonarola's Dominican successors at the Convent of San Marco, and his relationship with the Friars was close.

On May 16, 1610, a Dominican, Fra Antonio Berti, testified that in 1550, at the age of sixteen, he had been sent by his father from Florence to Rome in order to become a merchant. Later, when Philip became a priest, he started going to confession to him, and Philip encouraged him in a religious vocation. Antonio joined the Dominicans.[3] He seems to have known Philip for the rest of the Saint's life, and testified that, in the year before Philip died, the Saint told him that the Dominicans in Florence had been the source of everything good that Philip possessed.[4] The words Antonio ascribes to Philip are strong and unambiguous.[5] Father Cistellini points out that neither Elisabetta nor Gallonio make any mention of this influence, and that we have to wait until the second edition of Bacci's biography before it is mentioned.[6] But neither Elisa-

---

3. "...mi confessai dal Beato Filippo nella chiesa di S. Girolamo della Charità, al quale conferii l'inspiratione, che havevo, d'esser religioso; et egli, doppo alcune interrogationi, per prova della volontà mia, mi consigliò di farlmi religioso nella Minerva, dove havevo havuto l'inspiratione." (I made my confessions to the blessed Philip, in the Church of San Girolamo della Carità, to whom I disclosed my aspirations to become a religious; and he, after questioning me, to discern my will, advised me to become a religious at the Minerva, to which I had already a leaning.) Della Rocchetta and Vian, *Il Primo Processo per San Filippo Neri*, vol. 3, 176 (author's translation).

4. Professor Lorenzo Polizzotto has written me that: "The two friars of San Marco mentioned by San Filippo Neri as having had a great influence on him, present some difficulties. One, Fra Servanzio Mini is not mentioned in any of the lists of the friars of the convent (there is a Mini, but named Innocenzo, a converso, not a friar, who died in 1497). The second is very well known. He is described in the Chronicle of San Marco as one of the best preachers in Italy at the time who preached in many cathedrals with great success. Though of 'mediocre doctrine' once he began preaching he tackled the most difficult doctrinal questions with ease, causing great admiration in the people." Undated correspondence from Professor Lorenzo Polizzotto to the author.

5. "Attesto, come, l'istesso anno 1594 incirca, essendo andato a visitare il beato Filippo, in camera sua, alla Vallicella, mi disse, di propria bocca, queste parole: 'Quel che io ho havuto, da principio, di buono, l'ho havuto dalli vostri padri de S. Marco de Fiorenza.'" (I attest, that in the same year, about 1594, having visited the blessed Philip in his room at the Valicella, he himself said to me these words, "Everything I have that is good in its origin, I had from your fathers at San Marco's in Florence.") Della Rocchetta and Vian, *Il Primo Processo per San Filippo Neri*, vol. 3, 177 (author's translation).

6. Cistellini, *San Filippo Neri: Breve Storia*, 6–7.

betta nor Gallonio say everything and, as Berti did not testify until 1610, the information was not available to Bacci when he published the first edition of his biography in 1600.

In addition to this external evidence, there are also the internal pointers to the Dominican influence in what Philip taught and, more generally, what we might call his stance on the spiritual life. We do not have anything like a comprehensive account of St. Philip's teaching, but his approach is that of St. Thomas Aquinas. St. Thomas taught that perfection was open to everyone in no matter what state of life, and the gifts of the Holy Spirit, which become manifest in the unitive way, are in principle open to all. But the road to the unitive way passes through the way of the proficient, which itself is based on the way of the beginner. No one was ever stronger than St. Philip on the need to build the life of prayer on the spiritual combat, which fights the vices and helps to establish the virtues; and this emphasis, along with his belief that perfection is open to all, is clearly in line with the teaching of the Angelic Doctor. His own first contact with this teaching was in the Dominicanism of St. Catherine of Siena and Savonarola, as he found it in San Marco. Given Philip's lifelong friendship with the Dominicans and his debt to Dominican spirituality, I see no reason to doubt Fra Berti's testimony.

✣

It seems probable that the adolescent Philip's systematic early training in Christianity was through the *Confraternity of the Purification*, which was under the supervision of the Dominicans. Philip's education at Clemente's school was not overtly or consciously anti-Christian, but on the other hand, he would not have been taught specifically Catholic doctrine, either, regarding faith or morals. The humanist schools were concerned with instilling personal and social values, but their philosophical basis was an often-uneasy amalgam of Christian and classical sources. The need to instill specifically Catholic values, not only in the minority who attended classical schools but also for those in the *abbaco* and among apprentices learning a trade, was recognized. The youth confraternities provided a means both to supplement the religious education in classical schools and to reach the much larger group of working-class adolescents who did not attend any sort of school. Much importance was accorded to youth in Florence, and one of the ways young men were prepared and sustained for what the city expected of them was through its confraternities.

> Though not exclusive to Florence, youth confraternities were most numerous there. Only in Florence, moreover, were they formally

incorporated into civil and ecclesiastical life, being assigned specific roles regarded as crucial to the spiritual and material welfare of the city. Much was expected of them and of the children they nurtured.[7]

The most important of these groups was the *Confraternity of the Purification*. The primary purpose of the *Purification*, like all the other confraternities, was religious. It was, however, a religious aim that was clearly yoked to the civic dimensions of Florentine Catholicism.

> As expressed in the confraternity's statutes, however, a sound civic education could only be achieved if solidly grounded in religious principles. Catechetical instruction was thus the starting point of the educational process that would result in the formation of good citizens.[8]

Philip is thought, I believe correctly, to have belonged to this group. Cistellini points out that the *Purification* was connected with the Dominicans of S. Marco and that Philip frequented this *ambiente*. Cistellini, who thinks it probable that Philip was a member, writes:

> Si sa che frequentave l'ambiente domenicano de S. Marco, dove era vivissimo e venerato il recordo del Savonarola (del quale Filippo serberà amirata devozione), e dove probabilmente fu aggregato alla fiorente Compagnia di fanciulli intitolata alla Purificazione.... (Given that he frequented the Dominicans at S. Marco, where the memory of Savonarola was very much alive and venerated [and for which Philip kept a loving devotion], and where he was probably aggregated to the flourishing Confraternity of the Purification....)[9]

The relations between the Dominicans and the *Purification* were at times stormy,[10] but the link itself and the Dominican influence on the confraternity is undeniable. That in itself, of course, does not prove Philip was a member. On the other hand, Philip learned the elements of

---

7. See Polizzotto, *Children of the Promise: The Confraternity of the Purification and the Socialization of Youth in Florence, 1427–1785*, Introduction, 1. Polizzotto goes on to say, "Confraternities provided members with the opportunity to take a more active part in the religious and spiritual life of Florence. This in turn gave them the satisfaction of contributing to the welfare of their city. Confraternities also enabled Florentines to establish social and professional networks, and then to enlarge and strengthen them. Finally in Ronald Weissman's influential formulation, they provided a liminal refuge from the harshly competitive world of Florentine politics and society." Polizzotto, *Children of the Promise*, 1:14.

8. Ibid., 6.

9. Cistellini, *San Filippo Neri, L'oratorio e la Congregazione Oratoriana*, 19.

10. See Polizzotto, *Children of the Promise*, chapter 2, "The Medician Ascendancy, 1440–1490," and Chapter 3, "In the Shadow of Savonarola, 1444–1490."

the Christian faith and the spiritual combat somewhere; he was associated with the Dominicans who, at least by the time he would have been involved, were in effective control of the *Purification*. It would seem unlikely that he did *not* belong to the confraternity.

There is another consideration that lends support to this view. The structure of the meetings of the Confraternity, and many of its practices, were adopted by Philip when he began the Oratory for laymen in Rome. For example: the reading aloud by one of the members until sufficient numbers had arrived for a meeting, having boys preach sermons, picnics outside the city at holidays, the singing of sacred songs or hymns in the vernacular—all show that Philip was well acquainted with the particular practices of the *Purification*, and this knowledge was probably gained first-hand.

The only objection to this conclusion is based on a misreading of Philip's character. It might be said, that is, that "good Philip," so in love with God, would have had little time for the society of his peers. This interpretation goes with Philip the dreamer, who loved to be solitary and look at the scenery. But the evidence we have is all in the other direction: he loved people, he was popular with his contemporaries, and at this period of his life he liked to dress as well as he could afford. There is no evidence that he did this just so he could look in the mirror. He was a good-looking, well-turned-out teenager, and good-looking, well-turned-out teenagers want others of the same sort around them. Marco Antonio Maffa states that he remembers his father, who was born the same year as St. Philip and had known Philip as a young man in Rome, telling him that Philip had the most handsome features.[11] Ponnelle and Bordet seem to be expressing a tradition when they write:

> As a youth, he dressed elegantly, after the manner of the young men of his rank. We may picture him in the dress of the young sculptor painted about this time by Bronzino; in [a] black doublet, wide and flowing, cut to fit his figure, the neck loose, with the edge of the shirt gathered all round over the black of his doublet, and with a large cap. Perhaps he even wore a gold chain.[12]

One of the purposes of the *Purification* was to see that this natural propensity of adolescent boys, for the company of others of their own age and sex, did not turn to homosexual practices. Florence had a name for homosexuality, and in 1432 the authorities instituted a special magis-

---

11. "era di bellissima fattezza." Della Rocchetta and Vian, *Il Primo Processo per San Filippo Neri*, vol. 2, 89.

12. Ibid., 56–57. This contrasts strangely with Capecelatro's description, which he tells us is based on the portrait of him now in the Doria palace in Rome: "He was not

tracy to pursue and prosecute sodomy. Michael Rocke, in his book *Forbidden Friendships*,[13] has written:

> Largely as a result of this magistracy, prosecutions and convictions for sodomy in fifteenth-century Florence far exceeded those in any other late medieval or early modern city on record, both in Italy and elsewhere. In the much larger city of Venice, from 1426 to 1520, roughly the same years as the Night Officers' tenure, authorities prosecuted 411 individuals, and from 1406 to 1500 convicted 238.[14]

The Magistracy lasted until 1502, and the figures for the incidence of those charged by the authorities with homosexuality in Florence—a city of about 40,000 people—seem extraordinary. Rocke says that "taking into account the sentences handed down by other magistracies, the total number of convictions for homosexual sodomy in these years approached 3,000."[15]

> These extraordinary figures, partial though they certainly are, begin to furnish a sense of the dimensions, the vitality, and the contradictory significance of homosexuality in the sexual and social life of Florence. Sodomy was ostensibly the most dreaded and evil of sexual sins, and was amongst the most rigorously controlled of crimes; yet in the later fifteenth century, the majority of local males at least once during their lifetimes were officially incriminated for engaging in homosexual relations.[16]

Whether or not, as has been suggested, Rocke brings a certain enthusiasm to this subject, it is worth noting that neither Najemy nor Polizzotto contest the figures, and they are of the opinion that the practice was so widespread that, if it was not protected by the authorities, then there was "semi-official tolerance."[17] Philip was called "good Philip" because unlike many, or perhaps even most, of his contemporaries, he led a chaste life.

---

dressed in the new fashion which foreigners were at that time introducing into Tuscany, and which was eagerly adopted by lovers of change; he wore the old republican hood or cowl with its long strips to be wound around the back; and this hood was never taken off but to the Gonfaloniere of justice, or to prelates of highest degree." Capecelatro, *The Life of Saint Philip Neri*, 10. But the portrait of Philip in the Palazzo Doria, "of the School of Baraccio," shows him exactly as described by Ponnelle and Bordet; he is bareheaded, with a large ruff and a chain. See Rossoni, *Immagini di Santità Per un'iconografia di san Filippo Neri*, 124–125.

13. Rocke, *Forbidden Friendships*, 46–47.
14. Ibid., 47.
15. Ibid.
16. Ibid., 4–5.
17. The expression is Polizzotto's, *Children of the Promise*, 110.

This was the city in which Philip grew up, and yet a few days before he died, Philip told his confessor, Baronius, that he had been given the grace of maintaining perpetual chastity.[18] No one seems ever to have doubted this truth, and Bacci says that "the Sacred Congregation of Rites, at his beatification, declared it adequately proved."[19] Furthermore, Baronius says that Philip had told him that for many years he had never felt those motions of the flesh that young people are accustomed to have, and that he was also free from any natural pollutions.[20] I am sure all this is true, but while St. Philip Neri never had sexual relations, we learn little about the difficulties Philip might have had in establishing the virtue of chastity. We are again brought up against the fact that all witnesses at the process first knew him when he was middle-aged. Without exception, they all marvel at his purity,[21] but most attributed this to the grace of God in a way that robs the virtue of much interest; that is, we get the impression that Philip never had any real difficulty in establishing the virtue.

St. Thomas says that "chastity takes its name from the fact that reason chastises concupiscence, which like a child, needs curbing,"[22] and that, properly speaking, it is concupiscence relating to venereal pleasure that needs reining in.[23] If concupiscence never forces itself on someone as venereal pleasure, it is hard to see how he would have the virtue of chastity. This tendency to discount the presence of the raw material of chastity in Philip can be seen clearly in Cardinal Tarugi's testimony. Tarugi had been one of St. Philip's most spectacular converts. He was well-connected and apparently ambitious:

> A cousin of Julius III through his mother, who was one of the del Monte, and appointed by him chamberlain of honor at the court,

---

18. "A un bon proposito, mi disse, essendo suo confessore, dando gratia a Iddio delli sua doni, Chi Iddio haveva data gratia servar; perpetua verginità...." (As a matter of fact, he told me, his confessor, that, attributing to God's goodness the grace of this gift, he had been given the grace of preserving perpetual virginity.) Della Rocchetta and Vian, *Il Primo Processo per San Filippo Neri*, vol. 1, 138 (author's translation).

19. Bacci, *The Life of Saint Philip Neri*, vol. 1, 245.

20. "... da molti anni a dietro, non haver sentiti quelli commovimenti, che sogliono sentir li fanciulli, et esser libero ancora dalle pollutioni naturali." (...for many years, not to have felt those movements of the flesh that young people are accustomed to have, and that he was also free from any natural pollutions.) Della Rocchetta and Vian, *Il Primo Processo per San Filippo Neri*, vol. 1, 138 (author's translation).

21. Gallonio even makes the point that he made the saint's bed and that the bed-linen was always unspotted when Gallonio made Philip's bed in the mornings. Della Rocchetta and Vian, *Il Primo Processo per San Filippo Neri*, vol. 1, 159–160.

22. Aquinas, *Summa Theologiae*, 1, 2, q. 151, 1.

23. Aquinas, *Summa Theologiae* 1, 2, q. 151, 2.

where he inhabited the Borgia apartments with four servants, great was his disappointment when the death of the pope took him by surprise before he had attained to power. Had he not, a short time before, refused the bishopric of Aversa, either because he wished to remain a layman or because he entertained yet higher ambitions![24]

Furthermore, his talents both natural and acquired "made him a dazzling figure . . . and he was the perfect example of a courtier":

> He spoke wonderfully, being gifted with a natural eloquence, and inheriting from his uncle, Angelo Poliziano, a taste for literary beauty, and from his father, Tarugi Tarugi, a distinguished lawyer and a senator of Rome, a profound knowledge of the law.[25]

He was friendly, however, with some of the more morally suspect of the cardinals, including del Monte, who had started life on the streets of Piacenza before he was picked up by the then-Cardinal del Monte, who was to become Julius III.[26] The Cardinal had his brother adopt the boy, and, after his election as Pope, created—over the protests of many members of the Sacred College—his seventeen-year-old protégé a Cardinal. Ponnelle and Bordet point out that friendship with Cardinal del Monte points to a "certain libertinage," and Tarugi is described as "having gone completely astray."[27]

Tarugi had been to confession to Philip during the latter months of the reign of Julius III, and from that time on he tells us:

> I felt burning within me a bright flame, which my sins could not extinguish, and which never ceased to torment me until the time when I gave myself entirely into [Philip's] hands.[28]

One of the things that must have drawn Tarugi to the Saint was the living lesson that chastity can be not only possible, but even attractive. Tarugi, like all the rest of them, never knew Philip as a young man, yet he swore on oath in the year after Philip's death that chastity had been no problem for Philip:

---

24. Ponnelle and Bordet, *St. Philip Neri*, 198.
25. Ibid.
26. "The Venetian ambassador Dandolo relates how Julius III, when he was legate in Piacenza, took a boy of low extraction, from the streets, as it were, and made him keeper of his ape, because he had shown great courage when the animal caught hold of him. The keeper of the ape learned in a short time how to insinuate himself in the favor of his master, to such an extent, that the latter grew fond of him and prevailed upon his brother to adopt him." Pastor, *The History of the Popes from the Close of the Middle Ages*, vol. 13, 70.
27. Ponnelle and Bordet, *St. Philip Neri*, 198.
28. Ibid., 199.

It was believed that he was a virgin, because in Florence, from the time of his childhood he was called Pippo Buono. Pippo is the diminutive of Philip, and this is confirmed because he did not experience any disturbances (sexual motions) either when he was with women or with men.[29]

This sort of thing is repeated over and over by other witnesses. There are, however, indications of there being more to the story than this; indications that go some way to restoring our faith in Philip's humanity. In Gallonio's testimony in September 1595, there is the account of how once when Philip, as a young man in Rome, was passing the Coliseum, he saw three men who tempted him to sin.[30] In his life of the Saint, Gallonio writes:

> One day he was passing by the amphitheater built by the imperial Flavian dynasty (which we now call the Coliseum), intending to visit the Lateran Basilica, when he saw a demon in his way, in the guise of a beggar, completely naked. An impure thought did cross his mind... he was quite convinced that the beggar was indeed a demon, not a man, even though it presented itself to him under the attractive form of a man....[31]

Bacci says explicitly that the devil "often endeavored, not only by suggesting to him evil thoughts, which by his prayers and tears he always promptly overcame, but by various other artifices, to stain the whiteness of his purity."[32] Bacci then records two other incidents from the saint's early years in Rome, one clearly of a homosexual nature and the other heterosexual.[33] The point of retailing these stories is not to establish any particular view about what today we would call Philip's sexuality but merely to reinforce what should have been obvious: that he did in fact have a sexual nature and that his chastity was a virtue that had to be established.

Philip's purity was a real virtue won after a warfare with his own nature in a city where chastity was more highly spoken of than practiced. It was in Florence that he began to use this world well. His home, his schooling, and his membership in the Confraternity of the Purifica-

---

29. Della Rocchetta and Vian, *Il Primo Processo per San Filippo Neri*, vol. 3, 379.
30. Ibid., vol. 1, 193.
31. Gallonio, *The Life of Saint Philip Neri*, 11.
32. Bacci, *The Life of Saint Philip Neri*, vol. 1, 246.
33. "One day, whilst yet a layman, he was accosted when on a journey by some profligates, who, probably allured by his good looks, tempted him to sin.... Another time, also whilst he was a layman, he was obliged to lodge one night at the house of a friend, where there was a beautiful but immoral woman, who entered his room secretly during the night, and tempted him to sin." Ibid.

tion all played their part in establishing the foundations of Philip's mystical life. These foundations were laid in the ordinary life of his own times, and he fought the spiritual combat in the world in which he grew up. At the same time, though, he continued to love and to be fascinated by the very world and its people that provided the material for the battle against sin and the struggle to establish virtue. Good Philip was a good Florentine; what distinguished him from those around him was his goodness, but it was a goodness that showed itself to his contemporaries in the same secular guise they all shared.

Philip's victory over the flesh was a real victory in which he played his own heroic part. However we are to understand the work of grace in this victory, it should not diminish our wonder at Philip's loving cooperation with God's grace. We should also remark that, although Philip lived a chaste life, this victory over concupiscence and sin was not accompanied by either harshness towards other people or self-deception. The dominant note of Philip's dealing with those harassed by sexual difficulties was always patience and compassion, a patience and a compassion he had learned through his own struggles.

✢

Philip's practice of the virtue of chastity exemplifies St. Thomas's teaching that the way of beginners involves not only mortification but also the nourishment and the careful fostering of charity. Traditional Catholic thinking maintains that there is a vital connection between charity and the practice of all the virtues. It is true that charity is the supreme Christian virtue, but it is not the only one, nor does the belief that charity is the greatest of all the virtues serve as a dispensation from the obligation to practice and develop the other virtues. It is important to emphasize this last point especially today: the use of the word "love" is not a kind of permission that justifies any sort of sexual behavior.

Heaven, as Newman said, cannot change, and God's law is from everlasting to everlasting. It is *we* who must change and learn to live as God wants us to live.

> We must become what we are not; we must learn to love what we do not love, and practice ourselves in what is difficult. We must have the law of the Spirit of life written and set up in our hearts, "that the righteousness of the law may be fulfilled in us," and that we may learn to please and to love God.[34]

---

34. Newman, "The Strictness of the Law of Christ," *Parochial and Plain Sermons*, vol. 4, 742.

In this passage Newman is echoing the teaching of St. Paul, who is quite clear as to the centrality of charity as well as the truth that it does not stand alone. In his famous hymn in praise of charity, he says:

> If I speak in the tongues of men and of angels, but have not charity, I am a noisy gong or a clanging cymbal. And if I have prophetic powers, and understand all mysteries and all knowledge, and if I have all faith, so as to remove mountains, but have not charity, I am nothing. If I give away all I have, and if I deliver my body to be burned, but have not charity, I gain nothing.[35]

This teaching from St. Paul can be found all through the New Testament. Christ himself tells us that upon the love of God and of neighbor depend the whole law and the prophets. "Over all these virtues," says St. Paul, "put on love, which binds the rest together and makes them perfect."[36] Charity establishes the mutual love of friendship between God and ourselves. We were created to live in communion with God, united to God, as St. Augustine says, and it is by charity that we enter into this union. Indeed, the union itself is a union of love.

Yet, because nothing without charity is of any use, it does not follow that there is nothing else to strive after. This is a point about which a lot of people go wrong today. They seem to think that because of the central importance of charity it follows that the other virtues do not really matter. But faith and hope, as well as the moral virtues, have their own intrinsic importance and are of essential importance in living the Christian life. This is what St. Paul has to say:

> Charity is patient and kind; charity is not jealous or boastful; it is not arrogant or rude. Charity does not insist on its own way; it is not irritable or resentful; it does not rejoice in wrong, but rejoices in the right. Love bears all things, believes all things, hopes all things, endures all things.[37]

St. Paul teaches that charity requires other virtues like patience, kindness, and endurance, and that vices such as jealousy, boastfulness, irritation and resentment have a reality that can destroy charity. These virtues and these vices are something different from charity, and although closely connected to charity, they must be practiced—or fought, in the case of the vices—in order to develop real charity.

St. Thomas's treatment of the virtues is based on a distinction within our feeling nature between what he calls the powers of desire, or concu-

---

35. 1 Corinthians 13:1–3.
36. Colossians 3:14.
37. 1 Corinthians, 13:4–6.

piscence, and aggression.[38] The distinction goes back to Plato[39] and was used by Aristotle.[40] In natural, mortal things, Thomas explains, there is not only a bent toward what is beneficial and away from what is harmful, but there is also a tendency to fight against what we perceive as contrary and destructive forces to our well-being. We are attracted to what pleases the senses and we avoid what hurts them, and this is called desire. We also resist whatever threatens our pleasure or brings danger, and we call this reaction (to what is seen as harmful to us) aggressiveness.

It was the conviction of Plato, Aristotle, and St. Thomas that desire and aggressiveness could be educated into well-established patterns of behavior that they called virtues. Aristotle taught that the virtues, at least the moral virtues, are not born in us: they do not belong to us by nature. On the other hand, the acquisition of these virtues is not contrary to our nature, but it does presuppose a natural aptitude for receiving them. We are, he taught, born with the capacity to react in the right way both to pleasure and to what frustrates and threatens us, but without proper training we are just as liable to react wrongly. The aptitude, or capacity, has to be developed by practice or habituation into an established habit of feeling and reacting rightly. This is what we call a virtue.[41] It follows from this that the way a child is educated, or formed, is vitally important.

The difficulty in presenting the doctrine of the virtues today is that hardly anyone thinks of morality in terms of well-established habits of right conduct. Many profess a morality in terms of duty (what I am obliged to do, or what my conscience dictates); or else some doctrine of self-realization (for example, I should do whatever will help to develop my potential, or answer my needs); or finally, of some version of a utilitarian theory of the greatest happiness for the greatest number. The first of these, in theory anyway, takes no account of consequences, while the second has nothing but regard for consequences and deals exclusively

---

38. These expressions translate *appetitus concupisicilis* and *irascibilis* in a way accessible to the non-specialist. "Speaking in a general way, sense appetite is one power, called sensuality, but it is divided into two kinds, namely aggressiveness and desire." Aquinas, *Summa Theologiae*, Ia, 81, 2.

39. See, for example, Plato's *Republic*, Book IV, on the three parts of the soul, 434d–441c.

40. Aristotle, in fact, distinguishes desire (επιθυμία), spirit or anger (θυμός or οργή), and wish (βούλησις)—but this last seems to me to be a sub-class of desire; it is a desire for the agent's own good.

41. "The passage from the indeterminate δύναμις (the mere capacity) to the determinate ἕξις is effected by ἐθισμός (habituation), by constantly reacting rightly to feeling in particular cases." Joachim, *Aristotle, The Nicomachean Ethics*, 72.

with what is best for the individual actually involved in the moral reasoning, usually in terms of pleasure; and the third is the official philosophy of government and the social services and has really very little concern for personal morality. This list is not of course complete, but is comprehensive enough to cover most of the immediate responses to questions about morality; and none of them carry any suggestion that the good life might require a training of our nature that is ordered towards the acquiring of good habits.

If we are going to appreciate the strengths of the good life based on the virtues, we will have to clear our minds of most of the contemporary ways of understanding morality and of the automatic responses that go with them. If we do this we will discover an approach to moral living that is of perennial value.[42] This approach holds that morality requires that the two fundamental elements of human nature, that is the desiring and aggressive, should not be left to fight it out between each other for control of the individual, but that they must be brought into a pattern of established responses that is not merely theoretical but practical. What does practical mean here? It means that morality, besides being taught in an abstract way as a set of principles, must also be something actually lived in everyday life.

The everyday living we are concerned with here is morality under the aspect of its serving as the foundation of the mystical life. That is, a genuine Catholic mysticism begins, as the term suggests, with the way of beginners. And the way of beginners, or the purgative way, cannot be distinguished materially from the effort to live the moral life. The teaching of the moral life requires not only well-grounded instruction but also example. It requires teachers who practice what they preach, and instruction without living examples is not worth much. Baron von Hügel describes what he owed to a priest who did more than talk about Christian virtue:

> When I was young and tempted to fall into sin, no old woman with a tract could have saved me. But I came across a Dominican monk. What a splendid man he was! What a lot I learned from him! He saved me from sin. I remember he said to me once, "You think I do all this for

---

42. The work of Alasdair MacIntyre is an important example of the contemporary efforts to return to an ethics based on the virtues. He writes, for example, "What matters at this stage is the construction of local forms of community within which civility and the intellectual and moral virtue can be sustained through the new dark ages that are already upon us. And if the tradition of the virtues was able to survive the horrors of the last dark ages, we are not entirely without grounds for hope." MacIntyre, *After Virtue*, 263.

pleasure? For show? Give up marriage, live in discomfort and cold, eat fish all the year round, that I do it to please myself? I don't, I hate it, but I do it for God. I do it to keep alive in this world the spirit that the world forgets—the spirit of renunciation, sacrifice, the supernatural life."[43]

The impact of the good Dominican on Von Hügel was, from one point of view, a moral one; that is, the moral superiority of the Dominican hit Von Hügel hard enough to change his conduct. This experience of being struck by the moral superiority of another has nothing directly to do with Christianity. That is, the experience, while congruent with a life "hid in Christ," is certainly not identical to that life. Kant called this experience of being struck by the superior goodness of another person *respect*.[44] "Respect," he says, "is a *tribute* which we cannot refuse to [one who possesses] merit whether we will it or not; we may indeed outwardly withhold it, but we cannot help feeling it inwardly."[45]

Fontenelle says, "I bow before a great man, but my mind does not bow." I would add, before an humble plain man, in whom I perceive uprightness of character in a higher degree than I am conscious of in myself, my mind bows whether I choose it or not, and though I bear my head never so high that he may not forget my superior rank.[46]

I am not concerned here with how Kant uses this experience in his own system, or even, given his own views on the irrelevance of feeling for the determining of moral action, how this feeling can play the central role in his work that in fact it does. Instead I stress the reality of the experience itself. There is such a thing as moral authority, and it has an impact on others whether they admit it, even to themselves, or not. The experience is real, but it has nothing directly to do with life in Christ; the authority of Kant's "humble plain man" requires neither divine grace nor the assent of Christian belief. The dutiful life of Kant's good man, and the natural authority he possesses, will help to develop what St. Augustine called the human city, but his moral character and his authority exist on a different plane from those baptized into the City of God.

---

43. von Hügel, *Letters to a Niece*, xxiv.

44. The German word is *Achtung* which has also been variously translated as esteem, regard or reverence; in addition, *Achtung* also has the sense of "pay attention" or "watch out," and this is certainly part of the meaning Kant wanted to convey.

45. I have added the words in brackets to make it clear that it is to the person himself (who possesses moral worth), and not to some abstraction called "merit," that we are forced to give respect "den wir dem Verdienste nicht verweisen können." This is concealed by the translation. Kant, "The Analytic of Pure Practical Reason," *Critique of Practical Reason*, 169–170.

46. Ibid., 169.

None of this is said to denigrate natural goodness—and one could only wish there were more of it around—but we must develop a sense that baptism gives a new life, a new truth, and the means to live this new life. We have to begin to take more seriously Newman's insistence that Christianity has brought us a new way of speaking, and then we must begin to pay attention to what we are saying.

It is the sad teaching of experience that the outcome of the spiritual combat is all too often the reality of failure and a sense of hopelessness in a struggle against what may seem to be overwhelming odds. St. Paul's anguished cry that he did not understand his own actions, for he did not do what he wanted to do and did the very things that he hated,[47] is only a particularly striking and authoritative statement of this fact. Indeed, the experience of the power of sin at work in the baptized led Luther and a host of others to contend that there was no real change in the person baptized, but only in God's attitude towards sinful human nature. After Baptism, God was held to see in the new Christian the merits of his Son that covered, but did not change, the sinful nature of the one baptized. This theory certainly has its attractions, and one of these is that it seems to accord with so much of human experience. Even people seriously trying to be faithful Christians are sometimes caught up for years with sins they seem to be able to do nothing about. To such people, a view of the sacraments that teaches that what is important is a fundamental commitment, or option, in faith to the saving power of Christ's death and resurrection brings solace and peace. It is no surprise that such a commitment, which in principle has nothing to do with success or failure in the moral life, has always had its adherents.[48]

Attractive as the idea of a fundamental commitment may be from certain angles, it runs clear counter to the Catholic teaching that in our baptism we have been given the capacities necessary to work at living a Christian life, and that these capacities have brought about a real change in our human nature. The Christian's work is to struggle against the soul's sinful tendencies and so enter in a personal way into the Lord's passion and death. But in addition to this dying to the sinful self there is

---

47. Cf. Romans 7:15.
48. In recent years, especially since the Second Vatican Council, a version of this theory, or at least a theory that seems driven by the same dynamic, has made its appearance as the theory of the fundamental option. The incompatibility of this theory with orthodox Catholicism has been authoritatively argued by Michael S. Sherwin, O.P., in *By Knowledge and By Love*. The author shows himself to be sensitive to the pastoral reasons that have led to the formulation of this position, but at the same time shows why it will not do. See especially "Charity's Act: Contemporary Efforts at Renewal," 1–11.

also the call to vivify and cooperate with the grace of the risen Christ so as to "walk in newness of life."[49]

The example of the saints shows us the possibility of living a chaste life, but unless we accept the fact that the practice of the virtue involved struggle for them, it is difficult to see what they have to teach those who find the battle for chastity a long and often discouraging one. Philip was called "good Philip" because he had learned to live a chaste life in a difficult environment. Later on, as a priest in Rome, he brought the mercy of God to those who found chastity difficult. He had learned, first hand, what this meant in the Florence of his boyhood.

---

49. Romans 6:4.

3

Reform in Florence
St. Catherine and Savonarola

> Nothing an outsider can say about religion has the rooted violence of things the religious have themselves had it at heart to say: no brilliant attack by an outsider against (say) obscurantism will seem to go far enough to a brilliant insider faced with the real obscurity of God; and attacks against religious institutions in the name of reason will not go far enough in a man who is attacking them in the name of faith.
> Stanley Cavell[1]

ST. PHILIP'S remark to Fra Berti about all the good in him he had received from the Dominicans at San Marco is not a rather embarrassing exaggeration to be explained away as a formal nod in the direction of men who had been good to him as a young man; on the contrary, it was the avowal of a significant truth.

The Dominicans at San Marco were the heirs of a reform movement that sought to return to a more exact observance of the laws and customs of the first days of their Order's existence. This movement held that St. Dominic and his companions had set the standard for authentic Dominican life, and any genuine reform must return to the way of life of the earliest days of the Order's existence. The friars who tried to put this into practice were known as Dominicans of the Observance, and the Dominican Observants were introduced into Florence with the founding of San Domenico in Fiesole in 1406.

The Theological Mysticism of St. Catherine and Reform

Behind the beginnings of the institutional reform of the Order there stands the figure of St. Catherine of Siena (1347–1380), hardly a Dominican in any juridical sense. She belonged to a kind of pious association, or

---

1. Stanley Cavell, *Must We Mean What We Say?*, 174.

sodality, that was under the direction of the Dominicans. Nearly the whole of her adult life was spent in a very active and varied apostolate, and this is the place to point out that she was not what today we refer to, somewhat inaccurately, as a nun.[2] The society to which she belonged was called Mantellate; it was a group of laywomen "committed to service of the poor and sick of the city."[3] These women lived at home but wore the black-and-white Dominican habit, and they enjoyed "the great Order's protection."[4] Catherine joined this group as an adolescent over, it seems, the pretty stiff opposition of some of the older women. She continued to live at home, and in spite of her belonging to a group dedicated to helping others she "was more than ever bent on prayer in silence and solitude."[5] Then, when she was about twenty-one, she received what she believed was an order from Christ to begin to practice, in a more public way, the second commandment to love your neighbor as yourself. Her life from that time on was an astonishing fulfillment of the Dominican motto of *Contemplare et contemplata aliis tradere*—to contemplate and to hand on to others the fruits of one's contemplation. She became, like St. Philip afterwards, a mystic in the marketplace and not in the cloister.

Also like Philip, one dimension of her work involved her in the movement for reform in the Church. The hopes for the reform of both the Church and the Dominican order, as well as the efforts to realize these hopes, did not begin with Savonarola in the late fifteenth century. He was only one figure, even if a very important one, in a movement initiated not by him but by St. Catherine of Siena more than a century earlier. Her influence was enormous,[6] and nowhere is this more evident than in the work of Savonarola and of the friars of San Marco.

The source of Catherine's political activity was an overwhelming awareness first of the holiness of God and then of the Church as the mystical body of the Incarnate Christ. Her union with God was the mainspring of everything she said and did; the union came first and nourished and guided her struggles. The gulf between this vision of the reality of the presence of God and the tawdry, shoddy, and often sinful

---

2. She was not a vowed religious in the simple vows of a third order Dominican, much less in the solemn vows of the second order enclosed contemplatives.
3. Noffke, *The Letters of Catherine of Siena*, vol. 1, xiii.
4. Foster and Ronayne, *I Catherine: Selected writings of St. Catherine of Siena*, 13.
5. Noffke, *The Letters of Catherine of Siena*, vol. 1, xiii.
6. "L'influence de Catherine de Sienne fut immense. Elle le fut sur Grégoire XI et Urbain VI, sur plusieurs cardinaux et évêques, surtout sur le groupe de disciples qui la suivait partout et sur l'ordre de saint Dominique. C'est d'elle que partit l'idée de réforme." *Dictionnaire de Spiritualité*, vol. 5, column 1440.

actuality of the Church militant drove her like a whip. On the other hand, everything she accomplished in the public arena was done in the light of her unbreakable faith that anything done against or outside the visible Church would bring nothing but further disasters.[7] Explicitly or implicitly, this was her message for Philip Neri.

St. Catherine's self-disclosure about her life of prayer and its Christian substance is vivid and arresting, but the same thing cannot be said about what was written of Philip's mystical experience and virtues. The sixteenth-century lives of St. Philip are structured with the object of presenting a systematic and ordered account of miracles and virtues that could serve as a basis for the work of the Congregation of Rites. Neither Capecelatro nor Ponnelle and Bordet can be accused of this, and in their different ways, a living picture of St. Philip does come through. On the other hand, they both lack the order and coherence of their sixteenth-century predecessors, and I find their treatment of the philosophical and theological background to Philip's life inadequate when I do not disagree with what they say.[8] However, I am concerned to supplement rather than correct. The great themes of his mysticism, and of what they led to in practice, are to be found in the writings and life of the Sienese Saint. I am not suggesting that Philip used Catherine's work as a primer of spirituality or of action, but his whole cast of mind about God, faith, and the apostolate is Catherine's. To what extent he derived this directly by reading Catherine's writings it is impossible to say, but he was formed by men who knew her work well and valued it and shared her longing for the reform of the Church. In later life, Philip possessed a copy of her *Dialogue*[9] and talked about it at the meetings of the Oratory.

I am concerned with Catherine's teaching, and I will not be dealing here with the extraordinary paranormal experiences that accompanied St. Catherine from the time she was a child, and were also such a strik-

---

7. Foster and Ronayne, *I Catherine: Selected writings of St. Catherine of Siena*, 23. "For (Catherine) the indispensability of the Church consists precisely in this, that it is the medium through which the blood shed on the cross for the human race becomes not only the *sign* of God's re-creating love for sinners but also the vehicle of that love to this and that sinner individually. The Church holds 'the keys of the Blood,' the Blood reaches us 'through the ministers of holy Church.' Indeed the Church exists, for Catherine, only *in function of* Christ's blood; but that was enough to prostrate her in reverence before its meanest minister."

8. For example, as I have already indicated, I think Capecelatro, as well as Ponnelle and Bordet, are plainly mistaken about what they seem to regard as St. Philip's Platonism. See part two, chapter seven, "Studies and Books."

9. Catherine of Siena, *The Dialogue*, translation and Introduction by Suzanne Noffke, O.P., Preface by Giuliana Cavallini (New York: Paulist Press, 1980). Caterina da Siena, *Il Dialogo*, a cura de Giuilana Cavallini (Siena: Edizioni Cantagalli, 1995).

ing characteristic of Philip's later life in Rome. Both saints possessed preternatural powers such as prophecy, the reading of minds, visions, ecstasies, and even the working of miracles. Yet these powers and experiences do not constitute sanctity, even if they sometimes accompany it. Sanctity is constituted, as Fr. Kenelm Foster put it, "simply and sufficiently"[10] by love of God and of neighbor. The other gifts "do not make a saint, though they may help towards canonization. They are given for the sake of others ... as a means to an end ... to draw attention to something else that really matters, the loving union of human beings with God."[11]

It is this love of God and of neighbor that we must focus on. There is no doubt that St. Catherine sets a high standard that few attain, but I suggest that her discussion can and should be used to throw light on the foundations of Philip's mysticism. Later on in life, the Holy Spirit moved Philip into a mode of being in which the miraculous seems to have become almost an everyday occurrence, but that was later on, in Rome.

In the *Dialogue* and in her letters, Catherine lays bare the extraordinary tale of her encounter with God, an account voiced with a strange authority that even today compels attention, and which in Catherine's time not only engendered a movement for reform but also became an important aspect of the Dominican heritage. There is a great deal of St. Catherine in St. Philip: not merely particular doctrines possessed in common but also a similar cast of mind about the things of God and the Church of Christ. Judging by what people write today about spirituality, this outlook and practice on the things of God is called medieval and contrasted with a this-worldly, "life-enhancing" spirituality associated with the Renaissance.[12] It would be absurd to try to argue that there were no differences between the spirituality of the Middle Ages and that of the Italian Renaissance. On the other hand, our contemporary academic orthodoxy seriously underestimates the fully Christian nature of the medieval approach. Many contemporary academic discussions seem to lack an appreciation of the centrality of the sacraments for medieval man and of his concern for the mystical body of the Church. It is quite true that their perception of both the sacraments and of the Church was accompanied by a sense that, in the words of David's great prayer:

---

10. Foster and Ronayne, *I Catherine: Selected writings of St. Catherine of Siena*, 15.
11. Thomas Gilby, O.P., cited in Foster and Ronayne, 15.
12. This seems to be the theme of a thought-provoking article by Melissa Meriam Bullard, "Renaissance spirituality and the ethical dimensions of church reform in the age of Savonarola: the dilemma of Cardinal Barbo," in Fletcher, *The World of Savonarola*, 65–89.

... all things come from thee, and of thy own have we given thee. For we are strangers before thee, and sojourners, as all our fathers were; our days on earth are like a shadow, and there is no abiding.[13]

Any spirituality that tries to blur over this uncomfortable truth is defective from the Christian point of view. Whatever shortcomings may be attributed to the medieval understanding of the value to be put on the things of this world, they did have a firm grasp on the truth that "here we have no lasting city, but we seek the city that is to come."[14] It was Philip's achievement to maintain this Christian perspective on life and make it viable in the ambivalent world of Renaissance humanism. That marvelous achievement hardly involved giving up on the religion of St. Catherine.

The first few words of the *Dialogue* set the tone for the rest of the book, a tone that is both passionate and personal and distinguishes Catherine's work from a formal theological treatise. "A soul rises up," she says, "restless with tremendous desire for God's honor and the salvation of souls."[15] The desire for God is not for some vague or completely unknown absolute, but for union with the God who is Father, Son, and Holy Spirit. This is no desire for self-realization or a kind of moral perfection; it is a desire for a consummation of all we are with the reality of the living God, who is truth, goodness, and beauty.

The experience of following this desire leads to an awareness, which at the beginning is only half-realized, that all things, even our life of prayer, are guided and nourished by the providence of God. We obtain a real and explicit assent to this theological truth of the working of providence in our own lives through our efforts to lead a Christian life. This spiritual combat forces us to recognize the reality of our own sins and failures, and when we begin to see ourselves as we really are, we are overtaken by a sense of the mercy of God.

The love and service of other people is woven into the texture of Catherine's thought. All too often the love of neighbor is discussed as though other people were put in our path merely as occasions for the development of our own spiritual lives; to develop, as it were, our own virtues without any particular regard for anyone else. For Catherine, though, other people are there to be loved and cherished for their own sake, and without this love on our part we won't get very far in the love of God. Yet, left to ourselves, this love of God and love of neighbor would be something we could hardly begin, and certainly not persevere

13. 1 Chronicles 29:14–15.
14. Hebrews 3:15.
15. Catherine of Siena, *Dialogue*, 25.

in, as a way of life. Our sins and our failures show us that it is only by the mercy and grace of God that we have begun and persevered; it is because Christ has left us his Church and its sacraments that we can begin to live as Christ wants us to live; it is because Christ has left us his Church and its sacraments that we can persevere in our striving for union with God.

In the road to union, the blessed Virgin is our inspiration and the model of the virtue we will need to possess. Catherine does not devote a great deal of space to Our Lady, but it is clear that she is central to her prayer and affective life as the human instrument God chose for our redemption and as the exemplar we are to follow in her humility and self-oblation. And, finally, everything is summed up by, and depends on, what she calls *The Tree of Charity*.

If we place Philip's later practice and instruction within the context of Catherine's theological stance, with its precision and its passion, then Philip's teaching and example take on a coherence and a depth they might not at first appear to possess. Much of what first seems sketchy and disconnected in the way Philip instructed and formed his followers suddenly becomes more intelligible, and a good deal more attractive, against the backdrop of Catherine's teaching.

Savonarola

Hubert Jedin has reminded us that the call for reform is almost as old as the Church itself;[16] but by the time of Savonarola, who was born in 1452, there was substantial agreement about the shortcomings of the Church, although what was to be done about them was another matter.

> It almost seemed as if the disease would become chronic. At the turn of the century [of fifteenth into sixteenth] the tension became even more acute. The Church had to endure the pontificate of Alexander VI and to realize, as never before, the difference between theory and practice, between persons and office; it also heard the preaching of Savonarola.[17]

Philip came from a family that venerated the memory of Savonarola

---

16. "The call for reform, for a return to the primitive form of Christianity which had its roots in the very nature of revelation, and whose lineaments had been stamped on it by the early Church, became ever louder. This call originated in the consciousness that Christ's foundation, as historically realized in its individual members, no longer corresponded to the ideal—in other words, that it was not what it should be; and in this respect it was no new thing but was almost as old as the Church herself." Jedin, *A History of the Council of Trent*, vol. 1, 6–7.

17. Ibid., 30.

and thought that he was a saint.[18] Philip shared the Dominican's longing for reform in the Church, but he worked a different way towards this goal. On the other hand, Savonarola's memory and example came back time and again to haunt him: the Savonarola who was for Philip not only an unofficial saint but also a cautionary tale. The influence of the unofficial saint has often been remarked on, but the cautionary role of Savonarola's life and teaching has not been adequately discussed, at least by those who write about St. Philip. We must recall Savonarola more as actor than thinker.[19]

Savonarola's Life in Florence

Savonarola was born in Ferrara in 1452, and in 1475 he entered the Dominican Order at Bologna. In 1482, he was appointed to a position in the convent of San Marco in Florence, which was afterwards to be famous as the center of his attempted revival of religious and political life in the city. He does not seem to have made much of an impression on this first visit, and his early efforts at preaching were a failure. He left in 1487. Three years later, he was recalled by Lorenzo de' Medici to resume his post at San Marco and almost at once "began to preach the sermons which, in series after series, were to have such momentous repercussions on Florentine religious and political life."[20] Savonarola had learned how to preach. At first, his preaching was of an apocalyptic sort that, except for its impact, was a recognized genre and did not differ much in its content from a number of other preachers.[21] There was, however, a significant difference in how the preacher himself was regarded by the authorities.

Piero de' Medici, the *de facto* ruler of Florence, had succeeded his father Lorenzo in April 1492, and almost at once there was general dissatisfaction with him and hope for a change. There was serious rioting,

---

18. See chapter one, "Using this World Well," 51–53. Della Rocchetta and Vian, *Il Primo Processo per San Filippo Neri*, vol. 3, 399, n. 2416.

19. "Those who have discovered inconsistencies and contradictions in Savonarola's preaching and taken these as proof of insincerity or demagoguery have missed the point. Experience, not logic, in the key to understanding his prophetic message, just as passion rather than calculation is the key to understanding the character of the man." Weinstein, *Savonarola and* Florence, 160–161.

20. Polizzotto, *The Elect Nation*, 2.

21. Ibid. "Although he early assumed the prophetic mantle which was ever afterwards to clothe his utterances, at this stage his message, designed, by means of dire warnings to impending tribulations, to arouse the Florentines to a sense of their spiritual inadequacies and to prompt them to undertake a thoroughgoing moral and spiritual reformation, bore little that distinguished it from others of an apocalyptic sort."

and a year later, in 1493, there followed an unsuccessful attempt by some of the patrician families (the *ottimatti*) to raise the people against Piero. Although the hoped-for revolt came to nothing, unrest among all classes continued, at first expressed in an apolitical way: "in a visible but vague religious excitement, a mood of confused and contradictory expectations, and of mounting hatred for the Jews."[22] Naturally enough, this excitement was both expressed and encouraged by popular preachers who were closely involved with the general populace. The government was all too aware of what was going on and took steps to curb the preachers. The important thing for our purposes is that Savonarola was not looked upon at this stage as a danger to the state.

> When Parenti remarks that the people of Florence were putting their hopes in the promises of preachers who were telling them that God would bring men to the good life by means of a great scourge, it comes as a surprise to learn that he was not talking about Savonarola but about two Franciscan rabble-rousers, Bernardino de Feltre and Domenico da Ponzo.[23]

Savonarola was on good terms with Piero. He was, after all, the head of an important religious institution in the city and had no interest in civil disorder. His relations with the Medici were to change dramatically in 1494, when Charles VIII of France invaded Italy. Piero, acting on his own initiative, tried to buy off the king by giving up the Florentine fortresses that stood in Charles's way.[24] Piero's unauthorized surrender of the forts so enraged that Florentines that they expelled him, and Savonarola was sent as a member of a peace mission from Florence to the French king. The Medici were exiled from Florence, and Florence became in fact what it had always been in name: a republic. It was a republic with a very uncertain destiny:

> The Tuscan state which it had taken the Florentines over a century of labor to put together had come undone in a matter of days, this just when Florence found itself dangerously isolated from powerful neighbors on the north, east, and south who were furious with her for allying with the French invader.[25]

Internally, the situation was no better. The patricians, the *ottimatti*,

---

22. Weinstein, *Savonarola and Florence*, 125.
23. Ibid.
24. He also turned over the citadels of Livorno and Pisa, which were Florence's lifeline to the sea, then Pisa itself, Montepulciano, and Arezzo all declared their freedom from Florence.
25. Weinstein, *Savonarola and Florence*, 27.

who had led the uprising against the Medici and had intended to regain the control of Florence it had exercised before the rise of the Medici, now became itself the object of mounting suspicion:

> Having raised the cry "popolo e libertà!" against the Medici, they now found it being turned against themselves. The "good citizens" felt deceived; they had taken up arms for liberty only to find they had fought merely to perpetuate the same men in power. Returning exiles, suspicious of anyone who had stayed and prospered under Medici rule, added another divisive element.[26]

The French invasion and the establishment of the republic seemed to confirm all that Savonarola had predicted, and, in a sermon preached on the first Sunday of Advent 1494, he was not slow to point this out.[27] In another sermon on the text *Ecce gladius Domini super terram cito et velociter*,[28] preached earlier in the same year,[29] he explained the nature of prophecy along Thomistic lines by saying that "future things which depend on free will are uncertain to every creature, but they are certain to God and to those to whom He reveals them."[30] This is brought about by a special light which is "a participation in eternity, which God communicates to whomever he wants."[31] This light, he assures his hearers, has been given to him: "I say to you, Florence, that this light has been given to me for your sake, not for mine, for this light does not make a man pleasing to God."[32] He continues by saying that he "began to see these things more than fifteen, maybe twenty years ago," but only began to speak of them during the last ten years; first in Brescia, but "later God allowed me to come to Florence, which is the navel of Italy, so that you might give notice of them to all the other cities of Italy."[33] But Florence itself has heard the message directly from God, and "so you will have no excuse, Florence, if you are not converted; believe me, Florence, it is not I, but God, Who says these things."[34] The message of the sermon is clear:

---

26. Ibid., 28.
27. Savonarola, Aggeus, Sermon VII, *Selected Writings of Girolamo Savonarola: Religion and Politics, 1490–1498*, 139–150. This sermon was preached on the First Sunday of Advent, November 28, 1494.
28. *Behold, the sword of the Lord [will be] over the earth soon and swiftly.*
29. Savonarola, Renovation Sermon, Octave of the Epiphany, *Selected Writings of Girolamo Savonarola: Religion and Politics, 1490–1498*, 59–75. This sermon was delivered on January 13, 1494.
30. Ibid., 61.
31. Ibid.
32. Ibid.
33. Ibid., 61–62.
34. Ibid., 62.

Savonarola is a prophet who predicted a great danger, and the danger through the mercy of God has been averted; the Florentines should listen to its prophet, give thanks for God's mercies and do penance.

> I would like to be able to tell you this morning all the things I have said to you in the past about this (that is, the need to give thanks for a great danger adverted), but it is not possible. For now I will say to you only this, which I have had in my mind and have told you several times over the past year up to last Advent: do penance, do penance, and do not delay, for many then will not have time. Have you not already seen that this was true? Have you not been next door to great danger? Do you not remember how I often said to you, "Though it looks like fair weather now, soon it will be cloudy," and that I used to say, *Qui habet aures audiendi audiat* [e.g., Matt. 11:15], that is, "He who has ears to hear, let him hear." You have seen how it turned out for any who did not hear. You must recall how great a war the demons waged against us, and that God freed us from all those dangers, such that if I were to recount them all to you, you would be stupefied. I would like you to know that all my repeated saying and crying out to you, "Do penance," was not in vain.[35]

Savonarola's prophecies and his membership in the delegation that had brought peace and saved Florence from destruction resulted in an extraordinary degree of prominence and authority for the friar.[36] He suddenly found himself mediating between the religious and political spheres of Florentine life. Najemy writes that Savonarola was "catapulted" into this role by the fall of Piero's regime, which "unleashed the energy of Florence's volatile religious culture."[37] The republic of Florence was to be a Christian commonwealth in which Jesus Christ was to be the sole sovereign, and his Gospel the law. By the end of 1494, Savonarola began identifying the republic as the New Jerusalem, in which the reform of Christian society would begin. In order to fulfill its divinely appointed task, Florence must have a new constitution, and he and the Florentines he inspired devised one that lasted until the fall of Florence and the return of the Medici in 1512.

Savonarola himself, however, had a much shorter time to live. His

---

35. Savonarola, Aggeus, Sermon VII, *Selected Writings of Girolamo Savonarola: Religion and Politics, 1490–1498*, 142.

36. "Assured now of the attentiveness of those in high places, and enjoying great popularity and prestige amongst the populace in general, he began to develop a sweeping program of religious and political reform, based upon his divinations of God's will." Polizzotto, *The Elect Nation*, 2.

37. Najemy, *A History of Florence 1200–1575*, 392.

foreign policy alienated Florence from the rest of Italy, and more importantly, at least for the friar, he quarreled with the Papacy.[38] In the end, the Republic he had helped to create bowed to the will of Pope Alexander VI and allowed Savonarola to be condemned as a heretic; it had him hanged and burned in 1498.

Interpretations of Savonarola's Life

So much, then, for the biography; it is relatively straightforward, but the same cannot be said of its implications. The first and most obvious difficulty is that even after four centuries, the significance of Savanarola's life and work is contentious. Histories of the period in which he appears, as well as biographies of the friar, are so disparate in their evaluation of his life and work that it is easy to wonder if they are writing about the same man. These divisions are not drawn solely along religious lines. There are committed Catholics who believe that Savonarola was a saint, sent by God to decry the corruption of the Church of his time as well as to bring about a genuine reform of both personal morals and politics. The impassioned and still moving work of Ridolfi is a notable example of this genre.[39] Then there are those Catholics who, without denying the friar's saintly qualities, regard his life "as in the truest and fullest sense a tragedy."[40]

> For the very essence of tragedy lies in this, that under stress of critical circumstances, some flaw in a noble character leads by steps, slow perhaps, but sure, to a final catastrophe, and that in and through the catastrophe itself that which was imperfect or faulty is as it were purged out, while that which was noble survives in the mind and memory of men, and does its work more effectively that it would have

---

38. "Savonarola was a strict Thomist and a strict adherent to the doctrine of papal supremacy. For all that, in March 1498, even he entertained for a moment the idea of summoning a Council with the assistance of the Emperor and the Christian Princes for the purpose of calling Alexander VI to account ... Not a trace of conciliar theory but a Council is planned!" Jedin, *A History of the Council of Trent*, 40. This has to be balanced against the less anodyne view of Polizzotto about the stance of Savonarola's successors: "Years later [i.e. after the Council of Pisa, 1511] the Piagnoni were to claim that they, and the friars of S. Marco in particular, had never been conciliarists and had fought tooth and nail against the Council of Pisa ... but this was not the case. The chroniclers Giovanni Cambi and Luca Landucci, for example, had no hesitation in listing the Council's spiritual and political advantages. They saw it as a means to assuage the ills of the Church by remedying the depredations of its prelates." Polizzotto, *The Elect Nation*, 228.

39. Roberto Ridolfi, *The Life of Girolamo Savonarola*, translated by Cecil Grayson, (New York: Alfred A Knopf, 1959).

40. Lucas, *Fra Girolamo Savonarola*, 441.

done had there been no catastrophe to arouse attention and awaken sympathy.[41]

These two writers and many like them are concerned primarily with the implications of the life and teaching of Savonarola for the Church, and this perspective is fundamental when we begin to consider the influence of Savonarola on St. Philip.

Yet the implications of Savonarola's work and thought in the political and social order cannot be neatly hived off as irrelevant. His work at the end of his life centered on the theme that the city of Florence had a unique political role to play in world history; the reformation of both church and state were to come about through the agency of the Florentine republic. Donald Weinstein's *Savonarola and Florence: Prophecy and Patriotism in the Renaissance* is a brilliant account of this complex religious and socio-political reality.[42] *Fire in the City* by Mauro Martines[43] traces part of the same story from a more self-consciously political perspective; Martines, that is, has little time for Savonarola's religious convictions, but thinks they were important as they provided him with a firm standpoint from which to criticize the absolutist pretensions of the Medici. In connection with Philip's relationship to the Medici, it should be remembered that it was not under the Medici, but under the republic which Savonarola had helped create, that Savonarola was tried and executed. The complex story of both the friar's and the city's dealings with Pope Alexander VI, of Savonarola's excommunication, and of the threat of an interdict on Florence—all these factors played a role in the unhappy outcome. It is a mistake to attribute Savonarola's death exclusively to any one cause.

> No one ingredient precipitated the governmental decision to yield up its friar to the fire. Political considerations of various types, the fear of driving the city truly outside the pale of orthodoxy, simple exhaustion, fiscal needs, the economic condition within the city, all played their part. But the role played by the threat of the interdict cannot be gainsaid. It had hung over the city and its merchants since February. Every passing day made its actualization more terrifying.[44]

There is a further complication. The friar left a great deal more behind him than the ruins of his work: the memory of his life and an

---

41. Ibid.
42. (Princeton, New Jersey: Princeton University Press, 1970).
43. Lauro Martines, *Fire in the City, Savonarola and the Struggle for the Soul of Renaissance Florence* (Oxford: University Press, 2006).
44. Trexler, *The Spiritual Power: Republican Florence Under Interdict*, 176–177.

account of his teaching. These memories were carried on in a movement in both the Church and political life, and this movement had both political and social implications. Lorenzo Polizzotto's work *The Elect Nation: The Savonarolian Movement in Florence 1494–1545*,[45] is an account of a reform movement of the Church in Tuscany that was organized and carried on in the first place by the friars who had been expelled from San Marco after Savonarola's death, but was largely composed of lay people both in Florence and outside of it.[46] The members of this movement were known by their enemies by a series of derogatory epithets,[47] among which *Piagnoni*, the weepers, and *Frateschi*, the monkish ones, eventually predominated and were gradually adopted by the followers of Savonarola as a badge of pride.[48] Philip's family belonged or were sympathetic to this movement, and he was therefore brought up in an atmosphere in which the sanctity of Savonarola was beyond dispute.

Newman on St. Philip and Savonarola

The main lines of the modern account of St. Philip's connection to Savonarola were laid out by Newman, and his analysis appears to have been followed closely by Capelcelatro and those dependent on him. In his *The Mission of St. Philip Neri*[49] delivered "in substance in the Birmingham Oratory January 1850 and at subsequent times," Newman begins by contrasting Savonarola with St. Paul. Savonarola, Newman says, was:

> A true son of St. Dominic, in energy, in severity of life, in contempt of merely secular learning, a forerunner of St. Pius the Fifth in boldness, in resoluteness, in zeal for the honor of the House of God, and for the restoration of holy discipline.

Newman then goes on to say that Savonarola's vehement spirit got the better of him, and unlike St. Paul—whose "prudence, gentleness, love of

---

45. Polizzotto, *The Elect Nation*, 2.
46. See Herzig, *Savonarola's Women: Visions and Reform in Renaissance Italy*, and de Agresti, *Sviluppi della Riforma Monastica Savonaroliana*.
47. *Piagnoni, Frateschi, Collitorti, Stopiccioni, Masticapaternostri, Pinzoheroni, Ierosomiliatani, Hieronimini*: there and other names were applied with varying degrees of ferocity to the followers of Fra Girolamo Savonarola. Polizzotto, *The Elect Nation*, 1.
48. Though they responded with some imaginative name-calling of their own, the Savonarolans soon came to glory in these terms of abuse. They saw them, in fact, as a grudging admission of their strength and cohesiveness. Ibid., 1.
49. Newman, "The Mission of St. Philip" (Sermon XII), *Sermons Preached on Various Occasions*, 211. The quotations from Newman that immediately follow are all taken from this sermon, 211–218.

his kind, and human accomplishments are never more happily shown than in his speech to the Athenians" (Acts XVII)—the Dominican:

> ...burst forth into a whirlwind of indignation and invective against all that he found in Florence, and condemned the whole established system, and all who took part of it, high and low, prince or prelate, ecclesiastic or layman, with a pitiless rigor, —.

St. Paul had to be content to take away only two converts after his address to the Athenians, while Savonarola had "great immediate success, [for he] frightened and abashed the offenders, rallied round him the better disposed, and elicited and developed whatever there was of piety, whether in the multitude or in the upper class." Finally, though, "his innocence, sincerity, and zeal were too much for his humility. He presumed; he exalted himself against a power which none can assail without misfortune. He put himself in opposition to the Holy See, and, as some say, disobeyed its injunctions."

Newman then goes on to lay down what has become the canonical account of St. Philip's work and its connection to Savonarola: Savonarola did much good, but in a public, noisy, and political way, and so it did not last; while Philip, like St. Paul, began quietly, was obedient to the Church, and succeeded. Cardinal Capecelatro, who translated Newman's *Instruction* on St. Philip into Italian, gives a vigorous statement of the differences in character of the two men and of their work. First of all there are the differences in their characters:

> What contributed most to Philip's success was his incomparable greatness and suavity of manner; whereas Savonarola's greatest difficulties lay in his fiery, impetuous character and his inconsiderate zeal. While Philip expresses in his life the tender and subduing charity of Jesus Christ, the Redeemer of men, Savonarola stands forth stern and terrible as a prophet of the Old Testament; he reminds us of the denunciations of Ezekiel or Amos, and his preaching breathes the spirit of the ancient law.[50]

Then there are the reasons for the spectacular failure of Savonarola's work as contrasted with Philip's success:

> ...while Philip longed for reformation of those holding high office in the Church, he never forgot the reverence and submission due to ecclesiastical authority; he knew that without this reverent submission, attempts at reform could only aggravate the wounds they were intended to heal... Savonarola on the other hand, in his great strait,

---

50. Capecelatro, *The Life of St. Philip Neri*, 162.

when compelled to choose between obedience to the Pope of ill renown and his ardent longing for reforms, could not humble himself and wait; and ruined by his short-sighted zeal the work he strove to accomplish.[51]

Both Newman and Capecelatro do present us with a credible picture of Savonarola as a public and not very attractive religious reformer. Yet on their account, it is difficult to understand how the Old Testament prophet *redivivus* could have captured, both during his lifetime and afterwards, the hearts and minds of so many distinguished and even holy men and women. If Savonarola were nothing more than a religious fanatic whose "fiery and intemperate character" finally got the better of him, he could hardly be regarded even as a tragic figure, much less as a saint.

Savonarola the Dominican

The picture Newman and Capecelatro draw of Savonarola must be developed in a way that allows more scope for the complexity of the Friar's character and, ultimately, its influence on Philip. More attention must be paid first to the attractive and genuinely Catholic aspects of Savonarola's character. At the same time, though, there was a Millenarian streak in Savonarola's thinking and preaching that has not been given due weight by those writing about St. Philip. Millenarianism is based on a passage in the Book of Revelation in which the souls of the righteous who had been slain for their faithful witness to Jesus Christ "came to life and reigned with Christ a thousand years":

> The rest of the dead did not come to life until the thousand years were ended. This is the first resurrection. Blessed and holy is he who shares in the first resurrection! Over such the second death has no power, but they shall be priests of God and of Christ, and they shall reign with him a thousand years.[52]

This passage has often been taken to mean that in a particular moment in history Christ has come again and together with his saints has begun his thousand-year reign. This Millennium is not to be confused with the Last Judgment, when Christ the Messiah will come in glory and all things will be subjected to him.[53] The Millennium, for those who believe in it, is in the present, the here and now; Christ, for those who think this

---

51. Ibid.
52. Revelation 20:5.
53. "At Judgment Day at the end of the world, Christ will come in glory to achieve the definitive triumph of good over evil which, like the wheat and the tares, have grown together in the course of history." *Catechism of the Catholic Church*, 681.

way, has already come again, and with him are the "saints" who will not taste "the second death." Throughout history, Millenarianism has been associated with those who are convinced that revolution and violent change are the only ways to fight the forces of evil entrenched in the power structures of this present age.[54]

> The Antichrist's deception already begins to take shape in history every time the claim is made to realize within history the messianic hope which can only be realized beyond history through the eschatological judgment. The Church has rejected even modified forms of this falsification of the kingdom to come under the name of millenarianism, especially the "intrinsically perverse" political form of a secular messianism.[55]

Florence under Savonarola was to be the center of a renewal of both Church and state;[56] Christ was the King of Florence, and the reign of the saints had already begun.[57] Here was Millenarianism with a vengeance.

It is not merely that the Friar shared the "Myth of Florence," but also the way he grafted this millenarian dimension onto the myth, that was the source of both his political and religious influence and ultimately the cause of his downfall. It is one thing to believe, for whatever reason, that Florence had a special role to play in world history; but to hold that the Florentine republic inaugurated in 1494 was the beginning of the Millennium spoken of in the Book of Revelation[58] is a statement of a totally different order. It betrays a cast of mind that was repugnant to Philip, who all his life fought against taking seriously the content or message of

---

54. "The idea of the messianic kingdom has a potentially revolutionary character. The established, all-powerful rulers of this world are, ordinarily, evil and tyrannical oppressors in prophecy. They are, however, doomed to be overthrown in a great decisive revolutionary struggle." Philip A. Wiener, ed., *Dictionary of the History of Ideas*, 5 Vols. (New York: Scribner's, 1973). vol. 3, 224.

55. *Catechism of the Catholic Church*, 676.

56. "Florence would spread her empire to many places, and those who resisted her would be conquered and fall under her dominion, and the light would spread as far as the land of the Turks. Preachers would arouse the people of other cities to go to Florence, where they would find both the true light and the model form of government. And Florence would possess the inheritance of these other cities, dissipated by the devil, by sin, by tyrants, by famine and by war. And when the wicked are dead and the tyrants spent, then many good people will come to Florence and fill all the roads and fields of the land with goodness." Weinstein, *Savonarola and Florence*, 145–146.

57. "All the characteristics of the millenarian pattern as it has been delineated by scholars were present in Savonarolian Florence: social crisis, a charismatic leader, a view of the world as a battle ground between good and evil forces, a chosen people, a vision of the ultimate redemption in an earthly paradise." Weinstein, *Savonarola and Florence*, 33.

58. Revelation 20:1–5.

private revelations, even if, as was certainly the case, he never doubted their possibility. In an emotionally overcharged atmosphere engendered by those who professed to be the bearers of such revelations, as well as by the credulity of those who accepted them, Philip in later life directed the full force of his personality and all his authority. He set himself firmly against anything that even hinted at the presence of what would lead his penitents away from the ordinary and usual ways of Catholic living. He began, at least instinctively, to develop this stance in opposition to this aspect of the influence of Savonarola and the *Piagnoni*.[59]

It is very difficult to create a coherent picture of Savonarola's life that can do justice to both the political figure and the religious reformer; even so, it has to be said that neither Newman nor Capecelatro gives us much sense of the moral and religious greatness that was destroyed by the friar's faults. Without some sense of this greatness, gone wrong assuredly, we will miss the source of Savonarola's influence. Furthermore, we will have no understanding of what there was about Savonarola that left a lifetime impression on Philip. The fact of the influence is beyond dispute, and not only on Philip but also on other saintly people as well. Ridolfi sums up this influence:

> Since the word saintliness was used about Savonarola, it is my duty to record the witness to it of many people, starting from San Filippo Neri, Santa Caterina de' Ricci, the Blessed Colomba da Rieti, the Blessed Maria Bagnesi, the Blessed Caterina da Racconigi, the Venerable Maddalena del Paradiso, and Santa Maria de' Pazzi, who all revered the Friar, obtained miracles from him, saw him surrounded by the glory of the blessed; from all of which it would appear that not to believe in his saintliness is for a Christian tantamount to not believing in the sanctity of those witnesses.[60]

Lucas remarks correctly, if rather primly, that the testimony of the saints on such matters may be mistaken.[61] That may be correct, although the

---

59. One of the tools used in the development of this stance was the humorous, ironical streak in his character that was so prominent in later life. I discuss Philip's irony in the next chapter.

60. Ridolfi, *The Life of San Girolamo Savonarola*, 277.

61. "The questions arising out of the veneration paid to Savonarola by St. Philip Neri, St. Catherine de' Ricci, and S. Francis of Paula, it does not seem necessary to discuss. There will always be some who are of the opinion that it is safer to trust to the critical insight of these saints than to any merely critical or historical consideration, and such persons we cannot, of course, hope to convince. Others have held, and will continue to hold, that even saints might be unconsciously prejudiced in favor of a very distinguished compatriot and that the case of Fra Girolamo must, after all, be judged on its merits." Lucas, *Fra Girolamo Savonarola*, 441.

number of saints who were thus mistaken in this particular case must surely be taken into account; that is, it is not only Philip who made the mistake if such it were. We are not, however, trying to establish the sanctity or otherwise of Savonarola, but rather to determine how Philip Neri was in part formed by the Dominican tradition as he found it in San Marco in the generation after the friar's death. This tradition had been revivified and given its form by Savonarola; and so it is to Savonarola as priest and religious reformer that we turn.

Savonarola, like St. Catherine of Siena before him and Philip Neri after him, must have had an enormously attractive personality. This has been obscured because most of the lives written about the friar understandably concentrate on his efforts at religious reform, his political activities and apocalyptic preaching. In all these dimensions, he comes across as a single-minded, powerful figure who had little time for listening to others or for compromise. Yet there must have been more to him than that, because, to take a key issue, Savonarola's influence and his power derived from his reform of the Dominican Order. The story is a complex one, and it provoked bitter opposition within the Order itself, but it involved the restructuring of the internal Dominican governmental forms by setting up a new administrative unit, called a Congregation, with Savonarola at its head. Weinstein sums up the matter by saying: "This was the outcome of unceasing efforts on the part of Savonarola and his brethren in San Marco, and the political agencies of the Florentine state."[62] But this account leaves out an essential part of the story: Savonarola's "unceasing efforts" were successful because he had the manpower behind him to back up his claims. The new vocations he had attracted to the Order, vocations that were of the highest caliber, provided the ultimate proof that his strategies were successful. Polizzotto gives us an idea of Savonarola's extraordinary achievement:

> In the eight years of Savonarola's apostolate in Florence, no fewer than 143 friars were professed in S. Marco and in S. Domenico at Fiesole; the peak occurred in 1497 with an intake of 56 novices. Fra Giovanni Sinibaldi was later to charge that Savonarola pursued a policy of active recruitment with little thought to the suitability of the men seeking admission. But, as Savonarola often argued, these vocations were evidence of the achievements of his reforming program to date and a guarantee of its continuation in the future.[63]

62. "By a Papal brief of August 13, 1493, Savonarola became the first Vicar General of the new Tuscan Congregation, later renamed the Congregation of San Marco, which included San Domenico of Fiesole, the Dominican houses in neighboring Prato and Sasso, and St. Catherine of Pisa." Weinstein, *Savonarola and Florence*, 109.

63. Polizzotto, *The Elect Nation*, 187.

It does seem that Fra Sinibaldi suffered from the not unfamiliar complaint of clerical jealousy because Savonarola's recruits were so exceptionally good.[64] The number and quality of these men, who lived at close quarters with Savonarola, testifies to elements of sanctity in Savonarola's character; certainly such men were not attracted to San Marco because it was in the hands of an unattractive, fundamentally misguided, and self-deceiving religious fanatic. It was those elements of sanctity that Savonarola bequeathed to his followers at San Marco, and these were the elements Philip Neri found amid the ruins of the friar's work.

What were some of these elements? First of all, clearly, it was Savonarola's sincerity in living up to his commitments. If the zealous and charitable way he lived his religious life had attracted so many to the novitiate of San Marco, then it is not surprising that this example of a deeply serious Christian life should have been an inspiration to many others who were seeking after holiness of life, whether they were Dominicans or not. From the outset of his religious life, he had distinguished himself in the observance of the three vows of poverty, chastity, and obedience, as well as in the rules of his Order.

> His practice of poverty ... was most rigid, and deeply deplored the relaxations in this matter which had crept into the convents of the Order. His purity was altogether beyond reproach or even the suspicion of a fault. To his superiors he was, at least in these early days, most docile in all things, and his spirit of humble obedience showed itself in the deference with which he treated not merely his equals but even his inferiors.[65]

We are so used to the picture of Savonarola as the fiery and intemper-

---

64. "Savonarole continua de promouvoir le développement de la congrégation de Saint Marc. Cette année (1495) et les trois suivantes, il donna l'habit domincain à de nombre aux postulants, parmi lesquels le lettré milanais Niccolò Seratico; Pandolfo Ruccellai (fra Sante), homme riche, ami estimé et protecteur de beaucoup de 'spirituels,' auxquel très vite Savonarole confia le soin des novices et des finances de la congrégation; Abram di Christoforo di Spagna (fra Francesco Maria) Juif converti qui par la suite retourné en sas patrie, abandonna l'Ordre; Bettucio (fra Benedetto) di Paolo Luschino, un enlumineur; Francesco (fra Ambrogio) d'Andrea della Robbia; l'helléniste Zenobio di Raffael Acciaiuoli; le médicin Pietro Paolo da Urbino; Malatesta Sacramoro da Rimini; Stefano de Maldeo da Castrocaro, ancient chanceleir de Lorenzo de' Medici; le richissime Francesco (fra Francesco Maria) di Antonio Gondi; le maître de la jeunesse florentine depuis quatre décennies Giorgio Antonio Vespucci, oncle d'Amerigo; Niccolò di Teodorico Schönberg; et beaucoup d'autres." *Dictionnaire de Spiritualité*, vol. 14, column 375.

65. Lucas, *Fra Girolamo Savonarola*, 9.

ate public reformer that it is easy to overlook this deeply personal and tender love for Christ, the Church, and its sacraments, as well as for the simple ordinary demands of Christian living. The themes we encountered in St. Catherine are all to be found in his work: a great hunger for the honor and glory of God—Father, Son, and Holy Spirit; the working of Providence in everyday life as well as in the course of history; a love for the Church as the Mystical Body of Jesus Christ and as the keeper of the sacraments; and a tender devotion to the Blessed Virgin.

Let me cite some of Savonarola's works that show something of the gentler, attractive side of his personality. First of all, there is his ardent desire to be united with Christ.

> Omnipotent God
> You know what I need to do my work
> And what my longing might be.
> I ask you not for a crown or a treasure
> Like the blind and grasping man,
> Nor that a town or a fort be built for me.
> I ask only, My dear Lord,
> That you pierce my heart with your love.[66]

In the longer "Lauda II," two verses stand out as exemplifying the same theme:

> Jesus, my highest comfort,
> You are my only love
> You are my blissful harbor
> And saintly Savior true.
> O mercy great,
> And piety sweet,
> That man is glad who lives as one with you
>
> ✽✽✽
>
> Inflame my heart completely
> With your love so divine,
> Till deep inside I'm blazing as bright as seraphim.
> O mercy great,
> And piety sweet,
> That man is glad who lives as one with you.[67]

Then, like Catherine, he meditates on Providence and the "earth so oppressed with every vice":

---

66. Savonarola, "Lauda I," *A Guide to Righteous Living and Other Works*, 75.
67. Savonarola, "Lauda II," *A Guide to Righteous Living and Other Works*, 76.

> Though it is true, and I do so believe
> Your Providence to be, Lord of the World,
> Forever boundless (nor could I believe
> Its opposite, because *experience* proves it)
> At times it does seem colder still than snow
> When I behold the world turned on its head,
> And lifeless on the ground
> Lies every virtue, and every custom fair.
> I find no brilliant light,
> Or even someone shamed by all his sins,
> Some men deny you, others say you sleep.[68]

But it is not only the world that has been turned on its head with "virtue and every custom fair" lying "lifeless on the ground"; the Church as well is in ruins.

> She walks in poverty, her limbs uncovered,
> Her hair dishevelled and garlands broken;
> She finds no bees, but on the ancient acorns
> With hunger great, alas, she throws herself.
> The scorpion bites her and the snake perverts her
> And all the locusts seize the tender roots;
> And so she crawls on earth
> The crowned one and her holy hands,
> Cursed by the dogs,
> Who swindle all the Sabbaths and calends.
> Some can not and some perceive not.[69]

Some of the images may appear a bit opaque to the modern reader; perhaps they did even when Savonarola used them. In any event, he provided his own gloss on nearly every word of the *Canzone*. Without repeating all he had to say, here is his understanding of some of the words of the verse. The *she* referred to in the first line is not the Virgin Mary, but "the Virgin Church because the Faith was never corrupted in her." She walks in the poverty of virtue, and her limbs are uncovered because the members of the Church "are no longer ashamed of their sins not even the clergy." The ancient acorns are "the poets, the rhetoricians and philosophers," while the locusts are "false brothers, who claim to fly high and to be Christians, and yet they dwell on the earth." The crowned one is the holy Church and her works, which men will not help to cure or even to see it is in need of help.

The excerpts I have cited date from early on in Savonarola's life, but

---

68. Savonarola, "Canzone II," *A Guide to Righteous Living and Other Works*, 61.
69. Ibid., 64.

the same sentiments were still very much present at the end of his time as he lay in prison, tortured and waiting execution. During these last days, he penned a meditation on *The Miserere*, Psalm 51 (50), Have mercy on me O God:

> Woe is me, who am destitute of all aid! Who have offended both heaven and earth! Whither shall I go? Whither shall I turn? To whom shall I flee for refuge? Who will take pity on me?
>
> To heaven I dare not lift up my eyes, for I have grievously sinned against it. On earth I cannot find a refuge, for I have been a by-word unto it.
>
> What then shall I do? Shall I yield to despair? Away with the thought! God is merciful, righteous is my Savior. Therefore God alone is my refuge.
>
> He will not despise the work of his own hand. He will not cast from Him the image of Himself. To thee, therefore, most righteous God, disconsolate and full of woe, I come, since Thou alone art my hope, Thou alone art my refuge. But how shall I open my mouth before Thee, when I dare not lift up my eyes? Shall I pour forth words of lamentation? I will implore Thy mercy. I will say: —
>
> Have mercy upon me, O God, according to Thy great mercy.[70]

These passages give us some idea of a side of Savonarola's character that is overlooked. He was not in the first place a reformer or a politician but a serious Dominican who cared passionately about making Jesus Christ better known and more deeply loved. Whatever may have gone wrong, it was a case of something very good being ruined. "Zeal for your house has consumed me," said the Psalmist,[71] and these words were applied to Christ;[72] we may also apply them to Savonarola. That he was consumed and that things went disastrously wrong is only too evident. Yet his downfall and death were not the exposure of a fraudulent politician, nor the punishment of a cynical and corrupt unbeliever; they were rather the dreadful consequences of a man whose mistakes and weaknesses ruined the making of a saint. Yet it has to be said that there remained enough of the saint, or of the saint that might have been, to inspire his followers to work for personal holiness and the reform of the Church. Philip Neri was among their number.

---

70. Savonarola, *An Exposition of the Psalm Miserere Mei Deus by Fra Girolamo Savonarola*, 5.
71. Psalm 69:9.
72. John 2:17.

4

Art, Irony, and Eros

...he who wishes to go to paradise must be an honest man and a good Christian, and not a believer in dreams.

St. Philip Neri[1]

Just as existence is treacherous, so also is the speech of Socrates.

Soren Kierkegaard[2]

Socrates, by universal consent of his contemporaries, was a "lover," an erōtikos engaged in a passionate search for truth. But he made the important connection of truth and the love of truth with beauty and the love of beauty—in the first instance (at least in his own society) with the beauty of the human body.

John Rist[3]

WE HAVE been trying to obtain a picture of the young Philip in Florence by looking at some of the influences that were brought to bear on the growing boy in childhood and adolescence. Many of these were institutional ones, such as his education in a humanist school in Florence and his specifically Catholic training under the influence of the Dominicans, both in the *Confraternity of the Purification* and in Savonarola's old convent of San Marco. In this chapter I want to point out that Philip's reaction to the heritage of Savonarola was deeply ambivalent. We can begin to illustrate this by discussing Savonarola's attitudes towards art.

Philip grew up in a world that took for granted that art was an important aspect of life, and that the artist had an important role to play in society. Furthermore, given the *Piagnone* sympathies of his fam-

---

1. Quoted in Bacci, *The Life of Saint Philip Neri*, vol. 1, 360.
2. Kierkegaard, *Concluding Unscientific Postscript*, 7.
3. Rist, *What is Truth? From the Academy to the Vatican*, 147.

ily, and his own association with San Marco, what Savonarola taught about art and how he put this teaching into practice would have mattered to Philip. It was the Dominican successors of Savonarola at San Marco who developed and nourished Philip's aesthetic sensibilities, and who taught him, at least by example, about the integration of a concern for the beautiful with a deeply felt desire for "the secret and hidden wisdom of God."[4]

Although the importance of art was unanimously accepted, this must not be taken to mean that it was not talked about, nor that the way the artist pursued his art was of little concern to sixteenth-century man. It does mean, though, that for Philip's age, our present-day discussions about how to show that art really has an important role to play in life were of no concern. Art was thought to be important because the society as a whole was thoroughly imbued with the Catholic view that images had a central role to play in religious experience, and as religion was important, it follows that the production of images was important. On the other hand, although in this sense art was taken for granted, it was nonetheless also vital to see that its role was properly carried out. The question that mattered was how this important aspect of religious experience was to be understood and properly used. It is at this point that the real difficulties begin. Those who understand best the impact of art are often the most ambivalent about its place in society. Plato banished the artist from his ideal commonwealth not because he was aesthetically blind, but because he understood, probably first-hand, the dreadful havoc caused by art gone wrong. Rather than condemning out of hand those who worry about the influence of art, we might well ask with Iris Murdoch "the not uninteresting question whether Plato may not have been in some ways right to be so suspicious of art."[5] In the end, Plato wanted art to be carefully controlled because he thought that it distracted man from the pursuit of the good and the beautiful; and not only did it distract, but it also all too often led towards irrationality and to the establishment of habits that prevent the development of life based on the cultivation of the best elements in human nature.[6]

4. 1 Corinthians 2:7.
5. Murdoch, "The Fire and the Sun: Why Plato Banished the Artists," *Existentialists and Mystics*, 386.
6. "The poets mislead us by portraying the gods as undignified and immoral.... Neither should we be led to picture the gods as laughing. Poets, and also writers of children's stories, should help us to respect religion, to admire good people, and to see that crime does not pay. Music and the theater should encourage stoical calmness, not boisterous uncontrolled emotion. We are infected by playing or enjoying a bad role. Art can do cumulative psychological harm in this way." Ibid., 390.

Art, Irony, and Eros   111

It is not to be wondered at, then, that Christianity found, and still finds, its relation to art and artistic production to be a complex one; furthermore, ideas about the nature of this relationship have undergone a good deal of development. In the first place, it is obvious that Christianity has been an integral and important aspect in the development of European culture. On the other hand, it is often said that it would not have been easy to predict such a development from either the Bible or the earliest days of Christianity.[7] Christianity grew out of Judaism, and Judaism had drastic prohibitions against the making of images.[8] Yet, it does seem that, in spite of these prohibitions, Judaism, both before the destruction of the Temple in AD 79 and long afterwards, was very divided on the place of art both in society and even in religion.[9] It would seem, then, that while the earliest Christians may have been ambivalent towards artistic creation, it is also true that Judaism displayed the same sort of tensions.[10]

Yet it was not only the fact that art was engaged in making images that seemed to many a prohibited activity in itself; there was also the influence art had that strengthened the ambivalence of the early Christians towards it.

> The pagan background (not to speak of the related sexual overtones) of ancient art helps to explain a morally and religiously based ambivalence about beauty among the Fathers. Indeed from time to time throughout the history of Christianity preachers have sought to dismiss earthly beauty as at best irrelevant to religion, at worst a source of irreligion and immorality (which, as Plato already knew, it often is!).[11]

---

7. "The most casual reflection on the history of European culture will indicate the enormous influence of Christianity—for at least sixteen centuries of our era primarily Catholic Christianity—in literature, music, architecture, painting and sculpture. That is not something one could easily deduce or expect from reading the Bible or the writing of the earliest Christians." Rist, *What is Truth?*, 143.

8. "You shall not make for yourself a graven image, or any likeness of anything that is in heaven above, or that is in the earth beneath, or that is in the water under the earth...." Exodus 20:4.

9. See, for example: Fine, *Art and Judaism in the Greco-Roman World, Toward a New Jewish Archeology*; Kessler and Nirenberg, editors, *Judaism and Christian Art, Aesthetic Anxieties from the Catacombs to Colonialism*; and Epstein, *The Mediaeval Haggadah, Art, Narrative and Religious Imagination*.

10. "Clearly the earliest Christians regarded images of pagan gods as objects of idolatrous worship and they probably evinced a more generalized concern that any physical beauty could lead to the worship of created objects, including the human form and the universe itself: a problem already foreshadowed in the Wisdom literature (*Wisdom* 13:3; 13:7)." Rist, *What is Truth?*, 146. The proper use of images, then, was a problem not only for Christians but for Jews as well.

11. Ibid.

In spite of the doubts and hesitations about earthly beauty, the early Church finally came firmly down on the side of the representation of holy things. The Incarnation had revealed God in human form, and therefore, in spite of whatever dangers there might be, it must be not only lawful but also helpful to represent the divine in images. St. John Damascene argued that:

> Previously God, who has neither body nor a face, absolutely could not be represented by an image. But now that he has made himself visible in the flesh and lived with men, I can make an image of what I have seen of God... and contemplate the glory of the Lord, his face unveiled.[12]

This sort of argument and its conclusions were affirmed at the Second Council of Nicaea;[13] and the rejection of iconoclasm has justifiably been called "a decision of incalculable significance."[14]

> The great history of Western art is a consequence of this decision which still largely determines our own cultural consciousness. A common language for the common content of our self-understanding has been developed through the Christian art of the Middle Ages and the humanistic revival of Greek and Roman art and literature, right up to the close of the eighteenth century and the great social transformations and political and religious changes with which the nineteenth century began.[15]

Art is important, but art is dangerous. We have to remember this twofold contention when we try to understand Savonarola's public role as a censor and destroyer of beautiful artifacts. The one thing many seem to remember about the Friar was his organizing of the destruction of valuable works of art, the so-called burnings of the vanities, the *brucciamenti delle vanità*. Two of these burnings that had been directly inspired by Savonarola took place in Florence, one on February 7, 1497, and the other on February 27, 1498. The first of these is described both in the *Vita Latina*, an early sixteenth-century biography of Savonarola,

---

12. St. John Damascene, cited in the *Catechism of the Catholic Church*, 1159.
13. "We declare that we preserve intact all the written and unwritten traditions of the Church which have been entrusted to us. One of the traditions consists in the production of representational artwork, which accords with the history of the preaching of the Gospel. For it confirms that the incarnation of the Word of God was real and not imaginary, and to our benefit as well, for realities that illustrate each other undoubtedly reflect each other's meaning." Cited in the *Catechism of the Catholic Church*, 1161.
14. Gadamer, *The Relevance of the Beautiful*, 3.
15. Ibid., 4.

and in the diary of Luca Landuci, "an acute observer of events in Florence."[16]

> All the vanities and indecent things, they related, were brought to be burnt: wigs and other vanities of women, veils, cosmetic colors, perfumes, mirrors, and the like; games and gambling instruments; masks and beards of carnival. Interspersed through the inventory, the following works of the musical and literary arts are listed: books of music and harps, lutes, cithers, *buonaccordi, dolzemela,* bagpipes, cymbals, *staffete,* and horns; books of poems, both Latin and Vulgar, the *Morganti Spagne,* the *Dieci Novelle* of Boccaccio, the works of Dante and Petrarch, and other "indecent writings." Cited among the plastic arts were: paintings of beautiful figures showing much immodesty; beautiful ancient sculpted figures of Florentine and Roman women; sculptured portraits by the great masters such as Donatello and others; and all indecent painting and sculpture and prints. The author of the *Vita Latina* noted that the content of the pyre was so valuable that a Venetian merchant offered to buy it from the *Signoria* for the great sum of twenty-thousand ducats.[17]

The burnings are sometimes looked on as a typical, if extreme, example of Savonarola's Puritan, iconoclastic outlook.[18] By now it should be clear that Savonarola was not some sort of crypto-Protestant before his time, and in fact he also had very definite and influential views about the importance of art in a Christian commonwealth. Modern research leaves no doubt as to the fact of this influence, but the attempts to establish a one-to-one relationship between this influence on individual artists has been less successful.[19]

---

16. "While the former author may have been an eye-witness to the event, it is certain the latter was." Steinberg, *Fra Girolamo Savonarola,* 6.

17. Ibid.

18. Such an interpretation views the work of Savonarola and his reformed friars "as a mere anti-Humanist appendix to the evolution of the Italian Renaissance." Assonitis, "Art and Savonarolianism in Florence and Rome," 50.

19. "One of the great mysteries in the study of Renaissance Art is the extent of Savonarola's influence on the visual arts. Despite the rich testimony to Savonarola's charismatic effect on artists, art historians have never documented a fully convincing, direct connection between him and any single great work. Nonetheless, his impact was indisputably pervasive. Even as an old man, Michelangelo averred that he could still hear in his mind the voice of Savonarola preaching. Botticelli, in an act of contrition and repentance, placed his own art on the Bonfire of the Vanities. Fra Bartolommeo made a Dominican confession [sic] because of Savonarola and defended the convent of San Marco against its attackers." *Selected Writings of Girolamo Savonarola,* 136. *Confession* must be an error; it was presumably Bartolommeo's *profession* as a Dominican that is being referred to here.

These are large questions, and to try to deal with them directly would lead us too far away from Philip—although it is important to point out that such questions are real ones, and their existence shows us we are faced with a complex situation in which it is easy to go wrong. Here, we are concerned with Savonarola's teaching and the influence it may have had on Philip. To make any headway towards finding out what this may have been, we have to make a clear distinction between Savonarola's aesthetic theory and his practice as a Dominican prior, and how Savonarola the public figure carried these theories into effect in Florentine society. Very generally, we can say that Savonarola the prior encouraged the arts and artists at San Marco, and in this he was following in a well-established tradition to which even the strictest Dominican reformers had subscribed. Savonarola the prophet and reformer of the state, however, pushed what may have been an acceptable theory about art, and even a theory of art in the Christian commonwealth, to consequences that included the burning of the vanities. I think that Philip was deeply marked in these matters by Savonarola the prior, but that temperamentally he was repelled by the methods of the prophet and reformer.

Although Savonarola wanted to return San Marco to an exact observance of the primitive rule of the Dominicans, he nevertheless encouraged the *arti del disegno*, and in this he was not exceptional.[20]

> ... if the *Vita latina* is correct, Savonarola was merely playing his role in the Dominican tradition by asking his brethren to practice the arts. If the *Vita latina* in not correct, the Dominican author was simply trying to place Savonarola in that strong Dominican tradition.[21]

For Savonarola, art has a clearly defined function related to the ethical; good art helps men to live good lives, and bad art has a corrupting influence.[22]

---

20. "According to Marchese...the practice of the arts among the Dominicans in Tuscany and in San Marco was not exceptional. He recorded that from the thirteenth century through the fourteenth century there were at least sixteen Dominicans, all but one of whom were from Santa Maria Novella in Florence, who practiced as architects, *muratori*, and carpenters; there were also many other artists and artisans from Dominican monasteries in Bologna and Lombardy. Marchese also noted the existence, in the fourteenth and fifteenth centuries, of miniaturists at work in Santa Maria Novella primarily, but later in San Marco." Steinberg, *Fra Girolamo Savonarola*, 10.

21. Ibid., 11.

22. "According to Savonarola, art is fundamentally a potent instrument for universal edification. Stirring beholders of all social classes to action, private meditation and devotion, art is a mnemonic agent capable of guiding people in their pursuit of living the well ordered life." Beebe, *Savonarolan Aesthetics and their Implementation in the Graphic Arts*, 6.

> Art functions properly when it leads the beholder to worship and to emulate correct behavior. It functions inappropriately—or even erroneously—when it exists for its own sake, when its didactic message goes unheeded, or when it is the occasion of heterodoxy or sin.[23] ... art must always be "simple," didactic, and functional, whether commissioned by a cleric to improve his church, a printer to illustrate his books, or parents to grace their home.[24]

The power of art derives from the fact that the artist imitates nature, and nature is God's creation.

> As God's creation, Nature is the artist's teacher. In the same way, a student learns to draw by copying drawings produced by the master's intellect. Little by little, the student learns the style of the master, as the master learned to copy creation that in turn originated by the *ingenio* of God.[25]

But copying creation is going to involve copying human beings who do not always appear appropriately garbed in real life. It is a measure of Savonarola's consistency, if nothing else, that he did not condemn the painting of the nude qua nude. Art should reflect nature, and so there was need to study from models.

> The critical issue is not whether artists should make studies from the life but where those studies are displayed. Savonarola counselled that nude studies should remain in the studio, and that they should not be exposed to the public's attention, especially that of children.[26]

It may be that *pas devant les enfants* is hardly a satisfactory solution to the problem of what to do with the sort of beauty that is not obviously conducive to virtue in an immediate way. Besides illustrating Savonarola's consistency, though, the solution does show us he was no barbarian with a visceral hatred of beauty. This contention is only reinforced when the example of Fra Bartolommeo is cited. Bartolommeo was one of Savonarola's converts and a distinguished artist who painted from live nude models both as a lay *Piagnone* and as a friar at San Marco.[27]

It is this tolerant and understanding side of Savonarola's attitude and practice towards the work of the artist that Philip took to heart. The

---

23. Ibid., 8.
24. Ibid., 11.
25. Ibid., 34.
26. Ibid.
27. "Were life modeling totally outside of Savonarolan parameters, these drawings could not have been executed, and indeed would not have survived Fr. Bartolommeo's solemn vows." Ibid., 24.

brucciamenti, whatever Philip knew about them or thought about them in Florence, were alien to his way of dealing, as a mature man, with sin and error. The strain of impatience, harsh judgment, and anger that both Newman and Capecelatro so rightly ascribe to Savonarola are not to be found in Philip's character. Perhaps he began to react against these elements of Savonarola's public mission even in Florence, but certainly in later life he had no use for them. Excess, of any sort, he met with his own version of Socratic irony.

In 1591, towards the end of Philip's life, a book appeared entitled *Philip, or the Dialogue of Christian Joy* by Cardinal Valier, who was a friend if not a disciple of the Saint.[28] The Dialogue opens in the Palazzo di San Marco, the residence of the Venetian Ambassador, and quickly moves on to becoming a report of a conversation that had taken place at the Chiesa Nuova (the Church Philip had built in Rome) a few days earlier.[29] In the Dialogue, Philip is compared several times to Socrates:

> It is not without reason that in the Dialogue he is again and again called "our Socrates" or the "Christian Socrates," for like his prototype he was able, not only to give wise counsels, but to take an interest in the various aspects of the human soul, and lay bare the depths of each.[30]

Cardinal Valier thinks that this interest and concern with the human condition is enough to justify calling Philip another Socrates.[31] The

---

28. Valier, Agostino Valier e l'Oratorio Filippino, *Il Dialogo Della Gioia Cristiana*, xxvi–xxxiii. See part two, chapter seven, "Studies and Books," 170 *ff.* for a more detailed discussion of the dialogue.

29. "The Dialogue is supposed to take place, nor is there anything to show it did not take place, under Gregory XIV, at the Palace of San Marco in Rome." Ponnelle and Bordet, *St. Philip Neri*, 23. After a few pages of introduction, the dialogue becomes a report of an earlier dialogue held at the Chiesa Nuova at which Philip was present. "Il *Philippus* ... più che un dialogo, è un intreccio di due dialoghi: uno, il principale che ne è la sostanza, intersecato nell'altro, che a cornice al principio e alla conclusione e in certi punti lo interrompe con dargli maggio movimento." Cistellini, *San Filippo Neri: Breve Storia*, xxxix.

30. Ponnelle and Bordet, *St. Philip Neri*, 501.

31. "Assuredly may that great man [that is, St. Philip] be styled a Christian Socrates, who despises all outward things, who is the mightiest and most dreaded enemy of every vice, who follows after virtue, and who is the master and teacher of sincerity and a blameless life, who is in all his doing an example of humility, a man who gives himself in lavish charity to all, who compassionates the weaknesses of all, who aids all with his instructions and counsels, and commends all to the most high God with holy prayers, and who amidst so many cares preserves a constant and unclouded cheerfulness." Valier, Agostino Valier e l'Oratorio Filippino, *Il Dialogo Della Gioia Cristiana*, cited in Capecelatro, *The Life of Saint Philip Neri*, 461–462.

Cardinal shows, at least, that Philip's friends and admirers found it difficult to categorize him. There always remained about him an air of mystery that, certainly by the end of his life, inspired not only love, but love tempered with a sense of awe.[32] In addition to what the sixteenth century seems to have seen, in the comparison of Philip to Socrates, I want to suggest that there are two further considerations that are useful. The first of these is Socrates' irony, and the second is his love of beauty. Nello Vian has described Philip's character as he left Florence:

> di carattere gaio e intelligenza aperta, arguto e motteggiatore conforme all'indole Fiorentino. (Of a cheerful character and open intelligence, witty and facetious, in the Florentine way.)[33]

Philip's character is said to have been *arguto e motteggiatore*, which I have translated as witty and facetious. These two qualities are the marks of an ironical person, and irony was one of the dominant aspects of Socrates' character. In comparing Philip to Socrates, the sixteenth-century writers wrote more truly, I believe, than they may have realized. Philip's way of dealing with other people, with himself, and with his own troubles is Socratic and ironical. This ironical aspect of Philip's character sheds a good deal of light on his secularity, and in particular on his unwillingness, perhaps even his inability, to follow the path of reform traced out by Savonarola. Philip took his understanding of Catholicism from the Dominicans of San Marco, but his personal practice of that religion, and the means he later used to bring others to the practice of that faith, was a world away from his Dominican heritage; at least as that heritage was found incarnated in Savonarola.

Irony is a complex question, and the discussion of irony is still very much with us.[34] Rather than attempt a discussion of this complex and far-reaching subject, I want to take a modern description of Socratic irony and then show how it applies to Philip. Then I will go on to show that the question of irony is more complex than it appears at first, because irony is a kind of laughter, and laughter from the beginning has posed a problem for Christians. At his passion, Christ was derided with cruel games and sarcastic remarks, and on the cross he was subjected to sarcasm and mocking laughter. As a consequence of this association of

---

32. Ultimately, I think this difficulty in categorization and the sense of awe derived from the fact that Philip carried the weight of God, and his reaction to the increasingly insistent demands of the divine presence shaped him and gave him an authority, an authority that St. John of the Cross called "a terrible strength."

33. Vian, "Fiorentinità di san Filippo," *San Filippo Neri*, 112 (author's translation).

34. See Lane, *Plato's Progeny, How Plato and Socrates Still Captivate the Modern Mind*, especially 64–68.

laughter with the behavior of the enemies of Christ, some of the early Fathers—such as Clement of Alexandria, John Chrysostom and Basil of Caesarea—took a very dim view indeed of Christians who indulged in laughter.[35] Laughter may bring to our mind a set of ideas such as light-heartedness, joyfulness, and good-natured bantering between friends, but it also carries with it darker overtones of sarcasm, aggression, and mockery.[36] Yet even the good-hearted laughter between friends was frowned on by the early Fathers. "Christ himself wept.... We often observe him doing so, but never laughing—nor even smiling gently: none of the evangelists states that he did so."[37] St. Thomas rehabilitated laughter for Christians[38] through an Aristotelian discussion of the virtues. Aristotle had taught:

> As to jests. These are supposed to be of some service in controversy. Gorgias said that you should kill your opponents' earnestness with jesting and their jesting with earnestness; in which he was right.... Some are becoming to a gentleman, others are not; see that you choose such as become *you*. Irony better befits a gentleman than buffoonery; the ironical man jokes to amuse himself, the buffoon to amuse other people.[39]

Irony, then, is to be distinguished from buffoonery, and Philip was always insistent that buffoonery was destructive:

> It is very necessary to be cheerful, but we must not on that account give in to a buffooning spirit.[40]
>
> Buffoonery incapacitates a person from receiving any further spiri-

---

35. See Halliwell, *Greek Laughter*, chapter 10: "Laughter denied, laughter deferred: the antigelastic tendencies of early Christianity," especially 471.

36. In a more formal way, irony has been defined as "the conflict of two meanings which has a dramatic structure peculiar to itself: initially, one meaning, the *appearance*, presents itself as the obvious truth, but when the context of this meaning unfolds, in depth or it time, it surprisingly discloses a conflicting meaning, *the reality* measured against which the first meaning now seems false or limited and, in its self-assurance, blind to its own situation." *Dictionary of the History of Ideas*, vol. 2, 626–34. See also, Fowler, *A Dictionary of Modern English Usage*, entry for "irony."

37. St. John Chrysostom, cited in Halliwell, *Greek Laughter*, 471. As with all generalizations, there are exceptions. Julian of Norwich has several passages where laughter is central. For example: "And alle this sorrow that he [the devil] would make us to have, it shall turne into himself. And for this it was that our lorde skorned him, and shewde that he shalle be skorned, and this made me mightly to laugh." Julian of Norwich, *The Writings*, 365. See Appendix I, 273.

38. The capacity of laughing characterizes man: Aquinas, *Summa Theologiae*, Ia, q.3, a4.

39. Aristotle, *Rhetoric*, 1421b.

40. Neri, *The Maxims and Counsels of St. Philip Neri*, April 26.

tuality from God. Nay more, it roots up what little a man may have already acquired.[41]

In *The Death of Socrates*,[42] Romano Guardini gives us a characteristically insightful account of Socratic irony as it appears in the *Euthyphro* and makes the important point that Socrates used irony to help his interlocutors rather than destroy them:

> ... to attack directly shows one to be entangled in the situation, while the wielder of irony stands above it. He makes appreciative remarks, but in such a way that an unfavorable meaning appears through them. His assent only underlines the contradiction more surely. He assumes an inoffensive air only to wound the more surely. The ironic attack shows the aggressor in blithe security. All this could be said of irony in general but Socratic irony is more than this. In the last resort its object is not to expose, to wound, to despatch, but to help. It has a positive aim: to stimulate movement and to liberate.[43]

Savonarola certainly attacked directly, and Savonarola was all-too obviously entangled in the situation in which he found himself and in which he had, in part, created for himself. To use an image of Newman's, he was the hunter who scoured the forests with noise and guns to capture his foes, or the fisherman who sought his catch with large nets let down into the river or sea. Anger, the concentration on the big picture, and the apparent absence of self-doubt were the marks of Savonarola's approach to his public apostolate. There is nothing of this in Philip; his ironical, skeptical nature, an irony that he applied first of all to himself, is the antithesis of that self-righteous anger that keeps coming through much of Savonarola's later preaching. Philip's temperament led him to deal with the individual and not the crowd, to prefer an indirect method of teaching to the direct and often crushing exposition of the truth. As Newman put it, he fished quietly by the bank of the stream, and he won over his penitents one-by-one, or in small groups, with kindness and with wit. It is here, in the character of the two men, rather than in what they tried to do, or the forum in which they tried to do it, that we will find the difference between them.

The concept of irony, then, is a key concept for understanding Philip as a Christian Socrates, and we should examine the idea more closely. A

---

41. Ibid., April 27.
42. Guardini's observation should not be taken as extending to Socrates' use of irony in all the Dialogues. See Halliwell, "Laughter on (and behind) the Face of Socrates," *Greek Laughter*, 276–302.
43. Guardini, *The Death of Socrates*, 6.

contemporary author has described some of the main elements of Socratic irony:

> I treat Socratic irony for present purposes as involving a cluster of phenomena: among them, self-deprecation/depreciation (including professions of ignorance); feigned praise of others; an uncertain, fitful air of playfulness; and, more generally, an obliquity of speech that created an impression of *arrière-pensée* and leaves Socrates' feelings elusive.[44]

There are any number of indications of this ironical and self-deprecatory streak in Philip's character in later life. He refused both a canonry of St. Peter's as well as the Cardinal's hat. To Gregory XIII, who wanted to make him a canon, "he excused himself on the ground that he did not know how to wear a canon's dress," and when Gregory XIV wanted to make him a Cardinal, Philip turned "the whole affair into a joke."[45] On another occasion, Clement VIII sent some Polish nobles "to acquaint themselves with his eminent virtues and sanctity," and Philip told them to wait until the story that was being read to him was finished:

> "You see what capital books I keep, and what important matters I have read to me!" and similar words, without so much as touching on spiritual things.[46]

An example of his feigned praise of others is shown in the account of how he converted Francesco Zazzara by appearing to praise him:

> "O happy you!" he said, "now you are studying; after a time you will be made doctor and begin to gain money, and to advance your family; you will become an advocate, and then some day you may be raised to be a prelate," and so he went on describing step by step all the honors which the world could give, or which had ever passed through the youth's imagination, repeating again: "O happy you! Then you will be looking for nothing more." Francesco thought that the Saint meant what he said; but at last Philip pressing the youth's head to his bosom, whispered in his ear, "And then?"[47]

---

44. Halliwell, *Greek Laughter*, 277–278. Halliwell continues: "If we take account of both these fundamental (and inter-twined) factors—the subtlety of Plato's dramatic expressiveness, and the problematic indirectness of much Socratic speech—we should view with strong skepticism any claim to identify a one-dimensional Platonic verdict on laughter. What I offer here will necessarily be selective. But it will reclaim for Plato's writings, above all in relation to the enigmatic persona of Socrates, a rich set of perceptions of the psychological, social and ethical possibilities of laughter."

45. Bacci, *The Life of Saint Philip Neri*, vol. 1, 270–271.

46. Ibid., 295. The process makes it clear that the book being read was Arlotto's!

47. Ibid., 266.

The playful aspect of his irony is well shown in his advice to a lady who asked him if it was a sin to wear shoes with very high heels, to which the Saint only answered with the double-entendre, "Take care you don't fall."[48]

All this adds up to that obliquity of speech and or *arrière-pensée* of which Halliwell speaks. It is clear that Philip often hid his feeling behind his words.

> ... one day, meeting two Dominicans, he passed between them, saying, "Let me pass, I am without hope." The good fathers, understanding his words in their ordinary sense, stopped him and began to console him, and to ask him a number of questions; but at last he smiled and said, "I have no hope of myself, but I trust in God."[49]

Self-deprecation, feigned praise of others, playfulness, and an obliquity of speech were all aspects of Philip's irony in later life. They must have been part of his make-up, at least in germ, by the time he left Florence. In particular, I think his unwillingness to commit himself to a clerical career may have been the result of a combination of worldliness, coupled with distaste for the aggressive self-certainties of the Savonarolian movement in Florence. He was at this stage of his life unsure about many things and of how to put them together; rather than pretending this didn't matter, or trying to escape into a false sort of security by ignoring aspects of his nature, he refused to commit himself to anything in such a way that it would have involved being untrue to other aspects of his nature.

Aristotle pointed out in the *Ethics* that irony could be a sort of deficiency of truthfulness about oneself; on the other hand, he saw that it was a deficiency that, as the opposite of boastfulness, is often attractive for its apparent self-deprecation. This self-deprecation in Philip's case was due in part to his inability to make a coherent pattern out of his experience. He did not see things steadily, he did not see the whole, and that, I think, was clear to him. His inability to commit himself unreservedly to any one form of life led to an ironical attitude directed both at himself and at others. Irony, unlike laughter between friends, is a solitary activity. Laughter between friends is a social activity; irony is solitary in the sense that the people who are the object of the irony are not partners in the activity. This is especially true of the sort of irony that grows out of a somewhat uncommitted stance towards life; a habitual ironical attitude places a distance between the speaker and other people.

48. Ibid., 189.
49. Ibid., 278.

That distance was certainly there in Philip's later life, and it must have been there from the beginning. Irony can be cold and forbidding, and it can be cruel, but it need not be, and Philip's irony, like that of Socrates in the *Euthyphro*, was clearly attractive, witty, and graceful.[50]

What is missing in the sixteenth-century comparison of Philip to Socrates is any account of the dimension of desire. We have already drawn attention to the key role that desire played in St. Catherine's life, and we have noted that we could detect something of that same importance for Philip, under the reticence of his contemporary biographers. Yet the picture of Philip as a Christian Socrates is not really very helpful without some more explicit reference to the importance of desire for Socrates—and Philip—for "without a doubt no-one has succeeded in escaping *eros* nor will anyone in the future, so long as beauty (kallos) exists and there are eyes to see."[51] *Eros* is awakened by beauty, and the satisfaction of possessing what we desire brings, at least temporarily, peace and joy. Every account we have of Philip draws attention to his joyful nature, and I want to say something about a theological understanding of Philip's Christian joy.

Eros and the Beautiful

Capecelatro, in discussing Philip's education during his earliest years in Rome, writes:

> Philip, we may be sure studied ... scholastic philosophy; and if, as is possible he knew Plato (for from the time of Leo X most of the illustrious philosophers of Rome were Platonists), I can understand that the larger and more poetical genius of Plato would have a greater charm for him than the strictly logical and almost mathematical method of Aristotle.[52]

This linking of St. Philip to Plato is, I think, unhelpful. Here, however, I want only to show that it is positively misleading in trying to understand the saint's sacramental mysticism. The fabric of the language of Christian mysticism is woven out of Platonic threads. This is hardly sur-

---

50. Halliwell points out that "in categorizing self-deprecating irony, Aristotle uses the adjective *charieis* to describe the attractiveness of those who use it in moderation and discreetly (1127b31). *Charieis* (graceful, stylish, witty, etc.) occurs in EN 4:8 ... and undoubtedly has gelastic overtones. How, then, might Aristotle position irony in relation to *eutrapelia*? ... Where *eutrapalia* playfully promotes shared affinities *eironeia* retains the capacity to place a distance (a one-sided pretense) between speaker and hearer." Halliwell, *Greek Laughter*, 321.

51. Longus, *Daphnis and Chloe* (Preface), cited in Rist, *What is Truth?*, 143.

52. Capecelatro, *The Life of Saint Philip Neri*, 39.

prising, as until the recovery of Aristotle there was no other philosophical language to use. This does not mean that Christian mysticism is in essence Platonic or neo-Platonic, and it requires a certain amount of care and learning to make sure we are not misled by the use of Platonic language and Platonic themes into drawing the conclusion that Christian mysticism is nothing more than warmed over Plato, with a dressing of Christian terminology that does not go very deep.

Jean Daniélou is one of those fully alive to the magic of Plato's language—"his larger and more poetical genius," as Capecelatro would have it—but Daniélou is also keenly aware that the use of this language requires discrimination and a clear sense that Christianity is not Platonism. In his brilliant book *Platonisme et Théologie Mystique*, to which I have already referred, he discusses Gregory of Nyssa's analysis of turning inward away from external things, and writes that:

> ... l'intériorité de Grégoire n'est pas celle du néo-platonisme. Ce qu'il trouve en entrant en lui-même c'est la communication que Dieu lui fait de la vie surnaturelle... L'intériorité chrétienne, c'est l'approfondissement de la grâce baptismale et non la prise de conscience de l'esprit par lui-même. (... interiority for Gregory is not neo-Platonic. What he finds on entering into himself is the sharing in the divine life that God himself gives... Christian interiority is the deepening of baptismal grace and not the taking possession of itself by the spirit.)[53]

This turning away from external things and finding God through interior experience, an experience given by God himself, is not, then, a version of Platonism. It is not Platonic because it is the deepening of the divine life first given to us in baptism. Daniélou continues:

> Mais ce qui est remarquable c'est que cette expérience originale, Grégoire l'exprime dans les termes du néo-platonisme. Celui-ci lui fournit une structure que va lui permettre exprimer une expérience d'essence différente.... (But what is notable is that Gregory expresses this new sort of experience in neo-Platonic language. This language gives him a structure which allows him to formulate an experience that is essentially different....)[54]

Very few people possess either Daniélou's learning or discrimination, so it is easy to go wrong, either by assimilating Christian mysticism to Platonism or else by insisting that authentic Christianity should have nothing to do with it. It seems to me a futile and ill-conceived business to insist that Plato should be banished from the Catholic consciousness;

---

53. Daniélou, *Platonisme et Théologie Mystique*, 48 (author's translation).
54. Ibid., 48–49 (author's translation).

ill-conceived because he is and has always been a formative element in that consciousness, and futile because he is still too influential to be effectively ignored. He got too many things right. On the other hand, the suspicion that there is something radically wrong with Plato from the Christian point of view seems ineradicable. The suspicion is justified at least when it comes to understanding the nature of Christian mysticism, and this is what concerns us in this book.

The term or end of Christian mysticism is an awareness of a person; it is an encounter, however dark or veiled it may be, with "the countenance of the Incarnate and humiliated Son of God."[55] The term or end of Plato's search for ultimate reality is an idea: a very special sort of objective idea called a form, to be sure, but not in any sense a person. The fascination of Plato's account derives from his ability to force us to look at our own ordinary experience in a new way and then to go beyond, or transcend it; but, as I indicated above, he goes badly off the rails about where it is going.

> When a man has been...tutored in the lore of love,... in the right and regular ascent, suddenly he will have revealed to him, as he draws to the close of his dealings in love, a wondrous vision, beautiful in its nature, and this, Socrates, is the final object of all those previous toils.[56]

This beauty never "waxes nor wanes," it is eternally beautiful in all its parts and appears that way to everyone who beholds it. Furthermore, and this is crucial:

> Nor again will our initiate find the beautiful presented to him in the guise of a face or of hands or any other portion of the body, nor as a particular description or piece of knowledge, nor as existing somewhere in another substance, such as an animal or the earth or sky or any other thing; but existing ever in singularity of form independent by itself....[57]

Whatever such an idea or form might be, it is clear that it is not the beauty of God that is being talked about. Furthermore, the idea of beauty does not seem to be able to perform the function ascribed to it in Plato's philosophy. Very briefly, the difficulty is this: The experience of beauty in everyday life is supposed to lead beyond itself to a contemplation of what is everlasting and without change; and this contemplation is said to be a superior version of the experience of the beautiful that we

---

55. Von Balthasar, *The Glory of the Lord*, vol. 1, 285.
56. Plato, *Symposium*, 210e–211a.
57. Ibid., 211a–b.

can see and touch and hear. But in the end, we are left with an intellectual process that is a pretty feeble substitute for the experience.

There is a never-ending stream of books and articles on Plato's treatment of *eros* and its relation to the desire for the good. *Eros* is the origin of both sexual desire and the desire for beauty. Somehow or other, the experience of falling in love can be the key, although obviously most of the time it is not, to the beginning of the ascent to contemplation of the perfect beauty. Falling in love has a large sexual component, and such love involves a desire to possess the other person in a fairly literal way. Plato is all too aware of this, and physical love, he holds, causes the soul to be immersed in the particular and the sensuous things of this world. But the love of beauty in another person is also a call to go beyond, to transcend, the particular and the sensuous and to begin to participate in a world that is universal and spiritual. If the lover draws back and looks at, gazes on—in a word, contemplates—the beauty of the beloved, then he has taken the first step away from this world of appearance towards a participation in a beauty that is eternal. The lover and his beloved share a spiritualized love that will be "to participate in the divine version of reproduction, which is the understanding and the passing on of eternal truths."[58] Sexual desire becomes transmuted into something it is not, no matter how noble and inspiring this other might be. And again, what is put in its place is not a person, but an exchange of ideas. Roger Scruton put this in a brutal way, but it is about time something like it were said:

> But it requires only a normal dose of skepticism to feel that there is more wishful thinking than truth in the Platonic vision. How can one and the same state of mind be both sexual love for a boy and (after a bit of self-discipline) delighted contemplation of an abstract idea? That is like saying that the desire for a steak could be satisfied (after a bit of mental exertion) by staring at the picture of a cow.[59]

The Platonic ladder and the role of *eros* have played an important role in the mysticism of the Church, but the Christian ladder ends in a union with Jesus Christ and not with an intellectual facsimile of reproduc-

---

58. Scruton, *Beauty*, 41. Scruton continues: "That is the true kind of Erotic love, and it manifests itself in the chaste attachment between man and boy, in which the man takes the role of teacher, overcomes his lustful feelings, and sees the boy's beauty as an object of contemplation, an instance in the here and now of the eternal idea of the beautiful." The heterosexual version of the myth he also points out "had an enormous influence on medieval poetry and on Christian visions of women and how women should be understood, inspiring some of the most beautiful works of art in the western tradition...." (42).

59. Ibid., 42.

tion.⁶⁰ The nature of the goal is misrepresented by Plato, but his analysis of the starting point of the experience—of beauty and of falling in love—are still very much to the point. They also help us to understand Philip's own attitude towards these experiences.

Marco Antonio Vitelleschi testified a few months after the Saint's death that he heard him use some lines that express his continuing engagement with the whole question of the love of God, a love of God expressed in the tradition of Petrarch, a tradition that even before St. Philip's time was getting tired. The sonnet itself is thought to be a parody of Petrarch.

> Vorrei saper de voi com'ella è fatta
> Questa Rete d'Amor, che tanti ha presi;
> E come girar può tanti paesi
> Che 'l tempo alquanto omai non l; l'abbi sfatta.
> (I'd like you to tell me how this Net of Love is made, which has captured many; and how it can tour many countries, that time has not yet undone it.)⁶¹

Philip's use of this secular plea for an understanding of love is in keeping with his later practice in Rome, where he gave new words to popular secular songs as a way of attracting men to the exercises of the Oratory. So the fact that the poem had secular and even mocking overtones would not have bothered him. The words became for him an expression of his longing for a final and definitive union with Christ, which is expressed over and over again in what little of his work has come down to us. For example:

> I fain would love Thee my Jesus, but I do not know how.
> I shall never love Thee if Thou dost not help me, my Jesus.
> I would fain find Thee, my Jesus, and I do not know the way.⁶²

The love of beauty was the beginning, but the end was Jesus Christ.

---

60. See Daniélou, "Eros et Agapé," *Platonisme et Théologie Mystique*, 211–220.

61. Cited in Vian, "Un Sonetto Parodistico Petrarchesco Noto a San Filippo Neri." *San Filippo Neri*, 19–23. The text and a translation are in Appendix II.

62. Prayers of St. Philip from the testimony of Francesco Zazzara in the *Primo Processo per San Filippo Neri*, cited in Ponnelle and Bordet, *St. Philip Neri*, 591. "Prayers which the Blessed Philip Neri, my spiritual father, taught to me, although I have always been an unworthy, intractable and proud son. He many times recommended me to say, in the form of a chaplet, that is instead of the Pater and Ave, one or other of these ejaculatory prayers, which the said Father valued exceedingly. . . ."

5
The Philip Who Left Florence

The end of the virtuous life is likeness to God. Because of this, purity of soul and freedom from the disturbance of passion is exercised by attention to the virtues so that a certain form of the transcendent nature might become present in them due to their more refined way of life. Since the life of virtue is neither uniform nor the same, it is like the art of skillfully making a garment by weaving various threads; some threads are pulled straight and other drawn crossways against them. Therefore, it is necessary to have many elements concur to create a virtuous life.

St. Gregory of Nyssa[1]

THE READER who has got to this point in my book may well feel that no coherent picture has emerged of Philip's character, in spite of the fact that something has been said about his home; his love of everyday life; his humanistic schooling, with its unreconciled ambivalence towards Christianity and culture; and the moral, intellectual and religious formation he received from the Dominicans. Nonetheless, the reader may well ask: but who was Philip Neri? What was he like? Philip himself seems to elude us, it might be said, and he remains a shadowy figure with hardly enough substance to tie together the different elements of the various discussions. I have suggested that a step towards obtaining a more rounded picture would be to return to the old idea that Philip was a Christian Socrates; and I have already discussed the strain of irony in his character. We have to remind ourselves, though, that the key of calling Philip a Christian Socrates does not mean we will find a Philip who was all of a piece. That is to say, although our key may help us to get a better picture of Philip as one person, we are still a long way from being

---

1. St. Gregory of Nyssa, "Ninth Homily," *Commentary on the Song of Songs*, J. 271.12.

able to paint a picture that is a coherent one. It may be the case, and I think it in fact is, that there is no coherent picture to be painted because he was not, at this stage of his life at any rate, a young man who had it all together.

On the one hand there is the honest, likeable boy who was attractive to others both physically and morally, and who had been deeply marked by the sacramental and ecclesial attitudes of the spirituality of St. Catherine of Siena and the Dominicans at San Marco. This was the boy who had been taught that the serious practice of Christianity requires a spiritual combat, a combat that "is the hardest of all struggles; for while we strive against self, self is striving against us."[2] On the other hand, though, there is the Philip who was also influenced by the Petrarchan humanism of his schooling and of his native Florence, and one aspect of this humanism was an emphasis on "using this world well." There was a radical element of secularity in Philip; he remained a layman until, at the age of thirty-five, he was told by his confessor to become a priest.[3] His ordination did not put an end to this secularity, and for the rest of his life he continued his passionate involvement in the lives and occupations of every sort of human being. "I do not know that I have ever left the world,"[4] he said in later life. Philip was never just a spectator of the here and now, as it actually was, either before or after his ordination.

Philip had no role model for his particular mix of secularity and mysticism, and one reason it is difficult to form a clear picture of his character at this stage is that he lived with a variety of certainties that pulled him in different directions. If we concentrate, for example, on Philip the good Catholic boy growing up under the influence of the Dominicans, we get one sort of picture. On the other hand, if we think about the well-turned-out young man who delighted in the stories of Arlotto, and the very down-to earth-life they portray, then a different sort of portrait begins to emerge.

The "good Philip" who left Florence was a young man who had won the first rounds in the battle against the passions and had laid the foundation for a heroic practice of the Christian virtues. Nonetheless, as we have seen, the aim of the ascetical life is not only to lay the foundations of the moral life, but also to foster the growth of the life of grace in the soul. It is the flowering of this life of grace in the soul, a flowering which requires the foundations of the moral life, which is the final end or purpose of the first way.

2. Scupoli, *Spiritual Combat*, 5.
3. See Chapter Three, "Reform in Florence," 57.
4. Bacci, *The Life of St. Philip Neri*, vol. 1, 296.

This final stage of the way of beginners is marked by what Gregory of Nyssa calls *apatheia* and *parrhesia*.[5] *Apatheia* is the participation of the soul in the divine life through the possession of habitual grace. *Apatheia*, then, has a distinctly positive character, and it must not be understood as a condition in which the physical passions are destroyed, or in which we imagine they have been destroyed. *Apatheia* both brings about and is caused by arresting the process of building up the passions into vices, and the dismantling of these bad habits, or vices, which have been already established. The successful effort to develop the virtues, and at least partly to destroy the vices, is brought about not only by the spiritual combat but also through participation in the sacraments. This putting to death of the old man leaves the way open for the soul to participate more intimately in the life of grace. *Apatheia* has about it the characteristic of inner repose, but this serenity or equanimity is only one element in Gregory's understanding of *apatheia* and not the primary one.[6] Gregory's teaching on *apatheia* is couched in philosophical terms but teaches the Christian belief that, through the spiritual combat, the soul can at least partly subdue the old man and put on the new: that is to say, Christ himself.

The second mark of a serious and successful engagement in the spiritual combat is loving familiarity with God, or *parrhesia*.[7] The word in its secular sense has to do with political and psychological freedom and marks the disappearance of shame and fear. In a similar way, *parrhesia* in the spiritual life means a loving familiarity with God in which neither shame nor fear play any part. Prayer now becomes an expression of the realization of our divine filiation; "audemus dicere Pater noster," we dare to say our Father. The obstacles to this free and loving prayer of a son to his father are shame, which results from sin and demands purification; and fear, which shows a lack of faith. With the growth of *apatheia* in the soul, which is the result of a successful spiritual combat and a serious sacramental life, these obstacles to *parrhesia* begin to disappear.

Gregory's discussion of *apatheia* and *parrhesia* could have been written about Philip as he left Florence. There was a loving familiarity with God that was based on his possession of God's gift of habitual grace he had received at baptism. His struggle to develop the virtues and fight the vices was undertaken within a sacramental context. Philip had been

---

5. απαθεία and παρρησία.
6. See Daniélou, *Platonisme et Théologie Mystique*, 101.
7. Ibid., 110–123.

drawn, and had himself drawn, very near to God as he took the road to San Germano.

The young man who left Florence had the capacity for laughter and the love of friendship, but along with these there was the lonely, unintegrated side of his nature. This side was brought about, in the final analysis, by the providence of God, but it was fed by his own desire for holiness and complicated by his fascination with beauty and the things of this world. God had predestined Philip for sanctity and a sacramental mysticism of a high order, and in the words of the Psalmist, "deep calls to deep."[8] Probably he was already aware of a voice, "or the echo of a voice";[9] but as yet he did not adequately understand how to answer. He did know, as I have already said, that it was not going to be in Savonarola's way. The early years in Rome would see him working out his own unique response to the weight of God. In the light of his studies, and in the darkness of the catacombs, Philip Neri became a saint, but the foundations of this sanctity were laid in the Florence of his boyhood and youth.

Philip's departure from Florence has to be seen within the context of the dire straits to which Florence had been reduced by its internecine quarrels and external warfare. It seems probable that Philip had to leave for economic reasons and possibly even for political ones.[10]

Savonarola's Christian commonwealth of 1494, as we have seen, outlived its founder and survived until the return of the Medici in 1512.[11] In that year, the anti-republicans of the city, with the help of Pope Julius II and a Spanish army, put the Medici back in power. Najemy writes that this "was probably the most despised of all Florentine governments, and it lasted only fifteen years, until 1527."[12] It was during this period, in 1515, that Philip was born, and under which he spent most of his life in Flo-

---

8. Deep calls to deep / at the thunder of thy cataracts; / all thy waves and thy billows / have gone over me. Psalm 42:7.

9. The expression is taken from Newman's discussion of conscience in *The Grammar of Assent*: "... a voice, or the echo of a voice, imperative and constraining, like no other dictate in the whole of our experience." Newman, *An Essay in Aid of a Grammar of Assent*, 99.

10. The matter is carefully weighed up in Vian, 'Fiorentinità di san Filippo', *San Filippo Neri*, 114–115.

11. See chapter three, "Reform in Florence," 96.

12. "With more trappings of overt power, but less support that its predecessor of 1434–94, the new Medici regime soon alienated everyone. As Medici interests and the family's power base shifted to Rome under two popes, Leo X and Clement VII, they never found a family member suited to governing Florence and eventually entrusted the task to a series of functionaries detested by nearly all Florentines." Najemy, *A History of Florence 1200–1575*, 414.

rence; in 1527, when the Medici were once again forced to leave Florence, he was twelve years old. In 1530, the Medici were restored by the armies of Charles V, and this time they stayed for good; by this time Philip would have been fifteen. Najemy sums up this complex history, and it is a history that is important to keep in mind, as it explains Philip's leaving Florence:

> In the twenty years between 1512 and 1532 Florentines incessantly debated the fate of their republic only to see it decided by external power. Three times, in 1433, 1494, and 1527, the Medici were exiled, and three times they returned: recalled in 1434 by friends in the city; restored in 1512 by both internal allies and external armies; but imposed in 1530 on an unwilling and defeated city after a year-long siege by the armies of the Emperor Charles V, who two years later terminated Florence's long republican history and instituted the principate. This time the Medici returned to stay and to govern in relative stability until they died a natural death 200 years later.[13]

After the siege and the capitulation of Florence, the Medici returned in a vengeful mood. Guicciardini describes it this way:

> As soon as all the soldiers had departed, tortures and persecutions of citizens began in Florence; for those who had the government in their hands—partly to strengthen the state, partly because of the hatred stirred up against the authors of so many evils, and memory of abuses personally received, but principally because such was the Pope's intention...so interpreted the matter...that the article, whereby pardon was promised to those who had harmed the Pope and his friends, did not cancel the wrongs and crimes committed by them in matters concerning the Republic.[14]

Philip's family was too unimportant to have been in much danger by the imposition of what seems to have been a reign of terror imposed by the Medici and their friends. On the other hand, the family would not have escaped the economic consequences resulting from the warfare of the preceding years. Guicciardini continues:

> ...six of the leaders were decapitated, others imprisoned and a very great number banished. This weakened the city still more, and those who had participated in these things were reduced to even more dire necessity, while the power of the Medici remained freer and more absolute and practically regal in that city, bereft of money as a result of so long and dreadful a war, deprived of many of its inhabitants, both

---

13. Ibid., 446.
14. Guicciardini, *The History of Italy*, 1529.

within and without the walls, its houses lost, its goods and property elsewhere destroyed, and more than ever divided against itself—all this poverty made it all the more necessary to provide, for many more years, for their supplies from towns outside. For that year there had been neither harvest nor seed time, and the disorder of that year spread over the following years; with the result that more money left the city, afflicted and weakened as it was, for the purpose of buying grain in distant places and livestock outside of the dominion, than had been expended for so grave and costly a war.[15]

Successful lawyers usually manage to survive hard times, but relatively unsuccessful ones find themselves out of work like a lot of other people, and it is not difficult to imagine what the wrong political decisions, coupled with a lackluster legal career, would have meant for Francesco Neri. In any event, he packed Philip off to a rich relation, perhaps to restore the family fortunes, perhaps even to get him out of harm's way. However it was, Philip left Florence for San Germano, a journey of six hundred kilometers, on foot.[16]

---

15. Ibid., 1530.
16. Ponnelle and Bordet, *St. Philip Neri*, 68. "We must suppose he made the journey of six hundred kilometers on foot, by short stages, and almost as a beggar."

PART TWO
The Mystical Assault:[1]
Clouds and Light in San Germano and Rome

> I saw that he is to us all thing that is good and comfortable to our helpe. He is oure clothing, that for love wrappeth us and windest us, halseth us and all becloseth us [embraces us and wholly encloses us], hangeth about us for tender love, that he may never leeve us. And so in this sight I saw that he is all thing that is good, as to my understanding.
>
> Julian of Norwich[2]

ST. PHILIP'S mysticism was based both on the doctrinal and moral instruction he received in Florence and on his own efforts to put this teaching into practice. St. Gregory called this first training the way of light.[3] The newly converted soul is no longer dominated by error, sin, and darkness but has moved into the light of God's truth about how life should be understood and lived. Difficult as the struggles of beginners may be, they are based on knowledge of God and his law. They are not fought in the darkness of ignorance and confusion.

A successful struggle to control the passions and to lay the foundations of a virtuous life led to what Gregory called *apatheia* and *parrhesia*; that is, to the ability to live both in a state of grace and in a loving confidence and familiarity with God.[4] These endowments are prerequisites of a mystical life that is genuinely Christian. Yet while they are indispensable for such a life, they are not, in themselves, the guarantee of a call to such a life. The idea that "being good" entitles anyone to enter the illuminative way, much less the unitive way, is a false one. Bremond's expression *Invasion Mystique* reminds us that mysticism is

---

1. This is my translation of Henri Bremond's phrase *L'invasion Mystique*, the title of vol. 2 of *Histoire Littéraire du Sentiment Religieux en France*.
2. Julian of Norwich, *A Revelation of Love*, 139.
3. See Part One, "Light in Florence," 45.
4. See chapter five, "The Philip Who Left Florence," 129.

not the result of human efforts or techniques. "It is God who creates mystics," as Bremond puts it.⁵ If we take Christian mysticism to be marked very often by the three stages, or *studia*, of tradition, then we can say that the possession of *apatheia* and *parrhesia* is no guarantee that there will be any significant development in the nature of the individual's relationship with God. ⁶

It is true, of course, that the relationship may develop into a more intense and loving one, or it may go in the other direction and become routine and lukewarm, but it will still be the same kind of relationship based on a more or less successful moral life. It seems to be the case that there are many saintly Christians, and even saints, who have neither known nor experienced anything other than the demands and achievements of the purgative way. Yet God does call some men and women to sanctity by means of a new relationship with him, which involves more than the perfection of *apatheia* and *parrhesia*. Why this call does not seem to be more general, or if general why it is not more widely answered, is assuredly a difficult question, but it is not one I will try to answer here. It is St. Philip's life that is my concern, and it is clear that in his life there were changes in his relationship with God. These are reflected in the changing of the focus, or different *studia*, which followed the pattern of the three ways. St. Philip's journey was along this less traveled road.

In Gregory's description of the development of the mystical life, the new relationship of the second way involves leaving the clear light of the way of beginners and entering into a way characterized by both shadows and light. The certainties of the purgative way, which underlay the spiritual combat, become obscured. Things no longer seem quite so simple to understand, even if sometimes difficult to do, and we begin to look for deeper explanations of the meaning of existence and of how we should live. It is this search for understanding, and not necessarily sin, that leads us into what is hidden and dark to our ordinary ways of understanding. Gregory writes:

---

5. "C'est Dieu qui fait les mystiques." Bremond, *Histoire Littéraire du Sentiment Religieux en France*, vol. 1, 73. Bremond's first volume traces the development of Christian humanism (*l'humanisme dévot*) in France into the mystical tradition of the French School (1580–1660).This particular development does not concern us here, but what his expression conveys certainly does.

6. "... nous n'oublions pas que l'esprit mystique souffle ou et quant il veut. Aucune industrie humaine, aucune méthode, aucun effort personne ne serait du moindre secours au téméraire et qui flaterait d'atteindre a ces états supérieures." Bremond, *Histoire Littéraire du Sentiment Religieux en France*, vol. 1, 515.

Next, a more careful understanding of hidden things leads the soul through appearances to God's hidden nature which is symbolized by a cloud over shadowing all appearance and which little by little accustoms the soul to behold what is hidden.[7]

Gregory is putting this second way in relation to the Mosaic theme of the cloud. The cloud, which guides the soul, is the cloud that guided the Israelites through the desert, and brought them to Mount Sinai. When they arrived at the Holy Mountain:

> Then the clear light of the atmosphere was darkened so that the mountain became invisible, wrapped in a dark cloud. A fire shining out of the darkness presented a fearful sight to those who saw it. It hovered all around the sides of the mountain so that everything which one could see smoldered with the smoke of the surrounding fire.[8]

This describes the negative aspect of the second way; that is, the emptying out of the soul of the objects of sense, by persuading it of their vanity, and purifying it from its adherence to them. Gregory illustrates this passing beyond a reliance on sense experience by pointing out that:

> Every safeguard and precaution was taken against the approach of any animal to the mountain. If somehow it did happen that any animal at all showed itself at the mountain, it was stoned by the people.[9]

He understands this safeguard and precaution in this way:

> That none of the irrational animals was allowed to appear on the mountain signifies, in my opinion, that in the contemplation of the intelligibles we surpass the knowledge which originates with the senses. For it is characteristic of the nature of irrational animals that they are governed by the senses alone divorced from understanding.[10]

At the same time, this second way accustoms the soul to live with the invisible. The smoke and the fire struck terror into the hearts of the Israelites, and Moses went alone to the foot of the mountain:

> Since he was alone, by having been stripped as it were of the people's fear, he boldly approached the very darkness itself and entered the invisible things where he was no longer seen by those watching. After he entered the inner sanctuary of the divine mystical doctrine, there, while not being seen, he was in company with the Invisible. He teaches, I think, by the things he did that the one who is going to associate inti-

---

7. Gregory of Nyssa, *Commentary on the Song of Songs*, M. 1000 d.
8. Gregory of Nyssa, *Life of Moses*, paragraph 43, 42.
9. Ibid., paragraph 42, 42.
10. Ibid., paragraph 156, 93.

mately with God must go beyond all that is visible and (lifting up his own mind, as to a mountaintop, to the invisible and incomprehensible) believe that the divine is *there* where the understanding does not reach.[11]

This privation of the sensible, and this learning to be alone with God, are the fundamental notes of the illuminative way. It must be emphasized that this learning to be alone with God is not achieved, in Gregory's understanding of the matter, by any sort of downplaying of the importance of intellectual activity. The one who "is going to associate intimately with God" must indeed "go beyond all that is visible," but the purpose of this going beyond is to accustom the soul "to behold what is hidden." It is clear that this beholding is, for Gregory, an intellectual activity. Daniélou puts the matter very clearly:

> Enfin cette partie de la vie spirituelle est représentée comme une considération plus attentive (προσεξεστέρα) des choses cachées. Elle se présente donc comme une méditation d'ordre intellectuel. Ce n'est plus la purification morale qui caractérisait la vie purgative. Ce n'est pas encore l'union d'amour qui définira la vie mystique. La seconde voie est donc bien le domaine de l'intelligence. C'est à ce titre qu'elle correspond à ce qu'on appellera "vie illuminative." (Finally, this aspect of the spiritual life is [described as consisting in] a more attentive consideration of hidden things. It is put forward, then, as belonging to the intellectual order. It is no longer the realm of moral purification, which characterized the purgative way. Nor, again, is it the union of love, which defines the mystical way. The second way is thus the domain of the intelligence, and it is because of this aspect that it corresponds to what will be called the illuminative way.)[12]

In Chapter Seven, Studies and Books, we will see how this intellectual aspect of the illuminative way worked out in the development of Philip's embodied mysticism.

Gregory also, as we have seen,[13] associates the second way with the Sacrament of Confirmation. Confirmation has a special association with the Holy Spirit that completes and strengthens the grace of Baptism. The *Catechism* states this teaching in a way particularly applicable to St. Philip:

> Confirmation perfects Baptismal grace; it is the sacrament which gives the Holy Spirit in order to root us more deeply in the divine filiation, incorporate us more firmly into Christ, strengthen our bond with the

---

11. Ibid., paragraph 46, 43.
12. Daniélou, *Platonisme et Théologie Mystique*, 128.
13. See Introduction, "An Embodied Mysticism," 42.

Church, associate us more closely with her mission, and help us bear witness to the Christian faith in words accompanied by deeds.[14]

All his life Philip had a special devotion to the Holy Spirit, and at Pentecost 1544 he had an experience of the Holy Spirit that marked him for life.[15]

Among the gifts of the Holy Spirit is fortitude or courage. The change of focus brought about in the illuminative way requires great strength of character, a strength that is the fruit of the development of all the cardinal virtues, but especially that of courage or fortitude.[16] Gregory associates the sacrament of confirmation with the way of proficients because confirmation is the sacrament that helps the Christian to persevere through the trials and difficulties of life. This need for courage is especially evident in the development of the mystical life. The clear goals of the way of beginners disappear, and it requires courage to live in the obscurity that marks the second way. Courage, Thomas Aquinas says, can be taken in a general way to mean "a disposition of the soul to stand firm to what is in accord with reason amid the sundry assaults of passion or the hardship of practice."[17] The obscuring of the clarity of the beginner's life requires the virtue of courage because now "the hardship of practice" becomes very great indeed.

> ... I am well aware that the trials given by God to contemplatives are intolerable and they are of such a kind that, were He not to feed them with consolations, they could not be borne.[18]

---

14. *Catechism of the Catholic Church*, 1316.

15. See Introduction, "An Embodied Mysticism," 30–31.

16. "Fortitude," in the words of the *Catechism of the Catholic Church*, "is the moral virtue that ensures firmness in difficulties and constancy in the pursuit of the good." The text continues: "It strengthens the resolve to resist temptations and to overcome obstacles in the moral life. The virtue of fortitude enables one to conquer fear, even fear of death, and to face trials and persecutions. It disposes one even to renounce and sacrifice one's life in defense of a just cause. 'The Lord is my strength and my song.' 'In the world you will have tribulation; but be of good cheer, I have overcome the world.'" *Catechism of the Catholic Church*, 1808.

17. Aquinas, *Summa Theologiae*, 1a, 2ae, 61, 4.

18. St. Teresa of Jesus, *Way of Perfection*, Chapter XVIII, in *Complete Works* (ed. Allison Peers), 72. The writer of *The Cloud of Unknowing* teaches the same lesson: "And be not astonished with any unrestful dread, though the fiend (as he will) come with a sudden fearsomeness, pushing and beating on the walls of thy house where thou sittest; or though he stir any of his mighty limbs to rise and run in upon thee suddenly as it is without any warning. Thus shall it be, know thou right well, that whatsoever thou be that settest thee to work truly in this work, thou shalt verily see and feel, or else smell, taste or hear, some astonying made by the fiend in some of thy five wits without. All is done for to draw thee down from the height of this precious working." Anonymous, *The Epistle of Privy Counsel*, Chapter 5, in *The Cloud of Unknowing*, 83–84, f. 99a.

In sum, then, the second way begins in detachment from the world of appearances; this detachment is the result of what Gregory calls a diatribe[19] against the vanities of the sensible world. Then, the soul having detached itself from the things of sense, it rises in the spirit to invisible beauty. It seems clear from Gregory's discussion that these two aspects—of denial (of the ultimate reality of ordinary appearances) and affirmation (of truths which lie beyond)—are meant to be understood as one process with alternating aspects. The darkness helps the soul to fix on non-visible realities, while the contemplation of non-visible realities helps develop a firm conviction of the vanity of worldly pleasures and ambitions.

We find Gregory's two notes, of denial and affirmation, in this second *studium*, or stage, of St. Philip's embodied mysticism. There is, first of all, a determined effort to withdraw from the world of appearances into the darkness. This withdrawal began when he renounced his inheritance and continued when, in a literal sense, he left the world of ordinary experience for long periods spent in the catacombs. There is also the note of affirmation. In Philip's life at this stage, we find intensive intellectual studies that correspond to Gregory's "meditation on higher things." It needs to be emphasized that although Philip's formal studies were probably of fairly short duration,[20] his search for non-visible realities nevertheless continued for the rest of his life. In this search, the continuing cultivation of his intellectual life remained an integral aspect of his embodied mysticism.[21] For Philip, as for Gregory, the unitive way was achieved not by denying the importance or the value of the intellectual life, but by using it, and cultivating it, in order to go beyond it.

---

19. διαβολή.
20. See Part Two, Chapter Seven, "Studies and Books," 163.
21. See Part Two, Chapter Seven, "Studies and Books," 157*ff.*

6

San Germano

> The language of souls is their desire.
> Gregory the Great[1]

> God will be knowen, and him liketh that we rest us in him. For all that is beneth him suffiseth not to us. And this is the cause why that no soule is rested till it is noughted of all thinges that is made. When he is wilfully noughted for love to have him that is all, then is he able to receive ghostly reste.
> Julian of Norwich[2]

GALLONIO tells us that when Philip was eighteen, his father sent him to his uncle Romolo,[3] who lived at San Germano, a town in Campania between Rome and Naples,[4] lying at the foot of Monte Cassino. This would have been in 1533. Elisabetta, his sister, also said "he was eighteen when he left home."[5] Bacci, on the other hand, says Philip was sixteen at the time, which would mean he left Florence in 1531. The uncle had money: Bacci says he had a fortune of more than 22,000 crowns, and Gallonio makes this 22,000 gold pieces; in any case, the uncle was a childless merchant in comfortable circumstances, and Philip was sent to

---

1. Gregory the Great, *Commentary on the Book of Job*, cited in Clement, *The Roots of Christian Mysticism*, 22.
2. Julian of Norwich, *A Revelation of Love* in *The Writings*, 141.
3. Gallonio, *La Vita di San Filippo Neri*, 3. Capecelatro points out that Romolo was really Philip's second-cousin: "... if we look at the family pedigree we see that he was really his second cousin, being the first cousin of Ser Francesco [Philip's father]." Capecelatro, *The Life of Saint Philip Neri*, 20.
4. "Today San Germano is an unimportant speck at the foot of Monte Cassino. But at that time it was important as the intersection of the roads from Rome to Naples and the nearby port of Gaeta." Türks, *Philip Neri: The Fire of Joy*, 8.
5. Della Rocchetta and Vian, *Il Primo Processo per San Filippo Neri*, vol. 3, 402.

learn the business.[6] The tradition that Romolo was rich and wished to make Philip his heir[7] goes back to Philip himself. Baronius, among others, says that he had heard this from Philip:

> ... dal medemo p. Filippo, ho inteso più volte, che un suo zio l'haveva voluto fare herede della robba sua, et lui non la volse, perchè voleva attendere alle cose spirituali. (I heard from Fr. Philip himself that an uncle had wished to make him heir to his estate, but that he turned it down because he wanted to devote himself to spiritual matters.)[8]

In any event, San Germano proved to be only a stop on Philip's road to Rome, because Philip didn't want a career in business. That much is clear; it is not clear, however, how long Philip stayed with his rich relation, although everyone seems to agree that, long or short, the stay was of the greatest importance in Philip's development. We know neither his precise age when he left Florence, nor the exact year he reached Rome, although there is general agreement that it was 1532 or 1533, which would make Philip seventeen or eighteen when he arrived in the eternal city. Gallonio says that Philip spent only three days in San Germano.[9] Bacci, on the other hand, says he spent two years with his uncle.[10] Capecelatro cites an early seventeenth-century source that maintains that Philip spent three years in San Germano, although Capecelatro himself thinks "that he lived there between one and two years...."[11] Ponnelle and Bordet, with their unrivalled knowledge of the sources for St. Philip's life, come down on Gallonio's side and say that it was "after a

---

6. "Philip's father, Francesco Neri, had a cousin named Romolo, an industrious man, who went from Florence into the kingdom of Naples, and for many years was in business at San Germano, a town at the foot of Monte Cassino, until at length he had amassed a fortune of more than 22,000 crowns, which in those days was a very considerable sum." Bacci, *The Life of Saint Philip Neri*, vol. 1, 9.

7. "He [Francesco] sent him there not only that he [Philip] might join him in business, but in the hope that he might be named heir to his uncle's vast riches." Gallonio, *La Vita di San Filippo Neri*, 3.

8. Della Rocchetta and Vian, *Il Primo Processo*, vol. 1, 405 (author's translation).

9. "... Philip only stayed there a few days, fearing to injure his conscience, for he had in mind a much more valuable and influential line of business. He left his uncle and everything else, for the sake of Christ, for though he was rich, he wanted to make himself poor for our sake." Gallonio, *La Vita di San Filippo Neri*, 3–4. Germanico Fedeli, whose uncle had been an Oratorian with Philip, also says that Philip only spent a few days, "alcuni giorni," in San Germano and left because a life of business was not pleasing to him. Della Rocchetta and Vian, *Il Primo Processo per San Filippo Neri*, vol. 1, 158.

10. "He had now resided two years in those parts, and in 1533, after mature consideration, he departed for Rome...." Bacci, *The Life of Saint Philip Neri*, vol. 1, 12.

11. "Philip laid the foundations of a pre-eminent sanctity in San Germano and in Monte Cassino, in which places for three continuous years he drank in the spirit of piety

few days"¹² that he became disenchanted with his new life in San Germano. "He then left his uncle and commerce there in the lurch, took up his staff once more, and set out for Rome."¹³

As Capecelatro says, Philip's biographers "are not clear" about how long he stayed in San Germano, "and contradict each other."¹⁴ Yet his stay there was important in Philip's development because it was there he turned, and was turned, towards a new relationship with God and a re-ordering of his fundamental attitudes towards the world. Pastor sums up the standard accounts of this period of Philip's life:

> At San Germano . . . he gave himself up to exercises of piety, and soon he felt himself drawn to take a step as heroic as those once taken by Benedict of Nursia and Francis of Assisi, when they turned their backs upon the world and its brilliant allurements; Philip made up his mind to leave his cousin and to renounce his inheritance of 22,000 scudi and to begin a life of the greatest poverty and abstemiousness, so as not to be hampered in his relations with God and his thoughts of the things of heaven.¹⁵

If Pastor is right that "he gave himself up to exercises of piety" and "soon" decided to leave, then he cannot have made much of an effort to interest himself in the practical demands of his new life. On this view, he probably never intended to stay. And remember, it was his father's idea that Philip should go to San Germano.¹⁶ Philip left Florence because he was told to go, and left San Germano because he didn't like his new life. This fits in well with Gallonio's view that he only spent a couple of days with Romolo.

On the other hand, if Bacci is correct, and Philip left Florence at sixteen, then the view that he stayed longer with his rich relation becomes a possible option. The biographers of St. Philip who have opted for the

---

and holy virtues, mainly under the guidance of one of the most religious monks of Monte Cassino, Eusebio d'Evoli, a patrician of Naples." Capecelatro, *The Life of Saint Philip Neri*, n. 23.

12. "Au bout de quelques jours, il était dégoûté." Ponnelle and Bordet, *St. Philip Neri*, 21. Fr. Kerr translates this as "after a short time he was disgusted with it." Ibid., 68.

13. "Il plante là oncle et commerce, reprend son bâton et part pour Rome. . . ." Ibid., 21. Once again, this is stronger than Kerr, who renders this as "he left his uncle and the business." Ibid., 68.

14. Capecelatro, *The Life of Saint Philip Neri*, note, 23.

15. Pastor, *The History of the Popes from the Close of the Middle Ages*, vol. 19, 163.

16. "By order . . . of his father, he went to San Germano. . . ." Bacci, *The Life of Saint Philip Neri*, vol. 1, 9. "When he was eighteen, his father Francesco sent him to his uncle Romolo. . . ." Gallonio, *La Vita di San Filippo Neri*, 3.

longer stay have been swayed by the fact that at San Germano he came to a decision, which Pastor said was "as heroic as those once taken by Benedict of Nursia and Francis of Assisi."[17] Such decisions take time; they are not made in a matter of days. The good-looking young man who delighted in fine clothes, who left Florence fascinated with the human condition, was worldly. No one doubts there was a fundamental change in Philip either during or after his stay at San Germano. But whatever it was, and whatever may have brought it about, it cannot have happened in the space of a couple of days.

There is a roundabout confirmation of this in Ponnelle and Bordet, although it militates against their own view. They say that Philip experienced a conversion at San Germano from worldliness to a commitment to follow Christ. They go on to advance the view that Philip was slow to make the changes in his life that the experience would have required.

> He was chaste. Moreover, the love of money and ambition had played no part in his youth. But he felt an attraction to religion which, at the moment when circumstances were urging him towards worldly affairs, tore his soul in both directions. Between the career held out to him by his uncle Romolo, and which he looked upon as a brilliant one, and the gift of himself to Our Lord, he could not decide immediately, as the Apostles had done at the call of Jesus.[18]

But if there was a conversion, of whatever sort, and if Philip was slow to put into practice what this change of heart demanded, then an extended period of time would have been required. Philip, unlike the Apostles, did not answer immediately Christ's call to follow him.[19] The tradition, which goes back to Bacci, that Philip spent a substantial time at San Germano fits much better with his case. Bacci says that Philip's decision to renounce his inheritance and leave his rich relation was something that grew on him as a result of "retiring for prayer and meditation on the Passion of his Lord":

> It was during these retirements that his disdain of earthly things grew on him by little and little, and he deliberated on the best means of putting in execution the design which he had conceived ever since his coming to San Germano, of leaving trade, and giving himself up to God in a state of life in which he could serve Him with less hindrance.[20]

---

17. Pastor, *The History of the Popes from the Close of the Middle Ages*, vol. 19, 163.
18. Ponnelle and Bordet, *St. Philip Neri*, 69.
19. "And he said to them, 'Follow me, and I will make you fishers of men.' Immediately they left their nets and followed him." Matthew 4:19–20.
20. *The Life of Saint Philip Neri*, vol. 1, 10.

If we assume that Philip spent years rather than days at San Germano, then he must have done at least some work in his cousin's business, and the periods of "retiring for prayer" would have been at times before or after work. No matter how indulgent Romolo may have been, Philip would not have been allowed to spend all day praying. In line with this contention, Capecelatro says that "when Philip reached his cousin's house he was welcomed with joy, and began to learn the ways of commerce":

> Romolo loved him and frequently renewed the promise that Philip should be his heir. This loving union of hearts seemed to promise well, and Romolo looked forward to increased prosperity in his commerce, as well as to the brightening and gladdening of his daily life.[21]

Romolo's hope for an "increased prosperity in his commerce" could have been, presumably, the result of Philip's contribution to the business. This may have been the way things were, but Capecelatro's grounds for writing this rests on the tradition that goes back to Bacci that "Romolo soon discovered his good qualities, and before long determined to make him heir of all he had."[22] This is the sort of thing Bacci may have learned at the Roman Oratory, but this *might have been* is the only foundation for Capecelatro's words. Still, something like his account must be right if we assume that Philip's stay with Romolo was prolonged.

Bacci says that Philip's thought of changing his life "was quickened by a devotion which he adopted in those parts."[23] This devotion was to pray and meditate in a little chapel near Gaeta:

> Near to the harbor of Gaeta, not far from San Germano, there is a celebrated mountain which, according to a very ancient and common tradition, is one of those which were rent at our Savior's death. It belongs to the Benedictine fathers of Monte Cassino, who have a church there dedicated to the Most Holy Trinity. This mountain is split from top to bottom by three large fissures; and in the middle one, which is the largest, there is a little chapel on a rock, under the care of the monks, and on it a crucifix painted, which the sailors salute with their guns, as they pass beneath.[24]

Bacci's statement that the shrine is "not far" from San Germano is misleading. It is a good thirty miles away, and therefore too far for Philip

---

21. Capecelatro, *The Life of Saint Philip Neri*, 21.
22. *The Life of Saint Philip Neri*, vol. 1, 7.
23. Bacci, *The Life of Saint Philip Neri*, vol. 1, 10.
24. Ibid., 10.

to have gone and returned in a day. If we believe he was working at the time, even with little enthusiasm, it would have been something of an expedition to have reached the shrine. Yet Philip's visits to Gaeta are embedded in all the accounts of his life, with the exception of Gallonio's. Bacci, Capecelatro, Newman, and Türks all accept the tradition as true. Ponnelle and Bordet sound a note of caution:

> Did he, during his stay at San Germano, climb Monte Cassino and seek the counsel of the monks of that celebrated abbey? Did he visit the sanctuary of the Trinità at Gaeta, perched on the edge of the sea, and in the cliffs which, according to legend, had been split at the death of Christ? As to these matters we have only evidence of a later date.[25]

Father Kerr, the translator of Ponnelle and Bordet's work into English, maintains that: "There cannot... be any real doubt as to the authenticity of the tradition of the visits to the Chapel at the Rock at Gaeta, for it is given as an established fact by Bacci as early as 1622, at a time when several of the Fathers who had been companions of the saint were still alive."[26]

This is not altogether convincing. Gallonio does not even mention Gaeta, and he lived with the Saint. By 1622, the stay at San Germano was ninety years in the past; Philip had been dead for twenty-seven years. Furthermore, the editors of the *First Process* are inclined to think that the tradition of the visits to Gaeta may go back to the testimony of Elisabetta, who doesn't mention San Germano, but seems to imply he was sent to Gaeta.[27]

> Di Gaeta, anzi che di San Germano, parla qui, sola tra i testi, la sorella Elisabetta per il luogo dove andò F. Non sappiamo dire se, nel particolare, questa deposizione sia più esatta. A essa, in ogni maniera, potrebbe risalire la tradizione delle visite F. all famosa Montagna Spaccate sopra Gaeta, raccolta dal Bacci.
>
> (Philip's sister Elizabeth, alone amongst the witnesses, speaks here of Gaeta, rather than San Germano, as the place where Philip went. We do not know whether in this matter, her testimony is the most accurate. The tradition of Philip's visits to the fissured mountain above Gaeta may, in all events, go back to this testimony.)[28]

It is impossible to determine the length of Philip's stay with his rela-

---

25. Ponnelle and Bordet, *St. Philip Neri*, 68.
26. Ibid., translator's note.
27. "...una volta, quando era tornato de Gaeta a Rome..." Della Rocchetta and Vian, *Il Primo Processo per San Filippo Neri*, vol. 3, 402.
28. Ibid., note 2422 (author's translation).

tion in San Germano. The witnesses all agree, however, that he did go there. The roundabout journey from Florence to Rome is important because by the time he arrived at his final destination, he was a changed man. I think this change was largely due to a development in his inner life, for which the stay in the South was only the setting.

There are, however, two remarks to be made about this setting. The first is on the influence of the rugged landscape, and the second has to do with the influence of the Benedictines of Monte Cassino. Capecelatro, after describing the shrine itself, gives an account of the view to be had from the chapel.

> From the summit his eye might sweep over the Pontine Marshes, the bare and rugged Apennines, which cast their shadows on the blue waters of the bay, and, near at hand, over hamlets and dales with their gardens of oranges and olives.[29]

The contemplation of this magnificent vista, Capecelatro thinks, would have disposed Philip's soul to "silence and recollectedness, to a solemn awe, and a sense of eternal things."[30] This is the same sort of error writers make about the impression the views from Philip's house in Florence had on the spirituality of his early life.[31] It is anachronistic, an example of nineteenth-century romantic thinking, to imagine that a young sixteenth-century adolescent would have indulged in the *Sturm und Drang* sort of experience described by Capecelatro or Türks. This is even clearer when we come to the period at San Germano. At this stage of his spiritual development, it was not the landscape at Gaeta, however splendid, that moved Philip to silence and recollectedness. He had already begun an inward search for God, a search that involved silence and recollectedness. It is more likely that he sought out of the way places to be alone and quiet—not to look at the view.

San Germano lies at the base of Monte Cassino, and if Philip stayed any length of time with his rich relation, then "undoubtedly" (as Türks has it),[32] Philip would have visited the famous Benedictine monastery at the summit. Newman is especially strong on the importance of this Benedictine influence on Philip's development. In *The Mission of St. Philip*, Newman argues that:

> ...as from St. Dominic he gained the end he was to pursue, so from St. Benedict he learned how to pursue it. He was to pursue Savonar-

---

29. Capecelatro, *The Life of Saint Philip Neri*, 24.
30. Ibid.
31. See part one, chapter one, "Using this World Well."
32. Türks, *Philip Neri: The Fire of Joy*, 8.

ola's purposes, but not in Savonarola's way; rather, in the spirit and after the fashion of those early Religious, of which St. Benedict is the typical representative.[33]

Newman's view about the influence of the Benedictines on Philip's development is heavily influenced by the nature of his talk, which began as Chapter Addresses to his fellow Oratorians in Birmingham. Newman's little masterpiece is not solely a sketch of a biography of the saint, but it is a sketch from the point of view of the heritage Philip left behind him. An important part of this heritage was the establishment of the Oratory. The result is that Newman at times argues back from the nature of the Oratory, as it developed over time, to observations about Philip himself. That is fair enough; the Oratory was, after all, Philip's creation. The difficulty is the close identification of "those early Religious" with the Benedictines of Monte Cassino, as well as Newman's belief that what he views as the Benedictine characteristics of the Oratory in fact derive from the time of Philip's stay in San Germano. A quotation from "The Mission of St. Philip" will help to show this:

> Those early Religious lived in communities, which were detached from each other, not brought together under one common governance; they were settled in one place, and had no duties beyond it; they had little or nothing to do with ecclesiastical matters or secular politics; they had no large plan of action for religious ends; they let each day do its work as it came; they lived in obscurity, and laid a special stress of prayer and meditation; they were simple in their forms of worship, and they freely admitted laymen into their fellowship. In peculiarities such as these we recognize the Oratory of St. Philip. [34]

All this may have been true of the early monks, but it was not true of the Monks of Monte Cassino by Philip's time. In 1504, the Abbey of Monte Cassino had joined what came to be known as the Cassinese Congregation, which was a federation of all the Benedictine monasteries of Italy and Sicily. The Congregation was heavily centralized; monks could be moved from one abbey to another; and local superiors were all temporary.[35] Philip may have derived his idea of the autonomy of every Oratory from the history of the early, pre-Cluniac model of Benedictine government, but he certainly didn't learn it from the juridical set-up of

---

33. Newman, "The Mission of St. Philip," *Sermons Preached on Various Occasions*, 224.
34. Ibid., 225.
35. "The fifteenth century saw the rise of a new institution, the congregation, which more efficaciously guaranteed a lasting regular life. Luigi Barbo (d. 1443) became abbot of Santa Guistina at Padua in 1408 and instituted regular discipline in the decayed house.

Monte Cassino in his day. Of course, he might have been told about the history of the Order on a visit to the Abbey, but it stretches plausibility to think an eighteen-year-old boy would have been given lessons in monastic history, or that he would have been interested. Phillip's model for the government of the Oratory was that of a Dominican Priory with its Prior and his council.

There is, however, another and more interesting strand in Newman's discussion about Philip and Monte Cassino. Newman argues that Philip's love of the early Church stems from the influence of the Benedictines.

> Observe, my dear Brethren, Philip is now in quite a new scene (that is from Florence),—no longer amid the medieval grandeur, but among the Saints and associations of primitive ages... everything about Philip threw him back into the times of simplicity, of poverty, of persecution, of martyrdom; the times of patience, of obscure and cheerful toil, of humble unrequited service; ere Christianity had gained a literature, or theology had become a science, or any but saints had sat in Peter's chair; while the book of nature and the book of grace were the chief instruments of knowledge and of love.[36]

The fact of Philip's love of the early Church is beyond dispute. The exercises of Oratory itself were likened by Baronius to meetings of the early Church,[37] and Philip's preferred reading in later life was from the early writers of the Church:

> Si delettava, da giovane, come esso disse a me et a molti altri, leggere particolarmente le Epistole di S. Paolo; et poi, sempre, li piaque assai la lettione de libri santi, et, particolarmente, di Giovanni Cassiano et le vite de Santi Padri; et, ultimamente, essendo vecchio, se le faceva leggere da noi altri.
>
> (From the time of his youth, as he said to me himself and to many others, he delighted in reading the Epistles of Saint Paul, and then the

---

Recruits were so numerous that he was able to found new monasteries and reform existing ones, all of which were united in a congregation in 1419. To avoid the *commenda*, the office of local superior was made temporary, and all authority was concentrated in the annual general chapter. All monks made their profession for the congregation, and the chapter could move them about. All the monasteries of Italy and Sicily eventually joined the congregation, which, with the accession of Monte Cassino in 1504, called itself the Cassinese Congregation." *New Catholic Encyclopedia*, "Benedictines."

36. Newman, "The Mission of St. Philip," *Sermons Preached on Various Occasions*, 223.

37. "'Things being arranged in this manner, and approved by the Pope's authority, it seemed as if the ancient apostolical and beautiful method of Christian assemblies was renewed.'" Baronius cited in Bacci, *The Life of Saint Philip Neri*, vol. 1, 80.

reading of holy books always pleased him, and, in particular John Cassian and the lives of the Holy Fathers; and, finally, in old age he had them read to him by us.)[38]

Philip's love for the early Church and his devotion to its writers may have been acquired from the Fathers at Monte Cassino. The fact of the interest itself is clear, and he may very well have acquired some of this predilection from the Benedictines. On the other hand, Newman's view that some of the organizational aspects of the Oratory were derived from the Benedictines, seems to me to be mistaken.

San Germano was the scene of a radical shift in Philip's outlook, and as little as we may know about his stay there, it is important for that reason. If we are going to grasp the significance of the stay in San Germano, we have to view his time there as marking the transition from the purgative way, or the way of beginners, into the illuminative way, or the way of proficients.

The Second Conversion

The entry into the illuminative way is often presented as the consequence of a moral and spiritual inadequacy. The soul becomes convinced that it is all that God wants it to be, and so it falls into carelessness and over-confidence in its dealing with God. Then, as a sort of corrective, God leads the soul into a darkness which teaches the soul its own very real poverty. After this chastening, the humbled soul turns to God in a deeper and less self-interested way. This turning to God is often called the Second Conversion.[39]

The second conversion can be presented with a different emphasis, however. This presentation does not, of course, deny the need for the ascetical life. Rather, it presupposes it; although, it is important to emphasize today, it does take the necessity of the ascetical life seriously. Instead of fixing on the moral and spiritual inadequacies of the soul, this second account focuses on a new and intense desire for a personal and immediate experience of God. This is no natural desire for God, but is the work of the Holy Spirit, which moves the soul to say with the Psalmist:

---

38. Testimony of Cardinal Pietro Paolo Crescenzi in Della Rocchetta and Vian, *Il Primo Processo per San Filippo Neri*, vol. 2, 76 (author's translation).

39. "The necessity of a second conversion arises from all that remains in us of often unconscious egoism which mingles in the greater number of our acts." Garrigou-LaGrange, *The Three Ages of the Interior Life*, 27. Part 3, chapter 2, "The Entrance into the Illuminative Way," gives an authoritative account of this understanding of the matter and the need for the Second Conversion.

> As a hart longs
> for flowing streams,
> so longs my soul
> for thee, O God.
>
> My soul thirsts for God,
> for the living God.
> when shall I come and behold
> the face of God?[40]

This need for a second conversion stems from the apparent success in the spiritual combat. The landscape of the spiritual life has become so familiar that it is hardly thought about. St. Teresa describes people in this state in the following way:

> They avoid committing even venial sins; they love doing penance; they spend hours in recollection; they use their time well; they practice works of charity towards their neighbors; and they are very careful in their speech and in their dress, and in the government of the household, if they have one.[41]

It should not be supposed that everyone who has arrived at this condition fulfils it quite as well as St. Teresa's description might suggest. But the general lines are clear; she is writing about a person who has won a number of serious battles, and now rejoices in a peaceful and successful life in the service of God. She goes on to say that it is just this apparent absence of serious problems that is the source of another sort of difficulty. The carefully ordered existence begins to turn even the relationship with God into routine. The prayers are said, the spiritual exercises are fulfilled, but gradually the zest seems to go out of the relationship with God. St. Teresa says this stage is often a period of great aridity in prayer because the soul refuses to open the door any wider to God. God invites the soul, and the soul doesn't move. As a result, all the freshness and light of the spiritual life is darkened and may even be extinguished.

The ascetical life can take us only so far. It is true that its development provides the basis of Christian living. But this development is centered in building up the self. Once we realize that it is *my* pride, *my* anger, *my* lust that I have to overcome, and that this warfare is on home ground, then the home ground becomes a central aspect in the situation. The self, for example, seeks revenge, but the self, perhaps after a difficult and continuing struggle, successfully resolves not to take revenge. Well and good, but one does not need to be a psychologist to see that in one sense

---

40. Psalm 42:1–2.
41. Teresa of Jesus, *Interior Castle*, III.1., *Complete Works*, 221.

the self is still seeking its own way and the gratification of its own desires. It says "no" to sin, and at the same time it says "yes" to its desire to live an ordered and rational moral life. The achievements of the ascetical self are the victories of beginners. The best that can be achieved, even with grace, is to transfer the satisfactions of the self from a lower to a higher level of self-indulgence. All too often, active ascetics are "well-disposed, generously intentioned, heavily disguised, spiritual egoists."[42]

St. John of the Cross says that "however assiduously the beginner practices the mortification in himself of all these actions and passions of his, he can never completely succeed—very far from it."[43] The problem seems to be that the self that does the mortifying escapes the mortification. As this self becomes stronger and more successful in living a virtuous life, it falls prey to a spiritualized form of the very sins it has successfully fought in their obvious and gross form. Pride, avarice, lust, envy, and sloth all come back and they are all too likely to take possession of the very self that has tried to get rid of them. The fact that the self has conquered the more obvious expression of these sins only makes them subtler, harder to recognize, and so more difficult to deal with.[44] This built-in dynamic of self-gratification affects even the practice of the virtues.[45] Finally, the desire to possess for ourselves infects even our relationship to God. Religion goes wrong when it becomes the ultimate satisfaction. Von Balthasar puts this in a dramatic way when he writes that "we are capable of encircling in the narrow spell of our ego not only our fellow-men, but also the Creator himself, degrading him to the role of a lever for our egoistic yearning."[46]

---

42. Turner, *The Darkness of God*, 242.

43. St. John of the Cross, *Dark Night of the Soul*, I.7.5., *Complete Works*, vol. 1.

44. St. John of the Cross calls these spiritualized versions of the capital sins "the faults of beginners," and almost half of the text of the *Dark Night of the Senses* is taken up by his discussion of them.

45. The love of friendship, for example, is more generally talked about than practiced, because it is based on a giving of the good possessed by the lover to the one loved. Yet all human love is based on need. From the earliest times, when men began to think about these things, our human love has been viewed as based on need and poverty. Once we begin to understand our own solitude, or to experience it, we cannot bear it. Physical lust is one way of trying to evade the solitude. This escape does not work for very long, but a lot of people discover this only when they find it impossible to do without the physical expression of their need to escape the silence, and somehow to affirm the reality of their own self by imposing it on another.

46. Von Balthasar, *Heart of the World*, 40. "Under the weight of my good conscience and under the ample bosom of my great heart, the voice of Truth has been stifled. It's been silent for a long time now." Ibid., 96.

The cause of the final failure of a life determined purely in ascetical categories is its self-determining character. That does not mean, necessarily, that the person who begins by fighting sins and then developing the virtues actually creates his own moral standards. We are not dealing here with an ethics of authenticity or personal integrity, but with the strengths and weaknesses of people operating within a well-defined moral system; that is to say, within a system whose standards of behavior and levels of achievement are clearly recognized. The strengths of such an understanding of how life should be led are obvious. The morality of the way of beginners and of the proficients provides the foundations of Christian living, and it is essential for any sort of successful living with other people. Its strengths should be obvious.

It does not matter, to see the point, what precise model we adopt to understand the ascetical life. Practically speaking, there are only two. There is the Aristotelian-Thomistic view with its strong political dimension. This is the model for the classical formulations of the ascetical life, which are still to be found today.[47] Then there are views of moral living based on a version of Kantianism. These hold objectivity, and the self-legislating or free aspect of moral living, in an uneasy alliance. There are many other approaches to how life should be led.[48] But what we are concerned with here is not how moral living as such can go wrong,[49] but how Christian moral living can often defeat its own ends. This happens when morality gets above itself and makes a takeover bid for the whole of Christian existence. Then the troubles it leads to cannot be cured at the moral level.

If the spiritual sickness of the ascetical self cannot be cured by that self, then how is it to be cured? The answer, stated with great clarity by St. John of the Cross, is that it can be cured only by suffering. His answer is shared by many others, both before and after him, but the authority and compactness of his treatment puts him in a class by himself. This suffering, he teaches, is God's way of providing the cure we cannot impose on ourselves. It attacks the self's satisfaction in what it

---

47. E.g., Garrigou-Lagrange.

48. For example, there is the Nietzschean and existentialist understanding of the human condition, which leaves no room for rule-directed living. Again, there is the approach of a great deal of contemporary Anglo-American academic thought which *ex professo* has nothing to say about future conduct—although, of course, it has a good deal to say about what has already been done.

49. This corruption of morality by itself is a familiar theme in literature, we need only think of the novels of François Mauriac here. Hegel and Sartre have also found this subject a happy hunting ground. See my *Self-Deception and Hypocrisy in Hegel's Phenomenology of Mind*.

has become, and in how well it appears to fulfill the obligations of its state in life. The suffering, which appears under the guise of the darkness of God, overturns the well-organized life of prayer as well as the quiet satisfaction of duties efficiently and promptly carried out. St. John of the Cross calls this suffering the "Dark Night of the Senses." The landscape of our lives remains much the same, except for the significant fact that we no longer enjoy it much, or find it satisfying. As a result, the takeover bid of the whole of the Christian's life by the ascetical self is effectively defeated. A more radical application of suffering by God is then directed at the very identity of the self. The self, having lost any interest in the ascetical takeover bid, now becomes the object of a takeover bid itself. St. John calls this second application the "Dark Night of the Spirit."

The Dark Night of the Senses happens, St. John says, to most serious Christians. The sense of the presence of God no longer brings light and comfort, and suddenly our spiritual life becomes darkness and confusion. Even the awareness of God's presence seems to have been taken away from us, and our Christian life, which brought such strength and consolation, now appears pointless. St. John puts it this way:

> When they are going about these spiritual exercises with the greatest delight and pleasure, and when they believe the sun of Divine favor is shining most brightly upon them, God turns all this light of theirs into darkness, and shuts against them the door and the source of the sweet spiritual water which they were tasting in God whensoever and for as long as they desired.[50]

Now it is obvious that such a state may be the result of backsliding. Sloth and discouragement may have brought us to this state, and they are certainly not the result of God's action on us. St. John of the Cross, fully alive to this possibility, lists three signs to determine that this condition is not arising from "sins and imperfections, or from weakness and lukewarmness, or from some bad humor or indisposition of the body."[51]

First, the bleakness and lack of pleasure in the things of God has also to be matched by bleakness and lack of interest in the things of this world. If our hearts are really fixed on some temporal satisfaction, then we quickly become fed up with spiritual matters. St. John is not talking here about temptation but attachment to a satisfaction we are unwilling to give up. The usual reaction to the sin or imperfection that results

---

50. St. John of the Cross, *Dark Night of the Soul*, I.8.3.
51. Ibid., I.9.1.

from consenting to this attachment is disgust with self, including our efforts to lead a Christian life. If the sin is not a particularly gross one, then this may manifest itself as an impatience at the slowness of our spiritual progress. But in both cases, the spiritual tedium we then experience is self-induced. We have fixed our desires on the things of this world, we have become fed up with ourselves, and this overflows into our relationship with God.

The second sign is the positive side of the first one. The effect of the aridity and the darkness on us should be to realize, deeply, that we are not serving God, and this causes us pain and grief. At such times, St. John says, "the memory is ordinarily centered upon God, with painful care and solicitude, thinking that it is not serving God, but is backsliding, because it finds itself without sweetness in the things of God."[52]

Third, we find that we cannot meditate. It is not a question of not wanting to, it is a matter of not being able to. God leaves people in this condition "so completely in the dark they know not whither to go with their sensible imagination and meditation; for they cannot advance a step in meditation, as they were wont to do aforetime."[53] Abbot Chapman has the matter right when he writes that "the essence of the night of the senses is that the senses get into a night, in which they can't be used."[54] The world seems dreary and unattractive; God seems remote, puzzling yet somehow important; and when we come to pray we find we cannot use our imagination. As St. John says, everything seems to have gone wrong with us.

There are two responses to this darkness. The soul can try to hold its ascetical self as is, thus loosing its moorings in the darkness. It will begin to fall into depression. The self cannot face losing its carefully built system of virtues, which it has begun to identify with its essential nature. Its attempts to hold on to its former certainties now seem meaningless in the face of the present suffering and anxiety.[55]

The other response is to allow the growth of an awareness that it is possible to live without the constant pacifier of the ascetical self. The darkness leads not to another "super-self," but to a growing realization

---

52. Ibid., I.9.3.
53. Ibid., I.8.3.
54. Chapman, *Spiritual Letters*, 281. The passage continues: "St. John of the Cross means by 'senses,' all that satisfies the sensual and sensitive part of man; i.e. the imagination (by the help of which the intellect works, in this life), and the emotions and feelings which come from it. So long as these can work, a man *can* meditate, and *ought* to."
55. "What *can* happen next . . . is a crisis of self-knowledge, a crisis which gets its character from the nature of the self whose crisis it is. Depression is one form of that crisis. For in being . . . a self constructed upon anxiety, the ascetical self is especially prone

that "it is no longer I who live, but Christ who lives in me."[56] Our preoccupation with our self has been forcibly, even brutally taken away from us, and the encounter with the unknown God has become a real possibility.

St. Teresa and St. John describe the way the spiritual life often develops. Perhaps, they outline features which are always present but which are not always the most obvious characteristics of the entry into the illuminative way. St. Gregory of Nyssa describes the transition not so much in terms of moral failure or spiritual stagnation but as the consequences of an impetus or calling to draw closer to God. Apatheia and parrhesia are not obstacles to future growth, and for Gregory they are enduring aspects of the spiritual life. It is true that they may lead the beginner into tepidity and slavery to routine. But the call to a deeper or more authentic relationship with God is sometimes marked more by the desire for God, than as a cure from sin. Father Garrigou-Lagrange himself cites a passage from the fourteenth-century Dominican Johannes Tauler that sounds just this note of desire.

> From this pursuit of God . . . keen anguish results. When a man is plunged into this anxiety and becomes aware of this pursuit of God in his soul, it is then without doubt that Jesus comes and enters into him. But when one does not feel this pursuit or experience this anguish, Jesus does not come.[57]

It is "the pursuit of God" that is the dominant note in Tauler's description, not the cure from sin. Again, St. Bonaventure writes that "no one is in any way disposed for divine contemplation that leads to mystical ecstasy unless like Daniel he is *a man of desires*."[58] Philip was a man of desires, and that is the natural basis for understanding his conversion at San Germano. It is possible, of course, that Philip may have experienced temptations to lukewarmness, routine observance, and over-familiarity with God. Nonetheless, for someone who seems to have

---

to depression and is demolished by it. Disabled, if only temporarily, by depression, the ascetical 'I,' consisting in a moderate degree of smugness holding in precarious equilibrium of moderate degrees of self-indulgence and guilt, disintegrates into the warring factions of objectless anxiety and passionless obsession." Turner, *The Darkness of God*, 243. This whole chapter ten, "John of the Cross: The Dark Night and Depression," is a masterful treatment of St. John's doctrine that includes many insights from the development of psychology.

56. Galatians 2:20.
57. Cited in Garrigou-Lagrange, *The Three Ages of the Spiritual Life*, vol. 2, 35. The excerpt is from a sermon by Tauler for the Second Sunday in Lent.
58. Bonaventure, *The Soul's Journey into God*, 55.

had achieved both *apatheia* and *parrhesia*, it somehow misses the point to concentrate on how Philip may have failed. Philip was touched by God at San Germano. After that, nothing mattered to him so much as to find his way to touch his Maker, who had begun to take possession of Philip in a new and immediate way.

> And also our good lord shewed that it is full great plesance to him that a sely [innocent] soule come to him nakedly, plainly, and homely. For this is the kinde[59] yerning of the soule by the touching of the holy ghost, as by the understanding that I have in this shewing: "God of thy goodnes geve me thyselfe. For thou art inough to me, and I may aske nothing that is lesse that may be full worshippe to thee. And if I ask anything that is lesse, ever me wanteth. But only in thee I have all."[60]

Philip at San Germano was drawn into a cloud that made him realize riches and business were not for him; yet this happened because, like Moses, he began to understand that what he really desired, above everything, was to see the hidden God. So he set out for Rome, to the darkness of the Catacombs and the light of his studies.

---

59. *Kinde*, that is the natural *yerning*, but as transfigured *by the touching of the holy ghost*.
60. Julian of Norwich, *A Revelation of Love* in *The Writings*, 141.

7

Studies and Books

I cryde inwardly with all my might, seeking God for helpe, meaning thus: "A, Lorde Jhesu, king of blisse, how shall I be esede? Who shall tell me and tech me that me nedeth to wit, if I may not at this time se it in the?"
Julian of Norwich[1]

Kierkegaard perceived that the beginning of philosophy is not wonder, as the Greeks taught, but despair: *de profundis ad te, Domine, clamavi*. He realized that there was something to be found in the "private thinker" Job that had not occurred to the renowned philosopher, the noted professor.
Lev Isaakovich Shestov[2]

THERE IS general agreement that Philip left San Germano and arrived in Rome either in 1532 or 1533, that is, when he was eighteen or nineteen years old.[3] During his stay at San Germano, he had become increasingly disenchanted with the world of commerce and decided to give up his chances for a respectable career in business. There is nothing intrinsically evil in such a life, but it was not enough for Philip. His successful struggles to lead a serious Christian life had been fought within the well-defined parameters of the ascetical life. He had learned to live in God's grace (*apatheia*), and he had developed a loving familiarity with God (*parrhesia*). This deepening of his relationship with God had already breasted the surface of things. His openhearted worldliness,

---

1. Julian of Norwich, *A Revelation of Love*, Chapter 50, *The Writings*, 273.
2. Shestov, *Kierkegaard and the Existential Philosophy*, 11.
3. So say Bacci, Gallonio, and most of those who follow them. Capecelatro has 1534, basing his calculation on Philip's having left Florence at eighteen, coupled with a two-year stay in San Germano. Ponnelle and Bordet are silent as to the date.

with its frank appreciation of what the Italians call *la vita*, began to be clouded over by an effort to penetrate to the hidden meaning of life.[4]

Gregory of Nyssa had taught that this effort to penetrate into the hidden meaning of life was intellectual in character.[5] In harmony with this teaching, Philip's own mystical journey developed through a period in which studies and books became an essential element of that journey. His own search for God now took on the character of an effort to understand what Bremond called the *invasion mystique*,[6] the mystical invasion of God on Philip's soul. This chapter on studies and books is not, therefore, of merely biographical interest. It is also the discussion of an essential element of the embodiment of Philip's mysticism.

The chronology of Philip's early years in Rome from the time of his arrival until his ordination in 1551, a period of seventeen or eighteen years, is extremely difficult to work out. There are a few fixed dates—for example, the experience of the Holy Spirit in the catacombs at Pentecost 1544 and the founding of the Confraternity of the Most Holy Trinity in 1548—but there is a good deal of disagreement about the development of his life during this period. These disagreements do not stem from lack of knowledge about the sort of things Philip was doing during these years, but on how to fit them together.

We have to resist the hagiographical temptation to think that Philip was always perfectly clear not only that he wanted God before everything else, but also that he understood almost from the beginning how this was to be worked out in his own life. He was seventeen or eighteen when he arrived in Rome, an exceptional young man, no doubt, but a young man for whom the future was not laid for him to read beforehand, like a handbook on *theologica mystica*. In the end, he worked out a version of the Dominican formula, "*to contemplate and to hand on the fruits of one's contemplation to others*," but the way the formula was to be lived could not have been clear to him at the time.

Philip's life at this period was characterized by three as-yet-uncoordinated drives: one towards prayer and solitude, another towards studies and books, and finally one towards at least the beginnings of an apostolic life, a life of winning souls for Christ. Writers may take one or other

---

4. His life was to become a time of shadows and light: of a "pillar of cloud by day" and a "pillar of fire by night." "And the Lord went before them by day in a pillar of cloud to lead them along the way, and by night in a pillar of fire to give them light...." Exodus 13:21.

5. See Part Two, "The Mystical Assault: Clouds and Light in San Germano and Rome," 136, and Daniélou, *Platonisme et Théologie Mystique*, 128.

6. Bremond, *Histoire Littéraire du Sentiment Religieux en France*, vol. 1, 73. See Part Two, "The Mystical Assault: Clouds and Light in San Germano and Rome," 133.

of these themes and make it into the key for understanding the development of Philip's character. For example, Bacci—and he is not alone in this—concentrates on Philip's life of austerity and his attachment to prayer in a way that leads him to underrate the value that studies and books had for Philip. This lack of appreciation for the importance the intellectual life had for Philip leads Bacci, and those who follow him, to contract the amount of time he must have spent on his formal studies. It may be difficult to see quite how the different elements do fit together, but it is important to understand the complexity of Philip's nature, and that means taking account of the different elements before attempting any sort of synthesis. The only plausibility such a synthesis can have will rest on our grasp of these elements.

On his arrival in Rome, Philip sought out his Florentine countrymen and found lodging with a customs official called Galeotto del Caccia. In return for tutoring the two sons of the official, he was given a simple room and enough food to sustain himself. Most of the authorities say that he lived with Caccia until his ordination in 1551,[7] while others say he left when he gave up his formal studies.[8]

The sources all agree that during the early years in Rome, Philip led a life of great austerity. Bacci, for example, writes of his room:

> ... to say nothing of its extreme smallness, it was so poor, that there was nothing in it but a little bed, and some books; and his clothes, linen or woolen, were hung on a rope which went across the room. It was no rare thing for him to make the floor his bed. . . .[9]

His life and diet reflected a similar austerity:

> ... he led a life of great hardship and rigor, courting solitude as much as might be ... In food he was so abstemious that he seemed to take no thought either or eating or drinking. At first the people of the house were wont to reserve for him some part of their meals; but he, not wishing for anything, took a roll, and returned below into the courtyard near the well; there he ate his bread, and then drank some water, adding at times some few herbs or olives, In general he only ate once a day....

Such severe ascetical discipline should be viewed as a consequence of his turning away from the ordinary sort of life that would have been his

---

7. "... he retained a place of abode in the house of Galeotto del Caccia ... until the time of his priesthood in 1551." Ponnelle and Bordet, *St. Philip Neri*, 82.

8. "... 1537 quando lasciò la casa Del Caccia e gli studii." Cistellini, *San Filippo Neri*, 22. There does not seem to be much evidence for this contention.

9. Bacci, *The Life of Saint Philip Neri*, vol. 1, 13.

had he continued in his uncle's business. Philip had experienced a conversion during his time at San Germano, and by leaving San Germano he had burned his bridges. Now he had to learn how to live in a world in which there were no obvious signposts.

For an intelligent young man such as Philip, with a good education, his first instinct would be to try to understand what had happened to him. There is nothing to suggest that at this stage in his life, or at any other stage for that matter, that Philip thought that learning was necessarily inimical to the practice of sincere religion. He thought just the opposite: that is, that the use of reason was an integral part of the practice of Catholicism. The first movement of his spirit after his conversion, then, was to learn what philosophy and theology could teach him about the meaning of his conversion and of the new demands his conversion had laid upon him. This was not a detached speculative activity, but rather the natural expression of a deep need, perhaps even a desperate need, to come to terms with what had happened to him.

In addition to tutoring the two boys, Philip became a student. He also deepened his life of prayer and began to touch the hearts of others with the love of God. It is difficult to sort out the chronology of these years, and while obviously his formal studies had a beginning and an end, these three activities are different aspects in the formation of a rich and elusive character, not clearly marked stages of a temporal development. Even if his formal studies were confined to a definite period, this is not true of Philip's love for books, and especially, most assuredly, for the Bible. Philip's studies and this love for books are the subject of this chapter.

I have already pointed out that it is in Philip's studies and in his love for books that we find an important aspect of his embodied mysticism. Gregory of Nyssa understood the illuminative way as "a more careful understanding of hidden things,"[10] and in this sense the illuminative way is a darkness to the ordinary ways of knowing that are based on sense perception. The second way is dominated by a search for hidden truth beyond sense experience.

> What then is the mystic initiation which the soul experiences during this night? It is the Word touching the door. We understand by this door the human mind searching for what is hidden; through it the object sought after enters.[11]

---

10. Gregory of Nyssa, *Commentary on the Song of Songs*, 202. See Introduction, "An Embodied Mysticism," 42.

11. Gregory of Nyssa, *Commentary on the Song of Songs*, 202.

For Gregory, as for Bonaventure, the intellect's search for truth is an integral aspect of the mystic's journey into God. The intellectual search is itself the door though which Christ enters. This is also true of Philip. It was by using the intellect, not by crippling it, that Philip's embodied mysticism developed.

The usual account of Philip's studies goes like this: Philip arrives in Rome as a penniless stranger who almost at once, after he has got himself established at the Caccias', takes courses, first in philosophy and later in theology. After some time, his life of prayer becomes so important to him that he sells his books to help a poor student. He gives himself up to the spiritual life, and then, or perhaps at the same time, begins his apostolate of preaching, not only by word but also by the example of his attractive personality, to the young Florentines of Rome. He continues with this mixed life of prayer and teaching until he is ordained in 1551.

It does not seem that enough attention has been paid to the financial side of these years. Philip cannot have been literally penniless, as he had money to buy books, and presumably the studies must also have cost money. Perhaps the rich relation at San Germano gave him enough to get to Rome and establish himself there. This is not to cast doubt on the accounts of how simply Philip lived, but a strict ascetical life does not preclude the possibility of a little something tucked away to be spent on books and education. This is only a supposition, but there must have been some money somewhere.

Leaving this practical matter aside, there are two different sets of questions about these early years in Rome that it will be helpful to keep distinct. The first is historical: For how long, where, and what did Philip study? The second, which is more important for our purposes, asks: Why did he start studying in the first place, and what was his attitude towards book learning after he gave up going to class?

The first set of questions can be dealt with quickly, because we do not know very much. For the most part, from the first biographies, people have been so concerned with other aspects of Philip's life that they have paid little attention to his studies. This is understandable, because what we know of his life of prayer really is extraordinarily interesting in itself and was intimately connected with his apostolate, an apostolate that ended with his being called the Apostle of Rome. It is hardly surprising, then, that the question of his studies has seemed of relatively little importance.

Nevertheless, Gallonio says:

> Since Philip was living in Rome, the idea of studying philosophy came into his mind, with God's prompting. . . . He applied himself to philos-

ophy because he thought that would be pleasing to God, and in a short time made such progress that he was counted among the best in his class.... He was endowed with a very acute mind for study, particularly in disputations. When it came to theology, in which he was well skilled, he always followed the opinions of St. Thomas.[12]

Bacci says:

When the youthful Philip had led this austere life for about two years, he determined, in order the better to understand heavenly things, and to taste them more perfectly, to add the study of philosophy and theology to what he had previously learned.[13]

Philip studied philosophy at the Sapienza[14] and theology at the Augustinianum,[15] but there is no clear indication as to when he gave his studies up. The usual account is that he quickly mastered what he needed to know and then gave them up entirely because they interfered with his life of prayer. Gallonio seems to say the studies lasted for three years:

Once our dear Father had received sufficient education in the human sciences, to the extent that there were few of his contemporaries who could match him, he left secular learning behind him, to follow the call of Christ, giving himself totally to prayer and the contemplation of the things of God; this was, I think, at the end of the year thirty-seven of our century.[16]

Bacci is of even less help:

He had now made sufficient advancement in learning, not for his own use only, but also for the edification of others; and he began to consider the Apostle's words, *Non plus sapere quam oportet sapere, sed sapere ad sobrietatem.* (Rom. xii. 3.) Now therefore he laid his studies aside, and applied himself wholly to that science which is found in the crucifix.[17]

---

12. Gallonio, *The Life of Saint Philip Neri*, 5–6.
13. Bacci, *The Life of Saint Philip Neri*, 15.
14. "... alli studii di philosophia e theologia: e questo lo so, perchè il medesimo beato Filippo mi disse, più volte, ch'haveva inteso, in Sapientia, mio padre Alfonso Ferri, quale all'hora legeva, in Sapientia, philosophia...." Marcello Ferro in Della Rocchetta and Vian, *Il Primo Processo per San Filippo Neri*, vol. 3, 41.
15. "Soleva andare il nostro benedetto padre, come da lui ha inteso, a sentire, quando era laico, lettioni de theologia, allo studio de frati di S. Agostino; dove essendo un crocefisso, non sapeva far altro, che piangere e sospirare." Gallonio in Della Rocchetta and Vian, *Il Primo Processo per San Filippo Neri*, vol. 1, 175.
16. Gallonio, *The Life of Saint Philip Neri*, 7.
17. Bacci, *The Life of Saint Philip Neri*, 19.

Most modern writers take the view that these formal studies were of short duration, and nearly all mention Francesco Zazzara's evidence in the First Process that Philip had told him "he had studied little, and that he had not been able to learn much because he was occupied with prayers and other spiritual exercises."[18] A modern Italian scholar sums up this interpretation:

> In this connection, besides, the result is clear, from the assembled factors that the years of study could not have been many.[19]

There are two indications that this judgment is wrong. First, as we shall see, a good case can be made out that Philip did not sell his books before 1540 at the earliest. It is generally agreed that this marked the end of his formal studies. If Philip began studying almost as soon as he arrived in Rome in 1532 (Gallonio), or even two years later in 1534 (Bacci), this leaves between six and eight years for his formal studies. Second, there is evidence that Philip was one of the best students of his time in both philosophy and theology. There also exist lists of his teachers and contemporaries.[20] It is difficult to see how this reputation for learning could have been built up, nor how he could have impressed the wide range of people he did in fact seem to have encountered, in a very short time.

In May 1610, Pompeo Pateri, a priest of the Roman Oratory, testified that he had heard from Cardinal Tarugi[21] that St. Philip used to help poor students, especially those who were strangers in Rome. He then goes on to add that Philip sold his books to help a particular student who was broke and lacking the necessities of life.[22] The student's name was Sirleto, and he lived to become a Cardinal and the Prefect of the Vatican library as well as an important figure in preparing documents for the Council of Trent. He was a trusted advisor to the Cardinal Legates.[23]

---

18. As cited in Ponnelle and Bordet, *St. Philip Neri*, 81–82.

19. "A tal proposito, inoltre, risulta chiara, dagli elementi raccolti, che gli anni di studii non dovettero essere molti." Bella, *Philippo Neri*, 70.

20. There is an accessible and lively account of Philip's teachers and fellow-students in Trevor, *Apostle of Rome*, 22–24. I think, though, she is mistaken about Philip's cast of mind. See the discussion of Philip's Aristotelianism later in this chapter, 168 ff.

21. In a later deposition, he says he heard the same account from Cardinal Baronius.

22. "Il beato padre, prevendo, forse, in spirito, che quell giovane doveva, con le virtù sue, ascendere, alla dignità, dove ascese, non havendo danari, per soccorrerlo, vendè li libri, per zelo della charità." Della Rocchetta and Vian, *Il Primo Processo per San Filippo Neri*, vol. 3, 159.

23. Guglielmo Sirleto was born at Guardavalle near Stilo in Calabria in 1514; he died in Rome on October 6, 1585. "During the concluding period of the Council of Trent he was, although he continued to reside in Rome, the constant and most heeded adviser of

Sirleto arrived in Rome in 1540, and five years later, in March 1545,[24] he began earning "four gold ducats a month" as a translator from Greek to Latin. Philip, then, could not have sold his books to help Sirleto before 1540, and perhaps he sold them even later than that; in fact he might have done so at any time until 1545, when Sirleto began to earn his own keep.

Bacci says, in the continuation of the passage cited above, that when Philip gave up his formal studies, he sold all his books, "and gave the price away for the love of God."[25] If selling the books and quitting his studies happened at the same time, and that makes perfect sense, then we would have to conclude that his formal studies lasted between six and eight years.

This estimate is strengthened when we take into account his success with his studies and the number of people who either taught or studied with him. By the end of his life, it was generally acknowledged that Philip was a well-instructed theologian, able to hold his own with the most learned men of his time. "Men who loved him much did not hesitate, at the process of his canonization, to praise his learning."[26] We find, for example, Marco Antonio Maffa saying:

> ... the blessed father was most accomplished in philosophy and theology in which he was learned in a more than ordinary way. And it was a thing to be wondered at to see him in his old age of eighty years responding, without warning, to the most difficult questions on the Trinity, on the angels, the Incarnation, and to all other theological and philosophical matters; and of how the freshness of his memory retained all this.[27]

---

the cardinal-legates... he was named in 1570 librarian of the Vatican library. His influence was paramount in the execution of the scientific undertakings decreed by the Council of Trent. He collaborated in the publication of the Roman Catechism, in the reform of the Roman Breviary and Missal, and directed the work of the new edition of the Roman Martryology. Highly appreciative of Greek culture he entertained friendly relations with the East and encouraged all efforts tending to ecclesiastical reunion. He was attended in his last illness by St. Philip Neri and was buried in the presence of Sixtus V." "Giugliemo Sirleto," [Old] *Catholic Encyclopedia*, vol. 14, 27.

24. "Manca la data del fatto, ma questo si può collocare tra il 1540, quando il Sirleto arrivò a Roma, e il 1545, quando egli, a comminciare dal marzo, ebbi assignati Quattro ducati d'oro al mese, quale 'deputato a tradurre di greco in latino' a servizio del Concilio." Della Rocchetta and Vian, *Il Primo Processo per San Filippo Neri*, vol. 3, 159, n. 1996.

25. Bacci, *The Life of Saint Philip Neri*, 19.

26. Ponnelle and Bordet, *St. Philip Neri*, 81.

27. Della Rocchetta and Vian, *Il Primo Processo per San Filippo Neri*, vol. 2, 87. Maffa was an official in the household of Cardinal Cusano, and a penitent of St. Philip's.

Another example of this praise is to be found in the second deposition of the young Giacomo Crescenzi.[28] In a way similar to Maffa, he says that he had heard Philip praised as learned in both theology and philosophy by men outstanding and famous for their doctrine. He says he was present on an occasion when a group of learned scholars presented Philip with some very difficult questions that they had been discussing for several days and had not been able to answer. Philip solved their questions in very few words, in a way that convinced them and as though he had just been studying the material himself.

Giacomo then poses the question as to whether the profundity of Philip's doctrine or the freshness of his memory is more to be wondered at. It was a good question, because Philip's intellectual capacity and knowledge seem to have made such an impression on those who knew him best that some thought his knowledge was infused. The term "infused" denotes God's direct action on man in connection with either knowledge, the virtues, or contemplation; it is contrasted with the result of human efforts, called "acquired."[29] So, in Philip's case, it is claimed that the depth of his knowledge and his capacity to use it were the result of a special grace infused into Philip's soul. This might have been the case, but I believe that, to rephrase Ockham, *miracula non sit multiplicanda praeter necessitatem,* and there is no need to bring in the supernatural to explain Philip's learning. He was intelligent and studied hard over a number of years; he loved books and kept up his reading all his life;[30] and all these factors, allied to a natural intelligence, are enough to account for the depth of his learning and his skill in using what he knew.

It may be true that Philip was often the recipient of special graces when dealing with other people in a way that required the use of his learning or when he was presented with a difficult question in philosophy or theology; indeed, this was probably the case. On the other hand, the sharpening of his intellect, the strengthening of his memory, and a deeper penetration into a particular question through the working of grace are not at all the same thing as infused knowledge. This suggestion of the presence of infused knowledge is adduced to explain how

---

28. He was a young Roman nobleman who was twenty-six at the time he testified; like his father, he had been a penitent of St. Philip's.

29. "Le terme 'infuse' désigne le mode de l'action directe de Dieu dans l'homme aux plan de la science, des vertus ou de la contemplation; il s'oppose à 'acquis,' qui désigne ce qui est produit par l'effort humain." *Dictionnaire de Spiritualité,* "infuse," 1729–1730.

30. "Leggere gli piaque sempre, e lo trovano abitualmente con libri o corone tra le mani...." (He always took pleasure in reading, and he was usually found with a book or a rosary in his hands....) Vian, *San Filippo Neri,* 72.

someone who had studied for a short space of time, and who did not set much store on book learning, could have in fact known as much as he did, and have handled his learning so well. If in fact the formal studies lasted for a good number of years, and were accompanied by a genuine love of learning, then there is no need to invoke this miracle.

I contend that while it is understandable that Philip's studies have received little attention, that does not mean they were of no importance either to him personally or to our own understanding of his character. The fact that Philip left off his formal studies has served as grounds to paint him as an anti-intellectual. All this is mistaken. His whole life was deeply marked by a love of learning, and furthermore, the apostolate of the Oratory was based on the use of books.

The picture of a Philip unconcerned with book learning goes back explicitly to *The Lives of the Companions of St. Philip Neri*.[31] This work was written by Father Giacomo Ricci, a Dominican who wrote a revised second edition of Bacci that was published in 1678. Ricci, who knew the first generation of Oratorians, also made use of other contemporary works.[32] In the chapter devoted to Father Pietro Consolini, Ricci says that Consolini[33] often insisted that members of the Congregation should be "well grounded in the sacred learning so necessary to their vocation," but he also used to warn his hearers that "under pretext of instructing themselves they not infrequently neglected their own spiritual profit."[34] This, as it stands, is unobjectionable and could have been said by St. Philip; but then Ricci has Consolini say:

> He reminded them of the example of St. Philip, who after having devoted to study all the time and application which were fitting, at last entirely gave up this occupation, and sold his books to bestow their value on the poor. During the remainder of his life the saint's only book was the crucifix, and his only science charity.[35]

This statement is just untrue. Two days after the death of the Saint,

---

31. F. Giacomo Ricci, O.P., *The Lives of the Companions of S. Philip Neri*, translated by F. W. Faber (London: Thomas Richardson and Son, 1847).

32. See Ponnelle and Bordet, *St. Philip Neri*, 1–2.

33. Pietro Consolini was born at Fermo in the Marches in 1553 and joined the Oratory in 1590. He was the confidant of Philip's last years and provided a living link between St. Philip and the successors of the first Oratorians who had been the companions of the Saint. He was also the inspiration for Bacci's biography. "Il Consolini rappresenta infatti l'elemento di continuità fra S. Filippo e i Padri delle generazioni successive fino all metà del '600 e l'ispiratore del biografo spirituale del Santo, il p. Bacci." Gasbarri, *L'Oratorio Romano dal Cinquecento al Novecento*, 155.

34. Ricci, *The Lives of the Companions of S. Philip Neri*, 250–251.

35. Ibid., 251.

that is on the twenty-eighth of May, 1595, the Fathers had an inventory made of the contents of Philip's rooms, and, in addition to personal effects and other objects, there was a long list of 515 printed books and thirty manuscripts that were his own property.[36] The mere fact of a library of 515 books[37] should send up a warning that there is something seriously wrong with the common picture of Philip's attitude towards the intellectual life.

The apostolate of the Oratory depended upon books. To convey the truth to his followers in a way that would touch their hearts and change their lives, there was first the ministry of the confessional. But in a more public way, Philip developed a practice of extempory preaching on the Bible and other books he regarded as conveying the fundamentals of the Christian life. One of the principal exercises of the Oratory was this "speaking on the book," *il ragionamento sopra il libro*. This was an improvised talk that sprang from the reading of some inspiring text. In Philip's view, this "speaking on the book" left the way open for the Holy Spirit to infuse his power into the speaker. The absence of a prepared discourse meant that a living connection was set up between the speaker and his hearers.[38]

St. Philip's method of teaching was a development of the practice of *Lectio Divina*.[39] His own understanding of *Lectio* was traditional and straightforward:

> ...in order to make his reading...fruitful, he read slowly and pausingly, and when he felt himself moved by what he read, went no further, but stopped to ponder the text; when the feeling subsided he resumed his reading, and this went on with passage after passage.[40]

The practice of speaking on the book gave scope both for the use of a text and for the work of the Holy Spirit. The speaker expounded a given element of tradition and, at the same time, allowed scope for its living and creative aspect. The text provided control and discipline, while the improvised and immediate character of the talk ensured that it became a living development of Christian truth.[41] Note: you cannot have any "speaking on the book" without a book.

36. See Cistellini, *San Filippo Neri, L'Oratorio e la Congregazione Oratoriana*, vol. 1, 104.

37. The question of Philip's attitude towards books is beautifully discussed in Vian, "Messer Filippo Neri Bibliofilo," *San Filippo Neri*, 67–75.

38. See Cistellini, op. cit., 78–90.

39. See "Lectio Divina et Lecture Spirituelle," *Dictionnaire de Spiritualité*, vol. 9, especially columns 470–487.

40. Bacci, *The Life of Saint Philip Neri*, vol. 1, 176.

41. See I, 2.2 of Jonathan Robinson, "How St. Philip Taught," *On the Lord's Appearing* (Washington, DC: The Catholic University of America Press, 1997), 45–59.

It is worth pausing to ask why it was that Ricci, and perhaps even Consolini, should have left us with such a one-sided view of Philip's attitude towards learning. The answer is that they wanted to make clear that the source of Philip's influence and the ground of Philip's holiness were an overwhelming and apparently continuous awareness of the presence of God in his life. Philip's influence was, in fact, based on his sanctity. But his sanctity was embodied in a rich cultural and intellectual heritage.[42]

In the Letter to the Ephesians, St. Paul prays that the Ephesians may be so rooted and grounded in love that they may be able to "know the love of Christ which surpasses knowledge," in order that they might be "filled up to all the fullness of God."[43] This reality of Christ's love is so overwhelming—not only from the point of view of conversion, but also for continued growth in our relationship with Christ—that nothing can really be compared to it,[44] and certainly nothing should get in the way of it. Philip thought that intellectual abilities and studies could get in the way of our awareness of the love of Christ, and even block it out. In his determination to see that this did not happen to his disciples, and that they would continue to put first things first, he practiced a ruthless mortification of what he called the *razionale*, the thinking or reasoning aspect of our nature. He did this not to denigrate reason, but to ensure that the *razionale* did not blot out the love of Christ in the interests of intellectual pursuits. None of this, however, justifies our saying that Philip was anti-intellectual and had little use for books; he took intellectual questions very seriously and he loved books, which he used both for his own personal enrichment as well as for his apostolate of the Oratory.

It is one thing to say that books were important to Philip, but it is another to describe his personal attitude towards what he read. The view is often expressed that Philip, if he had a philosophical stance at all, was more of a Platonist than an Aristotelian. Cardinal Capecelatro, as we have seen, states this firmly enough, although he does admit it is his own opinion.[45] This "understanding" of the Cardinal is given added authority by Ponnelle and Bordet, who, in their discussion of Cardinal Valier's Dialogue concerning Philip, would have us believe that "... we

---

42. See part one, chapter one, "Using this World Well," 67–68.
43. Ephesians 3:19.
44. "No matter how much knowledge we have of Christ and his work, his love surpasses that knowledge. The more we know of his love, the more we are amazed by it." Hoehner, *Ephesians, An Exegetical Commentary*, 489.
45. See part one, chapter four, "Art, Irony, and Eros," 122.

may look upon the Vallicella[46] as a refuge of Platonism in the midst of a city where the influence of Aristotle was ever on the increase."[47] Finally, Meriol Trevor informs us that:

> According to Pateri Philip was well informed in the scholastic philosophy, though he was never fond of that type of thought; he did not encourage his young men to take it up, saying there were plenty of schools for that elsewhere. But many of them record that he always liked to follow St. Thomas Aquinas. It was the later scholasticism that he, like all good humanists, so much disliked.[48]

Philip was a humanist; but humanism, as we have seen,[49] is a term that requires careful handling. Taken by itself, it does not help us much to understand Philip's take on either Scholasticism or the learning of Greece and Rome. What is at issue here is the widely accepted view that Philip is a sort of Christian Socrates, and therefore (it is thought to follow) he must have been a kind of Platonist. If he were a Platonist, one assumes then that he cannot have been an Aristotelian, and this would have to mean that the repeated assertion by many that he preferred the teaching of St. Thomas, the Aristotelian, when it came to theology, really does not reveal his inner convictions. This supposition is flawed for many reasons.

It will be worth our while to examine the issue of Philip's supposed Platonism more closely. Most of the Greek Fathers were Platonists in some sense of this word, and contemporary scholarship on the great Scholastics is abandoning the view that their work represents a radical break with most Platonic themes. Yet this does not mean that if you "really" want to understand St. Thomas, you must understand that the traditional view of his using Aristotle in a new and unique way is false; it only means that what he accomplished has to be understood in a less-simple minded way.[50] I would say something analogous about St. Philip: that he was a Christian humanist (along with whatever that entails about the love of Plato). It would be wrong, though, to say this shows that Philip was a crypto-Platonist. His intellectual stance was Aristotelian and Thomistic.

I have already drawn attention to Cardinal Valier's work, *Philip, or the*

---

46. The "Vallicella" is a common way of referring to Santa Maria in Vallicella, the Church of the Oratory in Rome.
47. Ponnelle and Bordet, *St. Philip Neri*, 502.
48. Trevor, *Apostle of Rome*, 23.
49. See part one, chapter one, "Using this World Well," 61*ff.*
50. See, for example, Dauphinais, David, and Levering, Eds., *Aquinas the Augustinian*.

Dialogue of Christian Joy.[51] Ponnelle and Bordet say that this "delightful work in which the Cardinal emulates Plato," in casting his work as a dialogue, "merits, as truly as the *Fioretti* in the case of St. Francis of Assisi, to be included among the sources of Philip's life."[52] This may be true, but the dialogue cannot be used as evidence that Philip was a Platonist. Valier calls Philip another Socrates, although what he meant by that, as we have seen, is not all that clear. Certainly Valier provides us with no evidence for thinking that Philip was a Platonist who distrusted scholastic philosophy. This holds for Capecelatro, Ponnelle and Bordet, Trevor, and Türks. I think that all these writers, with the exception, obviously, of Valier, were reacting against a rigid and unattractive form of Neo-Thomism. These writers are correct in wanting to distance Philip from the spirit of many aspects of this Thomistic revival.[53] That in itself, however, doesn't make Philip into a Platonist.

The point is important and worth elaborating. Aristotle, in discussing Socrates, said:

> For two things may be justifiably and fairly ascribed to Socrates— inductive arguments and universal definition, both of which are concerned with the starting point of science.[54]

Socrates' intellectual development was away from cosmological speculations and towards the study of human morality and the life of man in the state. It is usually said that Socrates, in early life, acquired a full knowledge of the science of his age and a full mastery of its humanistic culture.[55]

It was the oracle of Delphi that seems to have convinced him he was a man with a mission. Chaerephon asked the Delphic Oracle whether there was any man living wiser than Socrates, and he received the answer no—that is, there was no man living who was wiser than Socrates. This helped to bring about the "conversion" of Socrates from a scientific to a moral philosopher. He was wisest because he recognized his own ignorance, and he came to conceive of his own mission to seek for the stable

---

51. Valier, *Il Dialogo Della Gioia Cristiana*. See Part One, Chapter Four, "Art, Irony, and Eros," for the historical setting of the dialogue.

52. Ponnelle and Bordet, *St. Philip Neri*, 21.

53. The questions of how the teaching of St. Thomas is to be understood, and then how it is to be used in the contemporary situation, are complex and controverted. What it is in neo-Thomism that seemed unacceptable to the above authors as a tool to understanding of St. Philip is ably discussed in O'Meara, O.P., *Thomas Aquinas, Theologian* and Etienne Gilson, *Thomistic Realism and the Critique of Knowledge*.

54. Aristotle, *Metaphysics* 1078 b 28.

55. See Part One, Chapter Four, "Art, Irony, and Eros."

and certain truth, true wisdom, and to enlist the aid of any man who would consent to listen to him.

It was in this search for the stable and certain truth that we can understand the importance of universals expressed as definitions. Socrates wanted objective definitions, not dependent on particulars, because of his interest in ethical concepts such as justice, piety, and the like.[56] In his search for these definitions, Socrates used what Aristotle called "inductive arguments." Looking back, that is, on what he knew about Socrates' actual method, Aristotle[57] called it inductive. He did not mean that Socrates was a logician, but that he had a practical method of doing philosophy that involved the use of particular examples. And this practical method took the form of *dialectic* or *conversation.*

Socrates would profess ignorance, then elicit definitions from his interlocutors, then refine them. His purpose was to discover the truth not as a matter of pure speculation, but with a view to the good life. He did not set out to humiliate or destroy, and his profession of ignorance was—I believe—sincere. Socratic irony is this profession of ignorance— "I really don't know, so you tell me." The early dialogues are concerned with ethical concepts such as courage, temperance, friendship, and piety, and all these early dialogues produce no satisfactory definition. He thought that clear thinking based on true definitions was indispensable for living the good life, and what he was interested in was precisely how to live the good life. As he came up with no definition that would stand up, it is hardly surprising he was looked on as a danger to the *status quo*.

It is also important to see that for Socrates, it is not enough to say that knowledge is an indispensable condition for right living; he also maintained that knowledge and virtue are one, in the sense that the wise man, he who knows what is right, will also do what is right. From this position, Socrates went on to argue that virtue was one, and that, furthermore, it actually consisted in knowledge. In other words, from the identification of wisdom and virtue he thought there followed the unity of virtue. Aristotle was one of the first in the long history of the critics of this position when he said that Socrates forgot the irrational part of the

---

56. Aristotle says quite clearly that Socrates did not think that universals had a separate existence: "Socrates did not make the universals or the definitions exist apart; his successor, however, gave them separate existence, and this was the kind of thing they called Ideas." Aristotle, *Metaphysics* 1078 b 29.

57. Socrates was born about 470 BC and was put to death in 399. Aristotle's dates are 384–322 BC, and so did not know Socrates personally. Aristotle, though, worked with Plato in Athens for twenty years at the end of Plato's life. This gave Aristotle abundant opportunity to learn about Socrates and his teaching from Plato.

soul, and what Aristotle called the experience of the weak-willed man who knows what the right thing to do is and doesn't do it.[58]

Now, given that Philip has been held up as "a Christian Socrates" or as "our Socrates," we might have expected Valier's Dialogue to contain the sort of tentative, exploratory inquiries characteristic of Plato's early dialogues. But we find nothing of the kind. The Dialogue is about a theme proposed by Philip himself, *Gaudete in Domino Semper*: rejoice in the Lord always. The participants are asked to state what seems to them to be the cause of Christian joy. The theme was certainly an appropriate one when it is remembered that Philip's rooms were looked on as a school for sanctity and of Christian joy; and that Philip himself always held that it was much easier to guide men of a joyous nature in the ways of holiness than those who were of a melancholy disposition. None of the contributions of the participants much resemble what we find in Plato's early dialogues. They are more like the longer-winded interventions in Plato's *Symposium*, a dialogue that ends with Socrates' account of what a wise woman had told him about the everlasting beauty that is the ultimate source of all love. Yet there is nothing analogous to this paean of praise in Valier's work. What we do find is Cardinal Frederico Borromeo asking Philip for a concluding explanation or summary of Christian joy to be expressed *dialectico more*, and to be phrased *breviter et lucide*, shortly and clearly. The Cardinal gets exactly what he asked for, and St. Philip frames his answer in terms of Aristotle's four causes:[59] the efficient cause is God; the material cause is everything we experience in creation; the formal cause is the providence of God; and the final cause is for a constant increase of joy until it flourishes in heaven. Furthermore, he follows St. Thomas by characterizing joy as a quality of the soul.

Neither in tone nor in content is there anything particularly Platonic about the Dialogue. Certainly there is nothing in it that would lead us to doubt that the repeated assertion that Philip preferred the teaching of St. Thomas to that of anyone else is anything but true.[60] Furthermore, his library shows what one Italian writer calls the "massive presence"[61]

---

58. Aristotle discusses this problem of *akrasìa* in book 7 of the *Nichomachean Ethics*.

59. Valier, *Il Dialogo*, 102. The Cardinal lists the four causes: efficient, formal, material and final. Philip's answer, in fact, mentions explicitly only *materia* and *finis*.

60. "Anche se il genere letterario stesso (il dialogo) e il riferimento al Socrate cristiano reconducono ai modelli classici, parebbe un'arbitraria forzatura pretendere di assumere il Diologo per qualificare la Vallicella un centro di cultura umanistica e un cenacolo di platonismo, quasi in contrasto con l'indirizzo aristotelico corrente, in auge soprattutto nelle scuole gesuitiche." This is from Cistellini's introduction in Valier, *Il Dialogo Della Gioia Cristiana*, LXXIII. Cistellini is certainly right about that.

61. "una presenze massiccia de opere filosofiche." Bella, *Filippo Neri*, 235.

of philosophical works, consisting largely of either texts of Aristotle or commentaries on his work, both old and new, including the work of Averroes.[62] This only serves to reinforce the view that Philip took his Aristotle seriously. When it comes to the work of St. Thomas, we find that there were eighteen books both of the texts of the Saint and of commentaries on his work. Then there were an added thirty-three works of theology in the technical sense, works on grace, faith, charity, the last things, and the sacraments. There was also a collection of works concerning heretics and heresy, both ancient and modern, including a text on Anglicanism. There is no support in all of this for the contention that Philip did not find Aristotle and St. Thomas congenial, let alone the more extreme view that after his student days his only book was the crucifix.

Philip collected books, and if we are to assume that they were more than expensive wallpaper, we must suppose that he read them. The evidence that he either had a book or a rosary in his hand should not be entirely discounted even if it is an exaggeration. Nello Vian, in a lovely passage, seems to me to have it exactly right:

> Like old men, he loved to collect and replace things. And he continued to collect books right to the end, and he was still accustomed to take them up in his white and restless hands. And also that which was collected by the pure innocent—and most wise old man, who humanly loved to act so that he entered his room loaded with little earthly treasures, but had a heart that was free and fixed solely on the heavenly treasure.[63]

Philip had a clear sense of what was appropriate for different activities and occasions. He did not want a parade of learning in preaching or at the exercises of the Oratory. He held that the Scholastic mode of exposition was particularly inimical to moving the hearts and wills of those who attended sermons and talks, and so he designed the preaching and talks at the Oratory to inflame the hearers with a love of God and a desire to lead a good life. It is hardly surprising that he banned scholastic modes of exposition from preaching. But it does not follow

---

62. "sessantacinque testi di cui ben quarantasei riguardanti Aristotele, le sue opere e i suoi commentari di ogni tempo tra i quali emerge la figura di Averroé." Ibid.

63. "Come i vecchi, amava raccogliere e riporre. E libri seguitò ad ammaddare fino all'ultimo, e costumava ancora di prenderne tra le mani bianche e nervosa. E anche questo è ammaestramento del candido, savissimo vecchio, che umanamente si diletta di aggirarsi per entro le sue stanze ingombre di un terrestre tessorato, ma ha il cuore libero e fisso unicamente al tesoro celeste." Vian, *San Filippo Neri*, 75.

that he thought the whole of the intellectual life consisted in the preparation of sermons. If it is true, for example, that he read Aristotle and St. Thomas, and it is also true that he did not want them used at Oratory, then the conclusion to be drawn is that he thought there was more to life than preaching at the Oratory.

Philip clearly thought that an intellectual life nourished by reading—reading not directly related to the apostolate—had its own intrinsic value; after all, he kept it up for a lifetime. Reading and intellectual conversation was an integral part of a well-rounded and civilized man, and Philip was both of those things. He was, and always remained, a citizen of that learned Florence that was the fatherland of humanism.[64] It was in that fatherland of humanism that his embodied mysticism took root, and which for the rest of his life gave to it a unique and unmistakable character. Like Gregory of Nyssa, Philip's studies and books became the door through which the hidden Christ was to enter.[65]

---

64. "Nativo della dotta Firenze patria dell'umanesimo...." Ibid., 67.
65. See above, this chapter, 158.

8

The Catacombs and the Apostolate

His life now became more retired than ever; indeed, he almost separated himself, like a hermit, from commerce with men.
                              Pietro Giacomo Bacci[1]

Philip having thus lived a retired life for some time, and feeling himself more and more called by God to the conversion of souls, resolved to quit in part the solitude for which he had the greatest attraction, and to give himself up with greater fervor to the assistance of his neighbor.
                              Pietro Giacomo Bacci[2]

GREGORY of Nyssa thought, as we have seen, that the way of beginners was a way of light. The spiritual combat to fight the vices is difficult, but it is fought out within a clearly perceived framework of moral principles and ascetical practices. Then this clarity becomes clouded over, and what was light becomes darkness, a darkness that obscures the awareness of the certainties that underlie the spiritual combat.

Gregory takes this darkness as a necessary continuation of the spiritual journey into the hidden depths of God's being. Darkness and quiet obscure the visible world, freeing the spirit to reach out to the invisible. Gregory said that at the beginning, religious knowledge "comes to those who receive it as light. Therefore what is perceived to be contrary to religion is darkness, and the escape from darkness comes about when one participates in light."[3] As the mind progresses, however, it begins to grasp that God's nature is hidden in a darkness it cannot penetrate. Nonetheless, the soul now also begins to understand that in this dark-

---

1. Bacci, *The Life of Saint Philip Neri*, vol. 1, 20.
2. Ibid., vol. 1, 30.
3. Gregory of Nyssa, *The Life of Moses*, 162.

ness it is closer to God than it was when living within the clarities of the ascetical life.[4] This darkness is not a threatening presence, but a necessary condition for learning detachment from the visible world, and so drawing closer to union with God. The growing awareness of a reality beyond sense, a reality that studies helped bring about, then leads the soul to "pursue the truth and clothe herself in it."[5]

St. John of the Cross called this change in the spiritual landscape the "dark night of the senses." It is a period when it is no longer possible to use sense experience in the development of the spiritual life, and we have to begin to learn to live without the clarity of the way of beginners. This night, he holds, is experienced by most serious Christians. Later on, there is what he calls the "dark night of the spirit." This involves not only the obscuring of faith, but, often enough, a positive, frightening, conviction of the absence of God, of the failure of hope, and drying up of charity. This night is the lot of relatively few. Since the time of St. John of the Cross, the dark nights have become associated almost exclusively with periods of trial and difficulty, of desolation and of purifying trials. St. John is the master of this interpretation, with his careful analysis of the dark night of the senses and the dark night of the spirit, and his interpretation, in which the darkness carries dread of the unknown, is by far the most general.[6]

St. Teresa Benedicta of the Cross, Edith Stein, in her *Science of the Cross*,[7] combines both views: of night as a time of peaceful seeking after God and night as mysterious and threatening. She distinguishes what she calls the cosmic night from the mystical night and then claims that there is an identity of content that entitles us to use the same name for both. It is not a relationship of likeness, but neither is it completely arbitrary. She holds that it is a relationship of *symbolic expression* such as commonly exists between the sensory and the spiritual. She shows what

---

4. "This is the true knowledge of what is sought; this is the seeing that consists in not seeing, because that which is sought transcends all knowledge, being separated on all sides by incomprehensibility as by a kind of darkness. Wherefore John the Sublime, who penetrated into the luminous darkness, says, *No one has ever seen God*, thus asserting that knowledge of the divine essence is unattainable not only by men but also any every intelligent creature." Ibid., 163.

5. St. Catherine of Siena, *Dialogue*, 25.

6. It is true that St. John does not actually identify night with desolation, because, in addition to the pains of purification, night also illumines the soul by its burning love. Nonetheless, I think it is true to say that since his time spiritual writers use night and darkness for any trial in a general sense.

7. Stein, "Cross and Night (Night of the Sense)," *The Science of the Cross*, 38–42.

she means by pointing out the way facial expressions are often said to express, or to image, spiritual characteristics.[8]

First of all, she describes the cosmic night:

> Night is invisible and formless. But still we perceive it, indeed it is nearer to us than all things and forms; it is more closely bound to our being. Just as light allows things to step forward with their visible qualities, so night *devours* them and threatens to devour us also. Whatever sinks into it is not simply nothing; it continues to exist but as indeterminate, invisible, and formless as night itself or shadowy, ghost-like, and therefore threatening.[9]

She explains that the *cloud of unknowing* of the mystics is not a simple-minded identification of natural darkness with a spiritual condition. That would be to identity the dark night with a regressive sort of stupidity, which would be less, not more, than human. Her description is very much in the Carmelite tradition:

> The *mystical night* is not to be understood in a cosmic sense. It does not impose itself on us from without but rather has its origin in the interior of the soul in whom it arises. The effects it produces, however, in the interior can be compared to those of the cosmic might: it entails the submersion of the exterior world even though outside it is bathed in bright daylight. It casts the soul into loneliness, desolation, and emptiness, stops the activity of all her faculties, frightens her by threatening horrors it conceals within itself.[10]

In addition, however, to this very effective statement of the views of St. John of the Cross, she shows the more positive aspect of the night of the senses:

> However, here there is also a *nocturnal light* that reveals a new world deep in the interior and at the same time illumines the outer world from within so that this outer is given back to us as entirely transformed.[11]

These words of the saint recall the earlier and more positive understanding of the darkness. When the visible world is no longer the focus of attention, our desire to understand our experience in the light of principles hidden from sense becomes a possibility. This longing to find the meaning of life, a meaning hidden not only from ordinary experience but also from the reach of reason itself, led Philip to the solitude

---

8. Ibid., 42.
9. Ibid., 39.
10. Ibid., 41.
11. Ibid.

and the darkness of the catacombs. Although Philip practiced great austerities during the early years in Rome, the ascetical life was no longer the focus of attention. He had fought the first rounds of the spiritual combat in a successful way, and the result of this, along with living in a state of grace and a loving familiarity with God, was a deeper need for prayer. The ascetical life and his studies led Philip to St. Catherine of Siena's "continual humble prayer,"[12] and he was drawn to the catacombs where, without distractions, he could "pursue the truth and clothe (himself) in it."[13]

Solitude, and dwelling in what St. Catherine called "the little cell of self-knowledge," is a necessary stage in the development of many people's spiritual lives. The effort to understand the meaning of a serious conversion—of who the God is who is doing the calling, of who this new self is, and what God wants of this self—these questions need time for solitude and reflection. This need to understand led Philip first of all to his studies, and then to a deeper life of prayer and solitude in the darkness of the catacombs.

The transition from a life whose focus was on the spiritual combat to one in which prayer and solitude became the principal aspects is clear in the development of Philip's own embodied mysticism. Gallonio tells us that:

> He often did the round of the Seven Churches of Rome, with no one to keep him company: these churches were the ones most distinguished for their liturgy and the indulgences granted them by the Popes. He was aware that Scripture says about a soul afire with the love of God, "I will lead her into the wilderness, and I will speak to her heart" [Hos. 2:14], and elsewhere "He will sit solitary and be silent, for she will lift herself up above herself" [Lam. 3:28].[14]

This aspect of Philip's life has justly been called eremitical. A dictionary definition of a hermit reads, "Early Christian recluse; person living in solitude,"[15] and that makes it clear that it is solitude that marks the hermit. Ponnelle and Bordet want to extend the use of the word to include those living in community:

> ...the first Capuchins...were very properly known at that time as the Franciscan "hermits"...for the "hermit," as we have described him, did not necessarily live alone, but was associated with others of

---

12. Catherine of Siena, *The Dialogue*, 25.
13. Ibid.
14. Gallonio, *The Life of Saint Philip Neri*, 6–7.
15. *The Concise Oxford Dictionary*, "hermit."

like ideas. And the greatest interest was aroused in Rome by the band of "hermits" who were to become the Capuchins.[16]

This is an interesting historical point, but not particularly helpful in explaining the usual use of the word. This extension of its use of would seem to be dictated by the fact that Philip, who did for a period of his life live in solitude, later collected a group of "others with like ideas."

In his desire for solitude, Philip spent a good deal of time in the Catacombs. Both Capecelatro and Ponnelle and Bordet stress the importance of Philip's frequenting of the catacombs at night to pray. Bacci discusses these visits, but usually in connection with other spiritual exercises of the saint, such as the pilgrimage to the seven churches and praying in the porticos of churches when he found them shut for the night.[17]

> He used to carry with him, either under his arm or in his hood, some devout book, and a roll, on which he lived all day. It was in consequence of these practices that a Dominican Friar, named F. Francesco Cardone da Camerino, master of the novices at the Minerva, used to propose him to the novices as a model of penance, and often said to them, "Philip Neri is a great Saint, and, among other wonderful things, he has dwelt for ten years in the caves of S. Sebastian in the practice of penance, and lived on bread and the roots of herbs."[18]

Gallonio does not mention the catacombs, although he does discuss the mysterious palpitation of St. Philip's heart that began during prayer in the catacombs. The catacombs, though, played a crucial role in Philip's development during this period.

One answer often given to this question of why Philip sought out the catacombs is that there his love for the early Church was nourished and may even, perhaps, have been born. Philip haunted these lonely places because, on this interpretation, he found there a more perfect image of the Church than was provided by sixteenth-century Rome. Capecelatro expresses this view in his usual lyrical way:

> ... under [the] stately Rome we see, there is another and a kindred Rome—hidden dark and underground—the Rome of the catacombs.... This subterranean Rome is a shadow of the Unseen and the

---

16. Ponnelle and Bordet, *St. Philip Neri*, 79.
17. Bacci, *The Life of Saint Philip Neri*, Vol, 1, 20.
18. " ... to attend with greater fervor to the contemplation of divine things ... he adopted the devotion of going every night to the Seven Churches, a distance of some twelve miles, and particularly to the Cemetery of San Callisto, generally called the catacombs of San Sebastian, and there he prayed for a long while." Ibid., 20.

Eternal, and in some respects surpasses in interest the Rome of which the sun reveals the majesty and splendor.[19]

The catacombs, then, are considered on this view to have been an outward and visible expression both of the Christian belief in immortality and of the unity of the Christian community, a unity that bound together the dead as well as the living. This belief in immortality, as Newman saw, was one of the appeals of Christianity in the first centuries. A twenty-first-century writer comments on this:

> One overpowering reason can be adduced for the appeal of Christianity in the third and fourth centuries: its attitude to death. Christians spoke confidently of an afterlife and of resurrection. They believed in the absolute value and the personal survival of every individual. Gradually, they enshrined that belief in the vast warren of underground cemeteries they dug around the city of Rome where the Christian dead could be laid reverently in peace. For the poor, the childless and slaves, being welcomed into this community not only in life but also in death was profoundly attractive.[20]

It should be noticed that the catacombs were not hiding places in times of persecution:

> The catacombs were never a place for the living to take refuge but they were a place where the living could gather in union with their dead in prayer and ritual meals. But above all, in an age when the Christians had few or no buildings of their own on the surface, they were an eloquent statement of the Christian understanding of death, encircling the vast, noisy, dangerous, filthy and glorious city of Rome.[21]

I suppose that Capecelatro, although he would probably have flinched from the forthright language, is allowing that one reason for Philip's frequenting the catacombs was his desire to escape from sixteenth-century Rome, which, as in earlier times, was "vast, noisy, dangerous, filthy and glorious." Philip put himself in contact with the remains of a primitive Christianity that was purer or more authentic than anything to be experienced above ground.

---

19. Capecelatro, *The Life of Saint Philip Neri*, 61.
20. Green, *Christianity in Ancient Rome*, 178. "Though Christians did not use the standard word for a graveyard, a *necropolis*, their cemeteries well suited that description. They were indeed cities of the dead, in which all slept together in a solidarity they had hoped to enjoy in life, united in a common citizenship with the dignity and order that many of them had not known in the teeming bedlam of the streets of Rome." Ibid., 186.
21. Ibid., 186.

This must have been one factor, but there was also his need for solitude. There, by himself, close to the bodies of the early Christians and of the martyrs, Philip continued to develop an understanding of realities beyond the reach of ordinary consciousness. His studies had been fuelled by a desire to understand the meaning of his conversion, and they had been the gateway to truths more fundamental than those found in experience open to sense-perception. He never denied the necessity of study, yet he began to see that even philosophy and theology pointed beyond themselves to a hidden mystery. The darkness, which hid appearances, also seemed to obscure the very intellect that had led him forward.

Solitude is the one of the notes of the illuminative way. It was a vital characteristic of Philip's early life in Rome. Yet solitude only makes sense if we realize that it has its foundation in the experience of the social. When we say we are alone, we mean in an obvious way that there is no one else around, and the only way we can say this is because we have had experience of the presence of other people. The meaning of solitude in this obvious sense is usually not even thought about. Nonetheless, this awareness of being deprived of the company of other people is important. It is important because when we begin to reflect on it, we see that our individuality, our being a person, has a foundation in the fact that there are other people from whom we are separated. At birth we are separated from our mother, and at death we are separated from everyone else, and this sort of exteriority is an essential aspect of the solitude that begins to reveal to us that we are individuals.

The process of recognizing our individuality, which is occasioned by solitude, is a painful business. Just as the need to fulfill the law of Christ brought about a spiritual combat, so the gradual awareness of individuality brings with it another sort of struggle. The experience of solitude in the illuminative way reveals man to himself as a spiritual being, but it also exposes him to the danger of regressive behavior. Withdrawing from other people, even if it brings a heightened awareness of individuality and the value of the self, opens up the danger of taking refuge in false and destructive pictures of who we are.

The idea of an interior life unrelated to everyday existence, with its ordinariness, its complexities, and confusion, is a mistaken one. Whatever Christian living is going to entail, it will require at least living in the world as it is, even if that world is a monastic one. Indeed, without this reference to existence as it really is, whatever remains of the self is of little importance. In the *Phenomenology of Spirit*, Hegel describes what he acidly calls "the beautiful soul," which:

lives in dread of besmirching the splendor of its inner being by action and an existence; and, in order to preserve the purity of its heart, it flees from contact with the actual world, and persists in its self-willed impotence to renounce its self which is reduced to the extreme of ultimate abstraction.[22]

The isolated self of the illuminative way is essential for the development of the soul towards union with God. But this self both depends for its existence on others, and it requires interaction with others for its development. Without others, it will sink into untruth and irrelevance. It is one more sign of the validity of Philip's journey towards sanctity that he realized this, in practice. The earliest tradition concerning the ascetical life insisted on the importance of living with other people for the development of the virtues. Solitude not only preserves but also intensifies the faults of those who are not subject to the correction that is brought to bear on the individual by living with others. Like a mirror, a community holds up the faults of its members, and without the reflector, it is easy to obtain a distorted view of ourselves. Cassian, for example, writes:

> For a man appears to himself to be patient and humble, just as long as he comes across nobody to interact with; but he will presently revert to his former nature, whenever the chance of any sort of passion occurs.[23]

St. Catherine of Siena develops this traditional teaching by emphasizing that without other people, we cannot be virtuous, and that our own sins affect other people. "I would have you know that every virtue of yours and every vice is put into action by means of your neighbors."[24]

> I have told you how every sin is done by means of your neighbor, because it deprives them of your loving charity, and it is charity that gives life to all virtue. So that selfish love which deprives your neighbors of your charity and affection is the principle and foundation of all evil.
>
> Every scandal, hatred, cruelty, and everything unbecoming springs from this root of selfish love. It has poisoned the whole world and sickened the mystic body of holy Church and the universal body of Christianity. For all virtues are built on charity for your neighbors. So I have told you, and such is the truth: Charity gives life to all the virtues, nor can any virtue exist without charity. In other words, virtue is attained only through love of me.[25]

---

22. Hegel, *Phenomenology of Spirit*, 400.
23. John Cassian, *Institutes of the Coenobia*, Eighth Book, xviii.
24. St. Catherine of Siena, *Dialogue*, 33.
25. Ibid., 35–36.

There is no need to think that Philip's period of solitude was the result of the spectacular sins, or the roots of these sins, that Cassian and St. Catherine describe. No doubt the punitive, re-aligning aspect of the night of the senses, which St. John of the Cross emphasizes, was an aspect of Philip's experience of the illuminative way. There was also, I think, at least at times, the night described by Edith Stein: a night that revealed a new world deep in the interior and at the same time illumined the outer world from within, so that this outer was given back to him as entirely transformed.[26] To nourish this inner darkness, he was drawn to the catacombs where, without distractions, he could seek the truth not only with his mind, but also with his whole being. Solitude is a genuine need, at least for a time, for those on the mystical road. It was his need for God, and not his past sins, that led Philip into the silence of the catacombs.

But there does remain the dangers of solitude to which Cassian and St. Catherine, not to mention Hegel, so pointedly refer. It is clear that Philip was never in any serious danger of falling into the self-deceiving state of Hegel's beautiful soul. Solitude had been necessary to help him fix his heart on the unseen God. But he never lost what I have called his worldliness, and the way his mysticism came to be expressed was in his love for other people.

The love of other people is not only a condition, or a means, to union with God. It is also the case that union with God expresses itself through the love of other people. Gregory held that the mystic is only given the graces of contemplation so that he can pass them on to others. He is essentially an instrument, a channel, a mediator. "Thus our Moses is shown as one who carries the prayers of men to God, and the graces of God to men."[27] Philip, at least in this respect of his embodied mysticism, is another Moses.[28]

If it is true that at the end of his life Philip, like Moses, was one who carried the prayers of men to God and the graces of God to men, then it would seem that the foundations of Philip's experience of the unitive way were laid at the same time as he was praying in the catacombs. The idea that the three ways of classical spirituality produce three different selves is a serious misreading of a rich and fruitful teaching. Philip's studies and his solitary prayer in the catacombs did not destroy those aspects of his self that were dominant in his days in Florence, even if

---

26. Stein, *Science of the Cross*, 41. See also Stein's discussion of the new world deep in the interior, this chapter, 176.
27. Daniélou, *Platonisme et Théologie Mystique*, 328.
28. See Part Three, Chapter Thirteen, "The Apostle of Rome."

they were placed for a time on the back burner. They were always aspects of his nature to be used in new ways when they were required.

In Philip's work for others at this period in his life, we can discern three characteristic elements of his apostolate. All three aspects can be found in the activities of his mature years, but we can see their beginning in his early life in Rome. These aspects of his apostolate were the means by which Philip, like Gregory's Moses, carried the prayers of men to God and the graces of God to men. First, there is his unstructured, freelance apostolate in the streets and workplaces of Rome, which he conducted among the young Florentines living in Rome. Second, we have his intensely personal, one-on-one encounters, of which the conversion of Prospero Crivelli is but one example. Finally, there is his often unremarked capacity for organization, as evidenced by the founding of the Confraternity of the Most Holy Trinity.

The Florentine bankers had been a powerful factor in the economy of Rome since at least the end of the fifteenth century,[29] even before the reigns of the two Medici Popes, Leo X and Clement VIII, who had patronized their fellow-countrymen and made use of their financial skills. By the time of the death of Clement in 1534, Rome could count thirty Florentine banks.

> These formed a rallying-point for the contingent of ecclesiastical dignitaries, artists, men of letters, musicians, buffoons, merchants of every kind; indeed people of all sorts, who came to Rome from the banks of the Arno.[30]

Topographically, the Florentines were gathered into a well-defined geographical area in the busiest quarter of the city.[31] Far from forgetting Florence when he left it, Philip made the Florentine section of Rome the scene of his earliest labors. Bacci describes these beginnings of Philip's work with others in a sober but impressive way:

> ...he began about the year 1538 to go about the squares, shops, schools, and sometimes even the banks, talking with all sorts of persons in a most engaging way about spiritual things. Amongst others,

---

29. "Since the end of the fifteenth century the Compagnia della Pietà, composed entirely of their nations, had given them a kind of civil status. In 1514, when it was already rich and numerous, it acquired an autonomous jurisdiction, the consulate, which as soon as he was elected (Bull of June 1515) Leo X approved and endowed with new privileges." Ponnelle and Bordet, *St. Philip Neri*, 84–85.

30. Ibid., 84.

31. "Between the Ponte Sisto and the Ponte Sant'Angelo, 'aristocracy, finance, art, business, industry were crowded together on the left bank of the Tiber, with their eyes fixed upon the other bank.'" Ibid., 85.

he exhorted young men in the warehouses to serve God, saying, "Well! My brothers, when shall we begin to do good?" and thus with his natural sweetness and wonderful power of attraction, he gradually gained such influence over them as to win them to God.[32]

This capacity to attract young men in groups and to win them over to a more Christian life—especially young Florentine men, given their age and where they came from—is something Philip retained until the end.

Capecelatro as well as Ponnelle and Bordet have extended passages on this aspect of Philip's early work. They both mention his good looks and the attraction this would have had for the young men from Florence, who had probably brought more than the commercial skills of their native city to Rome. The point to grasp here is that, explain it as you will, Philip had a phenomenal capacity to attract the young and to lead them to virtue.

But his influence was not limited to the young or to those in groups. Bacci tells us that by a "particular inspiration of God, he began to converse with men of the very worst lives, whose conversion he earnestly begged of God...."[33] The conversion of Prospero Crivelli, "a Milanese, and cashier of the principal bank of Rome,"[34] seems to have made a deep impression on Philip's contemporaries. Crivelli had a high position in the bank of the Cavalcanti, which "entered into usurious contracts,"[35] and had been refused absolution by his Jesuit confessor unless he quit his job. Understandably enough, Crivelli found he was not up to obeying his confessor, but he could not bear the thought that his sins would not be forgiven. So, having heard that Philip was a holy man, he went to him and explained his situation, and Philip spoke with him and prayed for him; shortly afterwards Crivelli broke with the occasion of sin and received absolution from his confessor.

Capecelatro, after telling that Philip spoke to Crivelli "with the most tender kindness and sweetness," says, "Would that we knew how he spoke to him!"[36] We don't know, but we know that whatever Philip said had a weight behind it that managed to pierce Crivelli's attachment to sin.

The third example of Philip's work for other people is his founding,

32. Bacci, *The Life of Saint Philip Neri*, vol. 1, 30.
33. Ibid., 31.
34. Ibid.
35. Ponnelle and Bordet, *St. Philip Neri*, 88 *ff.*
36. Capecelatro, *The Life of Saint Philip Neri*, 51. "He treated him with the most tender kindness and sweetness, uttered neither reproach nor rebuke, but strove to console him with gentle and encouraging words. Then he went on to speak to him of spiritual things, and to enkindle in his heart the holy love of God. Would that we knew how he spoke to him!"

together with F. Persiano Rosa, his confessor, of the Confraternity of the Most Holy Trinity. Bacci tells us:

> The object of this confraternity was then, as now, to receive for a few days the poor pilgrims who came daily to Rome, to visit the holy places. The institution of it took place in 1550, on occasion of the jubilee of Julius III.[37]

Philip must have had considerable organizational skills when he set his mind to use them. He started his group with about twelve or fifteen others, but the work expanded and flourished so that fifty years later, at the Jubilee of 1600, it is said that half a million poor visitors were looked after. Philip had the talent to begin a work with enough cohesion and structure to achieve immense social significance. Ponnelle and Bordet assert that:

> Philip and his companions were more intent on the mystical significance of the undertaking. In the poor they were receiving Jesus Christ, and they loaded them with tender attentions; they washed their feet and cleansed and kissed their wounds.[38]

This may very well be true, but whatever the motivation, practical skills made the ideal into a reality that was to endure for several hundred years.

In addition to his work caring for pilgrims Philip also worked in the hospital of San Giacomo, a "hospital for all the poor and the incurably ill."

> It is impossible for us to imagine realistically enough what it meant to serve in a hospital at the time... the conditions were indescribable. Nothing was known of hygiene. Of the "nurses," many were simply vagrants, when they were not outright criminals hoping to profit from their patients... serving the sick meant doing something about cleanliness, sweeping the sickroom, washing dishes, bathing patients, paying that kind of attention which everyone who is helpless needs.[39]

This hospital was of great importance in Philip's life. He himself served the sick there and later sent his companions to do the same. It is said he met St. Ignatius of Loyola and his early followers doing the same sort of service, and it is certain he worked with St. Camillus of Lellis, who was later to found an order for the care of the sick. The work was heroic, and given what we know of Philip's fastidious nature, he must

---

37. Bacci, *The Life of Saint Philip Neri*, vol. 1, 36.
38. Ponnelle and Bordet, *St. Philip Neri*, 108.
39. Türks, *Philip Neri: The Fire of Joy*, 22.

have found it particularly difficult.[40] This work was one more mark of the genuine character of his mystical journey, a journey that ended with Philip's loving his "even-Christian"[41] with God's own love.

It is clear that Philip, guided by the Holy Spirit, had an intense, sensible awareness of this growth in his love for God and neighbor. No doubt there was more to his charity than feelings, but there is also no doubt that his development was marked by intense emotions and paranormal experiences. Bacci writes:

> While he prayed he felt the incentives of divine love multiply with such power with him, and kindle such a flame in his breast, that besides continually weeping and sighing, he was often obliged, in order to moderate the fire, to throw himself on the ground, to bare his breast, and use other means to relieve his spirit which was overpowered by the impetuosity of the flame.[42]

Philip set little value on these physical phenomena of mysticism themselves, and he did his best to control them. But they are an inescapable and abiding aspect of Philip's journey. Ponnelle and Bordet write that, as astonishing as many of these experiences were, what is even more extraordinary was the continuity of the experiences during his life. They seem to have run side-by-side with Philip's normal life, "and at every moment threatened to invade it. Far from yielding himself up to it willingly, Philip fought incessantly against this invasion."[43]

These phenomena were bound up with the experience in the Catacombs on Pentecost 1544,[44] when he saw Holy Spirit as a ball of fire entering his mouth,[45] and which he then felt expanding in his breast. Ponnelle and Bordet devote twenty pages to the lifelong consequences of this experience. They conclude, after a careful reading of the sources and a meticulous collation of their findings, that Philip, after Pentecost 1544, experienced for the rest of his life most of the paranormal events associated with the physical phenomena of mysticism. Ponnelle and Bordet have no doubt as to the purpose of these phenomena. They

---

40. "St. Philip was by natural temperament of an extremely delicate sensibility amounting to fastidiousness." Capecelatro, *The Life of Saint Philip Neri*, 47.
41. That is, his fellow Christian. The expression is taken from Julian of Norwich.
42. Bacci, *The Life of Saint Philip Neri*, vol. 1, 19.
43. Ponnelle and Bordet, *St. Philip Neri*, 123.
44. See Introduction, 30–31.
45. This detail in the description is not found in the Process but was revealed by Philip's disciple Fr. Consolini, to whom Philip had confided his most intimate secrets. Out of respect for the Saint's confidence, Consolini refused to testify at the formal hearing for Philip's beatification and canonization.

think that they were given to Philip to help other people and to attest to the genuineness of what he taught. Taking the example of Philip's trembling, they write:

> Philip's emotion, whether he was praying, or discoursing upon pious subjects, or busying himself with sinners, was something quite out of the common. Everyone could see it and everyone was convinced that there was something mysterious about it. It gave the impression of a supernatural possession. This was the great reason why people placed themselves under his direction, and why they listened so eagerly to his advice. It was the sense of a divine presence when people approached him that drew to him his first disciples, and was always bringing him new ones.[46]

This judgment is in harmony with the Church's considered view on these matters. The physical phenomena of mysticism function in the same way in relation to the mystic's experience as they do in relation to prophecy. Prophets, in the Christian understanding, are not "fortune-tellers."[47]

> God appoints them rather as his messengers, spokesmen, and heralds. Again and again we read: "Go and say to this people" (Is. 6:90), "Thus says the Lord" (Am. 1:3, 6, among others). The prophets are to call the people back to obedience and justice on behalf of God; they are there to encourage and comfort them in the difficult time of the Exile.[48]

If we take St. Thomas's analysis of prophecy, we will find three elements in it that apply clearly to the mysticism of St. Philip. First, St. Thomas says there is a gift of the Holy Spirit, but it is not a permanent endowment of the prophet. It is not what the scholastics called a habitus,[49] a sort of skill that he possesses. Prophecy is a special grace clearly given and exercised for the benefit of other people. The *Catechism of the Catholic Church* describes such graces in the following way:

> There are... *special graces*, also called *charisms* after the Greek term used by St. Paul and meaning "favor," "gratuitous gift," "benefit." Whatever their character—sometimes it is extraordinary, such as the

---

46. Ponnelle and Bordet, *St. Philip Neri*, 115.
47. *The Church's Confession of Faith*, 55.
48. Ibid. On the other hand, prophecy does have to do, in part, with contingent happenings in the future. "... revelation of future events belongs most properly to prophecy." Aquinas, *Summa Theologiae*, 2a, 2ae, 171, 3.
49. See Aquinas, *Summa Theologiae*, 1a, 2ae, 68, 3. Objection 3 and its response: "Prophecy belongs to those gifts which serve to manifest the Spirit, but are not necessary for salvation," but, as the gifts are necessary for salvation and are permanent endowments of the spiritual organism, it follows that Prophecy is not such an endowment.

gift of miracles or of tongues—charisms are oriented towards sanctifying grace, and are intended for the common good of the Church. They are at the service of charity which builds up the Church.[50]

Second, the prophet has no control over the experience that is the source of his prophecy. The prophet is carried away by God[51] so that he can know what God wants him to communicate to others. Prophecy begins with this rapture, and it is one of its essential characteristics. Here again, the rapture of the prophet seems to describe Philip's experience of the Holy Spirit in the catacombs.

Finally, St. Thomas says that although the message of the prophet comes from God, it cannot be confirmed by human reason, and so "prophecy is concerned with the working of miracles, as a kind of confirmation of the prophetic utterances."[52] We can say then that, from at least one point of view, the physical phenomena of mysticism play the same role as do the miracles that accompany prophecy. The miraculous in both cases attests both to the authenticity of the prophet's message and to the genuineness of the activity that flows from the mystic's experience. In both cases, the miracles function "as a kind of confirmation."

This "kind of confirmation" was given to Philip in the darkness. But it was not given for himself, but for the sake of others. Through his studies, he had learned to seek the truth that lay veiled by sense experience. Then, through the mercy of God, he was drawn into the hidden world of the catacombs where the physical darkness both provided a refuge from the world of ordinary experience and reflected Philip's developing awareness of the God who lies beyond all affirmations. Philip's mystical journey did not end in some sort of personal satisfaction, but in his becoming a living icon, a visible channel, of the mercy of God for a sick and wounded humanity.

---

50. *Catechism of the Catholic Church*, 2003.
51. "Rapture denotes violence of a kind . . . and the violent is that which has its principle without, and in which he that suffers violence concurs not at all." Aquinas, *Summa Theologiae*, 2a, 2ae, 175, 1.
52. Aquinas, *Summa Theologiae*, 2a, 2ae, 171, 1.

PART THREE
Light from the Darkness

> If in Christ is resumed the full resources of our affirmations of God, so too in Christ are all affirmations transcended. If all creation leads to Christ and finds in Christ the perfect image of God, then Christ leads us to the Father, who is the *Deus absconditus,* hidden in the divine darkness of unknowing.
>
> Denys Turner[1]

AFTER St. Philip experienced his conversion at San Germano, he was driven to try to understand what had happened to him and what the consequences of this encounter with God would have for him. He first turned to studies and books to consolidate his knowledge of God and to learn more about the hidden Lord who lay beyond everyday appearances. During this period of learning and reflection, he began to sense that, while his studies had taught him a great deal about God, nonetheless they did not seem to put him into any closer contact with the Lord who had made himself known to him while he was still working for his uncle.

This awareness of something missing led him to an intense and solitary life of prayer. He began to pray at night in the porticos of locked churches, to make the pilgrimage of the seven Churches, and to haunt the catacombs. In the catacombs he had an overwhelming experience of the Holy Spirit. It was an experience that was the beginning of a new relationship with God, and it was also the beginning of a new relationship with other members of Christ's mystical body.

The soul is taught by solitude and the darkness that the true knowledge of God is to know, in St. Gregory's words, that "this truly is the vision of God: never to be satisfied in the desire to see him. But one must always, by looking at what he can see, rekindle his desire to see more."[2]

---

1. Turner, *The Darkness of God,* 131.
2. Gregory of Nyssa, *The Life of Moses,* paragraph 239, 116.

This is the true knowledge of what is sought; this is the seeing that consists in not seeing, because that which is sought transcends all knowledge, being separated on all sides by incomprehensibility as by a kind of darkness.[3]

The soul now discovers that to find God is to seek him without end, and "that to follow God wherever he might lead is to behold God."[4] The following of God consists in constantly going on with the soul's quest to see God, and the determination to remain unsatisfied with, and to reject, any image or any concept that the soul might be tempted to identify as an experience of God.

Gregory maintains that what is experienced in the darkness is the grace of Christ as conveyed by the sacraments. The darkness is not a cover for a flight from the world. On the contrary, the dark knowledge of God leads back to the wounded and suffering world of everyday life.

> Certes, toute l'oeuvre de Grégoire de Nysse est soulevée d'un ardent désir de Dieu. Mais ces biens spirituels, l'âme n'en est pas avare, elle désire ardemment les communiquer... L'image qu'il nous propose n'est pas celle du solitaire fuyant l'humanité pour assurer sa tranquillité personnelle. Les figures centrales de son œuvre sont entourées de tout un peuple et animées d'un mouvement continuel, d'une sorte de flux et de reflux, de contemplation et d'apostolat.
>
> (Of course it is true that all of Gregory's work is borne up by an ardent desire for God. But the soul is not a miser about these spiritual goods, and it passionately wants to share them... the image he puts in front of us is not that of a solitary running away from humanity to obtain his own personal peace of mind. The important people in his work are all surrounded by other people and motivated by a continual movement of a kind of flux and reflux between contemplation and the apostolate.)[5]

This interior, and radically personal, encounter with the grace of Christ in the darkness is united in an essential way with the Mystical Body of Christ. This union is expressed, and it is made possible, by Christ's sacrament of love, the Holy Eucharist. The third way is not the history of an isolated, disembodied spirit becoming united with an unknown God. It is rather the account of how men of flesh and blood are prepared and sustained for union in the darkness with the hidden God. In the Eucharist we partake of the body and blood of Christ and so become sharers in the divine nature of him who shared our humanity. This sac-

---

3. Ibid., paragraph 163, 95.
4. Ibid., paragraph 252, 119.
5. Daniélou, *Platonisme et Théologie Mystique*, 332.

ramental interchange shows us the dependence of the mystical life on the objective aspect of Christ's action through the sacraments.[6] Furthermore, the very possibility of the sacraments requires Christ's mystical body, which is the Church.

Philip gave himself over to the action of God in the dark night of faith. God then used Philip as his instrument to help bind up the wounds of a suffering humanity. Philip himself believed that his own experience of "knowing nothing among you except Jesus Christ and him crucified"[7] was best shared with others through the sacramental life of the Church. For all the desire that he had for union with the unknown God, it remains true that his means of access to Christ was through the Church, the Church that is the mystical body of Jesus Christ and the custodian of his sacraments. Philip approached his Maker in the company of the holy people of God, and he brought back to them what he had learned in the darkness. It was written of Philip that from his "burning love of God there sprang up in his breast the most ardent longings of charity towards his neighbor . . . his fervent zeal never grew weary of laboring for the conversion of souls."[8] It was the Church's message, and it was in union with the visible Church, that he did his work. In practical terms, this meant an apostolate that was centered on the sacraments. It was in the holiness of beauty, and not only in the beauty of holiness, that real men and women could best be led to Christ.

---

6. "L'action sacramentelle marque ainsi la dépendance de la vie mystique a l'égard de l'action objective du Christ. Elle est la source normale de la mystique catholique qui est transformation de l'âme et du corps du chrétien a l'âme et au corps du Christ." Daniélou, *Platonisme et Théologie Mystique*, 260.

7. 1 Corinthians 2:2.

8. Bacci, *The Life of Saint Philip Neri*, vol. 1, 183.

9

The Darkness of God

Do you know when people really become spiritual? It is when they become slaves of God and are branded with his sign, which is the sign of the Cross, in token of which they have given him their freedom.

St. Teresa of Avila[1]

(Faith), which is a black and dark cloud to the soul (and likewise is night, since in the presence of faith the soul is deprived of its natural light and is blinded), can with its darkness give light and illumination to the darkness of the soul. . . .

St. John of the Cross[2]

PHILIP'S spiritual state by the time he was ordained, in 1551, is well described by Gregory of Nyssa's third way. We saw that the illuminative way leads to an increasing awareness of the indwelling of God within us, but the more the soul makes progress, the more it discovers that God constantly escapes our efforts to understand him or to experience him in any direct way. At this point, the cloud becomes a permanent aspect of the soul's relationship with God. The knowledge of God, in this third way, is knowledge in the darkness.

This new relationship to God is not a static or a finished one; the third way is a journey. There is, at the same time, an awareness of the action of God and our own striving after God. Yet neither the action of God, nor our striving after God, is fixed and repeated. On the contrary, the sense of the presence of God, and our response to the presence, is always new. It is here that Gregory's doctrine of what Daniélou calls *epektasis* is of such importance. *Epektasis* is Gregory's expression for his conviction that perfection consists in a continual striving after transfor-

---

1. St. Teresa of Avila, *The Interior Castle*, book VII, chapter iv, *Complete Works*, 346.
2. St. John of the Cross, *Ascent of Mount Carmel*, Book II, Chapter III, 5, *Complete Works*, vol. 1, 69.

mation into the likeness of God in Christ. I have said that this stretching towards what is ahead, and the sense of zest and excitement that this passage conveys, fits very well with Philip's own journey into God.[3]

Philip's spiritual condition, after his experience of the Holy Spirit at Pentecost 1544, may be described as follows:

1. *There was a deep awareness of the darkness of God.* We have already seen that darkness is one of those ambivalent metaphors that can convey either a comforting solitude in which the spirit finds refreshment and opportunity for reflection, or, on the other hand, vague threats or even the source of active terror. Yet ambivalent or not, darkness is one of those metaphors that have always been used by Christians to describe aspects of our awareness of God.[4] It is has no necessary connection with either transcendence or immanence; it is darkness. In all this, Gregory is stating a doctrine that St. John of the Cross, in more modern times, was to make particularly his own. For St. Gregory and for St. John, the term "darkness" expresses the truth that the divine essence remains inaccessible (in this life) even to the mind that has been enlightened by grace. It is the awareness of this inaccessibility that constitutes the highest form of contemplation.

This awareness of the darkness of God was not a static condition, but one that Gregory of Nyssa described as a constant seeking.

2. *This new awareness was brought about by a painful deconstruction of the ascetical soul in favor of a growing sense of the divine agency.* It is not only our awareness of God that changes as we stretch forward to what is ahead; the soul itself is also recast in a radical way. In its striving, and through the trials and difficulties of living in the darkness of faith, the self becomes more sensitive to the action of God. The recognition of this action of God finally becomes the dominant factor in the Christian's experience. With St. Paul, he says, "it is no longer I who live, but Christ who lives in me."[5]

---

3. Gregory's doctrine is based on Philippians 3:11–14, where St. Paul writes: "Not that I have already obtained this or am already perfect . . . but one thing I do, forgetting what lies behind and straining forward to what lies ahead, I press on toward the goal for the prize of the upward call of God in Christ Jesus." See Introduction, "An Embodied Mysticism," 44*ff.*

4. "The metaphors—of 'interiority,' of 'ascent,' of 'light and darkness' and of 'oneness with God'—appear to have occupied a central role in the description of the Christian ways of spirituality for as long as Christians have attempted to give one. And they still do." Turner, *The Darkness of God*, Introduction, 1.

5. Galatians 2:20.

This belief—that the soul is no longer its own master in the way it once thought it was—requires a rethinking of our usual view of the self. We tend to think we have a clear awareness of, or privileged access to, our own personal identity. We then go on to build our knowledge of everything else on this primary awareness of who we are, or at least who we think we are. This fundamentally Cartesian view of the self and its knowledge is false, and it is an obstacle to understanding just how radical the tradition of Catholic mysticism really is.

3. *This awareness of the divine agency was manifested in the sacramental life of the Church.* The living awareness of the inaccessibility of God is an encounter with the grace of Christ, or the effects of that grace, conveyed by the sacraments. For Gregory, interiority is a deepening of the grace of Christ received in Baptism. This grace is then strengthened and deepened by the Eucharist, which is both the sign and the cause of our union with God and with each other. The darkness of the third way is not so much a deeper knowledge of the self as it is an awareness of the presence of God in the mystical body of Christ, that mystical body of Christ which is the Church.[6]

☩

The threshold of the third way, according to St. John of the Cross, is a period of intense suffering. During the first darkness, which Philip experienced in San Germano and in the early years in Rome, the darkness was a friendly darkness. Its function was to cast a shadow over the world of ordinary experience and accustom Philip to look for the meaning of life in his studies and books. Philip's studies went hand-in-hand with his prayer in the quiet of the catacombs and the porches of the silent churches in the night. Then things changed. The darkness, which had provided the setting for his peaceful prayer as well as the light provided by his studies, gave way to a violent darkness that destroyed his peaceful walk with God. This new element in Philip's prayer culminated in the overwhelming experience of the Holy Spirit that changed both his prayer and his body for the rest of his life.[7]

---

6. Cardinal Daniélou expressed this in a difficult, but important, couple of sentences: "What he finds on entering into himself is the communication made by God to him of his own supernatural life. And thus the aspect of interiority, the immanence of the spiritual life, joins up with the sacramental aspect, transcendence." Daniélou, *Platonisme et Théologie Mystique*, 48 (author's translation).

7. St. John of the Cross describes this transition from the illuminative way, with its light and darkness, to the unitive way as something sudden. This fits in well with Philip's

St. John of the Cross calls this "inflowing of God into the soul" a "dark night," which both purges and instructs it at the same time.[8] It is usually the purgative aspect of this "inflowing" that is emphasized. Certainly, this aspect of the matter does play a central role in St. John's thinking, as the dark night of the soul "purges it from its ignorances and imperfections, habitual, natural and spiritual."[9] This darkness, St. John goes on to say, is not only night and darkness for the soul, but is "likewise affliction and torment."[10] The soul is thrown into darkness and confusion, and it feels that is has been abandoned by God.[11] In addition, there is a sense of being deprived of all goods, whether they be temporal, natural, or spiritual, and coupled with this sense of deprivation there is a terrible sense of isolation. This makes it impossible for anyone else to help the person who is really suffering in this way. He does not believe anyone else has ever suffered quite the way he is suffering, and so he doubts the ability of anyone else to help or understand him. Not unnaturally, this condition results in an apparent destruction of the spiritual life. The soul:

> ...is unable to raise its affection or its mind to God, neither can it pray to him, thinking, as Jeremiah thought concerning himself, that God has set a cloud before it through which its prayer cannot pass.[12]

But the trials and difficulties of the contemplative life "instruct" as well as purify the soul. The instruction of the dark night is the establishment of the Fatherhood of God over the individual soul. The purpose of the realization of God's Fatherhood is not so that we may be dominated

---

experience in the Catacombs. "When they are going about these spiritual exercises with the greatest delight and pleasure, and when they believe the sun of Divine favor is shining most brightly upon them, God turns all this light of theirs into darkness, and shuts against them the door and the source of the sweet spiritual water which they were tasting in God whensoever and for as long as they desired." St. John of the Cross, *Dark Night of the Soul*, I, VII, 3, 350.

8. St. John of the Cross, *Dark Night of the Soul*, II, V, 1, 381.

9. Ibid., II, V, 1, 381.

10. Ibid., 11, V, 2, 381.

11. "But what the sorrowful soul feels most in this condition is its clear perception, as it thinks, that God has abandoned it, and, in his abhorrence of it, has flung it into darkness; it is a grave and piteous grief for it to believe that God has forsaken it.... when this purgative contemplation is most severe, the soul feels very keenly the shadow of death and the lamentations of death and the pains of hell, which consist in its feeling itself to be without God, and chastised and cast out, and unworthy of him, and it feels that he is wroth with it. All this is felt by the soul in this condition—yea and more, for it believes that it is so with it for ever." St. John of the Cross, *Dark Night of the Soul*, II, VI, 2, 385.

12. St. John of the Cross, *Dark Night of the Soul*, II, VIII, 1, 393.

or humiliated, but so that we can begin here and now to live the life of God himself. The relationship through which the Father eternally engenders the Son is meant to be reproduced in each individual. When this condition is brought about, the soul is now no longer self-determining in its love, because is it "not through itself ... (but) through the holy Spirit" that it loves.

> The soul now loves God, not through itself, but through Himself; which is a wondrous brightness, since it loves through the Holy Spirit, even as the Father and the Son love One Another, as the Son Himself says, in St. John: "May the love wherewith Thou hast loved Me be in them and I in them."[13]

This breaking down of the self-directed ascetical self through a series of deeper and increasingly painful experiences must not be thought of as just one more ascetical exercise.[14] The darkness reduces the soul to a state where God is able to take it over. The whole thrust of St. John's analysis is to establish the principle both that the self gradually loses control over the direction of its own spiritual life and that, finally, the isolated, self-determining self is replaced by a condition in which God's action dominates the life of the individual. This is not a matter of recognizing the reality of divine providence in a philosophical way. What St. John wants us to understand is that thinking about God, trying to do what God wants, and the efforts to love God, are replaced by the lived experience of God acting in and through the individual.

In the last book of the *Interior Castle*, St. Teresa traces this final reconstruction of the ascetical self, which ends in what she calls a spiritual marriage. The suffering described by St. John of the Cross has broken down the obstacles to a union between the will of the individual and the will of God. In other words, there is an identity of purpose between the soul, which has been purified by God, and the divine will. This union, however, leaves the identity of the human will intact:

> We might say that union is as if the ends of two wax candles were joined so that the light they give is one: the wicks and the wax and the light are all one; yet afterwards the one candle can be perfectly well separated from the other and the candles become two again, or the wick may be withdrawn from wax.[15]

---

13. St. John of the Cross, *Living Flame of Love* (second redaction), III, 82, 393.
14. See Denys Turner, "John of the Cross: the dark nights and depression," *The Darkness of God*, where, in a masterly fashion, Turner describes St. John's analysis of this dismemberment of the ascetical self.
15. Teresa of Jesus, *Interior Castle* VII, ii, *Complete Works*, 335.

It is clear from this passage that Teresa thinks that it is only temporarily that the individual soul is "submerged" in, or identified with, the will of God.[16] In the spiritual marriage, however, the element of discrete identities, which maintain themselves, disappears:

> ... here it is like the rain falling from the heavens into a river or a spring; there is nothing but water there and it is impossible to divide or separate the water belonging to the river from that which fell from the heavens.[17]

I want now to show how the role of suffering in the development of the spiritual life, as understood by St. John and St. Teresa, worked itself out in Philip's case. When Philip was first ordained, he went to live at San Girolamo della Carità, where he lived in a loosely knit community with a group of other secular clergy, among whom there "were several distinguished priests ... who were pious and devout...."[18] At San Girolamo, he was harassed for several years—Gallonio says persecuted—by two sacristans in everything that concerned the celebration of Mass. The sacristans "were two priests, men of depraved morals, who had abandoned their religious orders ... [and] began to persecute Philip, in the year 1552."[19]

> ... when they knew that Philip was heading for the sacristy, with the intention of celebrating Mass, they ... sometimes blocked his access to the place; or if he had got in, they used various means to obstruct him. To force him to leave without celebrating, they would sometimes hide the Missal, or the priestly vestments, or even his own Chalice; not stopping there, they would often order him to unvest after he was all prepared for the Sacrifice and was stepping out of the sacristy....[20]

It is difficult to think of a trial which could have affected Philip more. Even at this early stage in his priestly life, he already showed signs of the extraordinary devotion and absorption in the saying of Mass that always characterized him. In fact, at the end of his life, the intensity of his devotion forced him to give up saying Mass in public. The active hostility that surrounded him every time he celebrated the Eucharist, and the efforts to destroy his recollection and even to actively impede him, must have been extraordinarily hard to bear.

---

16. "... by union is meant the joining of two things into one, each of the two, as is a matter of common observation, can be separated and remain a thing by itself." Ibid.
17. Ibid.
18. Gallonio, *The Life of Saint Philip Neri*, 28, 21.
19. That is, in the year after his ordination.
20. Gallonio, *The Life of Saint Philip Neri*, 35, 29.

In the end, Philip's gentleness and patience brought the two sacristans to repentance, but not before Philip had learned some lessons himself. He prayed constantly for patience under the attacks, and he thought his prayer was left unheard. But, one day at Mass, an inner voice said to him:

> Why do you ask me for patience, Philip? I will strengthen you with patience, but my wish is for you to strive as hard as you can to acquire it by means of these attacks.[21]

Clearly, then, Philip had not left behind fighting sin and establishing the virtues. This shows us that the *ways* or the *studia* of the spiritual life are built on the preceding ones as foundations, and like all foundations they need to be kept in repair. On the other hand, the suffering involved in Philip's saying Mass were not self-imposed, but accepted as the will of God, which he could not change. The only way even a Philip Neri could escape the self-constructed prison of the ascetical self was by accepting a love that was given to him in mercy, a love he did not and could not control. The development of patience and perseverance, which was the outcome of the experiences with the two sacristans, was the means God took to furnish Philip with the strength required for the harsher trials that were in store for him.

The troubles with the two sacristans were in the earliest years of Philip's priesthood and lasted for about two years, probably from 1552 until 1554. These years also marked the consolidation and expansion of the apostolic work he had begun as a layman. The visits to the sick in the hospitals, the strengthening of the work with pilgrims, the Oratory itself, and the visits to the seven Churches: all these initiatives grew and flourished under Philip's guidance. By the end of the pontificate of Paul IV, in 1559, it has been estimated that between two and three thousand people took part in the pilgrimage to the seven churches. At the same period, the first Index of Forbidden Books was being prepared, and there was a move to include all the works of Savonarola in the list. The Dominicans at the Minerva spearheaded the opposition to the move, and Philip was involved in their efforts. Finally, the talks at the Oratory and the exercises associated with it were increasingly successful and well attended. Philip's very varied apostolate, for better or for worse, was no longer an unimportant work on the sidelines. This prominence brought about the second great trial in Philip's spiritual development.

The "terrible Paul IV," as Ponnelle and Bordet call him,[22] was a ruth-

---

21. Gallonio, *The Life of Saint Philip Neri*, 35, 30.
22. Ponnelle and Bordet, *St. Philip Neri*, 191.

less, high-minded reformer of pitiless severity.[23] He was afraid of no one, and, what is more to the point here, he trusted no one. He imprisoned cardinals;[24] he had no desire to reconvene the Council of Trent, which he seems to have regarded as a useless talk-shop.[25] Consultation with anyone about anything became more and more an anathema to him. The atmosphere in Rome was oppressive and threatening. Philip and the Oratory became the center of a very different approach to reform.

> With the accession of Paul IV, Philip became, in contrast to him, the man of the moment; he became so by reason of his lovable character, in proportion as the Pope showed himself intolerant and severe. He was the very man to free the reform to which all men of all sorts had to submit, whether they liked it or not, from its repellent aspects and make it attractive.[26]

The Pope, however, was not interested in other modes or models of reform, and, given his character and his history, it was inevitable that both Philip and his work were viewed with suspicion and finally with outright hostility. By the end of the pontificate, the Pope had quarreled even with his nephews, in whom he had unwisely, and uncharacteristically, put his trust. During the last months of his reign, the Pope carried out a reign of terror, and the executive officer of the new rigorism was

---

23. "Even more than in his measures for reform, Paul IV displayed, in his attacks on those who deviated from the true faith, that pitiless severity and impetuous violence which were characteristic of all his actions.... He proceeded methodically and according to plan, displaying in so doing, a severity that no less a person than the celebrated Augustinian, Seripando, has described as inhuman." Pastor, *The History of the Popes from the Close of the Middle Ages*, vol. 14, 259–260.

24. "The first moments of his reign were filled with rigorous measures. In August, 1555, there came the imprisonment of the grand treasurer, Francesco d'Aspra, of Michelangelo Spada, the confidant of Julius III, of Cardinal Santa Fiora and his secretary Francesco Lottini, of Camillo Colonna, Ascanio della Corgna, and Guiliano Cesarini, the brother of the Cardinal of the same name." Ponnelle and Bordet, *St. Philip Neri*, 194. By the end of his reign Cardinal Pole had been stripped of his Legatine Powers in England and ordered back to Rome, and Cardinal Morone, who had been a Legate at Trent was in the Castel San Angelo. There is a terrifying portrait of the Pope's treatment of Cardinal Pole in Fenlon, *Heresy and Obedience in Tridentine Italy: Cardinal Pole and the Counter-Reformation*, 276 ff.

25. "There had already been conferences, discussions and decisions concerning ecclesiastical affairs on the most extensive scale, and it seemed to the practical sense of Paul IV that the moment had now come to take the work in hand. He was therefore, from the first, not inclined to continue the Council...." Pastor, *The History of the Popes from the Close of the Middle Ages*, vol. 14, 177.

26. Ponnelle and Bordet, *St. Philip Neri*, 192.

The Darkness of God   203

Cardinal Virgilio Rosario, who was a man cast in the same mold as that of his master, the Pope. In Lent 1559, he forbade the pilgrimage to the Seven Churches,[27] and Philip was subjected to "endless enquiries, the constant burden of which was the formidable charge of fomenting a sect and of holding 'conventicles,'"[28] and it was even reported that Philip had been placed under arrest.

> ... in the course of a terrible scene he was treated as a proud and ambitious man and as the introducer of novelties, and in the end Rosario, pending fuller information, forbade him, at one and the same time, the pilgrimage to the Seven Churches, the Oratory, and confessional. This meant the destruction of all that he had done, and Philip lived through hours of anguish.[29]

Philip acted with complete obedience and even refused to listen to talk against Cardinal Rosario and his party. A few weeks later, in May, the Cardinal died unexpectedly on his way to an audience with the Pope, and, with Rosario dead, the Pope seems to have let the matter drop. The Pope himself had not much longer to live and died in August.

The tale of Philip's way of dealing with his painful experiences under Paul IV is usually adduced as a sign of Philip's great sanctity. This is entirely appropriate, because it is in fact just that: evidence of heroic virtue. On the other hand, many of the accounts do not seem to convey much sense of the very real danger Philip was exposed to personally, nor of how the months of suspicion and distrust by the highest authorities in the Church really affected him. Capecelatro seems to have understood the danger, and he writes:

> Everyone in Rome began to talk about Philip; many judged him unfavorably, and he was everywhere spoken against. The tide was rising; the waves grew into billows white with foam; and our dear saint stood without shelter in the unpitying storm ... they declared that Philip was a sower of scandals and of evil seed; and that he ought to be dealt with as a teacher of new doctrines and a *setter-up* of a *new sect* ... and when we think of Paul IV, and of the sensitiveness and activity of the Inquisition, we begin to tremble for our saint; great trials are surely

---

27. "Rosario feared the danger that might arise from these gatherings in the case of a popular disturbance, the more so as among them were to be found a number of gentlemen belonging to families hostile to the Carafa, as, for example the Massimi and the followers of Santa Fiora himself. Such fears were by no means chimerical, as was seen several months later at the events which followed the death of the Pope." Ibid., 230.
28. Ibid.
29. Ibid.

coming on him, and if they do not crush him, it will be that the loving providence of God rebukes and quells the storm.[30]

Capecelatro then goes on to describe how the distrust and persecution of the ecclesiastical authorities must have affected Philip. This account has the merit of making it clear the very real personal danger of Philip's situation and the anguish the apparent destruction of his life's work must have cost him.

> We can scarcely imagine the anguish of Philip's heart during this trial. It is hard to bear the sorrows that come on us from our own corrupted nature, and perhaps harder still to bear those laid on us by ignorant and corrupt men. But no sorrows are so keen as those inflicted on us by persons who are to us the representatives of God and his justice, and whom we therefore respect and love. To feel oneself despised by the good, when all the aim of our life is to do good; to be condemned by the ministers of God's truth and justice, when all our life is a sacrifice of self to justice and truth—this is indeed a keen and unutterable sorrow, and only he who has felt it knows how hard it is to bear.[31]

There is, however, another understanding of Philip's reaction to his trials. It is an understanding, moreover, that goes back to the earliest sources and leaves us with the sense that Philip rose above the dangers and the heartbreak in a way that allowed him to see clearly that he was suffering for and with Christ. Philip's reaction to his trials, so this view insinuates, was in no way destructive of some sort of inner citadel of self-possession and inner strength. This clear certainty, it is claimed, protected Philip in some fundamental way, and so he remained in peace and tranquillity. Gallonio writes that Philip received Rosario's prohibition to hear confessions, to continue the work of the Oratory, and to go on with the pilgrimage to the Seven Churches, "with a cheerful countenance."[32] Bacci says that after Rosario's accusation that Philip was trying to set up a party, "Philip turned to a crucifix that was there, and said, 'Lord, Thou knowest if what I do is to make myself head of a party, or for Thy service'; and then went away."[33]

It is true that one of the marks of Philip's character that is always noted is his joyful, apparently carefree nature. Capecelatro voices this common theme:

---

30. Capecelatro, *The Life of Saint Philip Neri*, 151.
31. Ibid., 152–153.
32. Gallonio, *The Life of Saint Philip Neri*, 76, 62.
33. Bacci, *The Life of Saint Philip Neri*, vol. 1, 98.

> ...Philip was always cheerful and even gay; his heart was never clouded with morbid melancholy, but bright with a serene and sunny gladness.[34]

It may be the case that Philip's heart was never clouded with "morbid melancholy," but the rest of the passage is one more example of that sort of hyperbole which eviscerates the human dimension from the virtues of the saints. We found the same exaggeration in discussing Philip's chastity. The virtues of the saints are the virtues of human beings, and language that obscures this clouds our understanding both of the virtues themselves and of the saints who possessed them. The extraordinary joy that so impressed Philip's contemporaries was indeed a dominant feature of his formed character, but it was not won without a struggle. It is unreal to think that Philip never suffered in any sort of real way. The saints are not exempt from the pain that comes from what Newman called "loosening" ourselves from the world.[35]

> No one can have his heart cut away from the natural objects of its love, without pain during the process and throbbings afterwards. This is plain from the nature of the case; and, however true it be, that this or that teacher may be harsh or repulsive, yet he cannot materially alter things.[36]

Newman was preaching here about the hard beginnings of the First Way. But St. John of the Cross has shown that these hard beginnings are only a foretaste of what is to come as the pretensions of the ascetical self are gradually worn away. The principle that the joy of the saints is never obtained without suffering, suffering that is both exterior and interior, was a real aspect of Philip's mystical journey.

In saying that Philip's joyfulness was the joyfulness of a human being and that it was obtained, and then maintained, only with a struggle, I am not trying either to depreciate its value or to deny that it marked his character in an extraordinary way. I do, though, want to insist that its source was supernatural in origin. In later life, Philip always insisted that a natural cheerfulness was the best foundation for the Christian life, and he said that: "The cheerful are much easier to guide in the spiritual life than the melancholy," and also that "excessive sadness seldom springs from any other source than pride."[37] There is every reason to think that

---

34. Capecelatro, *The Life of Saint Philip Neri*, 247.
35. Newman, "The Immortality of the Soul," *Parochial and Plain Sermons*, 19.
36. Ibid. Newman continues: "Let us then, seriously question ourselves, and beg of God grace to do so honestly, whether we are loosened from the world...."
37. Neri, *Maxims and Counsels*, for April 21 and 24.

Philip was of a naturally cheerful disposition. On the other hand, an outgoing and lively nature is not identical with Christian joy. Philip's joy that seems to have cast such a spell over his contemporaries may have been based on nature, but its pervasive impact was the work of the Holy Spirit, the Holy Spirit that began to live in Philip from the time of his baptism. St. Paul tells us that joy is one of the fruits of the Holy Spirit,[38] and St. Thomas says that a fruit is something that proceeds from a principle as from a seed or root.[39] Philip's joy, then, may have been built on a naturally cheerful temperament, but its capacity to draw men to God came from the Holy Spirit "as from a seed or root."[40] The gifts of the Holy Spirit make their home in human beings, and they help to recast the nature of those who receive them. On the other hand, they do not take the place of the human nature in which they find their home, and a human nature incapable of suffering is no Christian concept.

There are two pieces of evidence that suggest that Philip's experience in his periods of trial is better described by St. John of the Cross, in his treatment of the Dark Night of the Spirit, than by the picture painted by the early biographers or Capecelatro. The first of these indicators is a report, by Giacomo Crescenzi,[41] of Philip's distress at another trial that happened later in his life. The source of Crescenzi's account is one of Philip's first Oratorians, Father Giovanni Antonio Lucci.[42] The second piece of evidence is a brief letter from St. Catherine de' Ricci to Philip, which suggests that Philip's soul was not always the garden of peace and tranquillity which tradition ascribes to it.

Giovanni Antonio Lucci is reported to have said that one summer day Philip came to his room, immediately after dinner, and took him for a walk. Philip went at such a furious pace that his companion could not keep up with him. After they arrived at St. Peter's, Philip began to pray, "kneeling on a bench that was four paces in length and very heavy,

---

38. "But the fruit of the Holy Spirit is love, joy, peace, patience, kindness, goodness, faithfulness, gentleness, self-control...." Galatians 5:23.

39. Aquinas, *Summa Theologiae*, 1a, 2ae, 70.3: "Are the fruits suitably enumerated in Galatians 5:22?"

40. "Since a fruit is something which proceeds from a principle as from a seed or root, the division of these twelve Fruits may be considered in the light of the various ways in which the Holy Spirit proceeds within us." Ibid.

41. In one of his depositions to the process for the canonization, November 15, 1595. Della Rocchetta and Vian, *Il Primo Processo per San Filippo Neri*, vol. 1, 364.

42. Crescenzi says that Lucci told him that Philip came to his room at San Giovanni dei Fiorentini, and the Oratorians did not take over this Church until 1564. Ponnelle and Bordet think the incident refers to Philip's difficulties under Pius V, in about 1567.

which his emotion caused to shake." The two then left St. Peter's and went on to another Church, where Philip burst out and told Lucci all he was suffering, although Lucci did not tell Crescenzi anything about its nature.[43]

Near the end of his life, in 1587 or 1588, St. Catherine de' Ricci, the Prioress of the Dominican Convent in Prato, wrote a letter to Philip in which she tells him not to be afraid of death, and that it is unthinkable that anyone who has done as much for God as he had done should not be saved.[44] Philip's letter to Catherine is lost, but it sounds as though he must have been asking for consolation and support; certainly not giving it. At very least, his letter can hardly have breathed the imperturbable peace that is usually ascribed to him.

The trials and obstacles St. Philip encountered were real and dangerous, and the suffering they caused raked the center of his being. St. John of the Cross and St. Teresa have shown how such suffering is the pathway to a condition where the mystic begins to love God with God's own love, and also, in that love, to lose oneself in the love for other people. The end, or purpose, of an embodied mysticism is to love the Lord and neighbor as oneself; not as an ascetical practice or as effort to obey a precept, but with God's own love.

The great difficulty in accepting, or even understanding, what John and St. Teresa are writing about is not so much in what they say, but in the intellectual baggage we bring to their teaching. For we all bring a Cartesian view about reality when we begin to talk about the nature of the self and its relation to God. But the Cartesian view of the self really is

---

43. "...havendo il p. Filippo molte tribulationi, ando a S. Giovanni de Fiorentini, per piglir uno de quelli padri in compagnia sua. Et, arrivato alla camera di m.s. Giovanni Antonio, (Lucci)...le disse 'vien con me', ci ando. Et il padre se avvio verso S Pieto et verso il ponte di Sant'Angelo, et caminava tanto in furia, che m.s Giovanni Antonio no lo poteve seguitare: et questo era di estate, subbito doppo mangiare. Arrivato a S. Pietro, il p. m.s Filippo se pose a fare oratione avanti il Volto Santo, sopra un banco lungo quattro canne, assai grosso, et che lo faceva tutto tremare; et m.s. Giovanni Antonio osservava tutte queste cose et stave maravigliato.... Nel tornare, il padre...li racconto tutte le tribulationi che haveva (quale m. s. Giovanni Antonnio non me le disse)...." Della Rocchetta and Vian, *Il Primo Processo per San Filippo Neri*, vol. 1, 364–365.

44. "Viva pure spensierata perquanto rigurada la sua morte, perche a un servo fedele, come lei e stato. Per tutto il tempo della sua vita, Dio che e guitissimo non potra negare il premio de Paradiso." (Live without concern about your death, because God who is supremely just cannot deny the reward of Paradise to a faithful servant such as yourself who has served him all his life.) Anodal, *Santa Caterina de'Ricci*, 266 (author's translation).

incompatible with a serious attempt to understand mystical theology. This is because Cartesianism is the epistemological and metaphysical counterpart of the exaltation of the ascetical self, whose pathology was so clearly outlined by St. Teresa and St. John of the Cross.

The two Carmelite Doctors taught that over-confidence in the achievements of the ascetical self is the root cause of hypocrisy and self-deception. But an even greater malice of this overconfidence is the road jam it sets up on the journey towards the unitive way. It is only when confidence in the ascetical self is left behind, usually forcibly by the action of God, that God can begin first to reshape the soul, and then, finally, to make it a direct instrument of his providence. And it is only when we give up the distorted modern view of the self that the embodied mysticism of the Church can be presented in a coherent way.

We have seen that the self, when left to its own resources, is incapable of finally escaping from its own spiritual egoism. In its efforts to conform itself to the law of God, it builds up a self which may, in fact, represent a considerable human and Christian achievement. Still, the self remains a private citadel, which, having repulsed the grosser and more obvious sort of sin, is all the more vulnerable to the sins of the spirit.[45] It would seem that the dark night of the senses of the "good Philip" of the years in Florence and at San Germano was relatively mild. On the other hand, although we do not know a great deal, we do know enough to be sure that the picture of the Philip whose inner life was always serene and happy is a false one. The darkness of the Catacombs and his suffering in Rome both point to a series of encounters with the darkness described by John of the Cross as the Dark Night of the Spirit.

It is not clear, however, what is left of the individual once the dark night of the spirit has done its work. The deconstruction of the ascetical self may leave the way open to a union with God, but how are we to understand this union from the point of view of the individual who is united with God? St. John's analysis traces in a masterly way the destruction of the hard core in each one of us that repels what I have called the takeover by God. On the other hand, once this hard core has been dismantled, what is left?

The question can't be answered in the way it is asked, for two reasons. In the first place, St. John of the Cross leaves out an important part of the soul's approach to God. He has no discussion of the fact that the Catholic mystic is related to God not as an isolated individual, but as a member of the mystical body of Christ. It is not that he says anything

---

45. See Part Two, Chapter One, "San Germano," 148*ff*.

wrong, but he does not say enough. Again, secondly, the way the question is asked assumes an inadequate modern view of the self. This view looks on the self as a fixed, isolated unit, which is already formed and is essentially untouched by its relations to other people or other things.

Von Balthasar puts the first difficulty very clearly. There is, he says, "a remarkable lacuna in St. John's thought, the yawning gap where the Church should be."

> Where, in the whole of John's work, is the neighbor? Where is the communion of saints? Where is the Johannine criterion for love of God: love of the brother?[46]

Whether, in the final analysis, this criticism about St. John can be sustained might be questioned. On the other hand, it certainly does give expression to the suspicion that the spiritual life is essentially a selfish one: selfish because it is an isolated and introverted cultivation of the self that has no interest in or concern for other people. What is more to our interest here, though, is that in this failure to discuss the other members of Christ's body, St. John leaves the way open for a false idea of the self to take root. This false idea of the self effectively blocks the way to understanding the embodied mysticism of St. Philip, or of any other Catholic mystic. It is in Christ's body, which is the Church, that Catholic mysticism is embodied:

> For just as the body is one and has many members, and all the members of the body, though many, are one body, so it is with Christ. For by one Spirit we were all baptized into one body—Jews or Greeks, slaves or free—and all were made to drink of one Spirit.[47]

Christ's body, the Church, is a pre-existing reality into which individuals are baptized and so receive their identity and function as Christians.

> ... speaking the truth in love, we are to grow up in every way into him who is the head, into Christ, from whom the whole body, joined and knit together by every joint with which it is supplied, when each part is working properly, makes bodily growth and upbuilds itself in love.[48]

The Christian self only becomes what it really is, and what it should become, as a member of the community that is Christ's body. From this, it follows that a Christian must be understood and spoken about as a social being, a social being whose identity is constituted in an important

---

46. Von Balthasar, "John of the Cross," *The Glory of the Lord*, vol. 3, 166.
47. 1 Corinthians 12:12–13.
48. Ephesians 4:15–16.

way by his membership in the body of Christ. Any view of the self that views it as fixed, or finished, in abstraction from its membership in Christ's body, is inadequate. It is inadequate because, in St. Paul's words, "your life is hid with Christ in God."[49] The reality and the depth of the individual are created by his hidden membership in Christ's body. But Christ's body is one, and to ignore this aspect of the Christian's membership in the one body will leave us with a false picture of the self.

The foundation of this false idea of the self, to which today we all adhere in an unreflective way, is found in the philosophy of Descartes. No doubt, Descartes's own philosophy is considerably more sophisticated and compelling than my summary of its main points about knowledge might seem to show. I have not, though, simplified to the point of falsifying. Whether Descartes was articulating an almost instinctive set of beliefs or was the pioneer of a new way of thought does not matter very much here. What does matter is that we are all Cartesians at heart. That means that we all adhere to the following four propositions as self-evident,[50] and they are four propositions that effectively inhibit any coherent theory of the dark night theory of embodied mysticism. The purpose of flagging these propositions at this point is to make sure the reader does not automatically use them to understand my subsequent discussions.

The first thesis of Cartesian dualism is that the self "is most fundamentally a contingently embodied point of consciousness transparently knowable to itself via introspection."[51] That is to say, the self has no necessary connection with the body, that its nature is to be understood as consciousness, and that this self can be reached by looking inside oneself. Descartes's picture of the self as a contingently embodied point of consciousness transparently knowable to itself via introspection is deeply rooted in the way we all think nowadays,[52] but it is most certainly false. We have no direct awareness of ourselves by introspection. On the contrary, I come to know myself only through acts directed towards things other than myself. The awareness of self arises concomitantly with these acts. In perceiving a tree or a table, I am aware at the same time that there is an *I* doing the perceiving; that the act of perception is

---

49. Colossians 3:3.
50. My discussion is based on Gary L. Hagberg, *Describing Ourselves, Wittgenstein and Autobiographical Consciousness*.
51. Hagberg, *Describing Ourselves, Wittgenstein and Autobiographical Consciousness*, 3.
52. See Charles Taylor, *Sources of the Self*.

my act. And so this awareness involves the awareness of my existence as a self.[53]

The second Cartesian thesis can be taken as maintaining that the contents of the mind are known immediately, and this is to be contrasted to all knowledge of outward things, which is mediated.[54] That is, I know myself in an indisputable way as a thinking substance, and everything else I know is the result of some sort of illative process based on this starting point. This Cartesian thesis of establishing a starting point in an indisputable knowledge of the self through introspection, and then arguing from this starting point to a mediated knowledge of the external world, is a non-starter. It is a non-starter because there is no such knowledge to be had, and the knowledge of the self that we do possess is no more immediate than the knowledge we possess of anything else.[55]

The third Cartesian principle holds "that first-person thinking and experience is invariably private, thus presenting, as a brute first fact of human existence, an other-minds problem."[56] Descartes's understanding of what we are and of how we think does not give us any means of

---

53. "Concerning the actual cognition by which one actually considers that he has a soul, I say that the soul is known through its acts. For one perceives that he has a soul, and lives, and that he exists, because he perceives that he senses, understands, and carries on other vital activities of this sort. For this reason, the Philosopher says: 'We sense that we sense, and we understand that we understand, and because we sense this, we understand that we exist.' But one perceives that he understands only from the fact that he understands something. For to understand something is prior to understanding that one understands. Therefore, through that which it understands or senses the soul arrives at actual perception of the fact that it exists." Aquinas, *De Veritate*, Question 10, a. 8, reply. This non-philosophic awareness of the self is contrasted by St. Thomas with my (philosophical) knowledge of the self. "To know that I have a soul or that there is in me that by which I perceive, desire and understand is one thing: to know the nature of the soul in another. For the later knowledge deliberate reflection, 'second' reflection, is required; but the reflection by which one is aware of the self is a very general sense is not a deliberate reflection; and it is common to all human beings." Copleston, *Aquinas*, 27.

54. The contents of the mind "are known immediately by contrast to all outward mediated knowledge (and that the self is thus non-evidential)." Hagberg, *Describing Ourselves, Wittgenstein and Autobiographical Consciousness*, 3.

55. In Descartes's own case, the argument requires the establishment of the existence of God to assure the self that it is not deceived in its belief that there is an objective reality. Roger Scruton writes: "This argument exhibits a pattern that occurs elsewhere. It begins from the subject, and the sphere where he is sovereign. It then argues outwards to an 'objective' viewpoint. From that viewpoint it establishes the existence of an objective world, and the sphere of being is constructed from the result. Such a pattern of argument is typical of the epistemological position known as 'foundationalism.'" Scruton, *Modern Philosophy*, 47.

56. Hagberg, *Describing Ourselves, Wittgenstein and Autobiographical Consciousness*, 3.

access to other minds, assuming they do exist. If we accept Descartes's starting point there seems no escape from solipsism.

This statement clearly needs some unpacking, because in some sense it is nonsense to deny that there is something privileged or immediate in the knowledge of our own present experiences. If you are bored to tears at the present moment, it does seem odd to suggest that you have to make some sort of inquiry about this, or that you could be mistaken about your condition.[57] Let us call this personal experience, and the question then becomes: is this personal experience, in fact, private? Private, that is, in the sense that your experience is inaccessible to me? I see you yawning and coughing and looking out the window, and I conclude you are bored. So far, so good, but does that mean I cannot know what it is for you to be bored? Is the experience I have called personal also private in some radical sense? The Cartesians would hold that mental states are private in this straightforward sense of being accessible and knowable only to the person who has them.

Such a picture must be as wrong as it is internally incoherent. Here I would want to adopt the Wittgensteinian argument that if an object were really private, it could not be referred to.[58] In brief, Wittgenstein argues that the subject of an experience makes sense of himself only through applying concepts, and concepts are developed within a world of objects. The primary application of these concepts is to this world of objects, and it is within a world of objects that we learn how these concepts are applied correctly—or incorrectly. But what are concepts supposed to apply to when we start talking about private experience? There seem to be no criteria for the application of concepts, concepts derived from our experience of real objects, to a realm which by definition is not based on concepts abstracted from objects.[59] So, in a realm of pure pri-

---

57. "...there is a peculiar 'privilege' or 'immediacy' involved in the knowledge of our own present experiences. In some sense it is nonsense to suggest that I have to find out about them, or that I could, in the normal run of things, be mistaken." Scruton, *A Short History of Modern Philosophy*, 276.

58. Wittgenstein's argument is set out, *inter alia*, in his *Philosophical Investigations*, 288.

59. One could draw out the argument by pointing out that without the possibility of telling whether or not an object *remains the same* while I am aware of it, without being able to distinguish between *looking carefully* or *looking carelessly*, without anything that constitutes *making a mistake* or *getting it right* in identifying and referring to cannot be done, there can be neither experience of an object, nor any way to express what is experienced conceptually. But in the hypothetical domain of pure privacy, there exist no criteria (other than what *seems so to me at the time*) by which such distinctions can be drawn. For these distinctions to be drawn, the object of experience has to be accessible to others, in collaboration with whom it can be stabilized, attended to, and examined, and from which alone can arise the possibility of understanding it.

vacy, what we would be left with is something like this: it *seems to me* that I am experiencing or understanding something, perhaps "something I know not what," as Locke said in another context. If this is all pure privacy can give me, then both experiencing and understanding have been robbed of any sort of objectivity and also probably of any sort of coherence. But this is to deprive both experience and understanding of the objectivity that are essential to them.

The fourth Cartesian principle affirms that "language is the contingent and *ex post facto* externalization of prior, private, pre-linguistic, and mentally internal content."[60] This principle entails that there is a private sort of experience which can be grasped by a private language, and this language can be subsequently fitted or slotted, as it were, into a public language for purposes of communication.

This, too, must be wrong. Language is not some sort of externally related, *post factum* addition to a primitive, non-conceptual, and non-verbal experience. The forming and the testing of concepts are essentially public and collaborative activities. Concept-forming is embodied in the medium of human collaboration, and this medium of collaboration is language. Thus any viable meaning of objectivity that can be ascribed to our capacity to think requires also that we have the capacity to speak and that, when we speak, others can understand us. In this way, we are substituting a third-person approach to questions of objectivity for the Cartesian strategy, which begins with the first person. If we bring this third-person approach to discussions about knowledge in the darkness, then some of the more obvious difficulties will become easier to deal with.

In the first place, if the self is not, as Descartes held, "most fundamentally a contingently embodied point of consciousness transparently knowable to itself via introspection," then St. Gregory's contention that the third way is not a deepening of self-knowledge, but rather an encounter with the grace of Christ, becomes more intelligible. Gregory maintained, as we have seen, that the darkness of the third way does not bring with it a deeper knowledge of the self, but rather a heightened awareness of the presence of God. This living awareness is an awareness of the inaccessibility of God and is an encounter with the grace of Christ, or the effects of that grace, conveyed by the sacraments. Such an account of an encounter with God in the darkness does not depend on, nor is it accompanied by, a clear Cartesian grasp on the self as a clear and distinct idea. According to St. John of the Cross, there is only the

---

60. Hagberg, *Describing Ourselves, Wittgenstein and Autobiographical Consciousness,* 3.

presence of a darkness, a darkness that removes all the familiar landmarks of ordinary experience, including the certainty of the self. To try to construct a theory of mystical experience that depends on the self somehow at the same time being aware of itself as a starting point, and yet, because of the dark night, being totally immersed in that darkness, is not going to get us very far in understanding the third way. The whole thrust of St. John's description is that the darkness invades the citadel of the ascetical self and leaves it powerless to initiate any sort of activity.

The second Cartesian thesis was that the contents of the mind are known immediately, and this is to be contrasted to all knowledge of outward things, which is mediated. If Descartes is wrong about the first point, then he is wrong about this as well. The darkness of the third way is in no way dependent on a prior and indisputable awareness of the self. The darkness is all-encompassing, and the self is in no way exempt from St. John of the Cross's "sea that overflows into the soul and both purges and instructs it at the same time."[61] In the dark night, it is not a matter of reasoning from the knowledge of the self to the truth that "I am in darkness." It is the darkness that has the upper hand, and there is no reasoning involved in this direct acquaintance of God's work in the soul.

The third Cartesian principle was that first-person thinking and experience is invariably private. I am said to have a naked knowledge of myself that remains what it is before and after anything that happens to me. I know that I am in the dark night, and no one else does, because I have a privileged access to an interior reality (my self) that is what it is, and that only I can know about. If this were true, it becomes extremely difficult to see how experiences could ever be shared or known about. Contemporary philosophy has made this question of our knowledge of other minds into a central and very complex question. For our purposes, however, we need only ask ourselves how it could be, if Descartes is right, that the Christ encountered in the darkness could be one living reality, and not the conclusion of an argument.

Finally, the fourth Cartesian principle affirms that "language is the contingent and *ex post facto* externalization of prior, private, pre-linguistic, and mentally internal content." This is a crucial contention and implies that knowing and thinking about something is a private transaction between the mind and its object. I will return to this question in the next chapter, but here I merely want to note that Descartes is wrong about this. Knowledge and thought are necessarily embedded in lin-

---

61. See the discussion of the purgative aspect of the Dark Night earlier in this chapter, 198.

guistically-structured collaborative activities of familiar kinds. Furthermore, these activities are directed towards things that are publicly situated and accessible. This position means that there is no way of saying that I have an experience of the dark night that is not in important ways a public and recognizably public experience. Public, that is, in the sense that it is essentially a communicable one. Furthermore, I want to argue that the experience of the dark night must already be linguistically oriented before it can be thought of as a human experience.

I do not think these four Cartesian principles, or attitudes, will stand up to a careful philosophical examination. For the purposes of this book, though, it is enough to show that they are incompatible with a serious effort to come to terms with the darkness of God.

10

Towards an Account of St. Philip's Embodied Mysticism

"... for I bear on my body the marks of Jesus."
St. Paul[1]

I HAVE maintained that mysticism is embodied, embodied in a particular person, a particular subject, and this introduces an historical and biographical element into any account of embodied mysticism. It is an element that cannot be avoided if we are not going to fall into Bradley's "unearthly ballet of bloodless categories."[2] But the particular subject is himself ensconced, involved in, a complex communal, linguistic, and symbolic order of beliefs and practices.[3] In providing an account of St. Philip's journey towards union with God, I have used the tradition of the three ways as understood by St. Gregory of Nyssa, and I have expanded on this teaching with the writings of the Carmelite Doctors.

In this chapter I come to grips with the function of the physical phenomena of mysticism in the lives of many of the saints. Here I will use Wittgenstein's principle that telling the truth about an experience is not a description of an inner happening, which is essentially pre-linguistic. Next I put forth a theory, based on St. Thomas, of how a communication of the divine might be possible without infringing the principle

---

1. Galatians 6:17.
2. See Introduction, "An Embodied Mysticism," 30.
3. "Furthermore, this order of beliefs and practices is always an aspect of a wider societal context. For St. Philip Neri, these beliefs and practices were situated in the mystical body of Jesus Christ, which is the Church. Yet the Catholic Church as he experienced it was that of Renaissance Florence, and then of Papal Rome, with their own particular appropriation of Christianity. It was a Church with its own glories, but haunted by its own violent history." Ibid., 18.

that no direct apprehension of God is possible in this life. Third, I deal with the function of the personal in Philip's mysticism. Finally, I discuss the role that the physical phenomena of mysticism play in the Christian economy of salvation.

The Physical Phenomena of Mysticism

Philip was convinced that the operation of the Holy Spirit was the source of all the paranormal phenomena in his life. This certainty on his part seems to have stemmed from his experience in the catacombs at Pentecost in 1544.[4] Ideally, it is this experience we should now analyze in our efforts to understand the connection of his mystical experience to the strange phenomena by which it was accompanied. The difficulty in doing this, however, is that we know very little about the details of the incident. Except for the very broadest outline—that Philip had an overwhelming experience of the Holy Spirit—almost none of its details can be ascertained with any certainty. The traditional description, including the ball of fire that entered his mouth, were only revealed after Philip's death, and there is no account of these wonders in the Process.[5]

In view of the difficulties in discussing what has been called "Philip's Pentecost," I have taken a similar sort of experience, of what the mystical theologians call *transverberation*,[6] from the lives of Saint Teresa of Avila, a contemporary of St. Philip's, and of Saint Pio of Pietrelcina, 1887–1968, commonly known as Padre Pio. There is a good deal more material to investigate, in these cases of transverberation, than there is in Philip's experience in 1544. On the other hand, all three accounts are of experiences of the paranormal, and we can take the more richly documented happenings (of St. Teresa's and Padre Pio's) to throw light on the less detailed description from Philip's life.

The case of Padre Pio, whose experiences were as strange as anything recorded in the lives of the saints, shows that the need for a clearer understanding of the physical phenomena of mysticism has not disappeared with modern times.[7] The authorities of the Church were extremely suspicious in their dealing with him. If there had been any question of delusion or fraud, it would have been detected in the course of the many medical and theological investigations of the physical phe-

---

4. See Part Two, Chapter Eight, "The Catacombs and the Apostolate," 187.
5. Ibid., note 43.
6. There is an excellent treatment of this phenomenon in the *Dictionnaire de Spiritualité*, vol. 12, "Transverberation," 1174–1184.
7. There is a bibliography of the more reliable lives of St. Pio in the *Dictionnaire de Spiritualité*, vol. 12, "Pie de Pietrelcina," 1443.

nomena of the saint's mysticism. Nonetheless, the reality of the whole range of the physical phenomena of mysticism finally had to be acknowledged as genuine. There is enough hard evidence to suggest we should not be satisfied with any explanation that says that paranormal experiences are always based only on the credulity of the half-educated or a lack of respect for ordinary standards of proof. The attitude of Father Thurston, who spent a lifetime investigating the physical phenomena of mysticism, is instructive, and it could well be adopted by those who dismiss the paranormal experiences of many of the saints. He disliked and distrusted mysticism, but he was prepared to investigate and weigh up these experiences in a sober and careful way.[8]

On the fifth of August, 1918, Padre Pio was the subject of transverberation. St. Teresa describes this experience in her autobiography, where she writes:

> It pleased the Lord that I should sometimes see the following vision. I would see beside me, on my left hand, an angel in bodily form—a type of vision which I am not in the habit of seeing, except very rarely.... In his hand I saw a long golden spear and at the end of the iron tip I seemed to see a point of fire. With this he seemed to pierce my heart several times so that it penetrated to my entrails. When he drew it out, I thought he was drawing them out with it and he left me completely afire with a great love for God.[9]

In Carmelite tradition, St. Teresa had this experience on more than one occasion, but the account she writes about probably refers to the year 1559–1560.[10] The experience was taken seriously enough to have moved Benedict XIII, in 1726, to institute a Feast and Office in its honor.[11] Father Thurston observes that on Teresa's heart, which was extracted after her death, was found a wide horizontal fissure, "as those may see to this day who visit the relic in its shrine at Alba de Tomes, or who procure one of the many photographs of it which are in circulation."[12] Father Crehan, who edited Thurston's work for publication, gives two reasons to doubt this. First, he says, was there is no "satisfactory evidence that this wound was not made in the operation of removal, which

---

8. "Il se méfiait du mysticisme sous quelque forme que soit, le considérant comme la porte ouverte aux déceptions; il est impossible de tirer de ses écrits quelques enseignements qui approche le spirituel autrement que par le bon sens." *Dictionnaire de Spiritualité*, vol. 15, column 912.
9. St. Teresa of Jesus, "Life," *The Complete Works*, vol. 1, 192.
10. Ibid., editor's note, 193.
11. Ibid.
12. Thurston, *The Physical Phenomena of Mysticism*, 68.

was performed by unskilled hands."[13] It is difficult to know how to deal with such a sentence. There seems to be no way to refute the suggestion that the wound might have been made by unskilled hands, unless the writer gives reasons for thinking this must have been so. In fact, this is just what Fr. Crehan does, but he is not particularly convincing in what he says. First of all, he says that St. Teresa "seems (Vida, chapter xxvii, p. 4) to have had no *corporeal* visions."[14] What she actually says in chapter xxvii is that at one period of her life she saw Christ at her side, "or to put it better, I was conscious of Him, for neither with the eyes of the body nor with those of the soul did I see anything."[15] But, as we can see from her own description of the transverberation, she explicitly says that she had a vision of an angel in bodily form, "a type of vision which I am not in the habit of seeing, except very rarely."[16] *Rarely* is not never.

As his second point, Father Crehan then goes on to say that as the saint had no corporeal visions, "it is therefore hard to see how an intellectual vision resulted in a bodily lesion."[17] I suppose we are supposed to take from this that if St. Teresa had had a corporeal vision (which in fact she did), then it would be much easier to accept the possibility of the lesion being the result of the activity of God. I can't see how a corporeal vision has any clearer causal connection with a putative lesion than an intellectual one. It seems to be that Crehan's correction of Thurston is no correction at all. What we are investigating is the relation of the physical phenomena of mysticism to grace and the gifts of the Holy Spirit. Imaginative visions are as much a part of the natural order as corporeal visions. How we are to understand this relationship between grace and nature is not going to be clarified by drawing distinctions between natural phenomena. This is especially true in the case of St. Teresa's transverberation, as the distinction between intellectual and corporeal visions is one that does not even apply.

Padre Pio, as I have indicated, was also subject to a similar experience in the evening of August 5, 1918. He described it in a letter of August 21 of the same year at the request of his spiritual director, Father Benedetto:

---

13. Crehan quoted in Thurston, *The Physical Phenomena of Mysticism*, 68, n.3.
14. Ibid. Corporeal vision, which are also called apparitions, are an experience in which "the eyes perceive an object that is normally invisible to the sense of sight. This may be caused by an external object or by some power impressing an image on the sense of sight." *New Catholic Encyclopedia*, vol. 14, 717. Such visions are distinguished from imaginative, and intellectual visions. The classification goes back to Augustine.
15. St. Teresa of Jesus, "Life," *The Complete Works*, vol. 1, 170.
16. Ibid., 192.
17. Crehan quoted in Thurston, *The Physical Phenomena of Mysticism*, 68, n. 3.

For this reason [in obedience] I am led to manifest to you what happened to me on the evening of the 5th of this month and all day on the 6th. I am quite unable to convey to you what occurred during this period of utter torment. While I was hearing the boys' confessions on the evening of the 5th, I was suddenly terrorized by the sight of a celestial person who presented himself to my mind's eye. He had in his hand a sort of weapon, like a very long, sharp-pointed steel blade which seemed to emit fire. At the very instant that I saw all this I saw that person hurl the weapon into my soul with all his might. I cried out with difficulty and I felt I was dying. I asked the boy to leave because I felt ill and no longer had the strength to continue.

This agony lasted uninterruptedly until the morning of the 7th. I cannot tell you how much I suffered during this period of anguish. Even my entrails were torn and ruptured by the weapon, and nothing was spared. From that day on I have been mortally wounded. I feel in the depths of my soul a wound that is always open and which causes me continual agony.[18]

Padre Pio's account is considerably starker and more foreboding than Teresa's, but they are recognizably of the same kind. I have already said that I am not at this moment considering whether the experiences were genuine in the sense of being an objective vision of an angel, or what the purpose of the experiences may have been in the economy of salvation. What I am investigating is the relation the experiences themselves bore to the descriptions of them by the saints themselves.

Both Teresa and Padre Pio described an occurrence or a happening, and it is clear that they held their description to be true ones. At the same time, though, the truth of the account must consist in something more than a series of statements about what they remembered about their inner experience at the time the transverberation took place. In calling the transverberation an inner experience, I do not intend to cast doubt on the truth of what the two saints described. I am merely pointing to the obvious fact that the truth of the experience cannot be verified in the usual way. For example, if two people are sitting in a garden with a fountain, they can discuss the fountain as well as the different impressions the fountain makes on each one of them. One may focus on how refreshing the sound of running water is on a hot July day, while the other may be fascinated by the play of light on the water in the basin of the fountain. In both cases, there is a personal aspect to the experience, but these personal aspects are only possible because of the reality of the fountain, to which in some way the experiences of the two people can be

---

18. Padre Pio of Pietrelcina, *Letters*, 1186.

related. The fountain may not be the cause of the different experiences, but it seems to be at least the necessary condition for the occurrence of the subjective experiences. Again, to say that the different experiences are personal does not mean that they are necessarily subjective in the sense of being idiosyncratic, with no reference to the fountain.

It is clear, in the case of the transverberation of the two saints, that there is nothing that corresponds to the reality of the fountain. The angel, or the divine being with the sword, plays a role that is analogous to that of the fountain, as he is at least the occasion for very similar reactions in the two saints; that is, they both recognized a being other than themselves. On the other hand, the angel is not like the fountain, as he is not seen by anyone else, nor are the effects of his actions experienced by anyone else. Padre Pio sent the boy away from the confessional because the saint "felt ill, and no longer had the strength to continue." On the other hand, there is no suggestion in the saint's account that the boy would have seen the angel if he got off his knees and turned around. The saint sent the boy away because he (the saint) felt sick and weak; not because he was anxious the boy would be able to see the angel and be upset as well.

There is, then, an obvious sense that we can call transverberation an inner experience without thereby intending to cast doubt on the reality of the experience. Nonetheless, if we want to say that the experience is true, or that it is not merely subjective, then we will have to give an account of what truth would mean in such a case and how it would be described. We will, to put it simply but (I think) accurately, have to produce a factor that plays the same role as the fountain in the garden. The fountain in the garden provided not only an objective referent around which the inner experiences of the two men can be understood, but it also had some sort of causal connection, or at least stood in a necessary relation, with the experiences themselves.

In his *Philosophical Investigations*, Wittgenstein argues that there is a world of difference between telling the truth about an experience and describing an inner experience. He says:

> ... the criteria for the truth of the *confession* that I thought such and such are not the criteria for a true *description* of a process. And the importance of a true confession does not reside in its being a correct and certain report of a process. It resides rather in the special consequences which can be drawn from a confession whose truth is guaranteed by the special criteria of *truthfulness*.[19]

---

19. Wittgenstein, *Philosophical Investigations*, Part Two, 222*ff*.

We can apply this principle to our example of the transverberation of the two saints in the following way. First of all, we would say that the truth of their *confession* (we might want to say *avowal*), that they had both seen and been wounded by a celestial being, is not established by a description of what went on in their minds at the time of the vision. Secondly, we would then argue that it is only because what they described can be seen as both using and being congruent with the language of faith that their claims can be either accepted or rejected. Furthermore, it is only because of this use of language, with its third-person reference, that the saints themselves were able to understand their own experience. Finally, while a third-person reference is essential both for communicating the experience of transverberation, and even for the saints' own understanding of what had happened to them, it does not follow that there is nothing to the original experience but what can be described. Confession or avowal, as well as the establishment of truth, require language and a third-person reference. There is, however, the element of God's activity in genuine mystical experience; this can only be perceived and described in its effects, but it cannot be reduced to those effects.

a. *The truth of their accounts is not established by an account of what went on in their minds at the time of the vision.* It is clear from Padre Pio's account that the experience of transverberation was both sudden and momentary. It will be remembered that Padre Pio was "*suddenly* terrorized" by the sight of the celestial person, who "*. . . at the very instant*" he was seen hurled the weapon he held in his hand.[20] The experience itself is momentary, although the effects endure.[21] This sudden and complex experience had to be thought about and worked over before it could be conveyed to his confessor. It was, perhaps, like being hit by a bolt of lightning, and had to be reduced to a verbal form before it could be related to a third party. I am not arguing that this recasting of the experience in a verbal form was a distortion of the original happening. I am, though, maintaining that however the truth of the accounts is going to be verified, or even understood, it will not be through a description of what went on in the minds of the two saints at the time of the transverberation.

---

20. See Padre Pio's account of this mystical experience, quoted earlier in this chapter, 221.

21. The writer of the article "Blessure d'Amour" in the *Dictionnaire de Spiritualité* (vol. 1, 1724–1730), after an examination of several instances of this phenomenon, emphasizes this momentary character of the experience. He cites Scaramelli, who defines this wound of love, of which transverberation is a subset, as: "Une touche enflammée et brûlante d'amour par laquelle Dieu élève subitement l'âme à la possession affective et sentie de lui-même, et se retire aussitôt" (1725).

b. *It is only because what they described can be seen as both using and being congruent with the language of faith that their claims can be either accepted or rejected.* The experience of the two saints was not private in the sense of being incommunicable. Obviously, they both communicated as best they could what had happened to them. But the only way they could do this was through language, and not only language in a general sense but the language of Catholic Christianity. This language has a vocabulary for dealing with the physical phenomena of mysticism, including that of transverberation. The two saints recognized that this language was the best means of expressing what they had experienced.

c. *It is only because of this use of language, with its third-person reference, that the saints themselves were able to understand their own experience.* The language of Catholic Christianity, which was the inheritance of the saints, must have guided their own understanding of what they had been subjected to. Certainly it was the essential instrument in any attempt to communicate their experience. This principle must not be understood in a reductionist sort of way, which would reduce the transverberation to nothing more than the linguistic formulation of an experience which had no integrity or reality of its own.

d. *Although language is essential for both communicating and understanding the physical phenomena of mystical experience, it does not by itself create the experience.* In simple terms, what I am arguing for here is that there does exist an element in the physical phenomena of mysticism that is the result of God's action. We can see this in the experience of the angel, in St. Teresa's case, or of the "celestial being," in Padre Pio's, who wounds. It is the active side of the experience (that is, active from the side of the angel or celestial being), as well as its transitory and even momentary quality, that dominates their accounts. What we have to deal with, then, is not an analogue to an empirical reality that endures, but an action, a doing. And here the agent is not the saint, but God. Whatever objectivity we are going to be able to ascribe to the experience of the two saints will be have to be based on an analogy to the objectivity we are able to ascribe to actions, and not to that of a readily observable empirical reality.

We now have to examine the claim that an analysis of action will provide a clue as to how the truth of mystical experience might be established. I have argued above that there is objectively more to an experience than what appears immediately to the one having the experience. I have also said that this immediate object of experience—that is, what we are first aware of in a conscious state—bears no necessary relationship to objectivity or truth. The truth concerning our inner experiences, as Wittgenstein put it, "... does not reside in its being a correct and certain report of a process." Such a report, in the case of transverberation, would be the first-person description of the happening by Teresa or Padre Pio. But if we were interested in knowing what really happened, or in what sense their accounts were true, we would want something more than description of a mysterious inner process. Objectivity is going to require that the description measures up to some sort of standard of truthfulness. The importance of the saints' accounts will be found, once again, in Wittgenstein's words, "in the special consequences which can be drawn from a confession whose truth is guaranteed by the special criteria of *truthfulness*."[22] We can see how this works out by a consideration of St. Thomas's classic restatement of Aristotle's requirements for the goodness of an action. These requirements are four:

> First, its generic existence as an activity at all; secondly, definition by an appropriate object; thirdly, the circumstances surrounding the act; and fourthly, its relation to a goal. Actions are good in the straightforward sense of the word only when all these elements are present: as pseudo-Denys says, *any defect will make a thing bad; to be good a thing must be wholly good.*[23]

None of this is as simple as it appears on the surface. What I want to emphasize here, however, is that the activity of judging a particular action in terms of the four requirements has little relation to what goes on in the agent's mind when he does the action. What I want to underscore is that while the four requirements for an action to be good are a statement of what a good action will possess, they are not a kind of checklist that the moral agent ticks off in his head before he does a good action. Of course he may deliberate about what he should do, but the deliberation is not about the four characteristics possessed by a moral action, it is instead about what is to be done in the here and now. Practical reason or prudence is, Aristotle says, "a true state, reasoned and capable of action in the sphere of human goods."[24] There is a great deal packed into this that does not directly concern us here, but what does

---

22. See the discussion of truthfulness in St. Teresa's and Padre Pio's accounts of their mystical experiences, 221*ff.* Wittgenstein, *Philosophical Investigations*, Part Two, 222*ff.*

23. Aquinas, *Summa Theologiae*, Ia, 2ae, 18, 4. This is Timothy McDermott's rendering of St. Thomas's position (*Summa Theologiae: A Concise Translation*, 194); the Latin reads: Sic igitur in actione humana bonitas quadruplex considerari potest: una quidem secundum genus, prout scilicet est actio, quia quantum habet de actione et entitate, tantum de bonitate, ut dictum est; alia vero secundum speciem, quae accipitur secundum objectum conveniens; tertia secundum circumstantias, quasi secundum accidentia quaedam; quarta autem secundum finem, quasi secundum habitudinem ad bonitatis causam.

24. Aristotle, *Nicomachean Ethics*, 1140 b 21.

concern us is to see that moral reasoning about what one should do is not the same activity as reasoning about the nature of moral activity, nor is it the same thing as trying to evaluate the moral character of the act after it has been done.

I want to say, then, that what goes on in the agent's mind when he does a moral action, and how he would justify the action after it is done, are not the same. Yet, and this is also important (if somewhat puzzling), while the four requirements for an action to be good were not present to the man's consciousness when he acted, we would not want to say that they were something imposed later on, as it were, to the action after it was completed. Nor, furthermore, do we believe that the requirements were altogether external to the action when the action was actually being performed. Somehow or other, the four requirements qualified the act, yet they were not in any obvious way aspects of the consciousness of the man doing the act. It follows from this that a description of subjective, or personal, experience is not going to be enough to determine the moral goodness of real actions; that is, actions that are actually done. You can be as authentic as you like, and as truthful in talking about your authenticity as all get out, but still not be engaged in moral discourse.

To apply Wittgenstein's analysis to our discussion of the criteria for a moral action, we could say that the truth of the man's *confession*, or *avowal*, that he had done a good act, is not established by a description of what went on in his mind when he did the action, but rather from the moral implications that can be drawn from what he actually did. It is these moral implications, in the sense of the four criteria for a moral act, that answer to Wittgenstein's *special consequences* and that establish whether or not the action done was truly a good one.

We seem to want to say two things. First of all, there are good reasons for saying that the significance, or simply the truth, of an act is not achieved by the description of an inner process. The truth of the goodness or otherwise of the action is determined by objective criteria that seem to bear little relation to what went on in the mind of the doer. If this is the case, then describing what went on in the agent's mind is not going to be a justification for what he did. Yet, secondly, there must be some relation of these objective criteria to the act itself. The four requirements have to apply to, or qualify, what the particular agent actually does. Unless the criteria in some way grow out of, or are implicit in, the particular act that was actually done, then the criteria for the goodness of the action would seem to be something external to it and not enter in any way into the making of the act a good act. We should remember that we are interested in the action the man actually does, and not just in the thinking and talking about the action in the process of evaluating it after it is done. So we want to say that the criteria for a moral action are not external and imposed on something to which they have no intrinsic connection; yet, at the time the action was actually done, these were not the object of the agent's consciousness. The temptation to base the nature of the act on what went on in the agent's consciousness must be resisted.

How are we to understand such a contention? My answer is that the means used to establish the moral character of the act have characterized the action, as an action, from the beginning. This is the case because they have constituted the act as this particular kind of act. At the same time, though, this "integral" or "finished" or "completed" moral act has little, and often nothing at all, to do with what went on in the agent's private experience. In fact, I would contend that very often the moral character of action is better determined by a third person than by the agent himself.

We are now in a position to say the following about the experience of St. Teresa and Padre Pio when they saw and were wounded by a being that appeared to them as outside themselves. In the first place, the vision was not an experience of an objective fact in the ordinary empirical sense. This is confirmed by the fact that the boy in Padre Pio's case did not see what the saint saw. It would seem that seeing the being was an aspect of the experience of sitting in the confessional and listening to the boy. Secondly, the objectivity and truth of the experience of the two saints will be established by criteria of truthfulness that were not present as aspects of the immediate experience of transverberation. Whatever these criteria are going to be, they will not be an account of what went on in the saints' minds. The role these criteria play will be more like the criteria for the goodness of action. The goodness of the man's act is established, as we have seen, neither by an account of what went on in the agent's mind, nor *a fortiori* by anything like a photograph or a drawing of the action being done in the world of space and time.

All these considerations will apply to determining the genuine character of the extraordinary experiences of the saints. There is, however, an important difference in the experience of transverberation and the moral act. A moral act is by definition a free act, while there was no element of freedom in the experience of the two saints. It was imposed on them by some external power, a power against which they had absolutely no ability to resist. The element of freedom and of choice came afterwards, in their recognition and descriptions of what was entailed by the experience over which they had no control.

If we now apply these principles to St. Philip's case, we can see that my statement must be right that he had no privileged, private access to the fact that his paranormal experiences were the work of the Holy Spirit. The significance, or simply, the truth of his conviction that his actions were governed by the Holy Spirit could not have been achieved simply by the description of an inner process. His being governed by the Holy Spirit was determined by objective criteria that bore little relation to what went on in his mind. One such criterion would be what his contemporaries thought of him. Ponnelle and Bordet write:

> The contemporaries of Philip were attracted to him principally by the fact that they believed that his miracles, and the effusions of the Holy Spirit, were authentic proofs of his sanctity. The same applies to ourselves, and we are further confirmed in our conviction that he is a saint by the judgment of the Church.[25]

This is surely the case, but I would want to add that the recognition of his miracles as genuine, and the truth of "the effusions of the Holy Spirit" were not based on Philip's own avowals that his miracles were genuine, or that he was moved by the Holy Spirit, but by the fact that his experiences and his verbalization of them were perceived to satisfy a complex criterion of linguistic, moral, and doctrinal beliefs.

Philip's own assertion that his experiences were the work of the Holy Spirit bears the same sort of relation to those experiences as do the inner state of the man who, for example, spontaneously gives money to a beggar in difficult circumstances. The hesitations and considerations of the man who actually gives the money to the beggar bear little obvious relation to the criteria for a moral act, and they certainly were not directly before his consciousness at the time he gave the money.[26] If this is the case, then describing what went on in the agent's mind is not going to be a justification for what he did. In a similar way, Philip's own description of his own experiences requires a third-person perspective, and this is not to be obtained by a description of what went on in his personal experience at the time of the paranormal happening. Secondly, though, there must be some relation of these objective criteria to what went on in the doer's experience if the standards are to apply to, or to qualify, what actually happened to St. Philip. In the case of the moral agent, we saw that the criteria must in some way grow out of, or be implicit in, his doing of this particular action. Unless this is the case, then the criteria for the goodness of the action would seem to be something external to

---

25. Ponnelle and Bordet, *St. Philip Neri*, 165.
26. I have worked out this example in more detail in my "Changing the Subject: The Liturgy as an Object of Experience."

it, and not enter in any way into the making of the act a good act. In a similar way, we would want to say that the criteria employed in the third-person perspective of paranormal experiences must in some way qualify the act in a way that makes these experiences genuine or false. It follows from these arguments that the criteria for a contention that an experience is the work of the Holy Spirit are not external and imposed on something to which they have no intrinsic connection. Yet at the time the action was actually done, these criteria did not necessarily have an obvious connection with what the saints themselves experienced.

Unutterable Words

Objectivity, we have seen, does not consist in a report of what was directly present to an individual's consciousness at the time of a particular experience. In the last section, I discussed objectivity by considering the ascription of a moral character to an act. I argued that objectivity must somehow qualify the action itself. I then suggested that this sort of objectivity is only possible because the criteria for determining this moral nature in some way pertain to the act itself. We do not want to say, that is, that the four criteria of St. Thomas are only predicates applied externally to the completed action. What we do want to maintain is that the moral act, as an act, is qualified by the criteria. I have also put forward the thesis that the use of these universals, which are required for the establishment of objectivity, is only possible through our ability to use language.

Our consideration of moral acts has shown us, so far, that objectivity is not a simple matter of the mind mirroring an already established or completed reality. In one way, this should be obvious: an action is a doing, and until the action is brought into being, there is nothing in reality to which the standards can apply. What we have now to go on to examine is the contention that the moral act, as an act, is constituted in its objectivity by the four criteria. At the same time, though, we have to remember that these criteria are not the reflection of what went on in the agent's mind as he performed the act.

The question has now become: How is it that an action could be qualified by criteria of which the agent has no direct awareness at the time of his action? I will try to answer this question by examining a passage in one of St. Thomas's Biblical Commentaries. There is a famous passage in St. Paul's Second Letter to the Corinthians, where the Apostle, speaking about himself in the third person, writes:

> I know a man in Christ who fourteen years ago was caught up to the third heaven—whether in the body or out of the body I do not know,

God knows. And I know that his man was caught up into Paradise—whether in the body or out of the body I do not know, God knows—and he heard things that cannot be told, which man may not utter.[27]

This passage has often been taken as a description of a mystical experience, in the broad sense of a contact with the divine. In this case, St. Paul was caught up by a force outside himself and then placed in a situation in which he heard unutterable words. St. Thomas discusses this experience of the Saint in his treatment of rapture,[28] which along with prophecy and the working of miracles make up Thomas's discussion of gratuitous graces, or *gratiae gratis datae*.[29]

The aspect of the text from St. Paul which interests us is his statement that he heard things that cannot be told, which man may not utter. Does this mean that Paul heard words which it was impossible for him to repeat, or that he heard words which he could have repeated but was not allowed to do so? The Greek for this crucial phrase is καὶ ἤκουσεν ἄρρητα ῥήματα ἃ οὐκ ἐξὸν ἀνθρώπῳ λαλῆσαι, which seems to mean he heard unutterable words which man is not permitted to speak. This suggests that Paul could have spoken the words, but was not allowed to do so.[30] This ambiguity is present in most of the English words used to describe mystical experience, such as "ineffable" or "unutterable." These words may mean, on the one hand, what cannot be expressed or uttered, or what cannot be expressed or described by language, or what is too great for words. On the other hand, the words may be understood to point to what it is not permitted or allowed to be disclosed or made known. If we take the words in the second way, the implication is that what Paul heard could have been expressed or uttered, but there was a prohibition to doing so.

In his Commentary of 2 Corinthians, St. Thomas deals with the expression *audivit arcana verba, quae non licet homini loqui*—that is, that Paul heard words that cannot be told—in the following way. He says that there are two possible interpretations of the *non licet*: (i) that what Paul experienced cannot be spoken about at all, and (ii) that it can be spoken about, but it must not be spoken of to the imperfect.

So Thomas says that *non licet* can be interpreted in two different

---

27. 2 Corinthians 12:3–4.
28. Aquinas, *Summa Theologiae*, 2a, 2ae, q. 175, articles 3–6, inclusive.
29. See Aquinas, *Summa Theologiae*, 2a, 2ae, q. 171, article 1. These gratuitous graces are not given for the benefit or even for the sanctification of the person who receives them, but for the benefit of others, and are directed towards the building up and sanctification of the Church.
30. See Martin, *2 Corinthians, Word Biblical Commentary*, vol. 40, 405–406.

Towards an Account of St. Philip's Embodied Mysticism   231

ways. In the first interpretation, he treats it as meaning "conveying what was actually seen," and this he says is impossible. In the second, he treats "speaking about" Paul's experience as meaning "speaking about this episode in which Paul had a vision of the Divine Essence." Understood in this way, the meaning is that he should not speak (about the fact of the vision) to the imperfect, but only to the spiritual.[31]

> There is another point in St. Thomas's analysis which should be noticed: He says that he heard, that is he pondered hidden words (*arcana verba*); that is to say the splendor of the divinity, about which no man is able to speak; he says, however he heard in place of he saw, as this pondering (*consideratio*) pertained to the inner act of the soul, in which hearing and seeing are the same.[32]

This statement provides us with the basis for the unutterable character of the experience. The experience was a direct awareness of God that was given to Paul outside of the ordinary human modes of experience and intellection. One could say, in a non-technical way, that both what was experienced as well as the capacity to experience (what was experienced) were given to him by God in the experience itself.[33]

---

31. Thomas explains this interpretation by pointing to texts that speak of concealment ("Gloria Dei est celare verbum") and silence ("Tibi silet laus, Deus") concerning what pertains to God's glory.

32. Aquinas, *In Omnes S. Pauli Epistolas Commentaria*, volumum Primum, Caput XII, lectio II, 508 (Torino: Marietti, 1922). This is the author's translation of the original Latin: *Audivit, id est, consideravit arcana verba, quam nullus homo potest loqui; dicit autem audivit pro vidit, quia illa consideratio fuit secundum interiorem actum animae, in quo idem est auditus et visus, secundum quod dicitur in num. C xii: ore ad os loquitur ei et palam*, etc. See also Numbers 12:8—"With [Moses] I speak mouth to mouth, clearly, and not in dark speech; and he beholds the form of the Lord."

33. "Aquinas was convinced both that the human soul depends in this life on sense-experience for all its natural knowledge and that its highest activities transcend the capacity of matter. In other words, the highest activities of the soul, and so of the soul itself, are intrinsically independent of the body, in the sense that they can be exercised in the state of separation from the body; but at the same time they are extrinsically dependent on the body, in the sense that while the soul is united with the body it is dependent for its natural knowledge on sense perception." Copleston, *Aquinas*, 161–162. The argument in the *Summa* is couched in terms of phantasms which are required by the human intellect for any sort of thinking, even about abstract or purely intelligible objects. These phantasms are derived from sense perception, and if there were no sensible objects, then the intellect will have no phantasms, which are required for it to think about intelligible species. *Dicendum quod divina essentia non potest ab homine videri per aliam viam cognoscitivam quam per intellectum. Intellectus autem humanus non convertitur ad intelligibilia nisi mediantibus phantasmatibus, per quae species intelligibiles a sensibus accipit, et in quibus considerans de sensibilibus iudicat et ea disponit*. Aquinas, *Summa Theologiae*, 2a, 2ae, 174 a 4.

If it is the case that both the experience and the capacity to have the experience were given at the time Paul "heard and pondered hidden words," then the question presents itself as to how Paul could have known that he had even had the experience, much less communicated its contents. St. Thomas is alive to this difficulty and discusses it in one of the articles on rapture in which he deals with the question as to whether or not St. Paul was withdrawn from his senses.[34] Thomas argues that he must have been withdrawn from his senses because the Divine essence could not be seen by any phantasm of a created species.[35] Yet Paul did see the Divine Essence, and so "it is impossible for man while a wayfarer to see God in his essence without being withdrawn from his senses."[36] Thomas then explains that the Apostle was able to talk about the vision because the experience left some sort of intelligible species "by way of habitus."[37] Thomas answers the objection by saying that when Paul remembered and wrote about the experience, it was not the vision itself that he remembered and wrote about, but the traces that the experience had left in his intellect.

This objection and Thomas's answer to it present an extraordinarily fertile line of investigation. The form of his answer to what was, for him, the acute difficulty of how a wayfarer could see God in this life, and if he did see God how he could remember and report on the experience, provides a key to understanding how St. Philip's experience of God might be in some way an awareness of the divine presence, but one that required an articulated discourse not only for it to be talked about, but

---

34. Aquinas, *Summa Theologiae*, 2a, 2ae, 175, a 4: *Utrum Paulus in raptu fuerit alienatus a sensibus.*

35. Thomas has dealt with this point in detail in the *Prima Pars* of the *Summa Theologiae*, q. 12, art. 2: "Whether the essence of God is seen by a created intellect through a likeness." (Utrum essential Dei ab intellectu creato per aliquam similitudinem videatur.)

36. Aquinas, *In Omnes S. Pauli Epistolas Commentaria*, volume Primum, Caput XII, lectio 1, 506, reply. This is the author's translation of the original Latin: *sine abstractione a sensibus*. Aquinas continues: *Nam impossibile est, quod Deus videtur in vita ista ab homine non alienato a sensibus, quia nullum phantasma est sufficiens medium ad Dei essentiam ostendendam, idea oportet quos abstahatur et alienetur a sensibus.*

37. "Further, after seeing God in His essence, Paul remembered what he had seen in that vision; hence he said (2 Cor xii 4): *He heard sacred words, which it is not granted to man to utter*. Now the memory belongs to the sensitive faculty according to the Philosopher. Therefore it seems that Paul, while seeing the essence of God, was not withdrawn from his senses." (Praeterea, Paulus postquam Deum per essentiam viderat, memor fuit illorum quae in illa visione conspexerat; unde dicebat: *Audivi arcana verba, quae non licet homini loqui*. Sed memoria ad partem sensitivam pertinet, ut patet per Philosophum. Ergo videtur quod etiam Paulus videndo Dei essentiam non fuerit alienatus a sensibus.) Aquinas, *Summa Theologiae*, 2a, 2ae, 175, art. 4, objection 3.

for it to happen at all. Thomas holds, then, that the experience itself is indeed ineffable in the strict sense of the word; that is, it cannot be expressed or described by language. On the other hand, it leaves some sort of trace in the intellect, a trace that, although caused by a supernatural experience, is the same sort of trace an ordinary experience would leave. Working with, or on, this trace, a sort of derivative knowledge is achieved, and this knowledge can be spoken about.

> After Paul had stopped seeing God through his essence, *he remembered what he had known in that vision by means of certain species which remained in the understanding and were relics, so to speak, of the previous vision.* For although he saw the very Word of God through his essence, and from the vision of that essence knew many truths, (and thus neither for the Word Himself nor for the things which he saw in the Word did the vision take place through any species, but only through the essence of the Word), nevertheless, by reason of the vision of the Word, certain likenesses of the things which he saw were imprinted on his understanding. Later, by applying these intelligible species to the individual intentions or forms which were stored in his memory or imagination, he could remember the things which he had seen previously, and this even through the activity of memory which is a sensitive power. Thus it is not necessary to hold that in the act of seeing God something took place in his memory, which is part of the sensitive power, but only in his mind.[38]

For our purposes, however, I want to emphasize that according to St. Thomas, it was the divine initiative that was the source of the hearing of the words which could not be uttered. It follows from this that, however we are to account for St. Paul's capacity to receive the effects of this initiative, our account will also have to emphasize that Paul's experience was the encounter with an other, with an object. It was this object that informed his mind and so constituted the experience as objective. What went on in his mind was the effect of God's action, and we will miss an important aspect of St. Thomas's analysis if we take away from it only how it was that Paul was able to remember and talk about his own experience as personal. We can understand St. Philip's awareness of the divine presence on the model of St. Paul's hearing of the unutterable words.

---

38. Aquinas, *De Veritate*, Question 13: Article 3, Answers to Difficulties, 4 (emphasis added). The Latin reads: "memor fuit eorum quae in illa visione cognoverat, per aliquas species in intellectu ipsius remanentes, quae erant quasi quaedam reliquiae praeteritae visionis."

The Personal Aspect of St. Philip's Mysticism

It would be wrong to conclude from my arguments for the necessity of a third-person approach to understanding the paranormal experiences of the saints that there is no such thing as personal experience. Just because it is the case that objectivity cannot rest on descriptions of what is supposed to have gone on in our minds, nonetheless, this in no way entails that there are no such things as individual or personal experiences.[39] There has to be a subject of experience, and a view of objectivity that dismissed the reality of the subject would be in fact a very odd one. That is not to say we have a direct perception of ourselves as a thinking subject; that approach, as we know, St. Thomas rejects with good reason.[40] We are aware of our own existence because when we say, "I exist," we know we are enunciating a true proposition and cannot be skeptical about its truth.[41] This, I think, is in the same spirit of Newman's "We use, not trust our faculties."[42] The unknown fourteenth-century mystic who wrote *The Cloud of Unknowing* expressed, in another of his works, this irreducible basis of a sane approach to the reality of the self in a pithy and unforgettable way:

> For I hold him too lewd and too simple that cannot think and feel that himself is—not what himself is, but that himself is. For this is plainly proper to the lewdest cow, or to the most unreasonable beast—if it might be said, as it may not, that one were lewder or more unreasonable than another—for to feel their own proper being. Much more then

---

39. It should also be pointed out that Wittgenstein accepted this point: "Although he rejects the Cartesian interpretation of subjectivity, Wittgenstein does not on that account discard the subjective, but rather returns once and again to the 'experience of the meaning of a word,' and he insists on 'the visual experience' that accompanies the seeing of aspects." Day, William, and Krebs, "The Bodily Root," *Seeing Wittgenstein Anew*, 135.

40. See discussion earlier in the previous chapter, 211. "... no one perceives that he understands except through the fact that he understands something, for to understand something is prior to understanding that one understands. And so the soul comes to the actual realization of this existence through the fact that it understands or perceives." Aquinas, *De Veritate*, 10, 8.

41. "... it is to be noted that Aquinas does not say that a man perceives that he has a spiritual soul or that he affirms his existence a thinking subject, if by this we mean simply a mind. The awareness of one's own existence of which Aquinas is speaking is an awareness enjoyed also by those who are innocent of all philosophy; it is anterior to any metaphysical theory of the self." Copleston, *Aquinas*, 48.

42. "It seems to me unphilosophical to speak of trusting ourselves. We are what we are, and we use, not trust, our faculties." Newman, *An Essay in Aid of a Grammar of Assent*, 66.

is it proper to man, the which is singularly endued with reason above all other beasts, for to think and for to feel his own proper being.[43]

That we are is clear enough; *what* we are in another matter.[44] The distinction, which is surely a familiar one, is important when we come to think about the development of St. Philip's own embodied mysticism. I have already said that Philip's own journey to union with God was through the ordinary practices of the Catholicism of his time. Furthermore, this union was dominated by the sacrament of the Eucharist. Of course it is universally acknowledged among Catholics, with various degrees of enthusiasm, that the Eucharist is the highest form of worship. There is, however, more to the matter than this. For while the Mass did not constitute St. Philip in his being, it did shape the sort of being he became. The complex of words and actions of the liturgy not only molded his experience of the divine, but it also shaped him as the subject of liturgical experience: what Philip actually became. Let us say, then, that the words and actions of the Church not only create the reality of the sacraments, but they also, in part, structure what the worshipper becomes.

How are we going to understand this development of the worshipper without falling back into the sort of subjectivism I have been arguing against? In the first place, we must remember that we are not talking about experience, as it were, in the raw. We are talking about the sacramental experience of a Catholic. So we are talking about the personal

---

43. Anonymous, "The Epistle of Privy Counsel," *The Cloud of Unknowing and Other Treatises by An English Mystic of the Fourteenth Century*, 105. "Lewd" as used here means "ignorant" or "unlearned."

44. "This is little mastery for to think, if it were bidden to the lewdest man or woman that liveth in the commonest natural wit in this life, as methinketh. And therefore softly, and mourningly, and smilingly I marvel me sometimes when I hear some men say—I mean not simply lewd men and women, but clerks and men of great knowledge—that my writing to thee and to others is so hard and so high, so curious and so quaint, that scarcely it may be conceived of the subtlest clerk or witted man or woman in this life, as they say. But to these men must I answer and say that it is much worth to be sorrowed, and of God and his lovers to be mercifully scorned and bitterly condemned, that now on these days, not only a few fold but generally almost all—except one or two in a country of the special chosen of God—be so blind in their curious knowledge of learning and of nature that the true conceit of this light work, through the which the most simple man's soul or woman's in this life is verily in lovely meekness oned to God in perfect charity, may no more, nor yet so much, be conceived of them in certainty of spirit, for their blindness and their curiosity, than may the knowledge of the greatest clerk in the schools of a young child that is at his A.B.C. And for this blindness erringly they call such simple teaching curiosity of wit, when, if it be well looked upon, it shall be found but a simple and a light lesson of a lewd man." Ibid., 105.

experience of the worshipper as already objectified. And what might that be like? We can find the beginning of an answer by using a somewhat difficult discussion of St. Thomas's about the phrase "taste and see that the Lord is good." Thomas says:

> The experiencing of a thing is gained through the senses; but in one way, of a thing present, in another, of an absent thing. Of an absent thing, by reason of sight, smell and hearing; but of a thing present, by touch and taste—of a thing extrinsically present, by touch; by taste, however, of a thing intrinsically present. God, however, is not far from us nor outside of us but in us...; and therefore the experiencing of the divine goodness is called a tasting.[45]

I have no intention of trying to explicate how this experience is said to fit in with St. Thomas's system.[46] The point in adducing it here is to show that St. Thomas is perfectly aware that there is an element of personal experience in our approach to God, in tasting and seeing that the Lord is good. This personal and experiential aspect of prayer, then, is not an invention of the modern world.[47]

---

45. From Aquinas, *Lectura in Psal.* 33, vol. 9, quoted in Cunningham, *The Indwelling of the Trinity*, 198.

46. Cunningham comments: "The loving-knowledge rooted in grace which is implied by the inhabitation attains the Persons as objects present to us and within us. So it cannot be a discursive knowledge, which by definition has no direct contact with the thing known.... We know God as present in us and with us without reasoning to this presence, by a sort of contact, or, better, a sort of tasting. This does not mean, however, that we have an immediate knowledge of the Trinity, such as in the Beatific Vision or with the immediacy of sense experience ... we know God by means of an effect produced by God operating, intrinsic in our intellective powers, known without reasoning.... But not any effect of God suffices as a medium for the contuition of Him: it must be an effect within man, an effect to which God is immediately present, an effect immediately perceptible, an effect supremely expressive of God. And these conditions are realized only in the gifts of grace, but especially in the gift of the Holy Ghost of Wisdom and in the supreme theological virtue of charity.... Simply put ... we know the gifts of the Trinity by experiencing them; and by Their gifts we know, we experience, the divine Persons themselves. But this is to have and to possess and to enjoy (imperfectly) the Persons: God is present by this fact in a very special manner.... It is clear then that in the experimental knowledge that Wisdom gives birth to, whose cause and formal medium is divine Charity, the formal explanation of the Trinity in the souls of the just is found...." Ibid., 198–202.

47. Bernard McGinn has written: "Jean Leclercq, in his study of the difference between monastic and scholastic theology, expressed the difference between monastic and scholastic modes in terms of the former's emphasis on *credo ut experiar* (I believe in order to experience) and the latter's concentration on *credo ut intellegam* (I believe in order to understand)." McGinn, "The Victorine Ordering of Mysticism," *The Growth of Mysticism*, 367. He goes on to add, though, that this dissimilarity makes a difference in emphasis, not in goals.

But how are we going to understand this necessity for a personal element in liturgical experience without falling into the sort of private experience I have been arguing against? I have been at pains to reject what has sometimes been called *mentalism* or *psychological internalism*. The objectivity of thinking does not come from a report on what goes on in my mind, and it is language that creates the possibility of objectivity. I have insisted that objectivity cannot be the result of a description of private experience, and that it is our initiation into a verbal community that enables us to communicate with one another, but, furthermore, that our experience as individuals is at least partially molded by the language we use.[48]

The personal aspect of the ordinary practices of Catholicism, including liturgical experience, is no exception to this principle, and it has to be understood as involving the use of language. Furthermore, this use of language is not merely a report of what went on inside the head of the priest or the mind of the laity; it also partly structures the experience itself. If we understand this principle correctly, we will see that it is possible to accept that "personal, experiential, and psychological categories"[49] have indeed marked the consciousness of modernity, but that this emphasis on the personal need not involve principles and practices inimical to the principle that the personal is structured by the language that makes Catholic sacramentalism possible.

The Function of the Paranormal in Philip's Life

The physical phenomena of mysticism did not define the nature of St. Philip's, or any other mystic's, union with God. Yet, while they do not define this union, they were a constant element in his life. They should not be dismissed as irrelevant, even if a desire for a tidy account of Philip's union with God might tempt one to leave them aside. I have tried to show, in my discussion of transverberation and my outline of St. Thomas's treatment of "unalterable" words, how we might begin to understand the relation of the divine initiative to human experience.

---

48. See Taylor, "Language and Human Nature," *Human Agency and Language*, on what he calls the "expressive view" of human language. "The expressive theory opens a new dimension. If language serves to express/realize a new kind of awareness; then it may not only make possible a new awareness of things, an ability to describe them; but also new ways of feeling, of responding to things. If in expressing our thoughts about things, we come to have new thoughts; then in expressing our feeling, we can come to have transformed feelings" (232–233). Richard Moran in *Authority and Estrangement* argues correctly, it seems to me, that Taylor pushes this principle too far when it comes to the actual constitution of the self (42–44).

49. Von Balthasar, *The Glory of the Lord*, vol. 3, 106.

What, though, we might still want to ask, were their function in the life of St. Philip, or of any Christian saint? One answer is to say that Philip's visions, his miracles of healing, and his reading of souls should be understood as an authentication of what he taught. They were a sign of the truth of his message and of who he was.

When the Gospels talk about miracles, the writers often use the Greek word for "sign." For example, the chief priests and the Pharisees asked what they were to do with Jesus: "For this man performs many signs. If we let him go on thus, everyone will believe in him...."[50] The miracles of Jesus were signs that invited belief in him.[51] The physical phenomena of mysticism have a similar function. The miracles are said to be an invitation to belief; sometimes this invitation is accepted, but it is also often refused.[52] In a similar way, the paranormal can act as an invitation to belief.

In his sermon *Miracles No Remedy for Unbelief*,[53] Newman makes the point, and it is a true one, that if someone does not believe, then a miracle is not going to create belief. In the parable of the rich man and Lazarus, the rich man in hell asks Abraham for someone to be sent to his five brothers who are still living so that they, too, may not end up in this place of torment. Abraham refuses and says: "If they do not hear Moses and the prophets, neither will they be convinced if some one should rise from the dead."[54] Our Lord rose from the dead, and they still do not believe. So it is quite true that miracles cannot create belief.

On the other hand, the Gospels also make it quite clear that miracles did happen, and the lives of the saints make it clear they go on happening. Of course, if one has it as a philosophical principle that miracles cannot happen, and therefore it follows that any particular miracle did not happen, then there is no point in even beginning to discuss the physical phenomena of mysticism. Suppose, however, we have an open mind about the possibility of miracles: what are we to make of Newman's point that they cannot create belief? Or, perhaps we should put the question in a more positive way and ask what could miracles possibly be *for* in a Christian context?

First of all, there is the fact that the Gospels are full of miracles. These

---

50. John 11:47–48; πολλὰ σημεῖα ποιεῖ.

51. "The signs worked by Jesus attest that the Father has sent him. They invite belief in him. To those who turn to him in faith, he grants what they ask." *Catechism of the Catholic Church*, 548.

52. "Despite his evident miracles some people reject Jesus; he is even accused of acting by the power of demons." Ibid., 548.

53. Newman, *Parochial and Plain Sermons*, vol. 8, Sermon 6, 1611.

54. Luke 16:31.

seem to reinforce the message of Isaiah that God has mercy on whom he will have mercy—that there is something essentially unearned about the mercy of God; and that is an important lesson. I think, in addition, we could also say something like this: miracles call attention to the presence of something strange; perhaps, they call attention to the presence of a mystery that we are invited to accept. A holy man or woman who works miracles, or is the subject of some of the various physical phenomena of mysticism, provides a kind of evidence for what the mystic believes; what happens to him shows that his message is to be taken seriously. At the same time, it should be remembered that Philip neither looked for such experiences, nor took any delight in their possession.

11

The Apostle of Rome

(Chez Grégoire)... l'Apôtre n'est rempli de grâces contemplatives que pour les communiquer. Il est essentiellement un instrument, un canal, un médiateur.... Ainsi notre Moïse apparaît-il comme transmettant la prière des hommes a Dieu et les grâces de Dieu aux hommes.

(For Gregory)... the Apostle is only given the graces of contemplation so that he can pass them on to others. He is essentially an instrument, a channel, a mediator.... Thus our Moses is shown as one who carries the prayers of men to God, and the graces of God to men.

Jean Daniélou[1]

Je suis tout à fait vide et sec en moi-même; les lumières ne me viennent que pour les autres; au fur et à mesure qu'ils en demandent. Je ne sais jamais rien d'avance, je ne puis jamais rien rappeler après.

I am totally empty and dry in myself; the understanding I do possess comes to me only in relation to others; and to the extent that it is needed. I know nothing beforehand, nor can I remember anything afterwards.

l'abbé Huvelin[2]

GREGORY of Nyssa's doctrine of the three ways of the spiritual life has provided us with a framework to trace the development of St. Philip's mystical life. The term of this development was a loving awareness of the presence of God in the darkness. Gregory makes clear that this term is not a state in which nothing changes and where there are no difficulties. Using St. Paul's words, Gregory says: "one thing I do, forgetting what lies behind and straining forward to what lies ahead, I press on

---

1. Daniélou, *Platonisme et Théologie Mystique*, 328
2. Portier, *Un précurseur l'abbé Huvelin*, 47.

toward the goal for the prize of the upward call of God in Christ Jesus."[3] Julian of Norwich expressed this double experience of having found God and yet being driven by this experience to look for him once again:

> For I saw him and sought him. For we be now so blinde and so unwise that we can never seke God till what time that he of his goodness sheweth himself to us. And when we see ought of him graciously, then are we stered by the same grace to seke with great desire to see him more blissefully. And thus I saw him and sought him, and I had him and wanted him. And this is and should be our comen working in this life, as to my sight.[4]

Julian's experience of an arrival that is at the same time a starting point aptly describes the culmination of St. Philip's own mystical journey. The dominant note is now the quiet assurance of the presence of God, coupled with a hunger to deepen this awareness. Life dominated by the spiritual combat, as well as existence marked by the search for truth pursued in the light of studies and the anguished probing in the darkness, have given way to the loving awareness of the presence of God. St. Teresa says that the characteristic of this final stage is peace and quietness. "So tranquilly and noiselessly, does the Lord teach the soul in this state and do it good that ... he and the soul alone have fruition of each other in the deepest silence."[5]

We are not to take away from St. Teresa's description that the soul is no longer capable of suffering. Some of her own most severe trials followed on what she calls the mystical marriage between the soul and God.[6] The point is that, having given herself entirely into the hands of God, the search is no longer the focus of her life. The activity of God in her soul is now characterized by God's use of Teresa as an instrument in his own love for the suffering, wounded body of Christ. From the point of view of St. Teresa, or St. Philip, the dominant note becomes the need to share and communicate the riches of their union with God to other people.

How did this general description of a mystic's union with God work out in Philip's own life? How, that is, did Philip's own union with God show itself in his own experience and activity?

His own experience continued to be marked by the physical phenomena of mysticism. It is clear that these phenomena did not define the

---

3. Philippians 3:13–14.
4. Julian of Norwich, *A Revelation of Love*, 159, 10–15.
5. St. Teresa of Jesus, *Interior Castle*, VII.3, *Complete Works*, 342.
6. Burrows, *Interior Castle Explained*, 110.

nature of his union with God, yet they were a constant element in his life. They should not be dismissed as irrelevant, even if a desire for a tidy account of Philip's union with God might tempt one to leave them aside. Philip's visions, his miracles of healing, and his reading of souls should be understood as an authentication of what he taught. They were a sign of the truth of his message and of who he was.[7]

In addition to Philip's experience of mysticism, there is also the question of his own activity. There was a large measure of passivity in his union with God. Yet there was also an element of his cooperation in God's use of him as an instrument for the healing of the wounds and forgiving of sins in the mystical body. This apostolate was marked by a profound secularity. In Florence, he had begun to learn to use this world well,[8] and in Rome his ministry was directed in the first place, although not exclusively, towards the sanctification of the laity. Bacci remarks:

> [Although] he sent a great number of his spiritual children into religion, both men and women ... nevertheless, his greatest delight and his special desire was, that men should make themselves saints in their own homes. Hence it was that he would never permit many, who lived in court with great profit to themselves and edification to others, to leave it and go elsewhere.[9]

In this making of saints in their own homes, Philip turned to the ordinary and readily accessible practices of Catholicism. His embodied mysticism, in its final stages, showed itself in his love of neighbor, in his emphasis on the prayer of petition, and in his sacramental ministry of the Confessional and the Mass.

The Love of Neighbor

The development of the isolated soul in the illuminative way is essential to strengthen the self and detach it from sensible experience as it sets out on the way to union with God. But this withdrawal into pure subjectivity can only be a temporary phase in the mystic's journey. Unless the individual returns to interacting with others, and the world of ordinary experience, he will sink into what Hegel called "the beautiful soul," a soul so perfect in its own eyes that it refuses to become involved with other people for fear of compromising its purity of intention. The beau-

---

7. See part three, chapter ten, "Towards an Account of St. Philip's Embodied Mysticism."
8. See part one, chapter one, "Using this World Well."
9. Bacci, *The Life of Saint Philip Neri*, vol. 2, 47–48.

tiful soul becomes totally irrelevant.[10] In spite of Philip's love and need for solitude, he always remembered the second great commandment, that we should love our neighbor as ourselves.

Gregory of Nyssa is clear that the graces of union with God in the darkness have a social significance. There is a statement of this in the *Commentary on the Psalms*, where he teaches that the mystic shares in God's nature by imitating divine well-doing. The perfection of the Christian lies in doing what is proper to the divine nature, which is to know how to accomplish whatever is really required to help those in need:

> For the person who has attained this lofty height stands midway between the mutable and the immutable natures and intercedes for both extremes. He offers prayers to God for persons alienated by sin and transmits the mercy of God's transcendent authority to those in need ... he imitates God by good deeds and associates himself with God's own nature. I mean that God imparts his benevolence to all those in need.[11]

This effort on Philip's part, to deal with the needs and failures of a suffering humanity, should be viewed as one aspect of his mystical life. His concern for others is not a consequence of his embodied mysticism; rather, it is part of the way this mysticism was practiced. This gives to Philip's life a dimension that resonates with contemporary concerns. The absence of God in the dark night of the soul is for many today the existential beginning of an involvement with the hidden God.[12] This is not the way Philip's mystical development began, but it was the way it ended. His life in the dangerous world of counter-reformation Rome was marked by an effective concern for those on the margins of society and for the victims of injustice and prejudice. The interventions often, although by no means always, went against the known wishes and attitudes of those in authority. Here are a few examples of Philip's concern for those who were at the mercy of the powerful.

---

10. See above Part Two, Chapter Eight, "The Catacombs and the Apostolate," 181 *ff*.

11. Gregory of Nyssa, *Commentary on the Inscription of the Psalms*, 40, M 457, J 45. See Daniélou, *Platonisme et Théologie Mystique*, 328: "Les grâces mystiques ont une fin apostolique." (Mystical graces have an apostolic purpose.)

12. "Like Simone Weil, I prefer to begin thinking about our awareness of God with an account of human and historical awareness of innocent suffering.... What Weil suggests—though she never says so explicitly—is that one can begin mysticism with a tragic sense of innocent suffering." David Tracey, "Afterword" in Kessler and Sheppard, *Mystics: Presence and Aporia*, 242.

Ponnelle and Bordet draw attention to Philip's gentleness and concern for the Jews and contrast it with that of Pius V.[13] Philip's attitude in this matter, although it was not approved of, was at least tolerated. There was, however, another instance of Pius's activities that nearly led to Philip's having to leave Rome. The Papacy had promised a Papal fleet for the crusade which ended with the victory of Lepanto in 1571. There were not enough galley-slaves or prisoners to equip the number of galleys promised, so the Pope decided to round up the gypsies on the streets of Rome and send them to the galleys. Many theologians, so Ponnelle and Bordet inform us in a non-committal way, thought that there "was a violation of justice in this requisition of innocent men."[14] Certainly Philip thought so, and in company with a number of distinguished theologians, he signed a remonstrance to the Pope. The Pope changed his mind, but, with the exception of Philip, he banished all the signatories from Rome.

Philip also made his way to the side of heretics and those condemned to death. He had no use for heresy, but he had the inner freedom to try to save heretics if he possibly could. One of the most noteworthy examples of this was his dealing with Paleologus. Paleologus was an apostate Dominican friar who, in 1583, was condemned by the Inquisition to be burned and, still unrepentant, was on his way to the scaffold set up in the Campo de' Fiore.[15] He was met by Philip, who embraced him and touched his heart in such a way that Paleologus showed signs of yielding. Philip told the soldiers to stop what they were doing—"Don't you know who I am?" he is reported to have said. Evidently they did, and Philip at once sent to ask the Pope for a stay of execution. In the meantime, they shut Paleologus up in a shop, the condemned man finally got up on a bench, and he recanted his heresy. During Philip's absence, Paleologus is reported to have shouted, "Where is that man, who spoke in the simplicity of the Gospel?" The Pope granted Philip's request, and Paleologus was sent back to the prison so that Philip could complete his work of conversion. Philip visited him in prison,[16] but he was always

---

13. "Everyone knows of the rigorous measures taken by Pius V against the Jews, driving them out from the Papal States, and only tolerating them in Rome and Ancona if they were confined within a special quarter of the city with the 'yellow cap' upon their heads." Ponnelle and Bordet, *St. Philip Neri*, 268.

14. Ibid., 282.

15. The following account of Paleologus's trial and execution is taken from Ponnelle and Bordet, *St. Philip Neri*, 293ff.

16. Germanico Fedeli says Philip visited him every day (for two years). "... il beato padre andava ogni giorno, a vistarlo in Tor Nono." Della Rocchetta and Vian, *Il Primo Processo per San Filippo Neri*, vol. 4, 21.

uneasy about how genuine Paleologus's conversion was.[17] It appears he had good reason to doubt, since after two years Paleologus was executed as a relapsed heretic, although he professed his faith on the scaffold. He was assisted at his death by two of Philip's Oratorians, Baronius and Bordini. One of the ministries of the Oratory seems to have been the care of the prisoners of the Inquisition.

Jews, gypsies, and heretics were not high up on the papal government's list of favorites. They were all outsiders and often the object of suspicion. It is clear that Philip's concern for these marginalized people stemmed from his sense of justice and his feeling of compassion for those who had been wrongly treated. He was not, though, moved to act merely because they were poor and suspect. He was not a natural antagonist either to the idea of authority or to those possessing it. Philip supported those he thought needed supporting. He supported the poor and the outcast, but he was also, as Newman said, "the counselor of Popes."[18]

Capecelatro ends his chapter on "St. Philip and the Cardinals and Aristocracy of Rome" by telling us:

> (His) relations with princely families, and with others too numerous to mention, together with the reverence and love with which he was regarded by so many Cardinals, prelates, and men of learning, extended the influence and increased the fruit of Philip's apostolate, and gave him over all Rome a moral pre-eminence and sway.[19]

Ponnelle and Bordet cite Cardinal Cusano, a contemporary of Philip's, who said that:

> ... to his knowledge no ecclesiastic, whether religious or secular, had been held in greater veneration by people of all classes, common folk as well as nobles, courtiers, prelates, bishops, cardinals and popes.[20]

Philip's love for other people was not ideological. He loved with God's own love, and God's love does not exclude anyone on purely social or political categories. And yet there remains the intriguing question how Philip, the very human being, managed to deal with both the great and the good, as well with those on the margins of society; with the prisoners of the Inquisition, for example, and with those who had put them there. The answer must be his irony.[21] He was called a Christian Socrates, and

---

17. Alexander Alluminatus testified that "Et quello fu una conversione, che al padre non li piaque mai." Della Rocchetta and Vian, *Il Primo Processo per San Filippo Neri*, vol. 1, 380.
18. Newman, "Litany of St. Philip," *Meditations and Devotions*, 119.
19. Capecelatro, *The Life of Saint Philip Neri*, 467.
20. Ponnelle and Bordet, *St. Philip Neri*, 492.
21. See part one, chapter four, "Art, Irony, and Eros."

"self-deprecation, feigned praise of others, playfulness and an obliquity of speech"[22] were all aspects of Philip's irony in early life and later on, as well. What, one wonders, is one to make of the following?

> Whenever the cardinalate was spoken of, [Philip] would raise his eyes towards heaven and say with impassioned fervor: *Paradiso, Paradiso*. Sometimes he would throw his berretta in the air while uttering these words, or play with an old Cardinal's berretta he had by him, as though it were a ball.[23]

The conventional interpretation of this would have it that Philip's heart, in Capecelatro's words, "was set on a dignity higher still" (presumably not the Papacy). It was by repeating these words, we are assured, that Philip's sons "found strength to put aside the alluring vanities and ambitions of life."[24] Maybe, but it was hardly a typical way of treating the symbol of "the sublime dignity of the Cardinalate."[25] It is just as likely that the irony of the young man from Florence was still very much alive in the aged saint. The hat was, after all, the sign of everything many ecclesiastics wanted out of life, and Philip did not have a high opinion of that sort of clerical ambition. *Paradiso, Paradiso*, doesn't sound like Savonarola, but the judgment on clerical ambition and clerical success was not that different. Philip lived successfully through the snake pit of papal Rome by distancing himself from its cabals and ambitions. It was his irony, directed against himself as well as others, that gave him the balance to survive with his ideals intact.

In the museum of San Marco in Florence, there is a banner inscribed with the words *Christus et Ecclesia Romanus* (see p. 248, n. 27), that is, Christ and the Roman Church; it was used by Savonarola in one of his processions through Florence in 1496, although it probably predates his arrival in the city.[26] The motto proclaims Savonarola's professed ideal in his reforming work, and it sums up what he believed to be the real moti-

---

22. See Part One, Chapter Four, "Art, Irony, and Eros," 121.
23. Capecelatro, *The Life of Saint Philip Neri*, 512. This seems to be based on Bernardino Corona's testimony (Della Rocchetta and Vian, *Il Primo Processo per San Filippo Neri*, vol. 1, 287). The part about throwing the hat into the air, however, is missing. It must be derived from some other source.
24. Capecelatro, *The Life of Saint Philip Neri*, 512.
25. Cardinal Antonelli, Pius IX's Secretary of State, used the expression in a letter to Archbishop Manning in 1875. "In the Sacred Consistory of this morning, our Lord, His Holiness, deigned to promote to the sublime dignity of Cardinal Mgr. Henry Edward Manning, Archbishop of Westminster." Purcell, *Life of Cardinal Manning*, vol. 2, 533.
26. It was attributed to Fra Angelico, though it was probably painted much later (c. 1480–1490) by Botticini. See Scudieri and Rasario (eds.), *Savonarola e le sue "reliquie" a San Marco*.

vation for both his efforts to reform the Church and to establish a Christian commonwealth.[27]

It is not difficult to see why Savonarola ended up as he did, because the ideal itself has two sides that seem to point in opposite directions, and while these directions may be compatible, they are not obviously so. At least, that is what people seem to think. Many would say that a religious movement dedicated to making Christ better known, better loved, and better served is clear enough, but to say that this same movement is also forwarding the interests of the Roman Catholic Church is not so clear. Even if it is admitted that the two aims are compatible, they do not seem to be of the same order: to work for Christ is obviously a religious activity, but to work for the Roman Church is not so clearly religious in the same sort of way.

The response of Catholic orthodoxy to this dichotomy—between a spiritual realm of the truly religious and the visible community we call the Church—is clear. The Church maintains that the dichotomy does not exist. Catholicism is the religion of the Incarnation, of God's taking our human nature to redeem us through his death and resurrection, and the visible community continues the work begun at the Incarnation. The Church and its sacraments are the appointed, ordinary means of our approach to God through Christ, and without the Church these appointed, ordinary means disappear. Theology is not merely a statement of the truth, of the way things are, but it also indicates how this truth is to be assimilated into our very being so that we become something new and better. This renewal of our nature, as St. Paul calls it,[28] is only made possible through the grace of God, which works through the sacraments of the Church. Yet, at the same time, growth in the Christian life requires a spiritual combat against everything that draws us away from Christ, and the weapons for this warfare—that is, the truth of Christianity, with its moral and ascetical teaching, as well as the sacramental life, which is the source of the grace of God—are to be found in the mystical body of Christ that is the Church.

The Catholic view of the Church is complex and contrasts with the relative simplicity both of classical Protestantism as well as of a good deal of modern theological thinking. For classical Protestantism, the

---

27. Journet, *Savonarole en prison*, 17. Journet says that Savonarola was "fidèle jusqu'au bout à la devise . . . Christus et ecclesia Romana." 17.

28. "Put off your old nature which belongs to your former manner of life and is corrupt through deceitful lusts, and be renewed in the spirit of your minds, and put on the new nature, created after the likeness of God in true righteousness and holiness." Ephesians 4:22–24.

Church is invisible and its members are known only to God; for much of modern thinking, the Church is nothing but the visible community as it develops through history. For Catholicism, the Church is both visible and invisible, and sinners as well as saints belong to the visible Church here on earth. This doctrine is inexhaustibly rich and inspiring, but it has to be lived out in space and time, and we are not going to grasp the challenge of this teaching without understanding that it is not a paper theory, but a way of life that often demands heroism of a particularly difficult kind. The need for heroism is not difficult to grasp; if a Catholic believes that the structure of the Church is willed by God, then the possibility of clashes between the institutional and the charismatic aspects of the Church is pretty obvious. Savonarola didn't manage to keep the personal and institutional dimensions of the Church together, and he died rejected by both the Church and the city he had tried so brilliantly, but so tragically, to serve.

St. Philip shared the friar's longing for a reform of the life of the Church.[29] Like Savonarola, Philip believed that there could be no real reform without interior renewal, but he also believed this interior renewal had to be based on and nourished by the sacraments of the Church. Savonarola professed the same belief, but in the end he could not live it out and broke with the institutional Church.

St. Philip chose another path. When he was presented with choosing between his work, which he believed to have been divinely inspired, and obedience to those who disliked both him and his apostolate, he obeyed. Savonarola, when faced with going on with his work or disobeying the Pope, chose to go on with his work and ruined both himself and his political work as well. Savonarola's arguments were often sound, but his practice was not. Philip was not a great one for argument, but his way of living out his Catholicism turned him, with the grace of God, into a saint.

The Prayer of Petition

The prayer of petition is often the source of muted embarrassment today. People have a sense that it is an irrational activity, or that it is in some way unspiritual and hardly Christian, or they feel it is not compatible with the mentality of sophisticated modern man. Yet the prayer of petition, along with praise and thanksgiving, is a fundamental form of

---

29. See Part One, Chapter Three, "Reform in Florence: St. Catherine and Savonarola," particularly the sections titled "Interpretations of Savonarola's Life," 97–99, and "Newman on St. Philip and Savonarola," 99–101.

Christian prayer. In the prayer of petition, we open our hearts to God and acknowledge our need for salvation and assistance. The reason we ask for what we need, and the reason this not an irrational or un-Christian activity, rests on Christ's command that we should pray for what we need.[30] The prayer of petition was central to Philip's life of prayer. Bacci records:

> He always had recourse to prayer before transacting any business, especially if it was of importance; and such was the confidence in God which he thus gained, that he would say, "As I have time to pray, I have an assured hope of obtaining from our Lord whatever favor I ask." Sometimes he conceived so great a confidence, that he would say, "I wish such a thing to turn out in this way, and such a thing in that way," and so it would turn out in the event.[31]

A dramatic instance of Philip's use of the prayer of petition is found in the account of the cure of Baronius from what was taken to have been a fatal illness.

> And now, when the last ray of hope from man was gone, Cesare (Baronius) sank into a peaceful slumber, and had a vision which he himself related on oath in the process of Philip's canonization. He saw in this vision Philip prostrate at the feet of Jesus Christ, who appeared as in pictures of the Resurrection, and with him was the ever-blessed Virgin Mother. And he heard Philip plead again and again with Jesus, saying: "Give him back to me, Lord, give him back to me; give me back this my son; I want him!"[32]

Reading such accounts triggers today an automatic reaction of skepticism. It is one thing to say the Our Father, for example, but it is another thing to give wholehearted assent to what we are saying. So long as we keep the petitions general, we may derive a certain comfort in saying the words. But, when we bring them down to the particular, when we bring them down to praying for specific things in the real world of space and time, then we wonder whether we mean what we are saying. We are haunted with an uneasy sense that the prayer of petition is a pointless

---

30. "In prayer man lays bare to God his (or the Church its) own need of salvation and assistance, acknowledging that the exigencies of concrete earthly existence are in God's hands. This affirmation expresses the partnership that God himself has established with man by grace and always appeals to the mercy of God, who has provided for us before we ask him (Mt. 6:25–33)." Rahner and Vorgrimler, *Theological Dictionary*, "Prayer of Petition," 371.
31. Bacci, *The Life of Saint Philip Neri*, vol. 1, 173.
32. Capecelatro, *The Life of Saint Philip Neri*, 217–218.

activity. It may help us along the way psychologically, we are tempted to say, but we honestly don't think it changes much. Then again, even if, somehow or other, "it works," we are hit with a sense that it is demeaning to use it. The use of the prayer of petition displays, so we feel, cowardice in the face of the difficulties of life and reveals a childish dependence on God that is unworthy of free men. The imperative, as we see it, that we should respect the autonomy of our humanity is part of the cultural legacy of the Enlightenment.[33] The conceptual difficulties with asking things from God, as publicized by the Enlightenment, are not intrinsically foolish, and most people have from time to time felt the force of one or other of them. It is worth trying to unpack what is contained in these attitudes. There are two questions to be asked. First, is it foolish to pray? Second, is it Christian to pray?

One of the oldest and most obvious objections to prayer is that it is a pointless occupation. If God is a conscious being who is all-powerful and directs the universe, including all human activity, as he sees fit, then what effect could prayer possibly have? Or, if God is not that sort of being, then perhaps it is blind necessity that governs everything, in which case there is obviously nothing to be gained in praying that anything should change. Or again, some people say that we have an unworthy conception of God if we think his will can be altered by anything we could do.

St. Thomas sums up these objections and then answers them by pointing out that it is an aspect of God's Providence that some of the things that happen should be brought about through prayer. God's Providence does rule all things, and we do not change it by prayer, but prayer is a constitutive element in bringing about what God's Providence has decreed.[34]

Our prayer of petition is one of the means God uses for bringing about the realization of his purposes. We are not telling God what he does not know; we are not trying to alter his will. Yet at the same time as we make this prayer, we are affirming our freedom, with God's grace, to enter into the realization of our own destiny. The prayer of petition is

---

33. Pelikan, *The Christian Tradition*, vol. 5, 60: "When applied to the Christian tradition and its doctrines, the Enlightenment represented what has been called the 'revolution of man's autonomous potentialities over against the heteronomous powers which were no longer convincing,' namely, the heteronomous authority of the church and of its dogma and ultimately of the objective authority of Scripture and of transcendent revelation itself." The reference in Pelikan is to Paul Tillich's *Perspectives on 19th and 20th Century Protestant Theology*.

34. Aquinas, *Summa Theologiae*, 2a, 2ae, 83, 2: "In order to throw light on this question we must consider that Divine Providence disposes not only what effects shall take

a loving witness to the truth that the universe is not governed by iron necessity or blind chance. It is God's Providence that rules all things and, through his mercy, we can cooperate with that Providence.

The use of the prayer of petition establishes, and deepens, our relationship with a God we believe to be personal. When we ask for what we need in a simple and uncomplicated way, we enter into a living relationship with our Father. The Father uses our petition as an aspect of how he works out his purposes. Our relationship with this personal God is made real, and deepened, by the prayer of petition. As we begin to learn about ourselves through recognizing what we need, and through a growing sense of our own weakness and dependence, so, at the same time, we begin to know the merciful God who is the giver of all we need. The saints, through their use of the prayer of petition, have come to know God in a deeper and more intimate way than do most of us. They become finely attuned to the will of God, and their prayers are answered because they pray for what God wants them to pray.

It might be the case that the prayer of petition is not an irrational activity; however, it might yet still be true that it is not a particularly Christian one. People often say today that it betrays an unspiritual and even a magical frame of mind to ask particular things from God. The truly spiritual person should pray to be united to the will of God, so it is said, and what is the point of telling God a lot of things he must know already? Some might say that we are treating God as though we were children who expected everything we wanted from a kind of super Santa Claus. To do this, so it is maintained, is surely to display a very unworthy conception of God and very little respect for ourselves.

Even if our prayer is not an asking for unworthy objects, there always remains the suspicion that we are trying to bend God's will to our own. Would it not be a better indication of our belief in God's Providence merely to pray that God's will should be done and forget about praying for anything definite?[35] This view is only strengthened when we remem-

---

place, but also from what causes and in what order these effects shall proceed. Now among other causes human acts are the causes of certain effects. Wherefore it must be that men do certain actions, not that thereby they may change the Divine disposition, but that by those actions they may achieve certain effects according to the order of the Divine disposition: and the same is to be said of natural causes. And so it is with regard to prayer. For we pray, not that we may change the Divine disposition, but that we may obtain by asking (impetrate) that which God has disposed to be fulfilled by our prayers, in other words that by asking, men may deserve to receive what Almighty God from eternity has disposed to give, as Gregory says."

35. The attitude is not a new one. St. Teresa discusses it in the *Way of Perfection* in a passage that is included in the Office of Readings of *The Liturgy of the Hours*, for the

ber that it is often very difficult to know exactly for what we should pray. St. John Damascene says that "to pray is to ask fitting things of God,"[36] and it would follow from this that it would be wrong to pray for what is not fitting. Furthermore, we read in Romans, "we know not how to pray as we ought."[37] We might well conclude from this that it is impossible for us to ask for what is fitting, and Scripture seems to support this view. "You ask, and receive not: because you ask amiss."[38] If we cannot be sure of asking for things that God wants us to have, then it would appear to be better to leave the whole matter entirely in his hands and forget about the prayer of petition.

In answer to all this, it has to be remembered, first, that our Lord taught his disciples to ask definitely for those things contained in the petitions of the Lord's prayer. Again, the writer of the Letter to the Hebrews writes of Jesus "that he always lives to make intercession. . . ."[39] In response to the objection that only God knows what is good for us, and so we cannot pray for what we really need, St. Thomas reminds us first that the passage from Romans also includes the promise that the Holy Spirit will help us in our infirmities to ask for what is fitting. His main point, however, is that there are some things we cannot use badly, and these must be prayed for unconditionally:

> There are certain goods, which man cannot use in an evil manner and which cannot have bad results, such as the blessings by which we are sanctified and merit bliss. For these the good pray absolutely, as it says in the Psalms, "Show us thy face and we shall be saved (79:4)," and again, "Lead me into the path of thy commandments" (118:35).[40]

This unconditional type of prayer was central to Philip's own practice. Fr. Francesco Zazzara, in the Process for Philip's Beatification, gives a list of "prayers which the Blessed Philip Neri, my spiritual father, taught to me, although I have always been an unworthy, intractable and proud son."[41] These prayers for goods "which man cannot use in an evil

---

Wednesday of the thirteenth week of Ordinary Time. "O Eternal Wisdom, between you and your Father that was enough; that was how you prayed in the garden. You expressed your desire and fear but surrendered yourself to his will. But as for us, my Lord, you know that we are less submissive to the will of your Father and need to mention each thing separately. . . ." St. Teresa of Jesus, "The Way of Perfection," *Complete Works*, vol. 2, 123.

36. St. John Damascene quoted in Aquinas, *Summa Theologiae*, 2a, 2ae, 83.1.
37. Romans 8:26.
38. James 4:3.
39. Hebrews 7:25.
40. Aquinas, *Summa Theologiae*, 2a, 2ae, 83, 5.
41. Francesco Zazzara quoted in Ponnelle and Bordet, *St. Philip Neri*, 596.

manner" are the cry of a man who, first, has already found God, yet desires to find him more securely; and second, prays in a longing yet secure way for what he knows he will obtain.

> I shall never love Thee if Thou dost not help me, my Jesus,
> My Jesus, if Thou would have me, clear away all the hindrances which keep me from Thee.
> I would fain do good, my Jesus, and I do not know how.[42]

The purpose of the prayer of petition is not to bend the will of God, but to pray for what we need in conformity with his will. It is his will for us that we should pray in this way. In the prayer of petition, we grow gradually into a sense of the reality of our dependence on God and develop the confidence to ask him for what we need. The simple, familiar business of asking for what we require, if we are going even to begin to live the Christian life, is the foundation of our response to the call of God. It is through the prayer of petition that we begin to relate ourselves in a real way to the God who was before all things and is in all things.

One of the marks of genuine growth in prayer is a deepening sense of confidence in God. Modern man is afflicted with anxiety; that is, with a sort of fear that seems to have no definite object. Our attempts to pray and lead a good life sometimes seem to make existence more complicated. Our efforts to respond to God often bring confusion and suffering, but they do gradually develop in us a heightened awareness of the reality of God and of his care for us. This new sense of the presence of God is the best antidote for that formless fear and unease that we call anxiety.

This anxiety, as well as suspicion, pessimism about the future, and a distrust of human motives, often seems rooted in a particular sort of temperament, but no one is entirely exempt from these experiences. Little can be done to change first reactions or moods. On the other hand, the practice of the prayer of petition gradually develops a confidence in God, which is based on a growing realization of his loving Providence. This confidence runs deeper and is more enduring than either temperament or moods.[43] Philip's unceasing use of this prayer brought him both a loving confidence in the providence of God and a growing familiarity

---

42. Philip's prayers are included in Ponnelle and Bordet, *St. Philip Neri*, 596.

43. Aquinas, *Summa Theologiae*, 2a, 2ae, 83, 9: "Prayer is not offered to God in order to change his mind, but in order to excite confidence (fiducia) in us. Such confidence is fostered principally by considering God's charity towards us whereby he wills our good: hence we say 'our Father,' and to indicate this excellence which is powerful to fulfill his charity, 'who art in heaven.'"

with how he should cooperate with this providence to help bring about the coming of God's kingdom.

The Confessional and Philip's Influence

Everyone who has written about St. Philip emphasizes his love of the sacrament of penance. It was his preferred means of winning souls for Christ, and the exercises of the Oratory grew out of his efforts to solidify and extend the conversion of his penitents.[44] Bacci tells us that he was one of the first "who revived in Rome the practice of frequent confession and communion,"[45] and Gallonio stresses the fruits of Philip's constant work of hearing confessions.[46]

In his turn, Newman wrote, in one of his earliest chapter addresses to his Oratorian Community in Birmingham, that the confessional was St. Philip's great instrument of conversion.[47] "Though he can scarcely be said to have had a Parish in Rome, he was the father of parish Priests. He was the most unwearied of Confessors, the most gentle and wise of directors. And what he was, such were his followers in their measure."[48]

Capecelatro, in addition, strikes the right note in emphasizing that it was Christ's love for the individual sinner that shone in Philip's use of the sacrament of penance.

> As soon as he was a priest, he devoted himself with great love to this difficult and patient ministry. Throughout his life it was in this office that he most closely reproduced the living image of Jesus Christ, and that he gathered most abundant fruit.[49]

The validity of the sacrament of penance does not depend on the

---

44. "He was not content with having ... won a number of penitents, but, desiring to preserve them, he took care, like a good father, to invent spiritual exercises, by which they should not only maintain, but keep continually increasing their fervor, and advancing in spiritual things." Bacci, *The Life of Saint Philip Neri*, vol. 1, 43.

45. Ibid.

46. "He was very assiduous in the work of hearing confessions, to the extent that he hardly ever left the church, forgetful of himself. That in itself is a great thing, but to tell you something more remarkable, he would pass the greater part of the day in this work, without ever becoming tired. He was so eager to summon wandering souls back to their sense, the merely being seated in the chair which he used to hear confessions gave him the greatest refreshment and delight. You would not believe how many people, and what great ones, he enabled to bring forth ample fruit from the manure of their sins, and how many men and women were encouraged by his efforts to embrace the monastic life." Gallonio, *The Life of Saint Philip Neri* 26, 32.

47. "The confessional, as we know, was St. Philip's great instrument of conversion." *Newman The Oratorian*, 198.

48. Ibid., 187

49. Capecelatro, *The Life of Saint Philip Neri*, 107.

holiness, or otherwise, of the priest. The sacrament is the appointed means for the forgiveness of sins and operates in virtue of the merits of Christ. This teaching of the Church assures the laity that their sins are forgiven when the conditions for a valid confession are observed, and that they do not have to worry about the merits of the particular priest who hears their confession. On the other hand, the sacrament not only forgives sins but also gives the grace to turn to Christ in a deeper way. It is in this aspect of conversion to Christ that the role of the priest, as an individual, is important. A priest such as St. Philip, who was united to Christ, will lead his penitent with Christ's own love. He will do this because, having surrendered himself to God, it is God's purposes, and not the priest's own, that will be present in his activities. It was said of a priest of the French Oratory that he "wrote scarcely any books; he wrote in souls."[50] St. Philip wrote no books, but he also wrote in souls, and he was able to do so because Christ spoke in him.

St. Philip wrote in souls because, like the Moses of St. Gregory of Nyssa, he had forsaken 'what human nature can attain" and had "entered within the sanctuary of divine knowledge" where his soul was "hemmed in on all sides by the divine darkness."[51] Yet the darkness was not a cover for a flight from the world.[52] Rather, it was the case that this union with the Christ of the Eucharist led Philip back to the wounded members of the Lord's mystical body, where he wrote in souls what had experienced in the darkness.

This is not to say that Philip thought his spiritual direction was in any way a substitute for the sacrament of penance, or that confession was a mere adjunct to his own spiritual guidance. It is clear from his guidance of souls that he believed that sacramental confession was not only the indispensable beginning but also the continuing ground of any fruitful spiritual direction. Time and again, we see Philip doing everything in his power to persuade someone to go to confession even though the hoped-for penitent had almost no instruction in the faith. There is a striking modern example of this belief in the efficacy of the sacrament in the conversion of Charles de Foucauld. As a young man, Foucauld had given up the practice of his faith and had led a dissolute life in the

---

50. This was written of Fr. Charles de Condren, the second General of the French Oratory. Huvelin, *Some Spiritual Guides of the Seventeenth Century*, 52.

51. See Introduction, 43.

52. "... the image Gregory puts in front of us is not that of a solitary running away from humanity to obtain his own personal peace of mind. The important people in his work are all surrounded by other people and motivated by a continual movement of a kind of flux and reflux between contemplation and the apostolate." See Part Three, "Light from Darkness," 192.

army as a professed atheist. He was persuaded to meet the Abbé Huvelin and went into the church where the priest was hearing confessions.

> (He) did not kneel down; he just bent over and said "Father, I have not the faith; I have come to ask you to instruct me." M. Huvelin looked at him. "Kneel down, confess to God, you will believe." "But I didn't come to confess." "Make your confession." He wished to believe, and felt that, in his case, forgiveness was a condition for receiving light. He knelt down and made a confession of his whole life. When the Abbe saw his penitent stand up after receiving absolution, he resumed: "Are you fasting?" "Yes." "Go to Holy Communion at once." And Charles de Foucauld approached the Holy Table and made his "second first communion."[53]

This sort of incident is reported over and over in the life of St. Philip. Yet this more modern example, stripped of its sixteenth-century expression, may help to emphasize the reality of the power of the sacrament. When the sacrament is in the hands of a saintly priest, its power becomes almost visible. Certainly, it adds to the influence of the priest in question.

This brings us to the question of the nature of Philip's influence in his later years in Rome. This is sometimes contrasted with that of Savonarola. Thus, Cardinal Capecelatro writes:

> Philip's reformation succeeded better than Savonarola's, and was more lasting, because he kept it free from all alloy of civil or political reform; he trusted to its immense indirect influence on civilization and government. Savonarola, on the contrary, combined and confused the two reforms, and this limited and retarded both. It was not altogether his fault; the state of things in Florence was such that he could hardly avoid the combination.[54]

What, one wonders, is "indirect influence"? If indirect influence means not actually being the holder of an office, whether that office be ecclesiastical or political, and one that automatically carries with it *de facto* the possession of power and therefore of influence as well, then Philip's influence was not political in this direct sense. On the other hand, in the same way that knowledge is said to confer power, so influence confers power, and great influence confers great power. No one doubts that at the end of his life Philip possessed great influence on a succession of Popes, and in this sense he was certainly not without power.

It will then be said that this type of influence is indirect, and that is certainly true if, as I said above, by "indirect" we mean not formally con-

---

53. Huvelin, *Some Spiritual Guides of the Seventeenth Century*, "Introduction," L (50).
54. Capecelatro, *The Life of St. Philip Neri*, 162–163.

nected with an office of one kind or another. But such influence is, nonetheless, very real. Yet to argue from this premise—that is, that Philip's influence was indirect—to the conclusion that he was not interested in "civil or political reform" is a very dubious step on several counts. First, an important aspect of Philip's reform was concerned with the spiritual life of the clergy of Rome, and this necessarily involved a political dimension. The government of Rome was in the hands of the clergy, and the Pope and his Curia governed just as any secular state of the time governed. Of course, government in this sense was not all that occupied their attention, but it is very clear that they were not indifferent to the political aspects of their calling. To become involved, then, with the way the clergy lived and how they saw their role in life was to involve oneself in governmental matters. Philip's enemies saw this very clearly.

There is, however, a second consideration, which is that, in fact, Philip did involve himself directly in what can only be called political matters. We may take two examples. The first of these concerns Savonarola. In 1558, Paul IV, as we have seen, was preparing the first Index of Forbidden Books, and there was a determined effort on the part of the Jesuits and the Augustinians to have the works of Savonarola placed on this list. Philip, with the Dominicans of the Minerva, led the opposition to this move, and their efforts were in fact successful. We need only notice here that while Philip's motives may have been spiritual, they certainly had consequences in the political order. Then there is the question of the absolution of Henry of Navarre. Henry of Navarre was the heir to the French throne, but he was a Protestant. Should he be reconciled to the Church and allowed to become the Catholic King of France? The question most certainly had its religious aspects, but it is surely stretching things to say it has nothing to do with "political or civil reform," and in point of fact the question of whether or not the absolution should be granted was a political *cause celèbre*. Nevertheless, Philip threw himself into the campaign and told his disciple Baronius, who was the Pope's confessor, to refuse the Pope absolution unless Henry was absolved. Once again, this hardly supports the picture of Philip as a pious priest who took no interest in the political and civil world in which he lived.[55]

---

55. See Ponnelle and Bordet, *St. Philip Neri*, 543–550. "He (Philip) told Baronius, if his penitent remained deaf to his advice, to refuse to hear his confessions any more, and Baronius who was scrupulously conscientious, did not fail to carry out his injunction. With Philip and Baronius thus united against him, no more was required to bring Clement VIII to a decision; if two or three persons who alone enjoyed his confidence had not had recourse to these strong measures, no one knows, says the Venetian ambassador, how long his hesitation might not have lasted" (549).

Then, too, there is the evidence of Philip's influence on Baronius and the writing of the latter's *Annales*, or history of the Church. Philip not only inspired—"ordered" would perhaps be more accurate—Baronius to write his monumental work as the best means of combating the Reformation, but if one reads the dedications of the various volumes, and the letters Baronius wrote to influential people across Europe, one comes away with the impression that this disciple of Philip's was keenly aware of the "political and civil" dimension of his work; and Baronius would not have written anything in this public way against the mind of Philip. For example, Baronius dedicated Volume XI of the *Annales* to Sigismund III Vasa, the King of Poland. The King was involved in diplomatic and military efforts designed to restore Catholicism in Sweden and to gain control of the Russian throne, and Baronius encouraged him:

> Continue... and complete the glorious work you have undertaken. Fight the wars of the Lord.... You will have angels for your co-fighters.... The Catholic Church has already given her contributions of prayers, and the Supreme Pontiff who presides over her imparts the apostolic benediction over this. May Christ in whose name it is done assist you so that not only the tyrannical heretic [that is, Charles XI of Sweden] but even the chief infidel, the unjust possessor of the Oriental Empire [that is, Boris Godunov, the Czar], be brought under just arms.[56]

We do have to distinguish Philip's work from Savonarola's, but I do not think the difference is to be found in picturing Philip as so involved with spiritual things that he was unaware of what going on in the world around him or uninterested in influencing that world. It is just the contrary which was the case. Bacci says that although tried to make the world regard him as a man of "little judgment," he was, nonetheless, "esteemed as a man of the greatest enlightenment, not only in spiritual things, but even in worldly affairs."[57]

> ... indeed his prudence and gift of counsel caused him to be resorted to as an oracle by men of every rank and condition, and even the Sovereign Pontiffs set a great value on his judgment.[58]

Philip was not the loveable old duffer, as he is sometimes pictured. He not only survived the Rome of his time, but he influenced it as well.

---

56. Cited in Pullapilly, *Caesar Baronius: Counter-Reformation Historian*, 61.
57. Bacci, *The Life of Saint Philip Neri*, vol. 2, 30.
58. Ibid. Bacci continues and instances the case of Leo XI, who, when he was a Cardinal, "used to go to him several times a week, and remain four or five hours at a time in his room, partly because of the consolation he felt in conversing with him, and partly to confer with him about important business."

Somehow or other those powerful, able Cardinals and Popes recognized him as participating in the darkness of God, and out of that darkness bringing light. Philip's embodied mysticism grew out of the complex and practices that were sixteenth-century Catholicism. Yet these beliefs and practices themselves came to be influenced by Philip's union with his hidden God.

St. Philip's Mass

Philip's baptism was the foundation of Philip's mysticism. But it was in the celebration of Mass that his union with God was clearly visible. Like the tree of the Psalmist planted beside the water, his celebration of the holy mysteries overshadowed and nourished everything else he did.[59] Yet the Mass itself is the supreme example of Christ's saving work. Christ offered himself to the Father as a sacrifice for our sins, and that sacrifice is perpetuated in every Mass. Christ "is able for all time to save those who draw near to God through him, since he always lives to make intercession for them."[60] In every Mass, we have the lesson that at the heart of Catholicism is the self-offering of Christ on behalf of others. This interceding for others by Christ is what every priest offers for others as he joins his petitions to those of the eternal Son of God.

Gallonio tells us that as a priest, Philip never let a day pass without celebrating Mass, unless he was ill.[61] Yet right from the beginning of his priesthood, in spite of all his efforts to restrain himself, he was constantly in danger of going into an ecstasy. Finally, at the end of his life, he gave up saying Mass in public and, with the Pope's permission, said Mass privately in a little chapel beside his room.

Philip was upset and ashamed of what he clearly considered unsuitable displays of his closeness to God. He was extraordinarily strict in his dealings with the paranormal experiences of others, and it is clear that he tried to apply the same exigent standards to himself. What is equally clear, however, is that once he started saying Mass, he was not in control of his experiences. This general description is repeated, with a good deal of detail, over and over in the Process and in the other sources.

Philip's preparation for saying Mass was to try not to think about what he was about to do. Gallonio writes:

> In order to celebrate Mass without interference (being much afraid of raptures and ecstasies) he used to do anything he could to restrain that

---

59. "He is like a tree planted by streams of water, that yields its fruit in its season, and its leaf does not wither." Psalm 1:3.
60. Hebrews 7:25.
61. Gallonio, *The Life of Saint Philip Neri*, 23, 30.

ardour of spirit which usually affected him, before putting on his vestments. Since he would never have been able to complete the Mass if he were suddenly abstracted from his senses and totally rapt into heavenly contemplation, he set himself to concentrate on turning his thoughts away from God.[62]

In turning his mind away from God, he distracted himself with some birds or little dogs. He also had poems and jokes read to him, among them those of his favorite, Piovano Arlotto.[63]

This unheard-of preparation for Mass was often only partially successful. Once he actually started to celebrate, he was frequently overcome with tears, his body trembled, "and his hands would be raised up so that it looked as if he were dancing or jumping up":

> While he was saying Mass, particularly after he had arrived at the offertory, he would be affected with such delight that his whole body shook and quivered as he proceeded with the ceremony. To check this effect, he used often to look aside, now to the right, now to the left, and from time to time he would rub his head with his hand.[64]

Once he finished Mass "he was often so abstracted from his senses that you would think he was more dead than alive."[65]

Finally, when Philip was seventy-six, he gave up saying Mass in public, and in his private chapel he was able to celebrate without the constant tension of trying to restrain his fervor:

> There it was that, in his longing for ever closer union to God, after saying the words "Lord I am not worthy..." he would ask those who were present, including the server, to go out, remaining on his own in the chapel. Alone, and without witnesses, he would often not consume the sacred Eucharist, nor drink the Precious Blood, before he had passed two hours, more or less, in contemplation of the Blessed Sacrament, with deep feeling of devotion and much shedding of tears. Once he had received the Body and Blood of Christ, he would admit the server, and complete the ceremony.[66]

The extraordinary aspects of Philip's celebration of Mass are repeated and enlarged on in all the sources, including the Process. However we are to understand them, they are better attested than many other aspects of Philip's life, and there is no need to go on with the descriptions of the

---

62. Gallonio, *The Life of Saint Philip Neri* 24, 30.
63. See Ponnelle and Bordet, *St. Philip Neri*, 125.
64. Gallonio, *The Life of Saint Philip Neri*, 23, 30.
65. Ibid., 25, 31.
66. Ibid., 150, 169.

phenomena. What we have to try to do is understand their significance. As Gallonio puts it, "but not to expand pointlessly on a matter which is well known and familiar to all, I will pass on to something else."[67]

It would be idle to suggest that there were not aspects of Philip's liturgical life that were unique. On the other hand, what he taught by his devotion to the Mass was not the importance of the paranormal, but that the Mass is central to Catholic living. St. Philip's lesson to us is that we have to move the modern focus of attention away from what is subjective towards the wonderful reality of Christ acting in the liturgical life of the Church. But it is not enough to appropriate the truth—that it is Christ who operates through his sacraments—in a way that is only notional or abstract. Our acceptance that in the liturgy of the Church we are dealing with Christ's work, and Christ's words, has to be given a real, deep, and existential assent. This appropriation requires the practice of personal prayer. Newman treasured the words of St. Ambrose, who said that it was not by dialectic that God had saved his people (*non in dialectica complacuit Deo salvum facere populum suum*).[68] That is a large subject, but at least let us take away from it that somehow the truth must be made attractive and lovable: it must not appear as alien, threatening, and indifferent to our own needs. It is not enough to merely state the truth about public worship. There has to be a personal appropriation of Christ's self-giving in the Eucharist. Personal prayer is essential if we are going to develop a real sense of this self-giving of Christ. Personal prayer is an indispensable aspect of a Christian life; it is not an invention of the sixteenth century. It may be that a heightened sense of its importance may have developed around that time, but it is a mistake to think that an interest in the personal, as distinct from the subjective, is a product of a modern post-Cartesian mentality. The unknown author of the fourth-century work the *Liber Gradualium* was intent on showing that the liturgy of the Church was a "pattern" that had to be internalized. Christ gives us, he says, "the icon of the Church" in order that:

> ... faithful souls might be made one again and, having received transformation [*metabole*, a play on traditional language for the miraculous change of the Eucharistic elements], be enabled to inherit everlasting life.[69]

---

67. Gallonio, *The Life of Saint Philip Neri*, 25, 32.
68. He used this saying as the motto for *A Grammar of Assent*.
69. This is Alexander Golitzin's translation of a phrase from the *Liber Gradualium*, the work of an unknown fourth-century Syrian monk. See "'Suddenly Christ': The Place of Negative Theology in the Mystagogy of Dionysius Areopagites," in Kessler and Sheppard, *Mystics: Presence and Aporia*, 18. Brackets in original text.

This internalizing of the Christian message is what the author called "the little Church of the heart." At the same time, however, the *metabole* is only possible within the liturgical experience of the Church:

> The *Liber Gradualium* speaks of "three Churches": the heavenly church of the angels and saints, the earthly church of clergy and sacraments, and the "little Church of the heart." It is the middle term, this writer insists, the earthly church, that enables the believer "to find himself in the church of the heart, and [thence]," even if only momentarily in this life, "in the church on high."[70]

It is, then, no new or modern thing to insist that the liturgy must be reflected in the experience of the worshipper in a way that molds (*metabole*) his individuality as a Christian. The purpose of liturgical piety is not some sort of superior self-gratification; rather, it is a growing awareness that we must live to make intercession for others, and to work to bind up the wounds of sin and error in the real world of space and time. If we understand this principle correctly, we will see that it is possible to accept von Balthasar's claim that "the personal and the subjective" have indeed marked the consciousness of modernity, but that this emphasis on the personal need not involve principles and practices inimical to Catholic sacramentalism. Every one of us must seek to build the "little church of the heart." St. Philip's lesson is not an interest in the paranormal, but in the here and now of the daily Mass.

Ars Celebrandi

We are so accustomed to think about the freelance, spontaneous, and very personal character of Philip's apostolate in later life that there is a danger of forgetting that the Oratory he founded in Rome was marked by the splendor of its liturgy, the beauty of its music, and the high quality of its art. We have to thank the historians of art and culture who have drawn attention to the pivotal role of the Chiesa Nuova in fostering the arts in sixteenth- and seventeenth-century Rome.[71] Capecelatro, who, as I have remarked before, knew the Oratory from the inside, is one of the few ecclesiastical writers on St. Philip who seems to have appreciated in a serious way this side of the Saint's work:[72]

---

70. Ibid. Brackets in original text.
71. See, for example, Morelli, "The Chiesa Nuova in Rome around 1600: Music for the Church, Music for the Oratory," and Verstegen, "Federico Barocci, Federico Borromeo, and the Oratorian Orbit."
72. Capecelatro, chapter seven, "S. Philip and Music" in *The Life of Saint Philip Neri*.

S. Philip's Oratory was one of the great centers of sacred music in Rome. His singers, as well as his composers, were always chosen from amongst the most celebrated men in the city; and the Oratory offered to composers a new and a wider field for this art than even the great Basilicas and the Papal Chapel.[73]

In addition to the Masses, Psalms, and Antiphons, which were all rendered, as Capecelatro puts it, "in the style of that time," there was also the singing of sacred songs in the vernacular. The relation of these *Laude* to what we would now call an Oratorio is a complex one, but there is a relation, and it shows the importance that Philip and his Oratorians ascribed to music. Philip had learned the usefulness of vernacular songs for the apostolate in Florence, probably at the Confraternity of the Purification,[74] and he continued and enhanced the tradition in Rome.

The care and attention that Philip devoted to music is also evident in the visual arts.

> (The) plurality of artistic idioms in the church of the Valicella, "the most famous and well-attended in Rome for the fact of being ...decorated by the most talented painters in Italy, who rival each other," as Rubens himself testified in 1606... testifies not to decisions made in a casual manner, but, rather, to an ideological climate more open and sensitive to new artistic expression....[75]

Perhaps the most important experience of beauty that Philip had while in Florence was that of the liturgy. Even though Savonarola had inveighed against the newer traditions of polyphonic music, the Dominican rite had a solemn majesty about it, and its version of plainsong, which was unique to the order, only reinforced the beauty of the celebration of Mass and the Divine Office. Philip would also have had an opportunity to hear the newer music in other churches.

The beauty of the Liturgy is an ordered beauty, and the phrase *ars celebrandi*, the art of celebrating, refers to how the Mass and the other sacraments are to be celebrated in an ordered fashion. The use of the word "art" in this connection is important and requires some comment. *Ars* in ancient Latin, like τέχνη in Greek, meant a craft or a specialized skill that involved doing things, like building ships or shoeing horses or surgery. It is a conception that is totally foreign to our way of thinking. Making it even more difficult for us to come to terms with this view of

---

73. Ibid., 375.
74. See part one, chapter two, "Chastity and Charity," 75.
75. Morelli, "The Chiesa Nuova in Rome around 1600: Music for the Church, Music for the Oratory," 3.3.

art is the fact that the usage developed in the early Middle Ages, and early modern English borrowed these developments. By the time of Shakespeare, art meant any special form of book-learning, "such as grammar or logic, magic or astrology.... 'Lie there my art,' says Prospero, putting off his magic gown."[76] But the Renaissance, first in Italy and then elsewhere, re-established the old meaning, and the Renaissance artists, like those of the ancient world, did actually think of themselves as craftsmen.

This older view maintained that art, unlike prudence or practical wisdom, is focused on what is to be done.

> The moment the artist works well—the moment the Geometer demonstrates—"it makes little difference whether he be in a good temper or in a rage." If he is angry or jealous, his sin is the sin of a man, not the sin of an artist.[77]

Art, like science, on this scholastic theory, is concerned with an *object* (an object to be made), and "it is bound fast by rules."[78] You cannot build ships or practice surgery without rules. The Schoolmen, following Aristotle, affirm this constantly, and they make this possession of fixed rules an essential property of art as such. Now, if liturgy is an art, then it too is a kind of doing with rules. Liturgy, like any other sort of art when faithfully executed, results in something beautiful. That is not to say that liturgy is only the production of something beautiful, but it is most definitely to say that if it is not beautiful, it has ceased to be *the ars celebrandi*.

Saint Thomas said that the beautiful is that which, being seen, pleases: *id pulchra ... dicuntur quod visa placent.*[79] Whether or not such a view of art is found to be acceptable nowadays, and for most people, of course it is not, nonetheless it was the view that lay behind everything that Savonarola taught and Philip learned about art. It was, furthermore, the view that nourished Philip's conviction that liturgy, because it was beautiful, brought us into contact with God. I believe that Philip's response to God, and the foundations of his future apostolate, were marked by an overwhelming sense not only of the beauty of holiness but also of the holiness of beauty. This sense was based on the conviction

---

76. See Collingwood, "Introduction," *The Principles of Art*, 5–7.

77. Maritain, *Art and Scholasticism*, 12. Maritain is citing the *Summa Theologiae*, 1a, 2ae, q. 55, art. 3. In a note, Maritain goes on to cite Oscar Wilde: "The fact of a man being a poisoner is nothing against his prose" (117).

78. Ibid., 15–16

79. Aquinas, *Summa Theologiae*, I Pars, q. 5, art. 4, ad 1. Cited in Maritain, *Art and Scholasticism*, 19.

that the importance of art and the beautiful was self-evident, and the modern need to justify and to endlessly discuss the role of art and the artist was not an issue. That is to say that if we accept the view of art as a craft, a doing, then the modern need to justify art does not exist: plumbers, doctors, and artists are involved in activities that are focused on what is produced in and for society, and that is the end of the matter.

Once, however, we abandon the view that art is a craft, then the need to justify its legitimacy, and questions about the role of the artist in society, begin to appear. This need touches on the question of the beautiful in the liturgy in an immediate and important way. If the liturgy is not a "doing" of a particular kind, it becomes the vehicle for the individual ideas of the celebrant, or the liturgical committee, of the moment. It is no longer something to be done, something to be done with clear rules of how to do it, something to be done as well as one can; it has developed into a tool for getting across the personal slant on Christianity of those in charge of the celebration.

It is because so many Catholics have at least tacitly accepted the mistaken view that externals in religion do not really matter, and that images are of little account, that they feel that the beautiful is irrelevant to the practice of sincere religion. It is because Catholics have become vaguely uncomfortable about what Hegel called "picture thinking," and certainly do not want to be "sunk in images"[80] that they have accepted, and even come to prefer, a style of worship that is almost exclusively verbal.[81] It is on account of this morass of mistaken attitudes that we have been delivered into the hands of the new iconoclasts.

Hegel said that art is a "thing of the past."[82] He meant that it no

---

80. Hegel thought that "religious thought is a representative mode of the consciousness. It uses sensuous images, but not just to contemplate their sensuous referents, rather as symbols which strain to render a higher content. This description of a higher domain in images drawn from a lower one is typical of religious thought.... But what religion lacks even in its purer formulations is the grasp of the inner necessity which unites the articulations of the idea and brings them back to unity." Taylor, *Hegel*, 480.

81. Because, as Gadamar puts it: "Hegel's real thesis was that while for the Greeks the good or the divine was principally and properly revealed in their own artistic forms of expression, this became impossible with the arrival of Christianity. The truth of Christianity with its new and more profound insight into the transcendence of God could no longer be adequately expressed within the visual language of art or the imagery of poetic language. For us the work of art is no longer the presence of the divine that we revere." Hans-Georg Gadamer, *The Relevance of the Beautiful And Other Essays*, 4–6.

82. "Art, considered in its highest vocation, is and remains for us a thing of the past. Thereby it has lost for us genuine truth and life, and has rather been transferred into our ideas instead of maintaining its earlier necessity in reality and occupying its higher place." Hegel, *Hegel's Aesthetics: Lectures on Fine Arts*, 10.

longer stood on its own feet; its rationality, as merely artistic experience, is perceived to be defective. Hegel argued that art had to be shown to be part of that same process that leads to the understanding of all existence in terms of rationality. The rejection of the Scholastic view of art as a doing, a doing which is self-authenticating, coupled with Hegel's view that art no longer is self-justifying, effectively destroyed any real conviction that beauty "really" matters; that is just the way things are. It is surely a testimony to Hegel's malign genius that today his reduction of every sort of experience to a kind of Gnostic rationality hardly seems to need articulating, much less the furnishing of new arguments.[83]

Beauty matters, and, because it matters, then a liturgy that is beautiful also matters. The question is not peripheral or "merely aesthetic." This contention does not depend on an effort to revive a scholastic theory of art. What is important is to show that art has a transcendental reference that cannot be reduced to questions of either truth or morality—or, for that matter, to irrelevance. There are various ways this might be done, but we could do worse than to return to Kant's *Critique of the Aesthetic Power of Judgment*.[84] This is not a plea that we all become Kantians, but it is most definitely intended as a reminder that one of the most influential theories of beauty in modern times maintained that art has a transcendental reference—and that Hegel really should not have the last say.[85] It is true that this reference was connected, in Kant, both with morality and with truth, but again, for Kant this reference is neither authenticated, nor even seen to be important, only because it is connected with goodness and truth.

It is this irreducible autonomy of the beautiful that Von Balthasar sets out to explain, to vindicate, and to hymn in his great work *The Glory of the Lord*. It would be a good thing, I think, if we could talk a bit less about what he wrote and try to spend some time seeing what he wrote about. I mean we should try to contemplate the beautiful in nature, art, and music, because if we do not return to some sense of the importance of beauty we are not going to achieve any real contact with what is good, and we will probably end up not being able to love anything other than

---

83. See Robinson, Chapter Five, "Hegel: God becomes the Community," in *The Mass and Modernity: Walking to Heaven Backward*.
84. This is part of the *Critique of the Power of Judgment*.
85. "Kant's third *Critique*, even though often profoundly misunderstood, has been more influential on the subsequent history of aesthetics than any other single work... [this history suggests] the influence of Kant on subsequent aesthetics; a real history of that influence would be nothing short of a history of aesthetics since Kant." Guyer, "Kant's Ambitions in the third *Critique*," in *The Cambridge Companion to Kant and Modern Philosophy*, 578–579.

our own pleasure and particular power-trips. Von Balthasar's well-known words are true, even if their truth has become obscured by endless repetition:

> Beauty is the disinterested one, without which the ancient world refused to understand itself, a word which both imperceptibly and yet unmistakably has bid farewell to our new world, a world of interests, leaving it to its own avarice and sadness.[86]

This effective banishment of beauty from the modern consciousness has the result that morality, in whatever form it is presented to us, appears as something imposed and alien to our real needs and desires when we honestly consider them. One way or another, in spite of what the professional philosophers may say, morality comes across as duty for duty's sake, and it is not surprising that wrongdoing seems a perfectly rational and indeed acceptable option.

> In a world without beauty—even if people cannot dispense with the word and constantly have it on the tip of their tongues in order to abuse it—in a world which is perhaps not wholly without beauty, but which can no longer see it or reckon with it; in such a world the good also loses its attractiveness, the self-evidence of why it must be carried out. Man stands before the good and asks himself why it must be done and not rather its alternative evil.[87]

Nor does the Church take beauty very seriously any more,[88] and because of this, what the Church says both about truth and goodness becomes more and more meaningless and irrelevant to the modern world.

> No longer loved or fostered by religion, beauty is lifted from its face as a mask, and its absence exposes features which threaten to become incomprehensible to man.[89]

Von Balthasar is not arguing that a concern for the beautiful ought to take the place of the true and the good; to be concerned with the aesthetic dimension in religion is not a substitute for either holiness or truth. He is, though, arguing that we will not be able either to hold onto

---

86. Von Balthasar, "Seeing the Form," *The Glory of the Lord*, vol. 1, 18.
87. Ibid., 19.
88. Capecelatro, writing at the end of the nineteenth century, in a rather sad little comment, says: "... in these our days we greatly need some master mind, to revive the knowledge and love of good religious music, and give it back all its power to elevate and purify and refine the soul of man. Of the yearnings I have felt all along my life this has been the deepest...." Capecelatro, *The Life of Saint Philip Neri*, 372.
89. Von Balthasar, "Seeing the Form," *The Glory of the Lord*, vol. 1, 18.

the truth and goodness of our faith, much less interest others in it, if we go on treating beauty as an irrelevant and basically frivolous concern, a concern of those who are unable to cope with the real world without the rose-tinted spectacles of the aesthetic. The *de facto* contempt for beauty in the Church, as shown especially in the liturgy, has serious consequences in the very real world that we are constantly being admonished to take more seriously.[90] This is so because beauty "will not allow herself to be separated and banned from her two sisters without taking them along with herself in an act of mysterious vengeance."[91]

> We can be sure that whoever sneers at her name as if she were the ornament of a bourgeois past—whether he admits it or not—can no longer pray and soon will no longer be able to love.[92]

The apostolate of Philip's mature years in Rome shows he had grasped at least intuitively the truth of what Von Balthasar is saying here. Truth and goodness must be seen to be attractive, and the way things attract us is because they are beautiful. It was through a well-conceived and successful use of painting, music, and architecture as settings for the liturgy that Philip carried on his apostolate in Rome.

Afterwards

On May 26, 1595, very early in the morning, Philip Neri died. He died at the hour and on the day he had foretold. No one doubted that a great Saint had gone home to God. All over Rome, the Cardinals and the famous preachers of the day were bold to say that Philip had no need of prayers. The Preacher General of the Dominicans told a great congregation at the Minerva that there was no cause to pray for Philip, since he was most certainly living in the glory of paradise. Like the "faithful and wise servant" in the Gospel, whose master "had set over his household, to give them their food at the proper time,"[93] Philip's life had been devoted to revealing to others the mercy of God. It was effective because it was based on a first-hand acquaintance with God himself. With this

---

90. "It is the enthusiastic imposition on us by the Roman Emperors and their successive governments of one form or another of an intolerant Abrahamic exclusive monotheism which has at last brought largely justified revolt and led most people to see 'religion' as a dull, ugly, quarrelsome sub-department of life rather than the waking to the love of Beauty and its source, which can demand greater sacrifices than the fashionable cult of money and success." A.H. Armstrong cited in Rist, *What is Truth?*, 143.
91. Von Balthasar, "Seeing the Form," *The Glory of the Lord*, vol. 1, 18.
92. Ibid.
93. Matthew 24:45.

first-hand knowledge by acquaintance, he became the Apostle of Rome in his own time.

It was in the ordinary, accessible practices of sixteenth-century Catholicism that Philip's journey had begun,[94] and that was where it ended.[95] But there was a journey, a journey that is best described by the tradition of the three ways, as understood by St. Gregory of Nyssa.[96] The development of Philip's relationship to God is not to be understood as a conscious effort to put into practice what is often today thought of as mysticism. Rather, it was Philip's struggle to find and do the will of God in the here and now that led to what is best described as his embodied mysticism;[97] a mysticism embodied in the beliefs and practices of sixteenth-century Catholicism, but also embodied in Philip's own individuality and particularity.[98]

To say that Philip's mysticism was embodied in his individuality and particularity is to remind ourselves of two things. In the first place, Philip's education in Florence, his time in San Germano, the isolation in the catacombs, his studies, the beginnings of his apostolate, and the difficult years after his ordination—all these are not so many interesting but basically extraneous experiences to what was really going on. There was nothing really going on, in a disembodied way, apart from these experiences. If we are going to understand Philip's mysticism, we have to know how it was embodied in, and only in, Philip's own personal history as it developed within the particular cultural and ecclesial setting that was his own.

If Philip's mysticism is ineradicably meshed into the particularity of his own life, then it follows, secondly, that mysticism is not a readily identifiable concept that is essentially the same in all cases. If we cannot remove the element of the historical from a discussion of Philip's mysticism, because if it is in the historical that the reality of his mysticism is actually to be found, then any attempt to talk about his mysticism in abstraction from the historical becomes one more example of Bradley's "unearthly ballet of bloodless categories."[99] Furthermore, if we cannot discuss Philip's mysticism without recourse to his own particular history, then this applies to any other mystic. We must not ignore the ineradicably personal and particular interaction between the mystic under

---

94. See Preface, "People Not Arguments," 8–9.
95. See Introduction, "An Embodied Mysticism," section 4, "The Three Ways"; also, Chapter Nine, "The Darkness of God," 37–44.
96. See Introduction, "An Embodied Mysticism," 195*ff*.
97. Preface, "People Not Arguments," 41–43.
98. Ibid.
99. See Introduction, "An Embodied Mysticism," 30.

discussion and his religious and cultural context. There may be a family resemblance in what they experienced or taught, but that does not come from the fact that they were all practicing "mysticism."

To what, then, is this family resemblance to be traced? It is to be traced, first of all, to the fact that all Christian mystics were formed in, and practiced, the ordinary duties towards God and, as Julian of Norwich called them, their "even Christians." The way of beginners, with its spiritual combat against sin and learning to live as children of the light, is the beginning of all Christian mysticism, just as it is of the beginning of all Christian living.[100]

It is only with the beginning of what I have called the mystical assault[101] that the mystical road can be clearly distinguished from the often heroic struggles and genuine sanctity of those who remain in the first way. There are many saints who are not mystics. On the other hand, it is just as clear that many saints are mystics, and it is this mysticism of the saints that is our interest in this book.

The difference between the holiness of those who live in the first way and the journey of the mystics begins to be clear with the onset of the illuminative way. The light of the illuminative way comes not from the apparently clear certainties of the way of beginners, but from what Gregory calls "a more careful understanding of hidden things,"[102] and he puts the second way in relation to the Mosaic theme of the cloud.[103] This way is marked by the privation of the sensible and of learning to be alone with God. The cloud is brought about, in part, by a search for a deeper understanding of life than anything the first way can provide. But as Bremond said, "it is God who creates mystics,"[104] and the privation of the sensible and the search for hidden meaning are the result of the grace of God. St. John of the Cross examined and taught how this first darkness is the result of God's action, to which the soul responds.[105] Ultimately, then, the family resemblance between Christian mystics must be reduced to the mystical assault by God on the individual, and the irreducibly particular appropriation by real people.

---

100. See the Introduction to Part One, "Light in Florence," 45.
101. See the introduction to Part Two, "Clouds and Light in San Germano and Rome," 133.
102. The reference is from Gregory of Nyssa's *Commentary on the Song of* Songs; see above, part 2, 3.
103. Ibid.
104. See the introduction to Part Two, "Clouds and Light in San Germano and Rome," 134.
105. See Part Two, Chapter Six, "San Germano," 152.

It was during this period of Philip's studies, and then of his solitude in the Catacombs, that the physical phenomena of his mysticism began to appear.[106] These phenomena should not be used in a mistaken attempt to give an account of the essence of mysticism. On the other hand, they are so often present in the lives of the saints that they cannot be ignored. This observation certainly applies very clearly to St. Philip. In the previous chapter, "Towards an Account of St. Philip's Embodied Mysticism," I have attempted an account of mystical experience that shows, first of all, that such experiences require language to be experienced, but yet these experiences cannot be reduced to this necessary requirement of language. This exercise in the ontology of mystical experience is at best a tentative approach to a subject that can hardly be said to be an over-plowed field. I hope that my suggestions might point the way to questions that others will take up. My discussion of the role of the paranormal in the mystical life is based on the traditional teaching that such experiences are given for the benefit of others. Their role is to attest to the genuineness of the mystic's life and teaching.[107]

Finally, in the unitive way, Philip gave himself over entirely to the action of God.[108] God then used Philip to help bind up the wounds of a suffering humanity. In Philip's case, he believed this could best be accomplished by a mission centered on the sacramental life of the Church. Philip had approached his Maker in the company of the holy people of God and brought back to them what he had learned in the darkness.

But it was not only a verbal message that he took back with him. In the darkness, Philip had been taken over by his Maker, and he became a living icon of the radiance of the Father's glory. It was light he brought from the darkness, and the light was not his own.

---

106. See Part Two, Chapter Eight, "The Catacombs and the Apostolate," 187.
107. See Part Three, Chapter Ten, "Towards an Account of St. Philip's Embodied Mysticism," the section titled "The Function of the Paranormal in Philip's Life," 237*ff*.
108. See Part Three, Chapter Ten, "Towards an Account of St. Philip's Embodied Mysticism," 217*ff*.

Appendix I
Julian of Norwich on Laughter

This is the understanding, simply as I can sey, of this blessed worde: "Lo how I loved the." This shewed oure good lorde to make us glade and mery.

And with the same chere of mirth and joy, our good lord loked downe on the right side, and brought to my minde where our lady stode in the time of his passion ...

Julian of Norwich, *The Writings, A Vision Showed to a Devout Woman and a Revelation of Love*, 203 (end of tenth revelation and beginning of eleventh)

Appendix II

Vorrei saper da voi com'ella è fatta
questa Rete d'Amor, che tanti ha presi;
e come girar può tanti paesi
che 'l tempo alquanto omai non l'abbi sfatta.

E s'egli è cieco Amor, come s'adatta
a trar strali da sé di foco accesi?
E quanti al dì ne spende e quanti ha spesi,
vorrei saper da voi dove gli accatta?

E s'egli è ver, che dicono i poeti,
che lo stral ha una man, l'altra ha la face,
come può adoperar anco le reti?

Ma dica pur ciascun quel che li piace,
Anco l'arco, listrali e la sua face:
Sol è un bel viso che diletta e piace.

I'd like you to tell me how this Net of Love is made, which has captured many; and how it can tour many countries, that time has not undone it.

If it is blind Love, how does he launch burning darts (by) himself. And how many of them does he expend per day, and how many has he expended, I'd like you to tell me where does he scrounge them up.

And if it's true, what the poets say, that one hand has the dart, [and] the other has the flame, how can he use nets too?

But still may each tell what it likes, even the bow, darts and his flame: only a beautiful face, that delights and pleases.

Vian, San Filippo Neri, 20
(translation by Robert Pontisso)

Bibliography

Abbagnano, Nicola. "Renaissance Humanism." In *Dictionary of the History of Ideas*, vol. 4. New York: Scribner, 1973.

Andres, Glenn M. John M. Hunisak, and Richard A. Turner. *The Art of Florence*, two vols. New York, London: Artabras, 1988.

Annas, Julia and Christopher Rowe, eds. *New Perspectives on Plato, Modern and Ancient*. Washington, DC: Center for Hellenic Studies, 2002.

Anodal, Gabriella. *Santa Caterina de'Ricci*. Bologna: Edizioni Studio Domenicano, 1995.

Anonymous. *The Cloud of Unknowing and Related Treatises*. Edited by Phyllis Hodgson. Exeter: Catholic Record Press, 1982.

——— *The Cloud of Unknowing and Other Treatises*. Sixth and revised edition. Edited by Abbot Justin McCann. London: Burns Oates, 1952.

Anscombe, G.E.M. *Intention*. Oxford: Basil Blackwell, 1957.

Aquinas, Thomas. *De Veritate*, vol. 2 (Questions X–XX). Translated by James V. McGlynn, S.J. Albany, New York: Preserving Christian Publication, Inc., 1993.

——— *In Omnes S. Pauli Epistolas Commentaria*, Volumen Primum, Caput XII, lectio II. Torino: Marietti, 1922.

——— *Summa Theologiae. A Concise Translation*. Edited by Timothy McDermott. Westminster, Maryland: Christian Classics, 1989.

——— *Summa Theologiae, Latin Text and English Translation, Introduction, Notes, Appendices, and Glossaries*, 60 vols. Edited by Thomas Gilby. Blackfriars in conjunction with London: Eyre & Spottiswoode and New York: McGraw-Hill Book Company, 1964–1981.

——— *The Summa Theologica*. Allen, Texas: Christian Classics, 1948; originally published 1911.

——— *Summa Theologiae*. Ottawa: Institutio Studii Generalis, 1941.

Aristotle. *The Basic Works of Aristotle*. Edited and with an introduction by Richard McKeon. New York: Random House, 1941.

Arlotto, Piovano. *Facezie, Moti e Burle*. Edited by Chiara Amerighi. Firenze: Libreria Editrice Fiorentina, 1982.

Assonitis, Alessio. "Art and Savonarolianism in Florence and Rome." PhD diss., Columbia University, 2003.

Bacci, Pietro Giacomo. *The Life of Saint Philip Neri*. New and revised edi-

tion. Edited and translated by Frederick Ignatius Antrobus. London: Kegan Paul, Trench, 1902.
Baldassari, S.U. and A. Saiber, eds. *Images of Quattrocento Florence: Selected Writings in Literature, History, and Art*. New Haven and London: Yale University Press, 2000.
Beebe, Donald Paul Remy. *Savonarolan Aesthetics and their Implementation in the Graphic Arts*. PhD diss., Yale University, May 1998.
Bella, Luciano Guiseppe. *Philippo Neri: Padre Secondo lo Spirito*. Milano: Editoriale Jaca Book, 2006.
Boccaccio, Giovanni. *The Decameron*. Translated by John Payne. New York: Walter J. Black, Inc., 1930.
Bonaventure, St. *The Soul's Journey into God, The Tree of Life, The Life of St. Francis*. Translated and with an introduction by Ewart Cousins. New York: Paulist Press, 1978.
Bonniwell, William R., O.P. *A History of the Dominican Liturgy*. New York: Joseph F. Wagner, Inc., 1944.
Bradley, F.H. "On our Knowledge of Immediate Experience." In *Essays on Truth and Reality*. Oxford: Clarendon Press, 1914.
——— *The Principles of Logic*. Second edition, revised, with commentary and terminal essays. Oxford: Oxford University Press, reprinted 1950.
Brand, Peter and Lino Pertile, eds. *The Cambridge History of Italian Literature*, revised edition. Cambridge: Cambridge University Press, 1996.
Bremond, Henri. *Histoire Littéraire du Sentiment Religieux en France*. Paris: Bloud et Gay, 1923.
Burckhardt, Jacob. *The Civilization of the Renaissance in Italy*. Translated by S.G.C. Middlemore. London: Penguin Classics, 1990.
Burrows, Ruth. *Interior Castle Explained*. London: Sheed and Ward, 1981.
Capecelatro, Alfonso Cardinal. *The Life of Saint Philip Neri*. Translated by T.A. Pope. London: Burns, Oates and Washbourne, Ltd, 1926.
Cassian, John. *Nicene and Post-Nicene Fathers*. Vol. 11 of *Institutes of the Coenobia*. Grand Rapids, Michigan: Eerdman's, reprinted 1978.
Cassirer, Ernst, Paul Oskar Kristeller, and John Herman Randall, Jr., eds. *The Renaissance Philosophy of Man*. Chicago: University of Chicago Press, 1948.
Catechism of the Catholic Church. London: Geoffrey Chapman. Revised edition, 1999.
Catherine of Siena. *The Letters of Catherine of Siena*. Two vols. Edited and translated by Suzanne Noffke, O.P. Tempe, Arizona: Arizona Center for Medieval and Renaissance Studies, 2000 and 2001.
——— *The Dialogue*. Translated and with an introduction by Suzanne Noffke, O.P.; preface by Giuliana Cavallini. New York: Paulist Press, 1980.

——— *Il Dialogo*. Edited by Giuliana Cavallini. Siena: Edizioni Cantagalli, 1995.
The Catholic Encyclopedia. Edited by Charles G. Herbermann et al. Fifteen vols. New York: Robert Appleton Company, 1912.
Cavell, Stanley. *Must We Mean What We Say?* Updated edition. Cambridge: Cambridge University Press, 2008.
Cessario, Romanus, O.P. *A Short History of Thomism*. Washington, DC: Catholic University of America Press, 2003.
Chapman, John. *Spiritual Letters*. New edition. London: Sheed and Ward, 1983.
Chardon, Louis, O.P. *The Cross of Jesus*. Two vols. Translated by Richard T. Murphy, O.P., with an introduction by Jordan Aumann, O.P. St. Louis: B. Herder, circa 1957–1959.
The Church's Confession of Faith. San Francisco: Ignatius Press (Communio Books), 1978.
Cirri, Luciano and Enrico Malatesta. *Padre Pio da Pietrelcina: L'ultima inchiesta: Nel Nome del Padre*. Roma: Aquili Editore Roma, 1989.
Cistellini, Antonio. *San Filippo Neri: Breve storia di un grande vita*. Milano: Edizioni San Paolo, 2007.
——— *San Filippo Neri—L'oratorio e la Congregazione Oratoriana, Storia e Spiritualità*. Three Vols. Brescia: Morcelliana, 1989.
——— *Una pagina di storia religiosi a Firenze XVII*. Firenze: Leo S. Olschki, 1967.
Clark, Kenneth. *Landscape into Art*. London: John Murray, 1940.
Clement, Olivier. *The Roots of Christian Mysticism*. Translated by Theodore Berkeley, O.C.S.O., and Jeremy Hummerstone. Hyde Park, New York: New City Press, 1982.
Cole, Basil. *Music and Morals: A Theological Appraisal of the Moral and Psychological Effects of Music*. New York: Alba House, 1993.
Collingwood, R. G. *The Principles of Art*. Oxford: Clarendon Press, 1938.
Copleston, S.J. *A History of Philosophy*. Eleven vols. London: Burns and Oates Limited, 1961–1972.
——— *Aquinas*. Middlesex: Penguin Books Ltd, 1955.
Cunningham, Francis. *The Indwelling of the Trinity*. Dubuque, Iowa: Priory Press, 1955.
Daniélou, Jean. *God and the Ways of Knowing*. Translated by Walter Roberts. Cleveland and New York: Meridian Books, 1965.
——— *From Glory to Glory: Texts from Gregory of Nyssa's Mystical Writings*. Translated and edited by Herbert Musurillo, S.J. New York: Charles Scribner's Sons, 1961.
——— *Platonisme et Théologie Mystique*. Paris: Aubier, 1944.
Dauphinais, Michael, Barry David, and Matthew Levering, eds. *Aquinas*

the Augustinian. Washington, DC: Catholic University of America Press, 2007.
Day, William and Victor J. Krebs, eds. *Seeing Wittgenstein Anew.* Cambridge: Cambridge University Press, 2010.
de Agresti, Domenico. *Sviluppi della Riforma Monastica Savonaroliana.* Florence: Leo S Olschki, 1980.
Della Rocchetta, Giovanni Incisa and Nello Vian. *Il Primo Processo per San Filippo Neri.* Four vols. Città del Vaticano: Biblioteca Apostolica Vaticana, 1957–1963.
Dictionary of the History of Ideas. Five vols. Edited by Philip A. Wiener. New York: Scribner's, 1973.
Dictionnaire de Spiritualité. Seventeen vols. Paris: Éditions Beauchesne, 1932–1995.
The Dogmatic Constitution on the Church: Lumen Gentium. Vatican: The Second Vatican Council, 1964.
Douglas, Mary. *Natural Symbols.* London: Routledge, 1996.
Duffy, Eamon. *Saints and Sinners.* New Haven: Yale University Press, 1997.
——— *The Stripping of the Altars.* New Haven: Yale University Press, 1993.
Eisenbichler, Konrad and Nicholas Terpstra, eds. *The Renaissance in the Streets, Schools, and Studies.* Toronto: Centre for Reformation and Renaissance Studies, 2008.
Eliot, T.S. "The Dry Salvages." In *Four Quartets.* London: Faber and Faber, 1944.
Epstein, Mark Michael. *The Mediaeval Haggadah: Art, Narrative and Religious Imagination.* New Haven and London: Yale University Press, 2011.
Evagrius of Pontus. *The Greek Ascetic Corpus.* Translated and with introduction and commentary by Robert E. Sinkewicz. Oxford: Oxford University Press, 2002.
Fenlon, Dermot. *Heresy and Obedience in Tridentine Italy: Cardinal Pole and the Counter-Reformation.* Cambridge: Cambridge University Press, 1972.
Fine, Steven. *Art and Judaism in the Greco-Roman World: Toward a New Jewish Archeology.* Revised paperback edition. Cambridge: Cambridge University Press, 2010.
Fletcher, Stella and Christine Shaw, eds. *The World of Savonarola: Italian Elites and Perceptions of Crisis.* Aldershot, UK, and Burlington, Vermont: Ashgate, 2000.
Forman, Robert K.C., ed. *The Problem of Pure Consciousness: Mysticism and Philosophy.* New York: Oxford University Press, 1990.
Foster, Kenelm, O.P. *Petrarch: Poet and Humanist.* Edinburgh: Edinburgh University Press, 1984.
Foster, Kenelm, O.P. and Mary John Ronayne, O.P. *Catherine: Selected Writings of St. Catherine of Siena.* London: Collins, 1980.

Fowler, H.W. *A Dictionary of Modern English Usage*. Second edition. Oxford: Clarendon Press, 1965.
Gadamer, Hans-Georg. *The Relevance of the Beautiful and Other Essays*. Translated by Nicholas Walker. Edited by Robert Bernasconi. Cambridge: Cambridge University Press 1986.
Gallonio, Antonio. *The Life of Saint Philip Neri*. Translated by Jerome Bertram. Oxford: Family Publications, 2005.
——— *La Vita di San Filippo Neri, Edizione critica, con introduzione e note di Maria Teresa Bonadonna Russi*. Roma: Presidenza Del Consiglio Dei Ministri, 1995.
Garrigou-Lagrange, R., O.P. *The Three Ages of the Interior Life*. Two vols. Translated by Sister M. Timothea Doyle, O.P. St. Louis, Missouri: B. Herder Book Co., 1954.
Gasbarri, Carlo. *L'Oratorio Romano dal Cinquecento al Novecento*. Roma: Arti Grafiche, 1962.
Gilson, Etienne. *Thomistic Realism and the Critique of Knowledge*. Translated by Mark A. Wauck. San Francisco: Ignatius Press, 1986.
Goldthwaite, Richard A. *The Economy of Renaissance Florence*. Baltimore: The Johns Hopkins University Press, 2009.
Green, Bernard. *Christianity in Ancient Rome: The First Three Centuries*. London and New York: T.&T. Clark International, 2010.
Gregory of Nyssa. *Commentary on the Inscription of the Psalms*. Translated and with an introduction by Casimir McCambley, OCSO. Brookline, Massachusetts: Hellenic College Press, 1990 (reprinted 2004).
——— *Commentary on the Song of Songs*. Translated and with an Introduction by Casimir McCambley, OCSO. Brookline, Massachusetts: Hellenic College Press, 1987.
——— *The Life of Moses*. Translated by Abraham J. Malherbe and Everett Ferguson. New York: Paulist Press, 1978.
Grendler, Paul F. *Schooling in Renaissance Italy*. Baltimore and London: Johns Hopkins University Press, 1989.
——— *The Universities of the Italian Renaissance*. Baltimore and London: Johns Hopkins University Press, 2002.
Guardini, Romano. *The Death of Socrates*. Translated by Basil Wrighton. New York: Sheed and Ward, 1948.
Guicciardini, Francesco. *Maxims and Reflections (Ricordi)*. Translated by Mario Domandi. Philadelphia: University of Pennsylvania Press, 1972.
——— *The History of Italy*. Translated, edited, and with notes and an introduction by Sidney Alexander. Princeton: Princeton University Press, 1984.
Guyer, Paul. "Kant's Ambitions in the Third *Critique*." In *The Cambridge Companion to Kant and Modern Philosophy*. Edited by Paul Guyer. Cambridge: University Press, 2006.

Hagberg, Gary L. *Art as Language: Wittgenstein, Meaning and Aesthetic Theory*. Ithaca and London: Cornell University Press, 1998.

——— *Describing Ourselves, Wittgenstein and Autobiographical Consciousness*. Oxford: Clarendon Press, 2008.

Hall, Marcia. *After Raphael: Painting in Central Italy in the Sixteenth Century*. Cambridge: Cambridge University Press, 1999.

Halliwell, Stephen. *Aristotle's Poetics*. London: Duckworth, 1986.

——— *Greek Laughter*. Cambridge: Cambridge University Press, 2008.

Haskell, Francis. *History and its Images: Art and the Interpretation of the Past*. Third printing with corrections. New Haven: Yale University Press, 1995.

Hegel, G.W.F. *Phenomenology of Spirit*. Translated by A.V. Miller. Oxford: Oxford University Press, 1979.

——— *Hegel's Aesthetics: Lectures on Fine Art*. Two vols. Translated by T.M. Knox. Oxford: Clarendon Press, 1975.

——— *The Philosophy of History*. New York: Dover Publications, Inc., 1956.

Herzig, Tamar. *Savonarola's Women: Visions and Reform in Renaissance Italy*. Chicago and London: The University of Chicago Press, 2008.

Hibbert, Christopher. *The House of Medici*. New York: Harper Collins, reprinted 2003.

Hoehner, Harold W. *Ephesians: An Exegetical Commentary*. Grand Rapids, Michigan: Baker Academic, 2002.

Hood, William. *Fra Angelico at San Marco*. London and New York: BCA by arrangement with Yale University Press, 1993.

Huvelin, Abbé. *Some Spiritual Guides of the Seventeenth Century*. London: Burns Oates, 1927.

James, William. *The Varieties of Religious Experience: A Study in Human Nature, Being the Gifford Lectures on Natural Religion Delivered at Edinburgh in 1901–1902*. New York: The Modern Library, n.d.

Jedin, Hubert. "The Struggle for the Council." In *A History of the Council of Trent*, vol. 1. Translated by Dom Ernest Graf, O.S.B. Edinburgh: Thomas Nelson, 1957; reprinted ACLS History E-Book Project.

Joachim, H.H. *Aristotle, The Nicomachean Ethics: A Commentary by the Late H.H. Joachim*. Oxford: Clarendon Press, 1951.

John of the Cross, St. *Complete Works*. New edition. Translated and edited by E. Allison Peers. London: Burns and Oates, 1954.

Journet, Cardinal Charles. *The Dark Knowledge of God*. Translated by James Anderson. London: Sheed and Ward, 1948.

——— *The Meaning of Grace*. London: Geoffrey Chapman, 1962.

——— *Savonarole en prison, Dernière Méditation, texts traduits et présentés par le Cardinal Journet*. Paris: Desclée de Brouwer, 1968.

Julian of Norwich. *Showings*. Translated from the critical text with an introduction by Edmund Colledge, O.S.A., and James Walsh, S.J. New York: Paulist Press, 1978.

———— *The Writings: A Vision Showed to a Devout Woman and A Revelation of Love*. Edited by Nicholas Watson and Jacqueline Jenkins. University Park, Pennsylvania: The Pennsylvania State University Press, 2006.

Kant, Immanuel. *Critique of Practical Reason and other Works*. Sixth edition. Translated by T.K. Abbot. London, New York, Toronto: Longman's, Green and Co., reprinted 1948.

———— *Kritik der Praktischen Vernunft*. Hamburg: Felix Meiner, 1967.

Katz, Steven T., ed. *Mysticism and Language*. New York: Oxford University Press, 1992.

———— *Mysticism and Sacred Scripture*. New York: Oxford University Press, 2000.

Kenny, Anthony. "Intentionality: Aquinas and Wittgenstein." In *The Legacy of Wittgenstein*. Oxford: Basil Blackwell, 1984.

———— *Wittgenstein*. Middlesex, England: Penguin Press, 1973.

Kerr, Lady Amabel. *A Son of St. Francis*. St. Louis, Missouri: B. Herder, 1900.

Kerr, Fergus. *Theology after Wittgenstein*. Oxford: Basil Blackwell, 1989.

Kessler, Herbert L. and David Nirenberg, eds. *Judaism and Christian Art: Aesthetic Anxieties from the Catacombs to Colonialism*. Philadelphia and Oxford: University of Pennsylvania Press, 2011.

Kessler, Michael and Christian Sheppard, eds. *Mystics: Presence and Aporia*. Chicago: University of Chicago Press, 2003.

King, Archdale A. *Liturgies of the Religious Orders*. Bonn: Nova et Vetera, 2005.

Knowles, David. *The Historian and Character*. Cambridge: Cambridge University Press, 1963.

Kripke, Saul A. *Wittgenstein on Rules and Private Language*. Cambridge, Massachusetts: Harvard University Press, 1982.

Lane, Melissa. *Plato's Progeny: How Plato And Socrates Still Captivate The Modern Mind*. London: Duckworth, 2001.

Louth, Andrew. *Denys the Areopagite*. London and New York: Continuum, 1989.

———— *The Origins of the Christian Mystical Tradition*. Oxford: Oxford University Press, second edition, 2007.

Lucas, S.J., Herbert. *Fra Girolamo Savonarola*. London and Edinburgh: Sands and Company, 1906.

MacIntyre, Alasdair. *After Virtue: A Study in Moral Theory*. London: Duckworth, second edition, with postscript, 1985.

Malcolm, Norman. *Wittgenstein: A Religious Point of View?* Edited with a response by Peter Winch. Ithaca, New York: Cornell University Press, second printing 1995.

Mancinelli, Fabrizio. *The Catacombs of Rome and the Origins of Christianity*. Firenze: Scale, 2005.
Marion, Jean-Luc. *Étant donné*. Paris: 1998. Translated edition, *Being Given*. Stanford: Stanford University Press, 2002.
Maritain, Jacques. *Art and Scholasticism*. Translated by Joseph W. Evans. Notre Dame: University of Notre Dame Press, 1974.
Marrou, Henri. *A History of Education in Antiquity*. London: Sheed and Ward, Stag Books, 1981.
Martin, Ralph P. *2 Corinthians, Word Biblical Commentary*, 40. Waco, Texas: Word Books, 1985.
Martines, Lauro. *April Blood*. Oxford: Oxford University Press, 2003.
——— *Fire in the City, Savonarola and the Struggle for the Soul of Renaissance Florence*. Oxford: Oxford University Press, 2006.
McGinn, Bernard, ed. and trans. *Apocalyptic Spirituality*. New York: Paulist Press, 1979.
——— *The Foundations of Mysticism*, vol. 1 of *The Presence of God*. New York: Crossroad, 2000.
——— *The Growth of Mysticism*, vol. 2 of *The Presence of God*. New York: Crossroad, 1994.
McLure, George W. *The Culture of Profession in Late Renaissance Italy*. Toronto: University of Toronto Press, 2004.
Mediaeval Latin Lyrics. Translated by Helen Waddell. Harmsworth: Penguin Books, 1952.
Merriell, D. Juvenal. *To the Image of the Trinity—A Study in the Development of Aquinas' Teaching*. Toronto: Pontifical Institute of Mediaeval Studies, 1990.
Molinari, Paul, S.J. *Julian of Norwich*. London: Longman, Green and Co., 1958.
Moran, Richard. *Authority and Estrangement*. Princeton and Oxford: Princeton University Press, 2001.
Morelli, Arnaldo. Abstract: "The Chiesa Nuova in Rome around 1600: Music for the Church, Music for the Oratory," *Journal of Seventeenth-Century Music*, 9, no.1 (2003).
Murdoch, Iris. "The Fire and the Sun: Why Plato Banished the Artists." *Existentialists and Mystics*. London: Chatto & Windus, 1997.
Murray, Placid, O.S.B. "Newman's Oratory Papers," *Newman the Oratorian*. Dublin: Gill and Macmillan, 1969.
Najemy, John M. *A History of Florence 1200–1575*. Oxford: Blackwell Publishing, 2006.
Nelstrop Louise, Kevin Magill, and Bradley B. Onisha. *Christian Mysticism, An Introduction to Contemporary Theoretical Approaches*. Aldershot, UK, and Burlington, Vermont: Ashgate, 2009.

Neri, St. Philip. *The Maxims and Counsels of St. Philip Neri*. Toronto: The Oratory of St. Philip Neri, 1995.
——— *Gli Scritti e le Massime*. Edited by Antonio Cistellini. Brescia: Editrice la Scuola, 1994.
New Catholic Encyclopedia. Prepared by an editorial staff at the Catholic University of America, Washington, D.C. New York: McGraw-Hill Company, 1967.
Newman, J. H. *Meditations and Devotions*. Westminster, Maryland: 1975.
——— *Parochial and Plain Sermons*. San Francisco: Ignatius Press, 1997.
——— *An Essay in Aid of a Grammar of Assent*. Introduction by Nicholas Lash. London: University of Notre Dame Press, 1979.
——— *Fifteen Sermons Preached Before the University of Oxford*. Edited and with introduction and notes by James David Earnest and Gerard Tracey. Oxford: Oxford University Press, 2006.
——— *Sermons Preached on Various Occasions*. London: Burns and Oates, 1887.
——— *The Idea of a University*. Introduction by George N. Shuster. New York: Image Books, 1959.
Newman the Oratorian—His Unpublished Oratory Papers. Edited and with an introductory study by Placid Murray, O.S.B. Dublin: Gill and MacMillan, 1969.
Nichols, Aidan, O.P. *Divine Fruitfulness*. Washington, DC: Catholic University of America Press, 1988.
Noffke, Suzanne, O.P., ed. and trans. *The Letters of Catherine of Siena*. Two vols. Tempe: Arizona Center for Medieval and Renaissance Studies, 2000 and 2001.
Nussbaum, Martha C. *Love's Knowledge*. New York and Oxford: Oxford University Press, 1990.
O'Meara, Thomas F., O.P. *Thomas Aquinas, Theologian*. Notre Dame and London: University of Notre Dame Press, 1997.
Padovani, Serena, ed. *L'Età di Savonarola: Fra Bartolomeo e la Scuola de San Marco*. Giunta regionale Toscana: Marsilio, 1996.
Padre Pio of Pietrelcina. *Letters*. Edited by Melchiore of Pobladura and Alesssandro of Ripabottoni, vol. 1. English Version edited by Father Gerardo di Flumeri. Foggia: Edizione "Voce di Padre Pio," 1980.
Pastor, Ludwig. *The History of the Popes from the Close of the Middle Ages*. New York: Consortium Books, n.d. (first volume originally published 1885).
Pelikan, Jaraslov. *The Christian Tradition: A History of the Development of Christian Doctrine*. Five vols. Chicago: University of Chicago Press, 1971–1984.
Peterson, David S., ed. *Florence and Beyond: Culture, Society and Politics in*

Renaissance Italy. Toronto: Centre for Reformation and Renaissance Studies, 2008.
Petrarch, Francesco. *Canzoniere.* Translated by Anthony Mortimer. London: Penguin Books, 2002.
——— *On Religious Leisure.* Edited and translated by Susan S. Shearer. New York: Italica Press, 2002.
——— *The Secret.* Edited by Carol E. Quillen. Boston and New York: Bedford/St. Martin's, 2003.
Pieper, Josef. *The Four Cardinal Virtues.* Notre Dame: University of Notre Dame Press, 1966.
Plato: Lysis, Symposium, Gorgias, vol. 3. Translated by W. R. M. Lamb. Cambridge, Massachusetts: Loeb Classical Library (Harvard University Press), 1975.
Plato. *The Republic of Plato.* Translated and with an introduction and notes by F. M. Cornford. Oxford: Clarendon Press, 1955.
Polizzotto, Lorenzo. *Children of the Promise: The Confraternity of the Purification and the Socialization of Youth in Florence,* 1427–1785. Oxford: Oxford University Press, 2001.
——— *The Elect Nation.* Oxford: Clarendon Press, reprinted, 2003.
Ponnelle, Louis, and Louis Bordet. *St. Philip Neri and the Roman Society of His Times.* Translated by Ralph Francis Kerr of the London Oratory. London: Sheed and Ward, 1922.
Portier, Lucienne. *Un précurseur l'abbé Huvelin.* Paris: Les Éditions du Cerf, 1979.
Pullapilly, Cyriac K. *Caesar Baronius: Counter-Reformation Historian.* Notre Dame / London: University of Notre Dame Press, 1975.
Purcell, E. S. *Life of Cardinal Manning.* London: Macmillan and Co., 1895.
Rahner, Karl. "Reflections on the Problem of the Gradual Ascent to Christian Perfection." In *Theological Investigations,* vol. 3 (*The Theology of the Spiritual Life*). Translated by Karl-H. and Boniface Kruger. Baltimore: Helicon Press, 1967.
Rahner, Karl and Herbert Vorgrimler. *Theological Dictionary.* Edited by Cornelius Ernst, O.P., and translated by Richard Strachen. New York: Herder and Herder, 1965.
Ricci, F. Giacomo, O.P. *The Lives of the Companions of S. Philip Neri.* Translated by F. W. Faber. London: Thomas Richardson and Son, 1847.
Ridolfi, Roberto. *The Life of Girolamo Savonarola.* Translated by Cecil Grayson. New York: Alfred A. Knopf, 1959.
Rist, John M. *What is Truth? From the Academy to the Vatican.* Cambridge: Cambridge University Press, 2008.
Robinson, Jonathan. "Changing the Subject: The Liturgy as an Object of Experience." *The Thomist* 75, no. 3 (July 2011): 365–391.

——— *Duty and Hypocrisy in Hegel's Phenomenology of Mind*. Toronto and Buffalo: University of Toronto Press, 1977.
——— *The Mass and Modernity: Walking to Heaven Backward*. San Francisco: Ignatius Press, 2005.
——— *On the Lord's Appearing*. Washington: Catholic University of America Press, 1997.
Rocke, Michael. *Forbidden Friendships, Homosexuality and Male Culture in Renaissance Florence*. New York and Oxford: Oxford University Press, 1996.
Rossoni, Elena. *Immagini de Santità: Per un'iconografia de san Filippo Neri*. Parma: Tipolitografia Benedettina Editrice, 1995.
Sells, Michael A. *Mystical Languages of Unsaying*. Chicago: University of Chicago Press, 1994.
Savonarola, Girolamo. *A Guide to Righteous Living and other Works*. Translated and edited by Konrad Eisenbichler. Toronto: Centre for Reformation and Renaissance Studies, 2003.
——— *De Simplicitate Christianae Vita*. Edited by Pier Giorgio Ricci. Roma: Angelo Belardetti, 1959.
——— *An Exposition of the Psalm Miserere Mei Deus by Fra Girolamo Savonarola*. Translated by F.C. Cowper, B.D. Milwaukee, Wisconsin: The Young Churchman Co., 1889.
——— *Selected Writings of Girolamo Savonarola: Religion and Politics, 1490–1498*. Translated and edited by Anne Borelli and Maria Pastore Passaro. New Haven and London: Yale University Press, 2006.
——— *The Triumph of the Cross*. Translated by John Procter, S.T.L. London: Sands and Co., 1901.
Screech, M.A. *Laughter at the Foot of the Cross*. London: Allen Lane, the Penguin Press, 1997.
Scruton, Roger. *A Short History of Modern Philosophy*. Second edition. London and New York: Routledge, 1984.
——— *Beauty*. Oxford: Oxford University Press, 2009.
——— *Modern Philosophy*. New York: Allen Lane, the Penguin Press, 1994.
——— *The Aesthetics of Music*. Oxford: Oxford University Press, 1997.
——— *Understanding Music*. London and New York: Continuum, 2009.
Scudieri, Magnolia e Rasario Giovanni, eds. *Savonarola e le sue Reliquie a San Marco: Itinerario per un Percorso Savonaroliano nel Museo*. Firenze: Museo di San Marco in cooperation with Taylor and Francis, 1999.
Scull, Andrew. Review of *Modernists and Mystics*. Edited by C.J.T. Talar. *Times Literary Supplement*, May 21, 2010.
Scupoli, Lorenzo. *The Spiritual Combat, Together With the Treatise on Spiritual Peace*. London: Burns Oates, 1963 (Printed in Belgium by N.V. Splichal-Turhout).

Sherwin, Michael S., O.P. *By Knowledge and By Love.* Washington, DC: Catholic University of America Press, 2005.
Shestov, Lev Isaakovich. *Kierkegaard and the Existential Philosophy.* Athens, Ohio: Ohio University Press, 1968.
Stein, Edith. *The Science of the Cross.* Translated by Josephine Keoppel, O.C.D. Washington, DC: ICS Publications, 2002.
Steinberg, Ronald A. *Fra Girolamo Savonarola: Florentine Art and Renaissance Historiography.* Athens, Ohio: Ohio University Press, 1977.
Stevenson, James. *The Catacombs: Life and Death in Early Christianity.* London: Thames and Hudson, 1978.
Stolz, Anselm. *The Doctrine of Spiritual Perfection.* Introduction by Stephen Fields, S.J. New York: The Crossroad Publishing Company, 2001. Originally published under the title *Theologie der Mystik,* 1936.
Tacchi Venturi, Pietro, and Mario Scaduto. *Storia della Compagnia di Gesu in Italia.* Roma: Civilta Cattolica, 1950.
Talar, C.J.T., ed. *Modernists and Mystics.* Washington, DC: Catholic University of America Press, 2009.
Taylor, Charles. *A Secular Age.* Cambridge, Massachusetts, and London: The Belknap Press of Harvard University, 2007.
——— *Hegel.* Cambridge: Cambridge University Press, 1975.
——— *Human Agency and Language, Philosophical Papers 1.* Cambridge: Cambridge University Press, 1985.
——— *Philosophy and the Human Sciences: Philosophical Papers 2.* Cambridge: Cambridge University Press, 1985.
——— *Sources of the Self.* Cambridge, Massachusetts: Harvard University Press, 1989.
——— *Varieties of Religion Today.* Cambridge, Massachusetts: Harvard University Press, 2002.
Teresa of Jesus, St. *Complete Works.* Translated and edited by E. Allison Peers. London and New York: Sheed and Ward, 1946.
Thompson, Augustine, O.P. *Cities of God: The Religion of the Italian Communes, 1125–1325.* University Park, Pennsylvania: The Pennsylvania State University Press, 2005.
Thurston, Herbert, S.J. *The Physical Phenomena of Mysticism.* London: Burns Oates, 1952.
——— *Surprising Mystics.* Edited by Joseph Crehan, S.J. London: Burns Oates, 1952.
Trevor, Meriol. *Apostle of Rome: A Life of Philip Neri, 1515–1595.* London: Macmillan, 1966.
Trexler, Richard C. *The Spiritual Power: Republican Florence Under Interdict.* Leiden: E.J. Brill, 1974.
Trinkaus, Charles. *In Our Image and Likeness: Humanity and Divinity in Italian Humanist Thought.* Two vols. Notre Dame: University Press, 1995.

——— *The Poet as Philosopher: Petrarch and the Formation of Renaissance Consciousness*. New Haven and London: Yale University Press, 1979.
Tugwell, Simon, O.P. *Ways of Imperfection*. Springfield: Templegate Publishers, 1985.
Türks, Paul. *Philip Neri: The Fire of Joy*. Translated by Daniel Utrecht. New York: Alba House, 1995.
Turner, A. Richard. *The Vision of Landscape in Renaissance Italy*. Princeton, NJ: Princeton University Press, 1966.
Turner, Denys. *Eros and Allegory*. Kalamazoo: Cistercian Publications, 1995.
——— *Julian of Norwich, Theologian*. New Haven and London: Yale University Press, 2011.
——— *The Darkness of God: Negativity in Christian Mysticism*. Cambridge: Cambridge University Press, 1995.
Valier, Agostino Cardinal. *Il Dialogo Della Gioia Cristiana*. Translated and with an introduction by Antonio Cistellini, D.O. Brescia: editrice La Scuola, 1975.
Verstegen, Ian. "Federico Barocci, Federico Borromeo, and the Oratorian Orbit." *Renaissance Quarterly* 56, no. 1 (Spring 2003): 56–87.
Vian, Nello. *San Filippo Neri: Pellegrino Sopra La Terra*. Brescia: Morcelliana, 2004.
von Balthasar, Hans Urs. *Heart of the World*. Translated by Erasmo S. Leiva. San Francisco: Ignatius Press, 1979.
——— *Prayer*. Translated by A.V. Littledale. London: Geoffrey Chapman, 1961.
——— *Seeing the Form*. Vol. 1 of *The Glory of the Lord*. Translated by Erasmo Leiva-Merikakis. San Francisco: Ignatius Press and New York: Crossroad Publications, 1982.
——— *Clerical Styles*. Vol. 2 of *The Glory of the Lord*. San Francisco: Ignatius Press and New York: Crossroad Publications, 1984.
——— *Lay Styles*. Vol. 3 of *The Glory of the Lord*. San Francisco: Ignatius Press and New York: Crossroad Publications, 1986.
von Hügel, Baron Friedrich. *Letters to a Niece*. Edited and with an introduction by Gwendolen Greene. London: J.M. Dent and Sons, Ltd, 1928; reprinted 1950.
——— *The Mystical Element of Religion*. London: J.M. Dent and Sons. Ltd, 1961.
Weinstein, Donald. *Savonarola and Florence*. Princeton, New Jersey: Princeton University Press, 1970.
Wharton, Edith. "Autre Temps." In *Xingu and Other Stories*. New York: Charles Scribner's Sons, 1916.
William of St. Thierry, *The Golden Epistle*. Translated by Theodore Berkeley OCSO. Spencer, Mass.: Cistercian Publications, 1971.
——— *On Contemplating God, Prayer Meditations*. Translated by Pene-

lope Lawson CSMV. Collegeville, Minn.: Cistercian Publications, Liturgical Press, 1970.

Witt, Ronald G. "What did Giovanni Read and Write? Literacy in Early Renaissance Florence." *I Tatti Studies, Essays in the Renaissance* 6 (1995): 83–114.

Wittgenstein, Ludwig. *Philosophical Investigations*. Second edition. Translated by G.E.M. Anscombe. Oxford: Basil Blackwell, 1958.

Index

abacco 64, 73
Alba de Tomes, Spain 219
alchemy 53, 71
Alexander VI (Pope) 97, 98
Alighieri, Dante 113; *The Divine Comedy*, 52
Ambrose, St. 262
Animuccia, Tullia 53
anxiety 153–54, 254
apatheia 47, 129, 133–34, 154–55, 157
Apostle of Rome, second (*see* Neri, St. Philip)
Aquinas, St. Thomas 73, 77, 137, 162, 169–70, 172–73, 205, 217, 225, 229, 234, 236, 237, 265; on illuminative way (way of light) 137; influence on St. Philip Neri 40, 172–74; on mystical theology in the *Summa Theologiae* 16–18, 21–24, 26–28, 30–31, 33, 34; on St. Paul's mysticism 230–33; on the Prayer of Petition 251–53; on prophecy 188–89; on purgative way (way of beginners or first way) 80–82; and the tradition of the three ways 38, 45, 48
Aristotle 66–67, 82, 118, 121, 168–74; on the four characteristics for a good action 225–26, 229
Arlotto, Piovano (Arlotto Mainardi) 68–70, 128, 261
ars celebrandi 264–65
art 59, 109; in the Christian faith 110–15; destruction of (iconoclasm) 111–15, 116; as part of liturgical practice in Catholicism 263–69
asceticism 35, 47, 128, 148–154, 175, 178, 199; and depression 153, 153 n.55
Augustine, St. 22 n.27, 46, 81, 84, 220 n.14
Augustinian Order 258
Augustinianum (Instituto Patristico Augustinianum) Rome 162
Averroes, 173

Bacci, Pietro Giacomo 12, 30, 53, 72, 77, 79, 139, 140, 141, 142, 143, 144, 159, 162, 163, 164, 175, 179, 184–85, 187, 250, 255, 259
Baccio della Porta (*see* Bartolommeo, Fra)
banks, Florentine 184; of the Cavalcanti 185
Baptism 85–86; in Renaissance Italy 52; of St. Philip Neri 51, 260; and the tradition of the three ways 42–43, 47
Baronius (confessor of St. Philip) 77, 140, 147, 246, 250, 258–59; *Annales* 259
Bartolommeo, Fra (Baccio della Porta) 113 n.19, 115
Basil of Caesarea 118
beauty 109, 111–12, 115, 117, 122–36, 267–69
Benedetto, Fr. (spiritual director of Padre Pio) 220
Benedict of Nursia, St. 141
Benedict XIII (Pope) 219
Benedictine Order 143, 144–48
Benivieni, Girolamo 50–51
Berti, Fra Antonio 72–73, 87
Boccaccio 69 n.68, 113
Bonaventure, St. 154, 161; *The Soul's*

289

Journey Into God 23–24
bonfires of the vanities (*brucciamenti delle vanità*) 112–14, 116
Bordet, Louis 13, 53, 55, 63, 66, 68, 71, 75, 78, 89, 140, 141, 144, 168, 170, 178–79, 185, 186, 187, 201, 228, 245, 246
Bordini (Oratorian in Rome) 246
Borgia family 78
Borromeo, Frederico (Cardinal) 172
Bradley, F. H. 24, 25, 30 n.51, 217, 270
Bremond, Henri: "*Invasion Mystique*" 133, 157, 271
Bronzino, Agnolo 75
Bruni, Leonardi 50, 67

Caccia, Galeotto del 159, 161
Camerino, Fra Francesco Cardone da 179
Camillus of Lellis, St. 46, 186
Capecelatro, Alfonso (Cardinal) 12–13, 58–60, 66, 71, 89, 99–101, 103, 122, 140–41, 143, 144, 145, 168, 170, 179–80, 185, 203–05, 246–47, 255, 257, 263–64
Capuchin Order 58, 178–79
Carmelite Order 34, 38, 177, 208, 217, 219
Cartesian philosophy (*see* Descartes, René)
Cassian, John 148, 182–83
Cassinese congregation 146
Castelfranco, Italy 53
Catacombs, Rome (*see* Neri, St. Philip, in the Catacombs)
Catechism of the Catholic Church 136, 163 n.23, 188
Catherine de' Ricci, St. 207
Catherine of Siena, St. 48, 73, 87–92; *Dialogue* 89, 90, 104, 106, 121, 178, 182–83
Catholicism, practice of (*see* liturgical practice, Catholic)
Cavell, Stanley 87

Chapman, John (Abbot) 153
Chardon, Louis: *The Cross of Jesus* 38
charity (Christian virtue) 26, 80–81, 182; practiced by St. Philip Neri 186–88, 193
Charles V, Holy Roman Emperor 131
Charles VII of France 94
Chesterton, G. K. 15
Chiesa Nuova (Santa Maria in Vallicella) (*see* Oratory of St. Philip Neri, Rome)
Christian joy 13, 122, 172, 205–06
Chrysostom, John 118
Cioni, Antonio 53
Cioni, Elisabetta 52–56, 72, 139, 144
Cistellini, Antonio 53, 72
Cistercian Order 34
Clement of Alexandria, St. 118
Clement VIII (Pope) 184
Clemente (childhood teacher of St. Philip Neri) 64
Cloud of Unknowing (Anonymous) 9, 16, 234–35
Coliseum, Rome 79
Confession (*see* Penance)
Confirmation: and the tradition of the three ways 42, 136–37
confraternities in Florence 73–75
Confraternity of the Most Holy Trinity, Rome 158, 184, 186
Confraternity of the Purification, Florence 73–75, 79, 109, 264
Consolini, Fr. Pietro 166, 168
Council of Trent 51, 201
Counter-Reformation 66, 116, 244, 263
Crehan, Fr. Joseph 219–20
Crescenzi, Giacomo 165, 206–07
Crivelli, Prospero 184, 185
Cusano, Nicola (Cardinal) 246

Daniélou, Jean (Cardinal) 34, 123,

136, 195, 241
Dante (*see* Alighieri, Dante)
dark night of the senses/spirit (*see* John of the Cross, St., *Dark Night of the Soul*)
del Monte, Francesco Maria del (Cardinal) (*see* Julius III)
Delphic Oracle 170
Denys the Areopagite (Pseudo-Denys) 38, 225
depression 153 n.55
Descartes, Rene 197, 207–08, 210–12; rebuttal of 212–15, 262
Domenici, Ludovico 70
Dominican Order 17, 38, 48, 51, 71–72, 83, 87, 114, 158, 179, 207, 245, 258, 269; and church reform 87–88, 90, 93–108, 201; Dominicans of the Observance 87; and Girolamo Savonarola 101–08
Donatello 113
Douglas, Mary 5–6

Ecclesiastes, biblical book of: and the tradition of the three ways 43, 44
ecstasy (*see* raptus)
Eliot, T. S. 25
Enlightenment 251
epektasis 195
eros (desire) 122–26
Eucharist 235; and the tradition of the three ways 43–44, 192–93, 197; St. Philip Neri's celebration of 2, 200–01, 235, 243, 256, 260–63

Facezie (*see* Arlotto, Piovano)
Felice of Cantalice, St. 58–59
Fiesole, Diocese of 69. *See also* San Domenico, Fiesole.
First Process for Philip's Beatification (*Il Primo Processo per San Filippo Neri*) 12–13, 52, 163, 165, 253

first way (*see* purgative way)
Florence 8–9, 48, 49–56, 174, 183, 208; confraternities of 73–75; education in 61–68; Florentine Republic 94, 95, 96, 98, 102, 130–31; French invasion of 94–95; and Girolamo Savonarola 93–99, 102; homosexuality in 75–76; siege of (1529–30) 130–31. *See also* Confraternity of the Purification; San Marco, convent of; San Giovanni; San Pier Gattolino; Medici family.
Forbidden Books (*see* Index of Forbidden Books)
Foster, Kenelm 62, 90
Foucauld, Charles de 256–57
Francis of Assisi, St. 31, 141, 170
Frateschi, 99

Gaeta, Italy (*see* Monte Cassino)
Gallonio, Antonio 12, 53–54, 56, 72, 79, 139, 140, 144, 161, 162, 163, 178, 179, 200, 255, 260, 262
Garrigou-Lagrange, R. 17, 38, 154
Gregory of Nyssa, St. 1, 10, 15, 45, 123, 127, 129, 157, 174, 175, 191–92; *Commentary on the Psalms* 244; on the illuminative way 133–38, 154, 160–61, 195, 271; on Moses 41–43, 135, 183–84, 241, 256, 271; and the tradition of the three ways 41–43, 45–46, 47, 48, 217, 241, 270; on the unitive way (third way) 193–97; St. Philip Neri and 40
Gregory XIII (Pope) 120
Gregory XIV (Pope) 120
Grendler, Paul F. 66–67
Guicciardini, Francesco 8, 131
gypsies 245–46

hagiography, Catholic 46
Hegel, Georg Wilhelm Friedrich 34, 181–83, 243; on art 266–67

Henry of Navarre 258
heresy/heretics 245–46
hermit 178–79
historical theology 1, 12
humanism 112, 169, 174; Christian humanism 60, 65–68, 169; humanist education in the Renaissance 61–68, 73, 91, 109. See also Neri, St. Philip, humanist education of.
Huvelin, l'abbé 241, 257
hysteria 20 n.22

iconoclasm (see art, destruction of)
Ignatius of Loyola, St. 3, 46, 186
illuminative way 43–44, 133–38, 148, 154, 160, 181–83, 195, 243, 271
Index of Forbidden Books 201, 258
Inquisition 69, 203, 245–46
Instituto Patristico Augustinianum (see Augustinianum)
Invasion Mystique (see Bremond, Henri)
irony 116–22, 127, 171, 246–47

James, William: on mysticism, in *The Varieties of Religious Experience* 16–21, 23, 30; "four marks" of mysticism 18–20
Jedin, Hubert 92
Jesuit Order 258
Jews (see Judaism)
John Damascene, St. 111, 253
John of God, St. 46
John of the Cross, St. 9, 10, 33, 34–35, 150, 151, 183, 194, 195, 197, 200, 205, 207–08, 217; *The Living Flame of Love* 36, 199; *Dark Night of the Soul*, 36, 152–54, 175, 177, 198–99, 205, 208–10, 213–14, 271
Journet, Charles (Cardinal) 35
joy (see Christian joy)
Judaism 94, 111, 245–46
Julian of Norwich 133, 157, 242, 271, 273
Julius II (Pope), 130
Julius III (Pope) 77–78; Jubilee of 186

Kant, Immanuel 84; *Critique of the Aesthetic Power of Judgment* 267
Kerr, Amabel, Lady 58
Kerr, Fr. Ralph 13, 144
Kierkegaard, Soren 109, 157
Knox, Ronald (Monsignor) 15

laughter 117–18, 120 n.44, 121, 273
Lectio Divina 167
Leo X (Pope) 184
Lepanto, Battle of 245
Liber Gradualium (Anonymous) 262–63
liturgical practice, Catholic 8–10, 17–18, 32, 47, 59, 235–37, 260, 263–69, 270, 272
Locke, John 213
Louth, Andrew: *Denys the Areopagite* 38
Luca Landuci 113
Lucas, Herbert, S.J. 96, 103
Lucci, Fra Giovanni Antonio 206–07
Luther, Martin 39, 85

Maffa, Marco Antonio 75, 164
Mainardi, Arlotto (see Arlotto, Piovano)
Mantellate Order 88
Martines, Mauro 98
martyrs, Christian (see Saints)
Mass, sacrament of (see Eucharist)
Medici family 96, 98, 130–31, 184. See also Leo X; Medici, Alessandro de'; Medici, Lorenzo de'; Medici, Piero.
Medici, Alessandro de' (Cardinal) 52
Medici, Lorenzo de' 50–51, 93

Medici, Piero 93–94, 96
Middle Ages: attitudes toward art 112, 265; education in 62–63; spirituality in 90–91
Millenarianism 101–102
Minerva (*see* Santa Maria sopra Minerva)
miracles 238–39, 243
Monte Cassino (Chapel at Gaeta) 143–48
Monteperstoli, Italy 53
Mosciano, Lucrezia da 53
Moses 41–43, 135, 155, 183–84, 238, 241, 256, 271
Murdoch, Iris 110
music 59, 267; in the Christian faith 110–15; at Oratory of St. Philip in Rome 263–64; vernacular music 74–75, 264
mystical assault (*see* Bremond, Henri, *"Invasion Mystique"*)
mystical theology (*see* mysticism)
mysticism 16–17; role in Christian life 46–47; definitions of 7, 10, 15, 18, 32; "embodied mysticism" 2, 8–10, 15–17, 25, 32, 34–35, 37, 45, 47, 48, 207–10, 217ff, 243–44, 269, 270; "four marks" of 18–20; God's action in 11, 36, 40, 193, 195–99, 208, 224, 233, 271–72; individual experience of 25, 29, 32–33, 37, 234–37; and intellectual life 59, 158; and language 27–28, 215, 224, 230–33, 237, 272; roots in liturgical practice 47, 59, 235–37, 260; mystical theology 15, 21–31, 158, 208; physical phenomena of 17, 29–31, 188–89, 217–25, 227, 237–39, 242–43, 272; Platonic themes in 123–26; prophecy and 188–89 (*see also* Savanarola, Girolamo, prophecies of). *See also* Neri, St. Philip, mystical life of; Neri, St. Philip, physical experience of mysticism.

Najemy, John M. 76, 96, 130–31
Neo-Platonism (*see* Platonism, Plato)
Neri, Caterina 53, 54
Neri, Elisabetta (*see* Cioni, Elisabetta)
Neri, Francesco 53, 71, 132
Neri, St. Philip: as "second Apostle of Rome" 3, 10, 270; apostolate of 161, 166–68, 172–74, 184–88, 193, 201, 243, 263; influence of St. Thomas Aquinas 40, 172–74; and Benedictine influence 145–48; biographical sketch of 2–3; biographical sources 12–13; birth and baptism of 51; in the Catacombs 30, 130, 155, 158, 178–80, 183, 187–89, 191, 197, 208, 218, 270, 272; chastity of 77–80, 86; cheerfulness of 116 n.31, 117–18, 147, 204–06; childhood stories of 54–55; as a "Christian Socrates" 116, 122, 127, 169–70, 172, 246; and Church reform 249, 257–260; death of 269–70; and Dominican influence 71–73, 104, 109, 127–28, 158; celebration of the Eucharist 200–201, 243, 256, 260–63; family members of 53; Florence upbringing of 48, 49–56, 109, 208, 243, 270; departure from Florence 130, 132; historical view of 2, 4; humanist education of 61–68, 109, 127–28, 169; humor and 68–70, 117–18, 120–22, 247; intellectual life of 158–74, 191, 197, 270; mystical life of 1–2, 8–11, 15–18, 44, 191–200, 205, 217–19, 232–33, 243–44, 270–72; ordination of 57, 128, 159, 161, 200, 270; physical appearance of 55, 75, 142, 185; physical experience of mysticism 30–31, 89–90, 187–89, 218, 227–28, 237–39, 242–43, 260–61, 272; use of the Prayer of Petition

250, 253–55; Penance, practice of 255–57; "Pippo bono" (Good Philip) 56, 75–76, 79, 80, 86, 128, 208; arrival in Rome 140, 157–59; religious education of 74–75, 109, 133; sainthood of 46–48, 55–56, 77, 130, 249; sale of books 161, 163–64, 166–67; in San Germano 139–48, 157, 154–55, 160, 208, 270; and Girolamo Savanarola 51, 92–93, 99, 102–04, 108, 109–10; and the tradition of the three ways 40–44, 45; writings of 109, 126, 253. *See also* Oratory of St. Philip Neri, Rome.

Newman, J. H. 1, 3–4, 6, 9, 15, 48, 49, 59–60, 67, 80, 85, 119, 180, 205, 262; writings on St. Philip Neri 12–13, 99–101, 103, 144, 145–46, 246, 255; *The Idea of a University* 60; *Miracles No Remedy for Unbelief*, 238

Nicea, Second Council of 111, 112

Nicholas, St. 46

Ockham, William of 165

Olivarez, Countess of 57

Oracle of Delphi (*see* Delphic Oracle)

Oratory of St. Philip Neri, Birmingham (U.K.) 99, 146, 255

Oratory of St. Philip Neri, France 256

Oratory of St. Philip Neri, London 13

Oratory of St. Philip Neri, Rome (Santa Maria in Vallicella) 3, 75, 143, 147, 163, 166–68, 169, 173–74, 201–02, 204, 246, 255, 263–64

Origen 41–42, 45, 48

ottimatti 94

Paleologus 245–46

panegyrics 50

parrhesia 47, 129, 133–34, 154–55, 157

Pastor, Ludwig 3, 141

Pateri, Pompeo 163

Paul IV (Pope) 201–202, 258

Paul, St. 2, 34, 40–41, 46, 47, 81, 85, 99–100, 147, 168, 196, 205, 210, 229–33, 241, 247

Penance, sacrament of: and the tradition of the three ways 42–43; St. Philip Neri's practice of 255–57

Pentecost: St. Philip Neri's mystical experience during 30–31, 137, 158, 187–89, 196, 218

Peter, St. 46

Petrarch 61–62, 67, 68, 113, 126

Piacenza, Italy 78

Piagnoni 99, 109, 115

pilgrimages/pilgrims (*see* Rome, pilgrimages in)

Pio, Padre 29, 218–25, 227

Pistoia, Italy 65

Pius V 245

Plato 66–67, 82, 168–70, 172; influence on mystical theology 122–26; and art 110; and *eros* 122–26

Platonism 38, 122–26, 169, 172. *See also* Plato.

Polizzotto, Lorenzo 76, 99, 104

Ponnelle, Louis 13, 53, 55, 63, 66, 68, 71, 75, 78, 89, 140, 141, 144, 168, 170, 178–79, 185, 186, 187, 201, 228, 245, 246

Prato, Italy 207

Prayer of Petition 249–55

Primo Processo per San Filippo Neri (*see* First Process for the Beatification of Saint Philip Neri)

Protestantism 248–49, 258

Proverbs, biblical book of: and the tradition of the three ways 42, 44

Pseudo-Denys (*see* Denys the Areopagite)

purgative way (way of beginners) 43, 83, 129, 134, 137, 148, 271

quasi-cognitio experimentalis 24, 26, 32

Rahner, Karl: on the tradition of the three ways 38–39, 44
Rangona, Marchesa 57
rapture (*see* raptus)
raptus 30 n.52, 35–37, 189, 230–32
Reformation, German 34
Ricci, Fr. Giacomo: *The Lives of the Companions of St. Philip Neri* 166, 168
Ridolfi, Roberto 97, 103
Rist, John 109
Rocke, Michael 76
Rome 2, 3–4, 8–9, 18, 75, 79, 116, 126, 130, 140–41, 155, 157–67, 184–87, 202–04, 243–47, 255–60, 263–64, 269; Florentines in 159, 161, 184–85; pilgrimages in 2, 179, 186, 191, 201, 203, 204. *See also* Augustinianum; Catacombs; Coliseum; Confraternity of the Most Holy Trinity; Neri, St. Philip, apostolate of; Oratory of St. Philip Neri, Rome; San Giacomo; San Girolamo della Carità; San Marco, Palazzo di; San Pietro; Santa Maria sopra Minerva; Sapienza; Seven Churches.
Romolo (second cousin of Philip Neri) 139–43, 161
Rosa, Fr. Persiano 57, 186
Rosario, Virgilio (Cardinal) 203–04
Russia 259

saints, Catholic 6–7, 17, 86, 252, 272
San Domenico, church of, Fiesole 87, 104
San Germano, Italy 130, 132, 139–48, 160, 161, 191, 197, 208
San Giacomo, hospital of, Rome 186
San Giovanni, Baptistry of, Florence 51

San Girolamo della Carità, church of, Rome 3, 200
San Marco, convent of, Florence 72, 73, 74, 87, 88, 93, 104–05, 109, 114, 115, 127–28
San Marco, Palazzo di, Rome 116
San Pier Gattolino, church of, Florence 71
San Pietro, basilica of, Rome 206
Santa Maria in Vallicella, church of (Chiesa Nuova), Rome (*see* Oratory of St. Philip Neri, Rome)
Santa Maria sopra Minerva, church of, Rome 201, 258, 269
Sapienza (University of Rome) 162
Savanarola, Girolamo 8, 48, 51, 53, 72, 73, 88, 201, 247–49, 257–59; and art 109–10, 112–15, 265; biography of 92–97; historical view of 97–108; imprisonment and execution of 97, 98, 108; and irony 119; prophecies of 95–96; writings of 106–09
Scholasticism 169, 173, 267
second conversion 148–154; and depression, 153 n.55
Second Vatican Council 57–58
second way (*see* illuminative way)
secularization 4–6
sermo de Deo 22–24, 28, 31
seven Churches of Rome 178–79, 191, 201, 203–04
Shestov, Lev Isaakovich 157
Siege of Florence (*see* Florence, siege of)
Sigismond III Vasa of Poland 259
Sinibaldi, Fra Giovanni 104–05
Sirleto, Giuglielmo 163–64
Socrates 116, 170–72; and irony 117–20, 122, 171; and beauty 117, 122
Song of Songs, biblical book of: and the tradition of the three ways 44
spiritual combat 46–47, 56, 71, 73, 75, 80, 85, 91, 128–29, 134, 149, 175, 178,

181, 242, 248, 271
St. Peter's basilica (*see* San Pietro, basilica of)
Stein, Edith (St. Teresa Benedicta of the Cross): *Science of the Cross* 176–77, 183
Stolz, Anselm 32, 33
Sweden 259

Tarugi, Francesco Maria (Cardinal) 77–79, 163
Tauler, Johannes 154
Taylor, Charles 5
Terence (Publius Terentius Afer) 67
Teresa Benedicta of the Cross, St. (*see* Stein, Edith)
Teresa of Avila (or Teresa of Jesus), St. 10, 19, 34–35, 149, 154, 194, 207–08, 217; *Interior Castle* 199–200; physical experience of mysticism 218–25, 227, 242
third way (*see* unitive way)
three ways, tradition of the 37–44, 45, 134, 183. *See also* purgative way; illuminative way; unitive way.
Thurston, Fr. Herbert 29–30, 219
transverberation 218–25, 227, 237. *See also* mysticism, physical phenomena of.
Trevor, Meriol 53, 169, 170
Tugwell, Simon: on the tradition of the three ways 39, 44

Türks, Paul 144, 145, 170
Turner, Denys 32, 33, 48, 191

unitive way 43, 138, 183, 192–97, 208, 213, 272
University of Rome (*see* Sapienza)

Valier, Agostino (Cardinal): *Dialogue of Christian Joy* 116, 168, 169–70, 172
Vallicella (*see* Oratory of St. Philip Neri, Rome)
Vian, Nello 13, 68, 173, 272
virtue ethics 46
Vitelleschi, Marco Antonio 126
von Balthasar, Hans Urs 17, 31–33, 150, 209, 263; on the tradition of the three ways 38; *The Glory of the Lord* 267–69
von Hügel, Baron 83–84

way of beginners (*see* purgative way)
way of light (*see* illuminative way)
way of proficients (*see* illuminative way)
Weinstein, Donald 98, 104
Wharton, Edith 4–5
Wittgenstein, Ludwig 212, 217, 222–26
World War I 13

Zazzara, Francesco 120, 163, 253

www.ingramcontent.com/pod-product-compliance
Lightning Source LLC
Chambersburg PA
CBHW020325170426
43200CB00006B/270